TREES™

VOLUME ONE
IN SHADOW

TREES, VOLUME ONE:
IN SHADOW. First printing.
February 2015. Published by Image Comics,
Inc. Office of publication: 2001 Center Street,
Sixth Floor, Berkeley, CA 94704. Copyright © 2015
Warren Ellis & Jason Howard. Originally published in single
magazine form as TREES #1–8. All rights reserved. TREES, its
logos, and all character likenesses herein are trademarks of Warren
Ellis & Jason Howard unless expressly indicated. Image Comics® and
its logos are registered trademarks and copyrights of Image Comics,
Inc. All rights reserved. No part of this publication may be reproduced
or transmitted, in any form or by any means (except for short excerpts for
review purposes) without the express written permission of Warren Ellis
& Jason Howard or Image Comics, Inc. All names, characters, events,
and locales in this publication are entirely fictional. Any resemblance
to actual persons (living or dead) or events or places, without
satiric intent, is coincidental. Printed in the USA. For information
regarding the CPSIA on this printed material call: 203-
595-3636 and provide reference # RICH–603185.
FOREIGN LICENSING INQUIRIES WRITE TO:
foreignlicensing@imagecomics.com
ISBN 978-1-63215-270-1

WARREN ELLIS
WRITER

JASON HOWARD
ARTIST

FONOGRAFIKS
LETTERING &
BOOK DESIGN

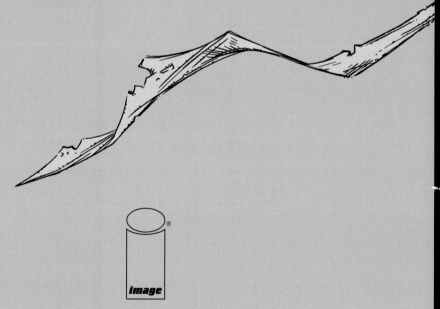

IMAGE COMICS, INC.

ROBERT KIRKMAN Chief Operating Officer • ERIK LARSEN Chief Financial Officer
TODD McFARLANE President • MARC SILVESTRI Chief Executive Officer • JIM VALENTINO Vice-President

ERIC STEPHENSON Publisher • RON RICHARDS Director of Business Development • JENNIFER DE GUZMAN
Director of Trade Book Sales • KAT SALAZAR Director of PR & Marketing • COREY MURPHY Director of Retail
Sales • JEREMY SULLIVAN Director of Digital Sales • EMILIO BAUTISTA Sales Assistant • BRANWYN BIGGLESTONE
Senior Accounts Manager • EMILY MILLER Accounts Manager • JESSICA AMBRIZ Administrative Assistant
TYLER SHAINLINE Events Coordinator • DAVID BROTHERS Content Manager • JONATHAN CHAN Production
Manager • DREW GILL Art Director • MEREDITH WALLACE Print Manager • ADDISON DUKE Production Artist
VINCENT KUKUA Production Artist • TRICIA RAMOS Production Assistant

IMAGECOMICS.COM

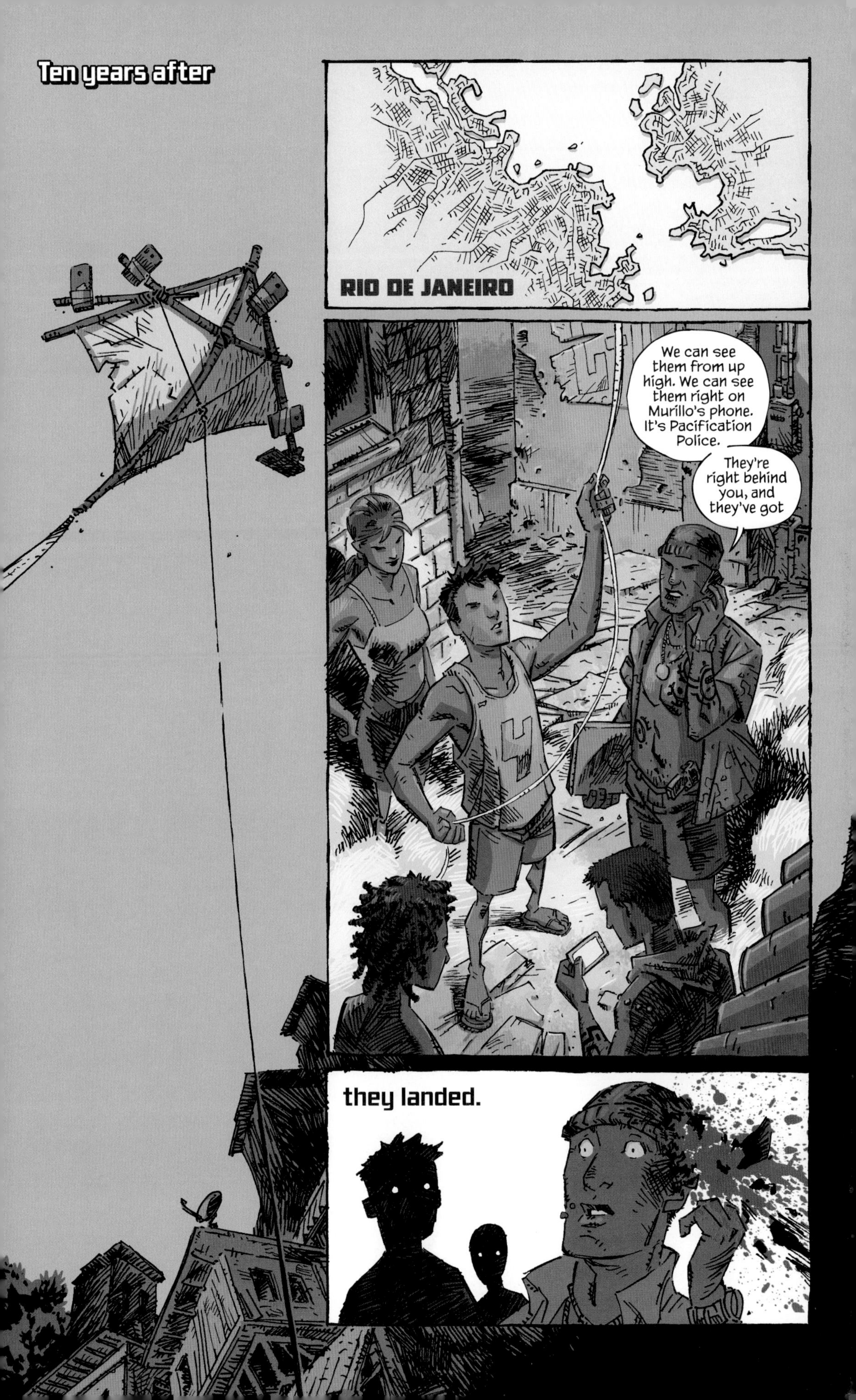
Ten years after
RIO DE JANEIRO
We can see them from up high. We can see them right on Murillo's phone. It's Pacification Police.
They're right behind you, and they've got
they landed.

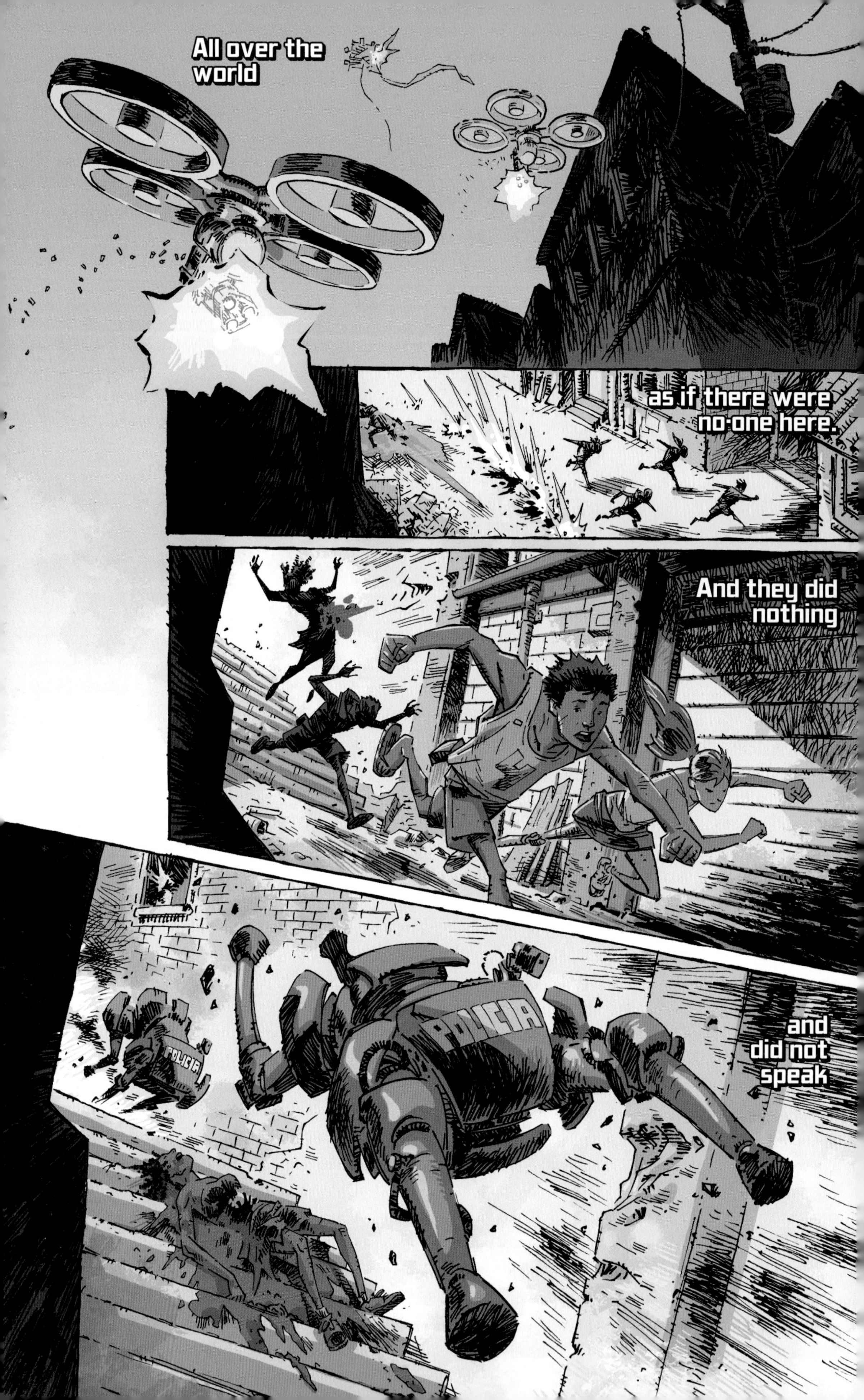
All over the world
as if there were no-one here.
And they did nothing
POLICIA
POLICIA
and did not speak

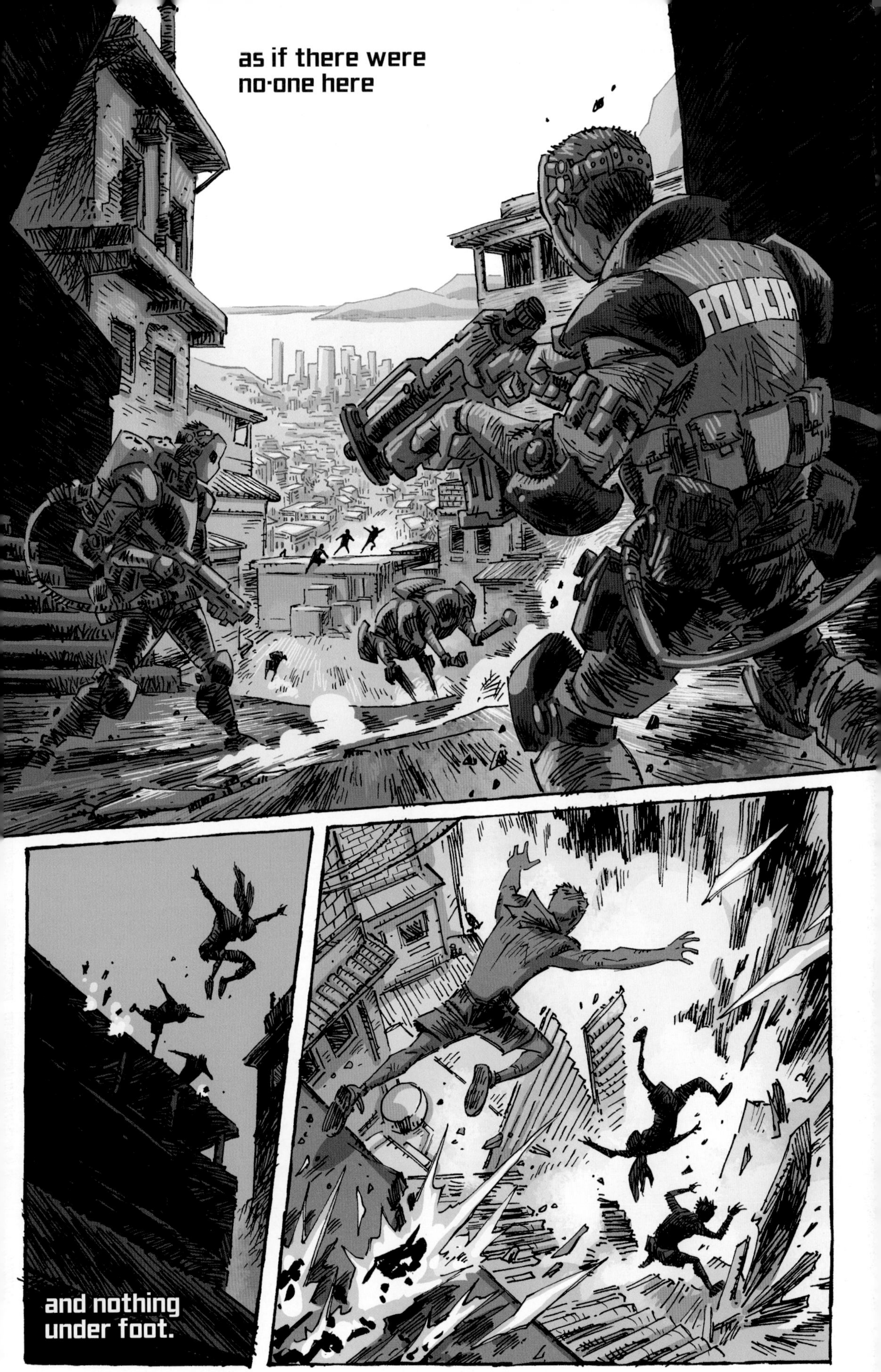
as if there were no-one here
POLICIA
and nothing under foot.

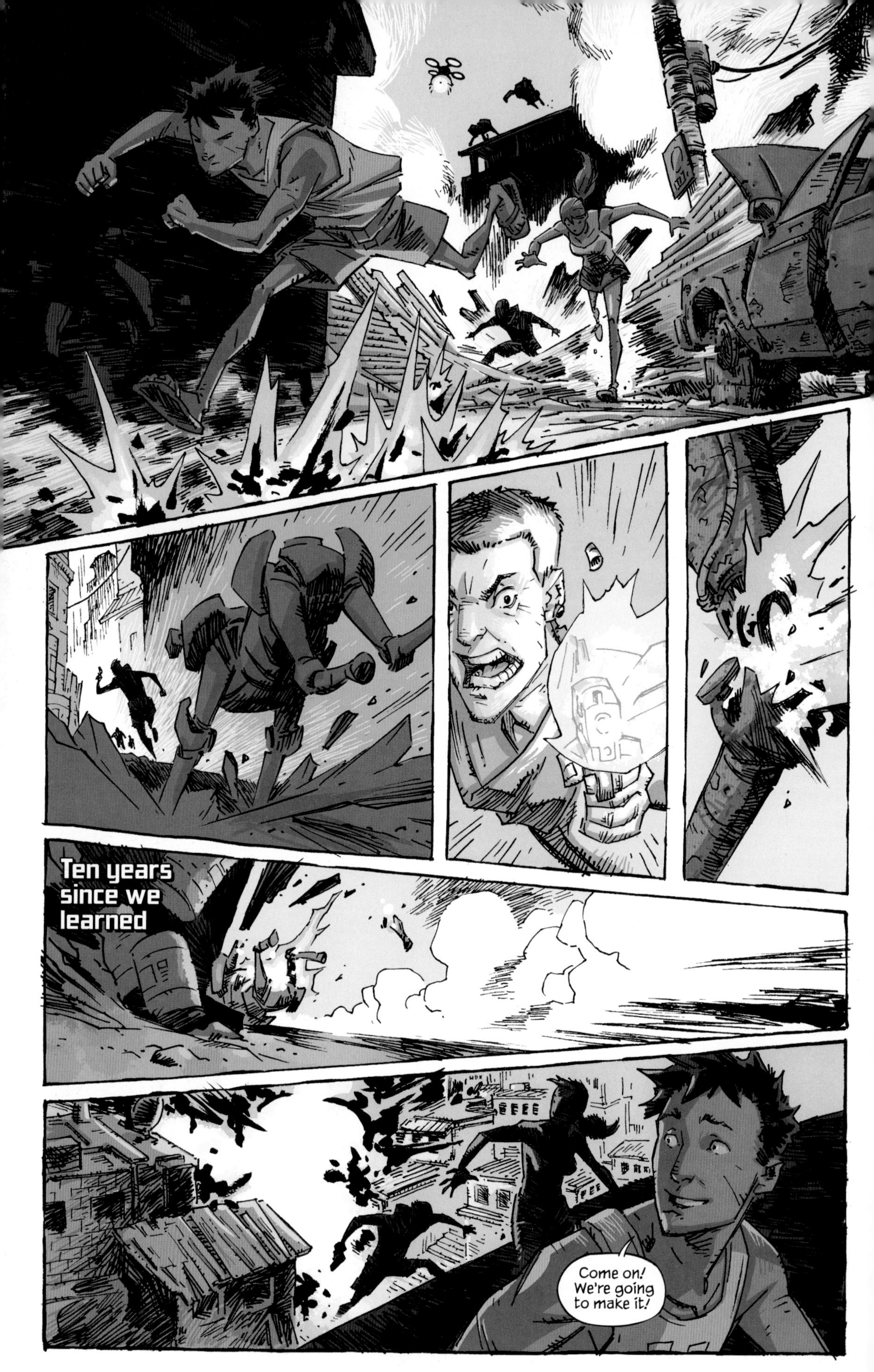
Ten years since we learned
Come on! We're going to make it!

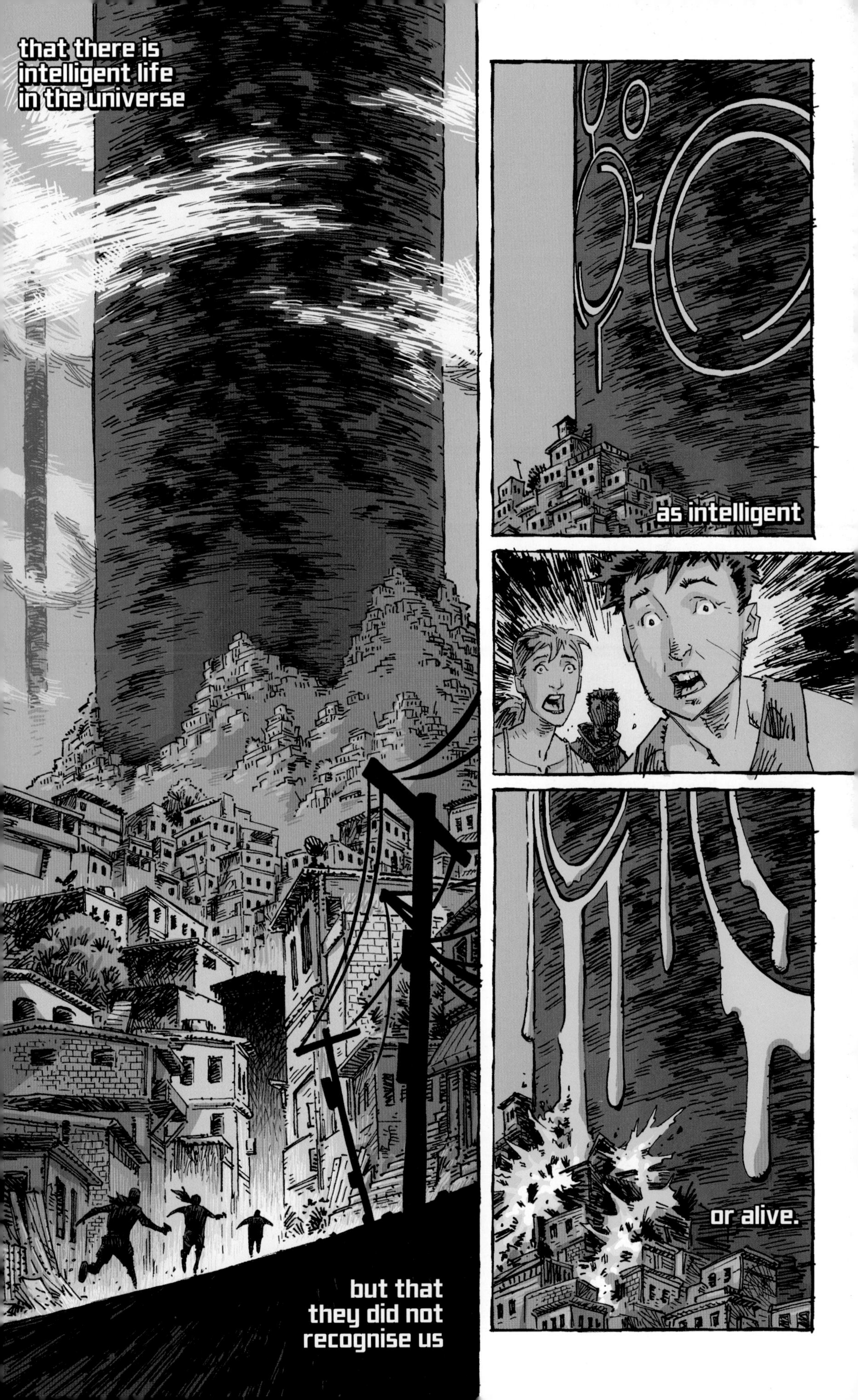
that there is intelligent life in the universe
but that they did not recognise us
as intelligent
or alive.

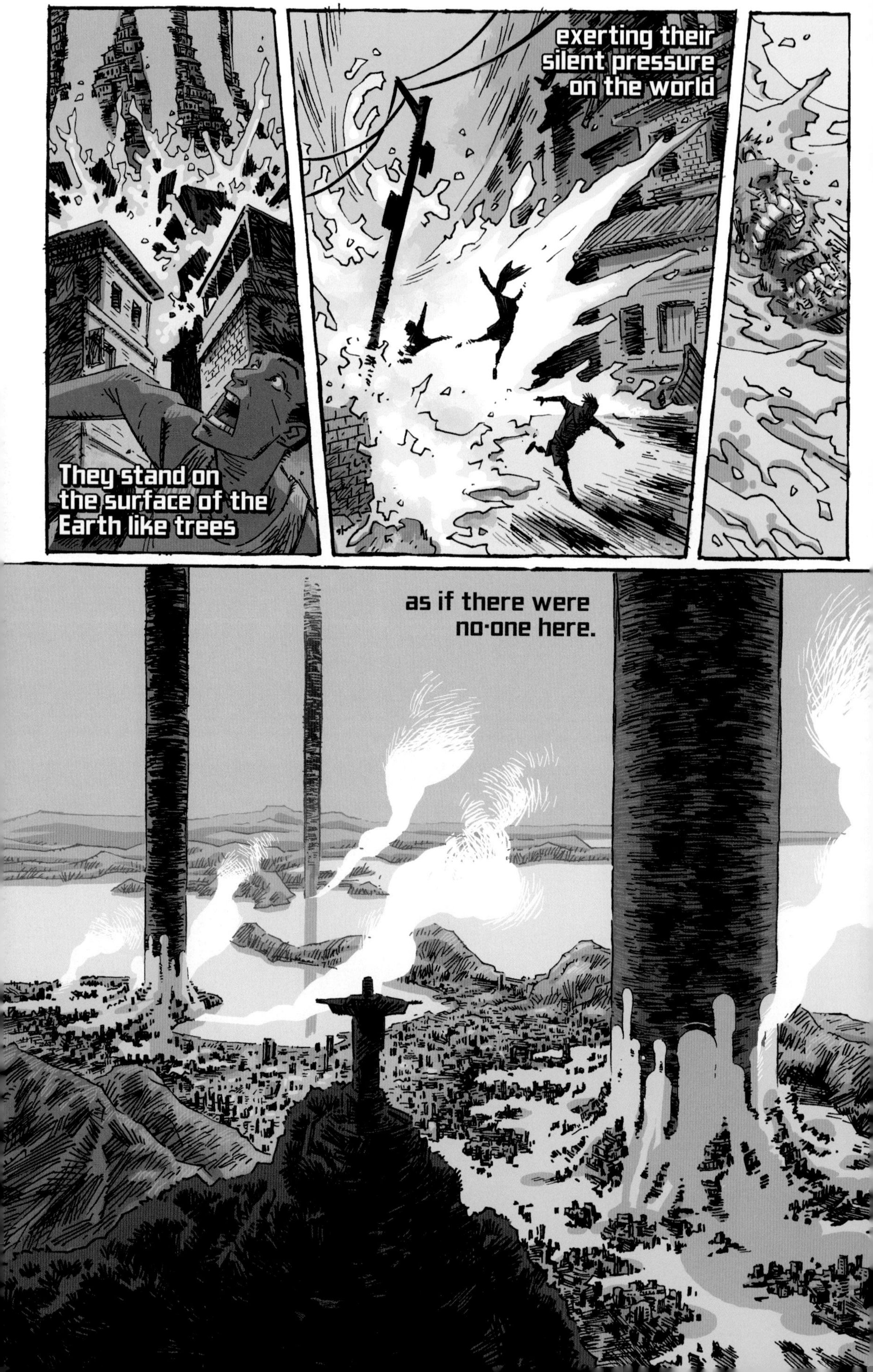
They stand on the surface of the Earth like trees
exerting their silent pressure on the world
as if there were no-one here.

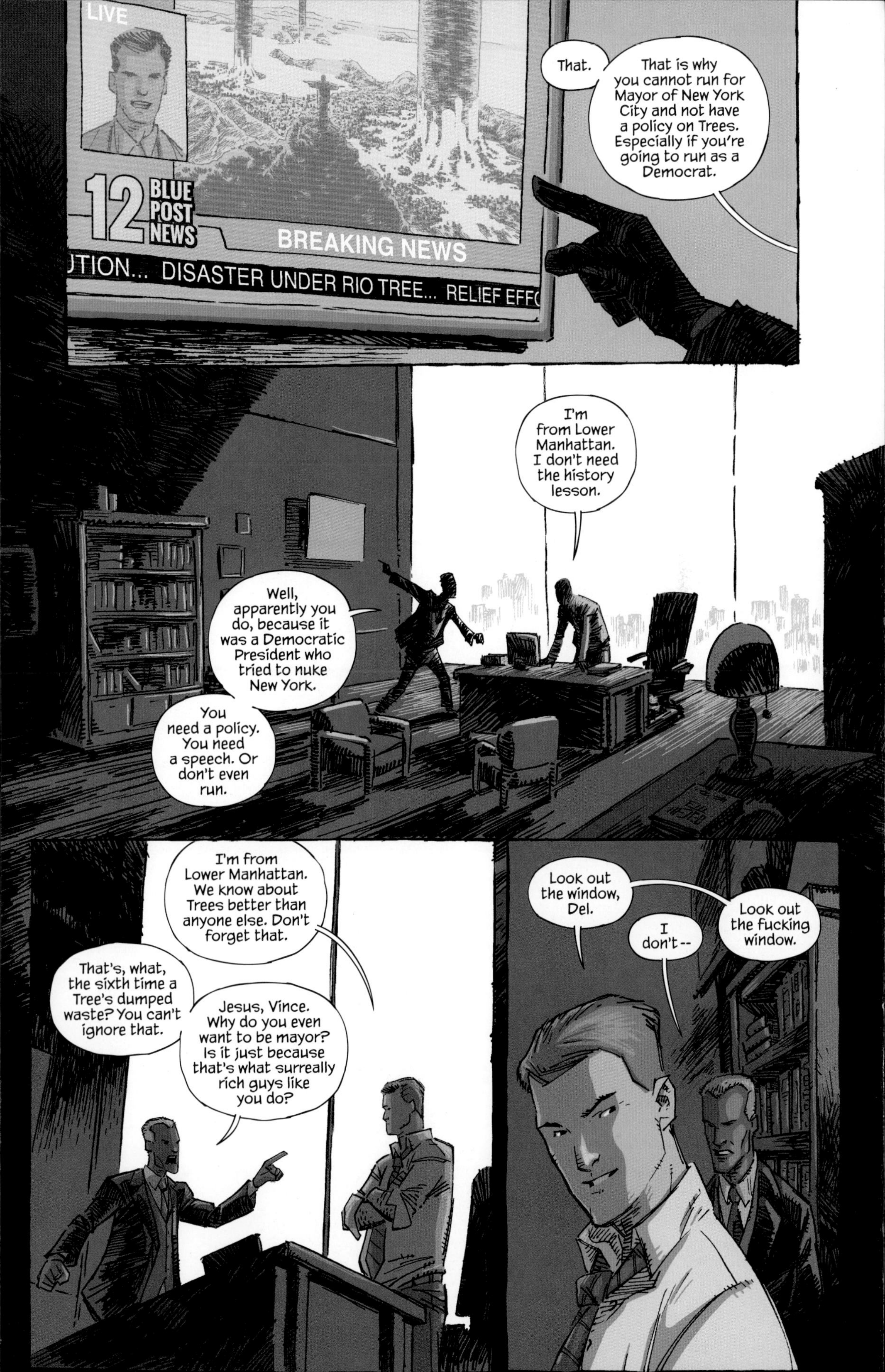
LIVE
12 BLUE POST NEWS
BREAKING NEWS
UTION... DISASTER UNDER RIO TREE... RELIEF EFFO
That.
That is why you cannot run for Mayor of New York City and not have a policy on Trees. Especially if you're going to run as a Democrat.
I'm from Lower Manhattan. I don't need the history lesson.
Well, apparently you do, because it was a Democratic President who tried to nuke New York.
You need a policy. You need a speech. Or don't even run.
I'm from Lower Manhattan. We know about Trees better than anyone else. Don't forget that.
That's, what, the sixth time a Tree's dumped waste? You can't ignore that.
Jesus, Vince. Why do you even want to be mayor? Is it just because that's what surreally rich guys like you do?
Look out the window, Del.
I don't --
Look out the fucking window.

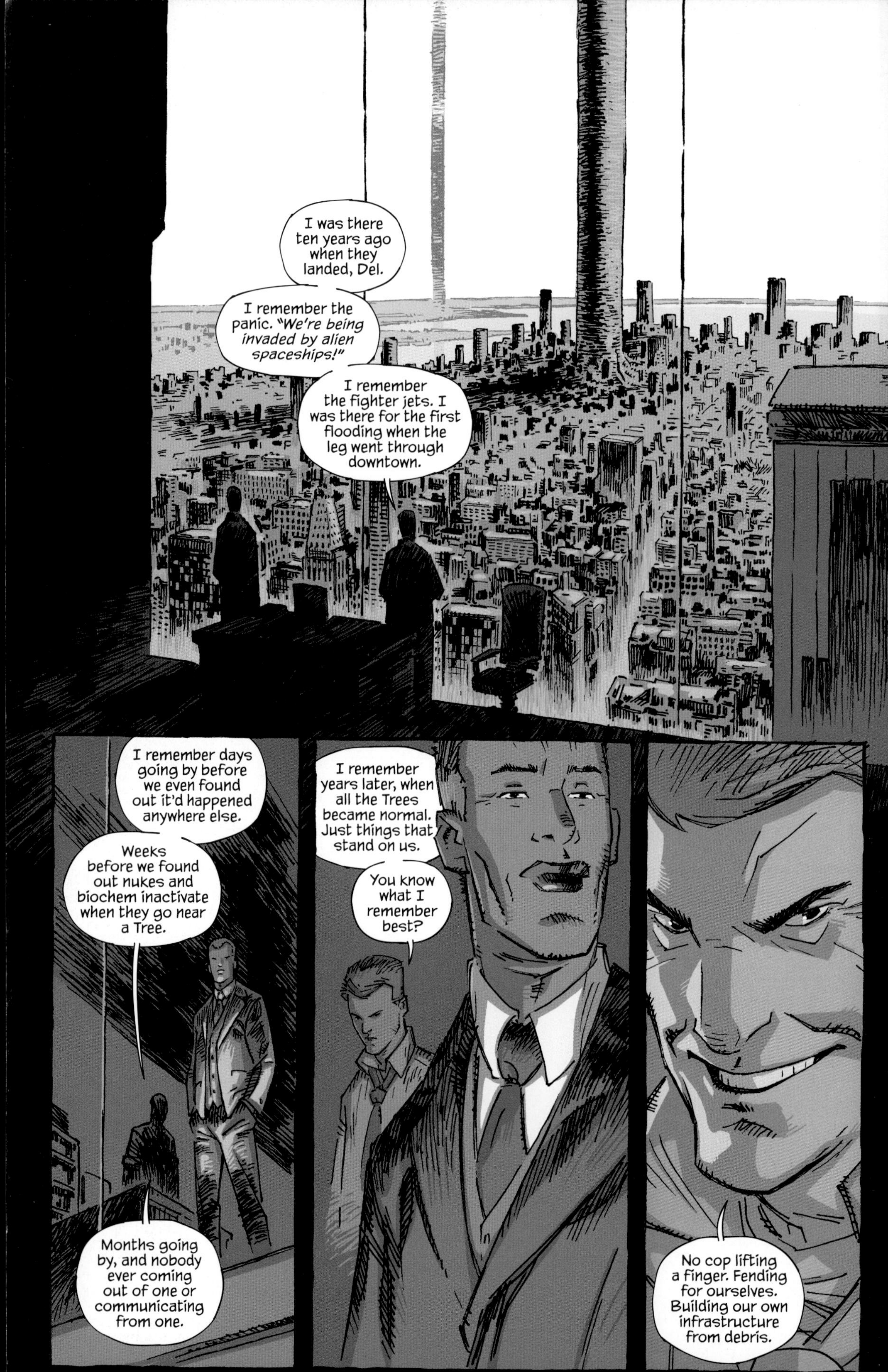

I was there ten years ago when they landed, Del.
I remember the panic. "We're being invaded by alien spaceships!"
I remember the fighter jets. I was there for the first flooding when the leg went through downtown.
I remember days going by before we even found out it'd happened anywhere else.
Weeks before we found out nukes and biochem inactivate when they go near a Tree.
Months going by, and nobody ever coming out of one or communicating from one.
I remember years later, when all the Trees became normal. Just things that stand on us.
You know what I remember best?
No cop lifting a finger. Fending for ourselves. Building our own infrastructure from debris.

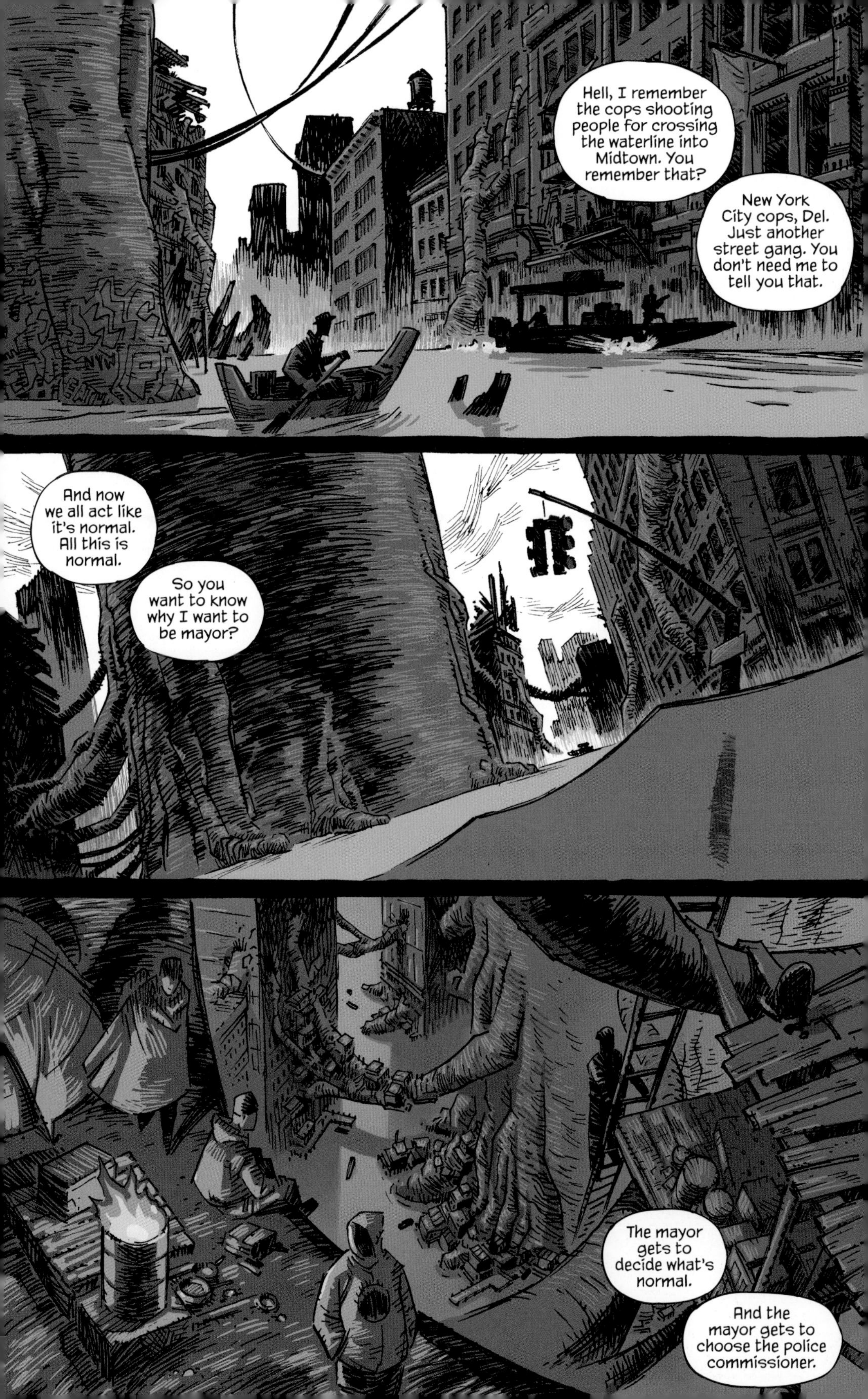
Hell, I remember the cops shooting people for crossing the waterline into Midtown. You remember that?
New York City cops, Del. Just another street gang. You don't need me to tell you that.
And now we all act like it's normal. All this is normal.
So you want to know why I want to be mayor?
The mayor gets to decide what's normal.
And the mayor gets to choose the police commissioner.

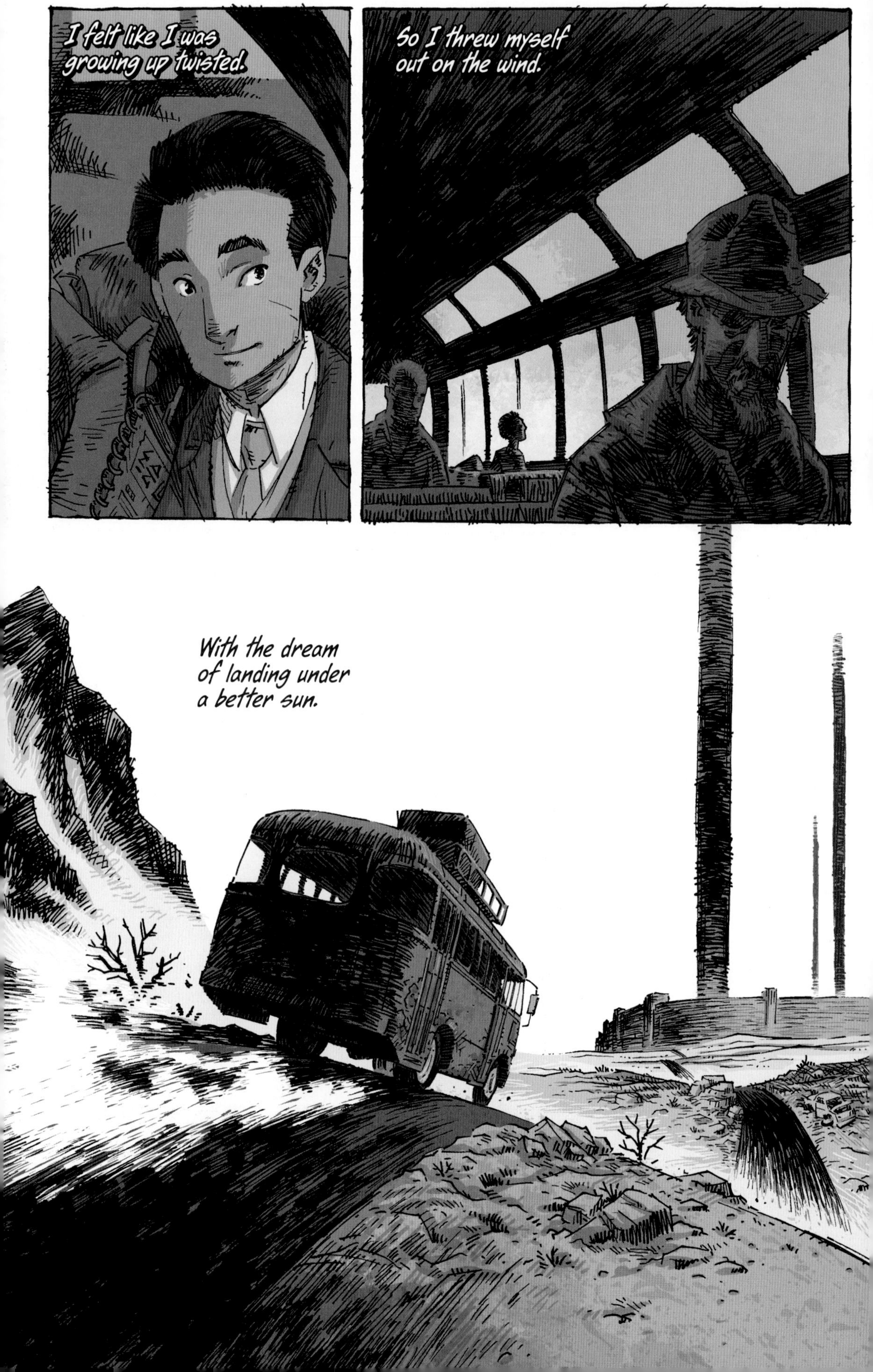
I felt like I was growing up twisted.
So I threw myself out on the wind.
With the dream of landing under a better sun.

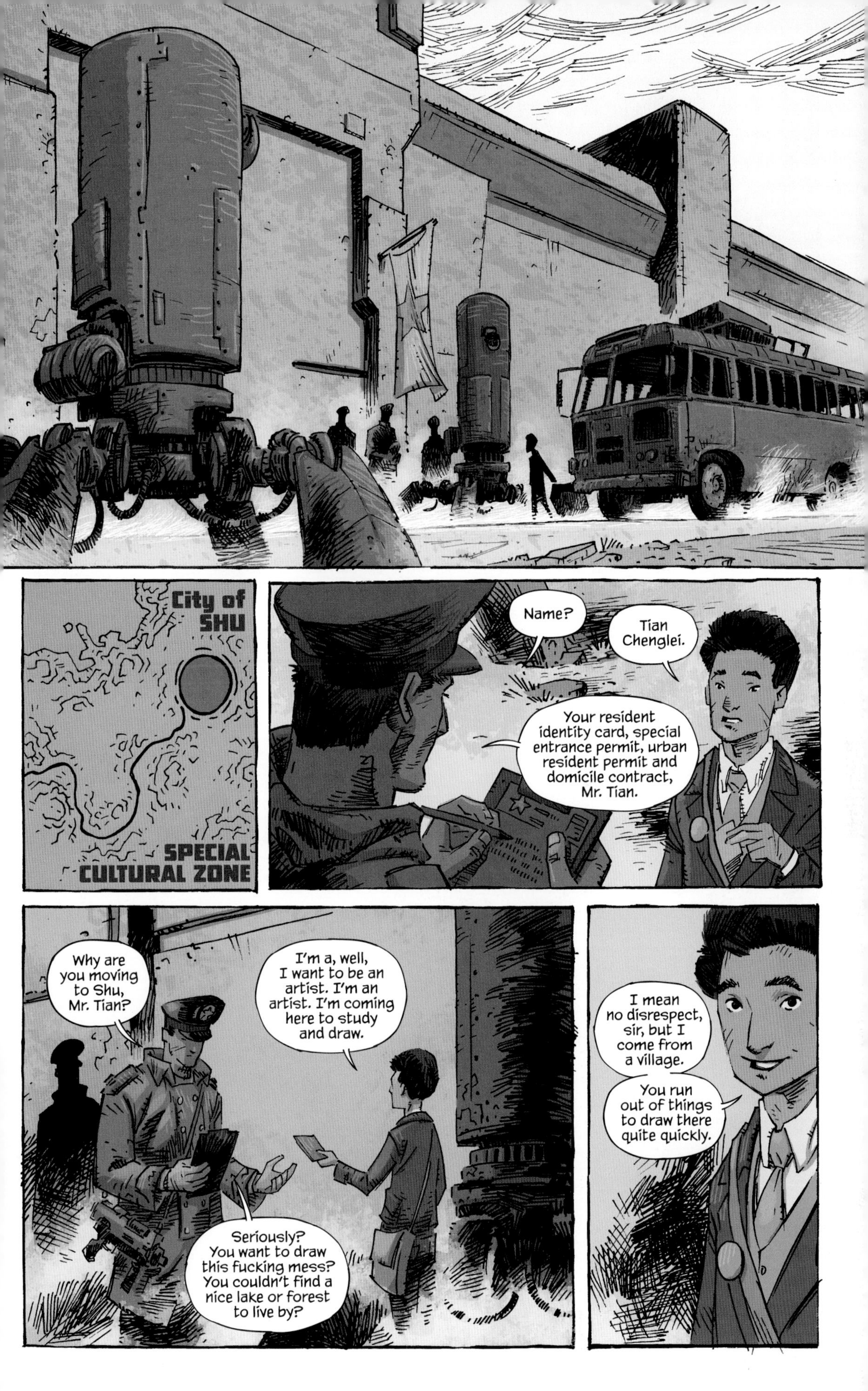
City of SHU
SPECIAL CULTURAL ZONE
Name?
Tian Chenglei.
Your resident identity card, special entrance permit, urban resident permit and domicile contract, Mr. Tian.
Why are you moving to Shu, Mr. Tian?
I'm a, well, I want to be an artist. I'm an artist. I'm coming here to study and draw.
Seriously? You want to draw this fucking mess? You couldn't find a nice lake or forest to live by?
I mean no disrespect, sir, but I come from a village.
You run out of things to draw there quite quickly.

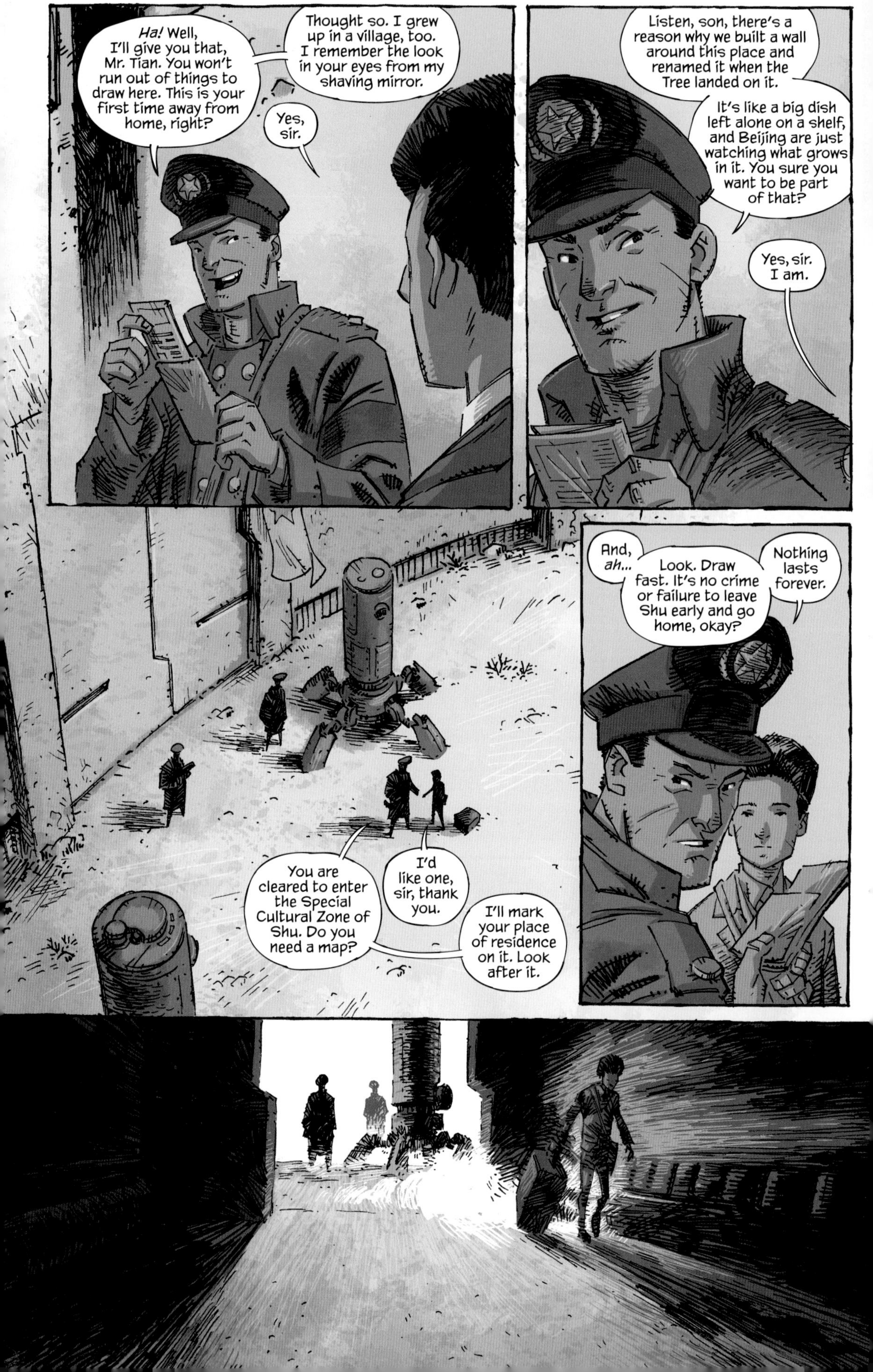
Ha! Well, I'll give you that, Mr. Tian. You won't run out of things to draw here. This is your first time away from home, right?
Yes, sir.
Thought so. I grew up in a village, too. I remember the look in your eyes from my shaving mirror.
Listen, son, there's a reason why we built a wall around this place and renamed it when the Tree landed on it.
It's like a big dish left alone on a shelf, and Beijing are just watching what grows in it. You sure you want to be part of that?
Yes, sir. I am.
You are cleared to enter the Special Cultural Zone of Shu. Do you need a map?
I'd like one, sir, thank you.
I'll mark your place of residence on it. Look after it.
And, ah...
Look. Draw fast. It's no crime or failure to leave Shu early and go home, okay?
Nothing lasts forever.

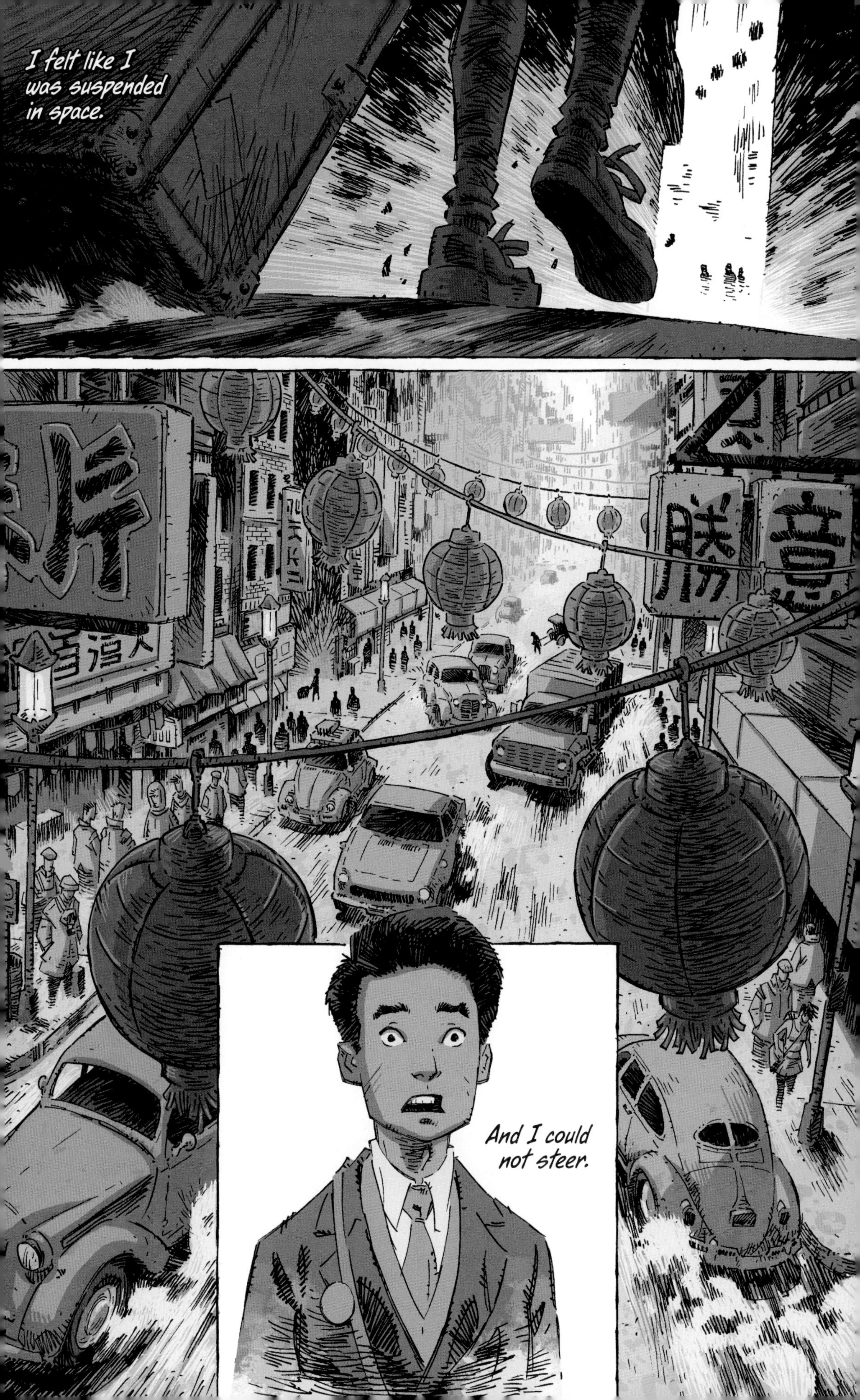
I felt like I was suspended in space.
And I could not steer.

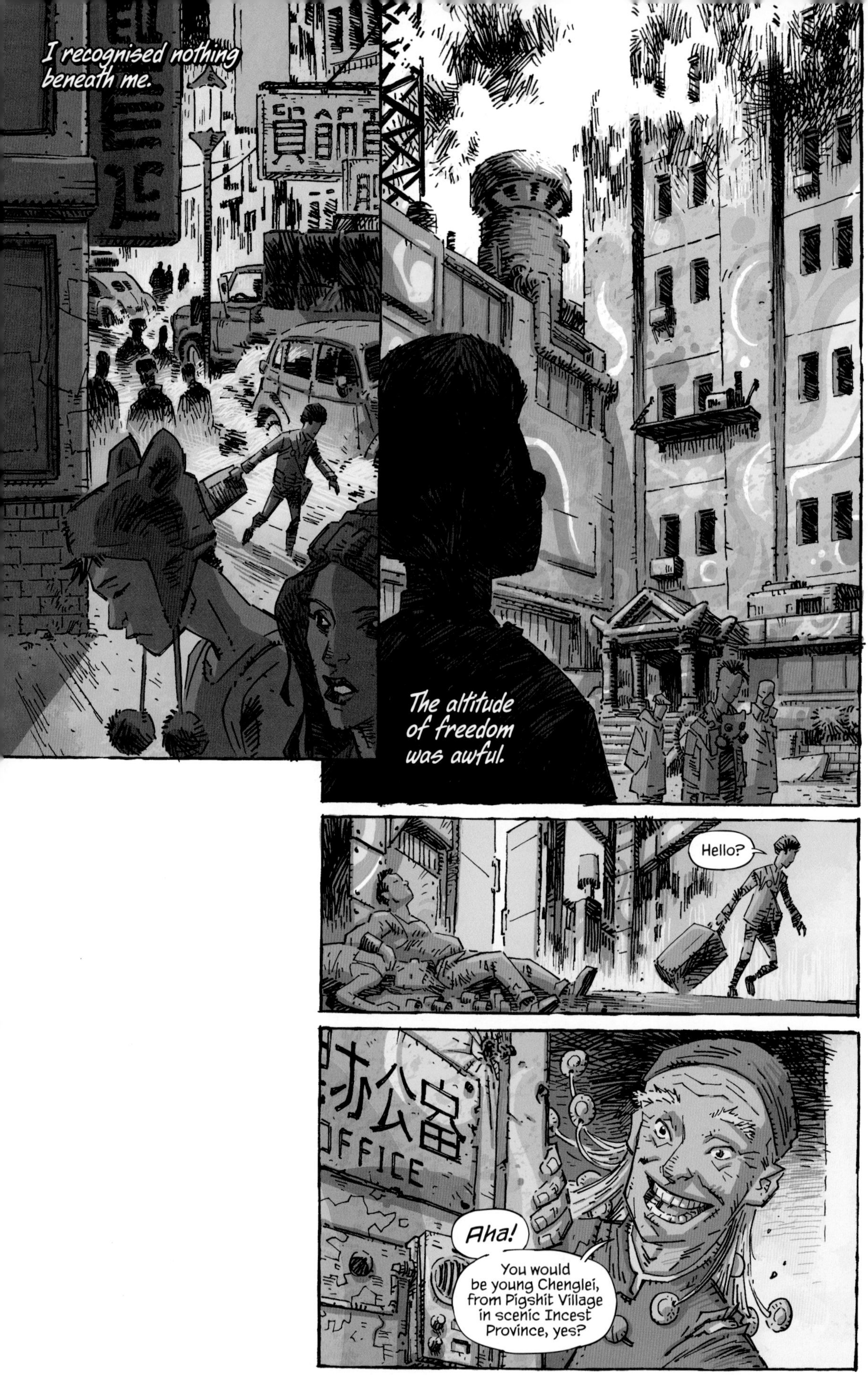

I recognised nothing beneath me.
The altitude of freedom was awful.
Hello?
Aha!
You would be young Chenglei, from Pigshit Village in scenic Incest Province, yes?

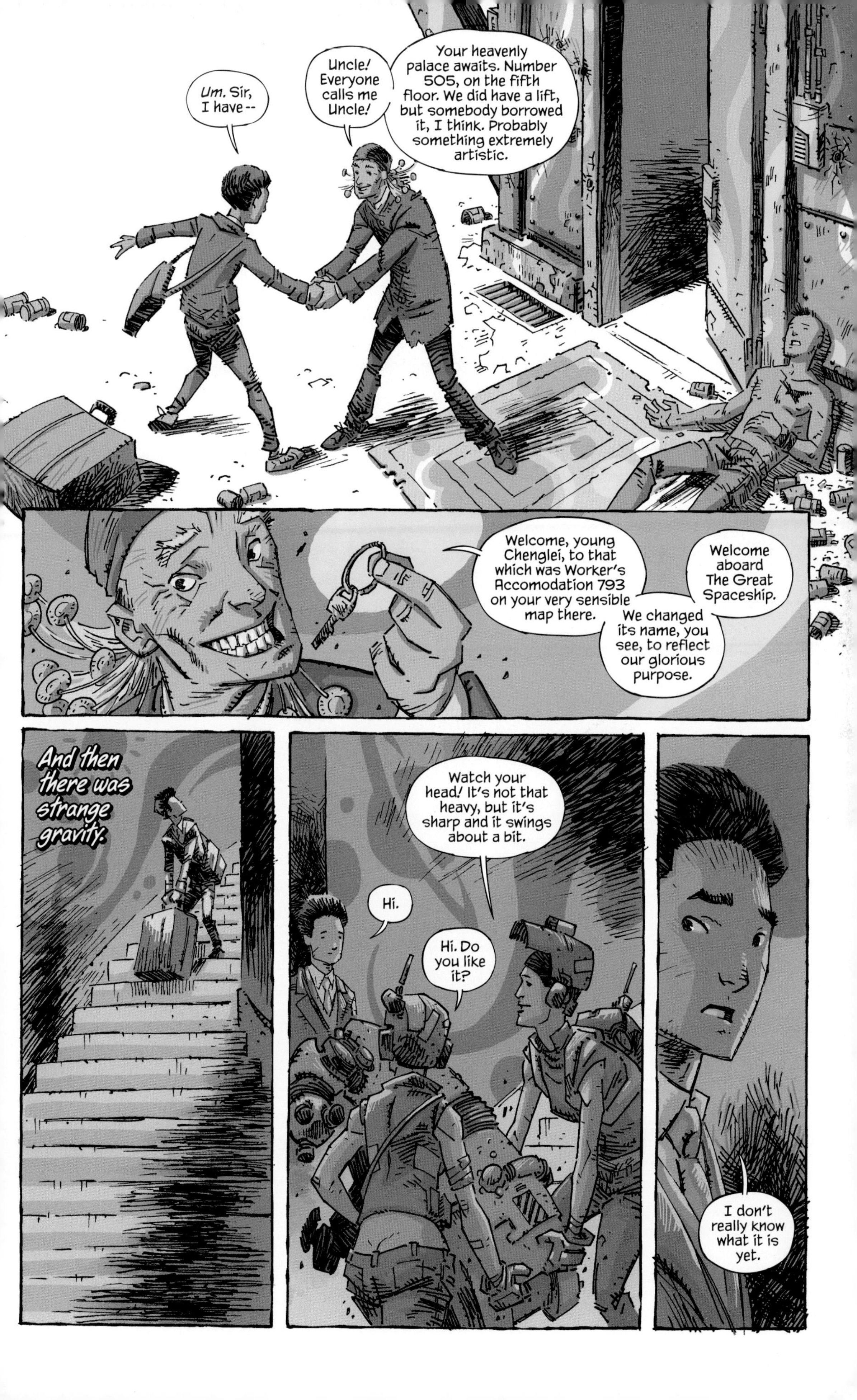
Um. Sir, I have --
Uncle! Everyone calls me Uncle!
Your heavenly palace awaits. Number 505, on the fifth floor. We did have a lift, but somebody borrowed it, I think. Probably something extremely artistic.
Welcome, young Chenglei, to that which was Worker's Accomodation 793 on your very sensible map there.
Welcome aboard The Great Spaceship.
We changed its name, you see, to reflect our glorious purpose.
And then there was strange gravity.
Watch your head! It's not that heavy, but it's sharp and it swings about a bit.
Hi.
Hi. Do you like it?
I don't really know what it is yet.

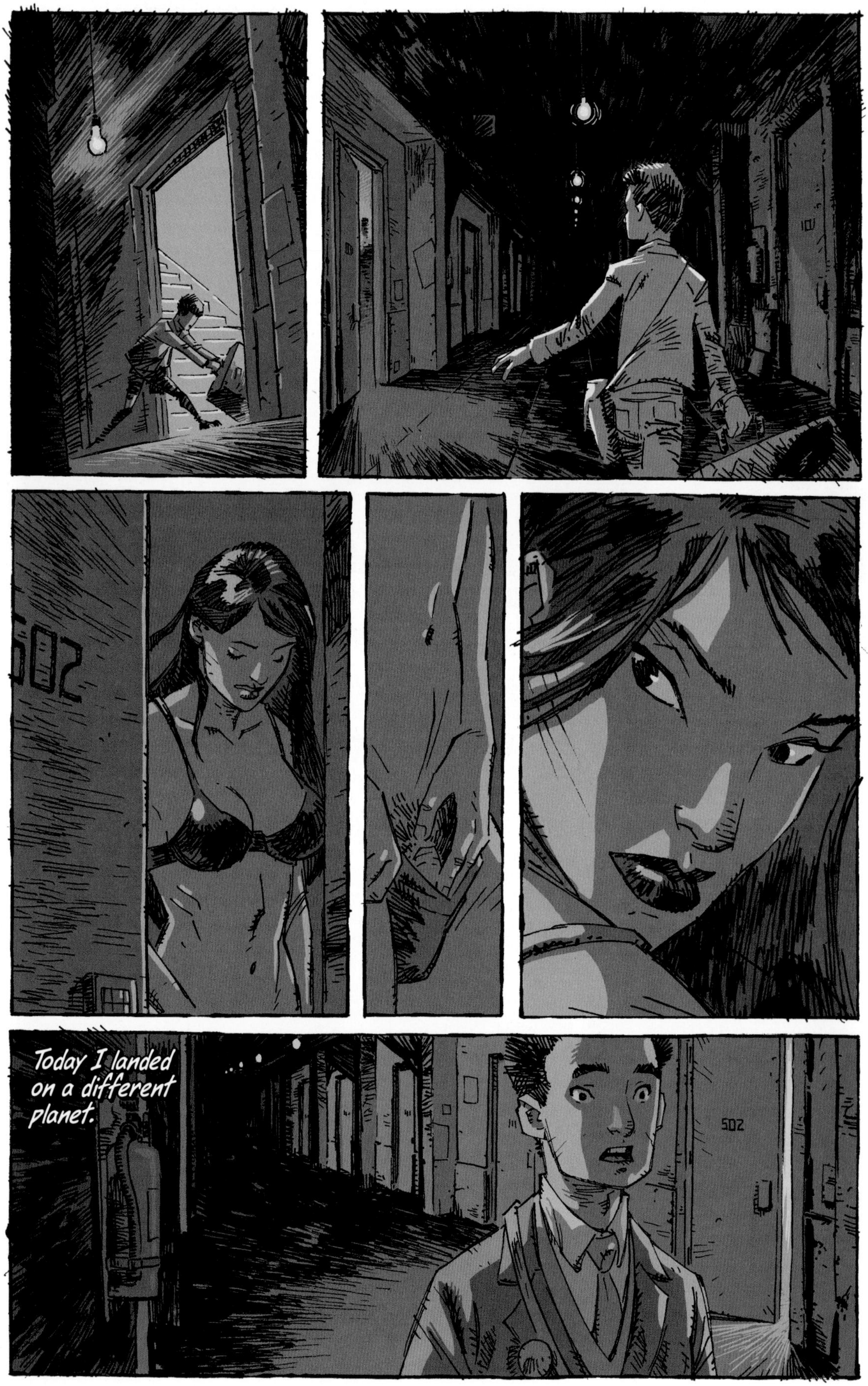
502
Today I landed on a different planet.
502

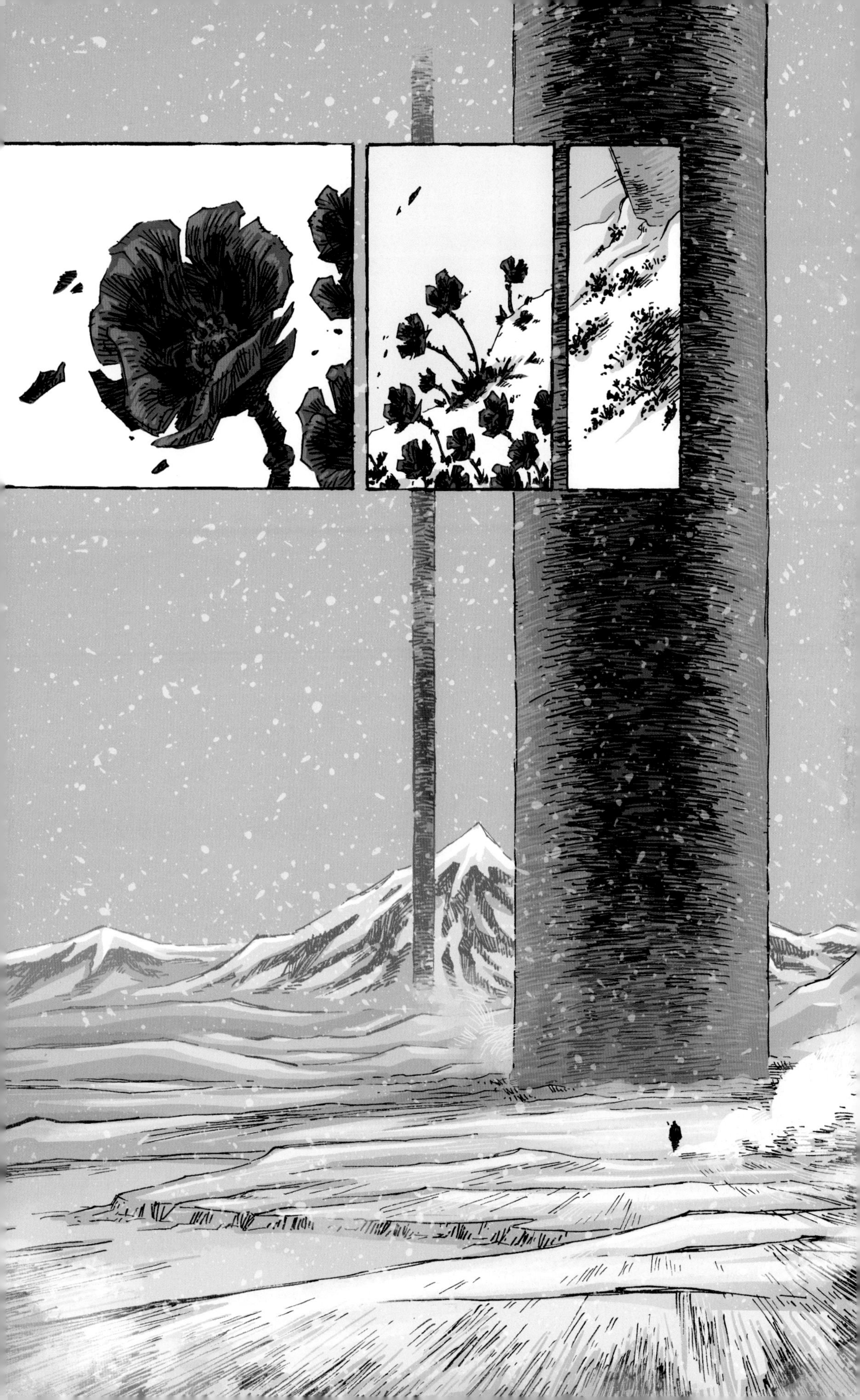

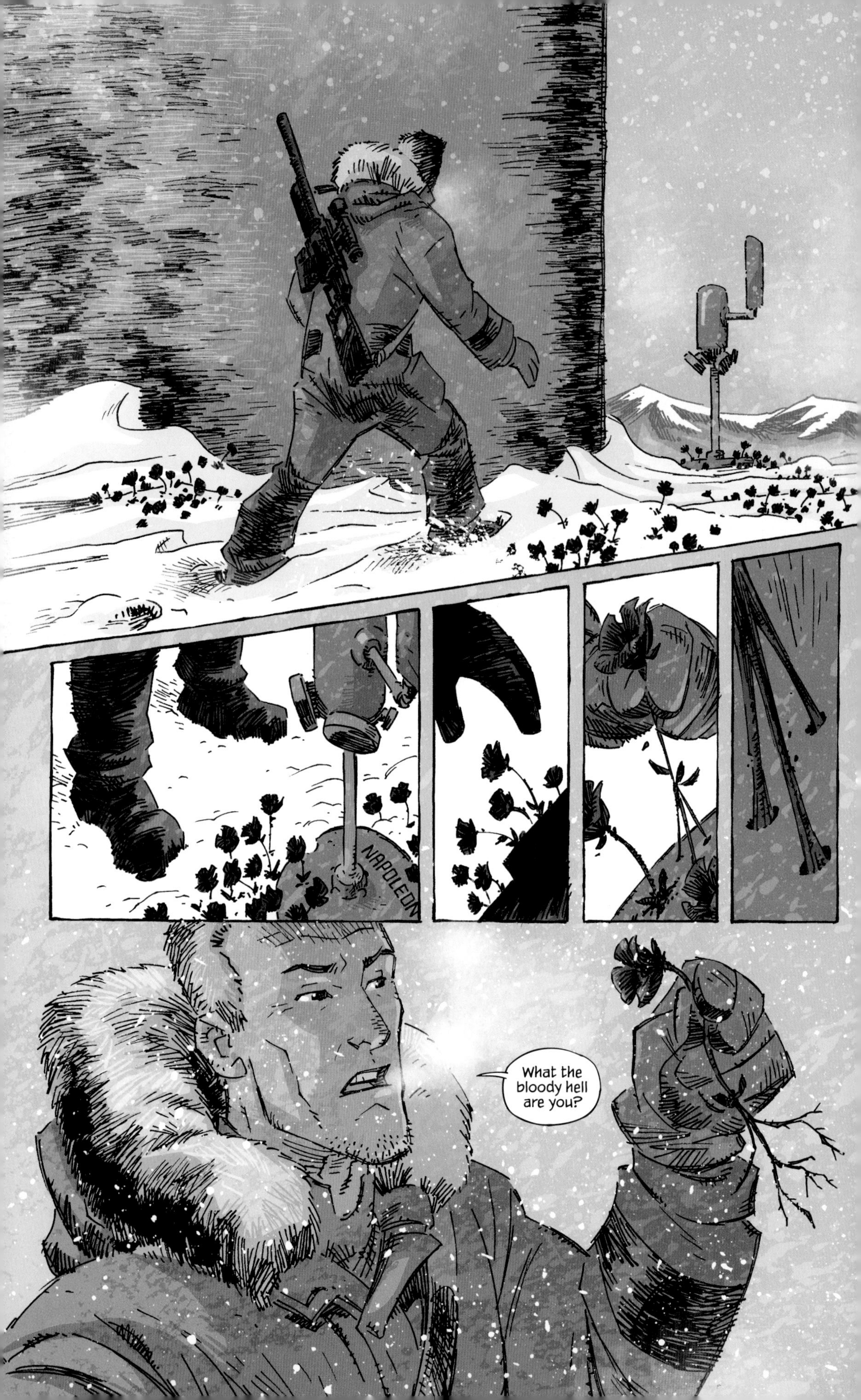
NAPOLEON
What the bloody hell are you?

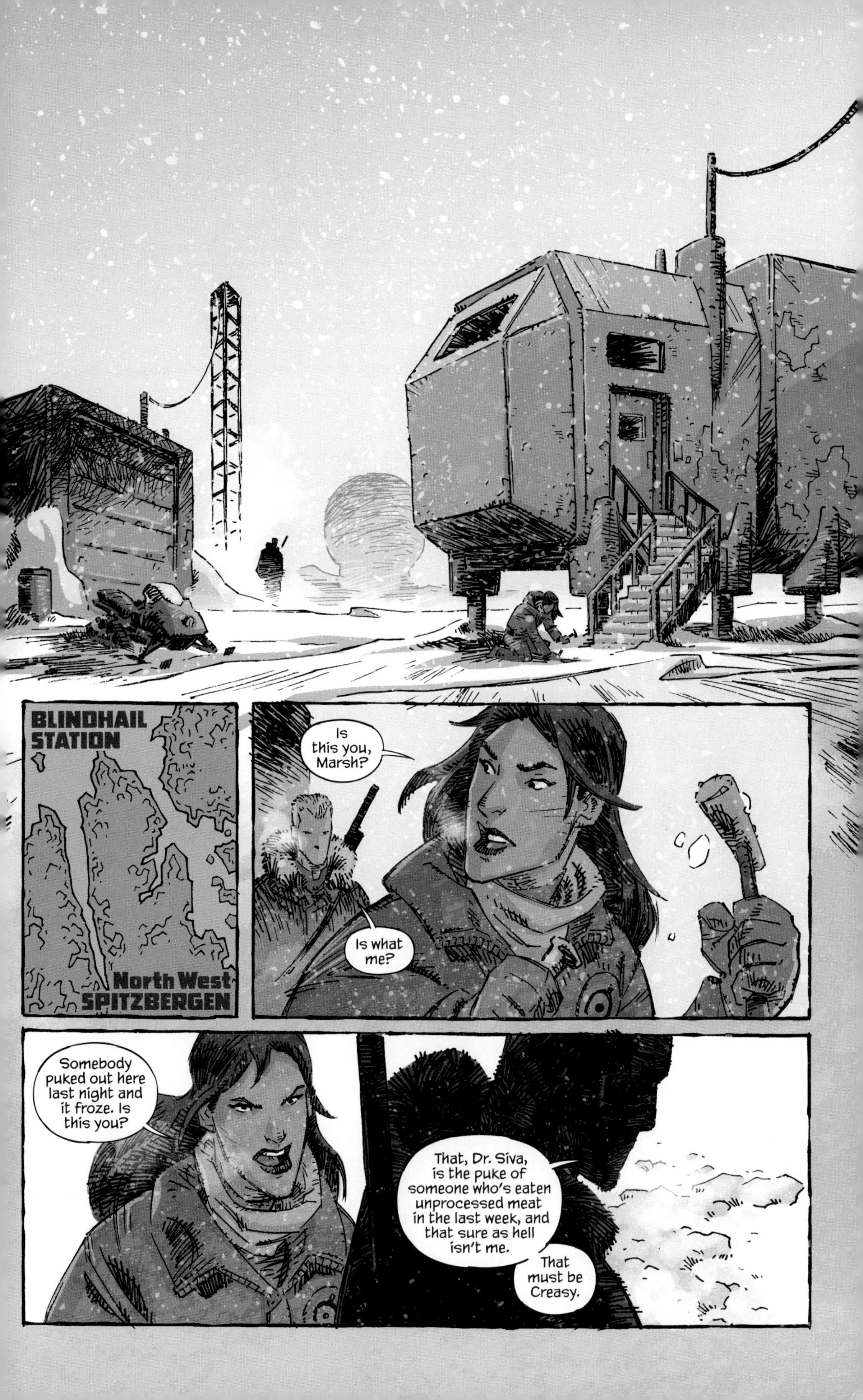
BLINDHAIL STATION
North West SPITZBERGEN
Is this you, Marsh?
Is what me?
Somebody puked out here last night and it froze. Is this you?
That, Dr. Siva, is the puke of someone who's eaten unprocessed meat in the last week, and that sure as hell isn't me.
That must be Creasy.

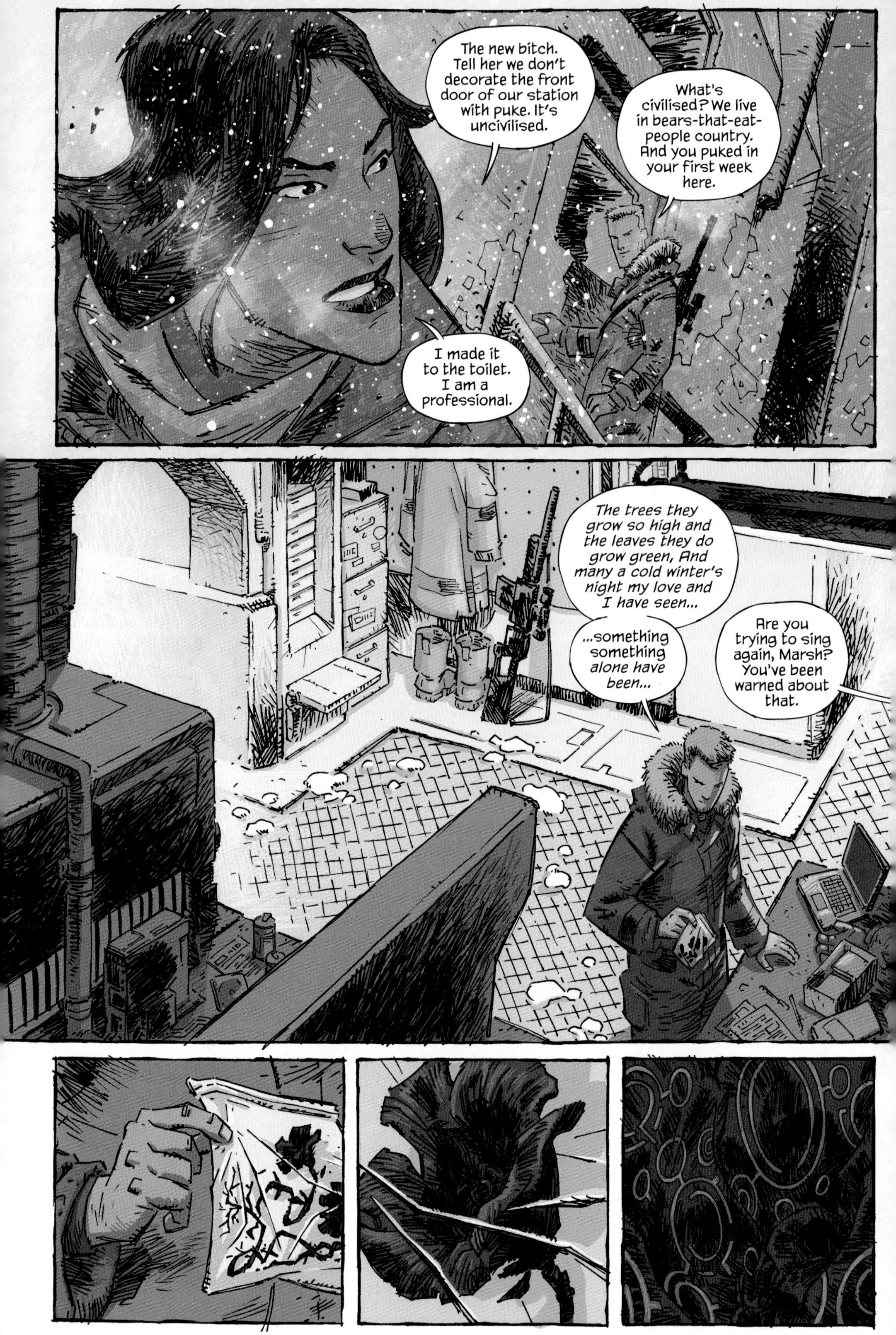
The new bitch. Tell her we don't decorate the front door of our station with puke. It's uncivilised.
What's civilised? We live in bears-that-eat-people country. And you puked in your first week here.
I made it to the toilet. I am a professional.
The trees they grow so high and the leaves they do grow green, And many a cold winter's night my love and I have seen...
...something something alone have been...
Are you trying to sing again, Marsh? You've been warned about that.

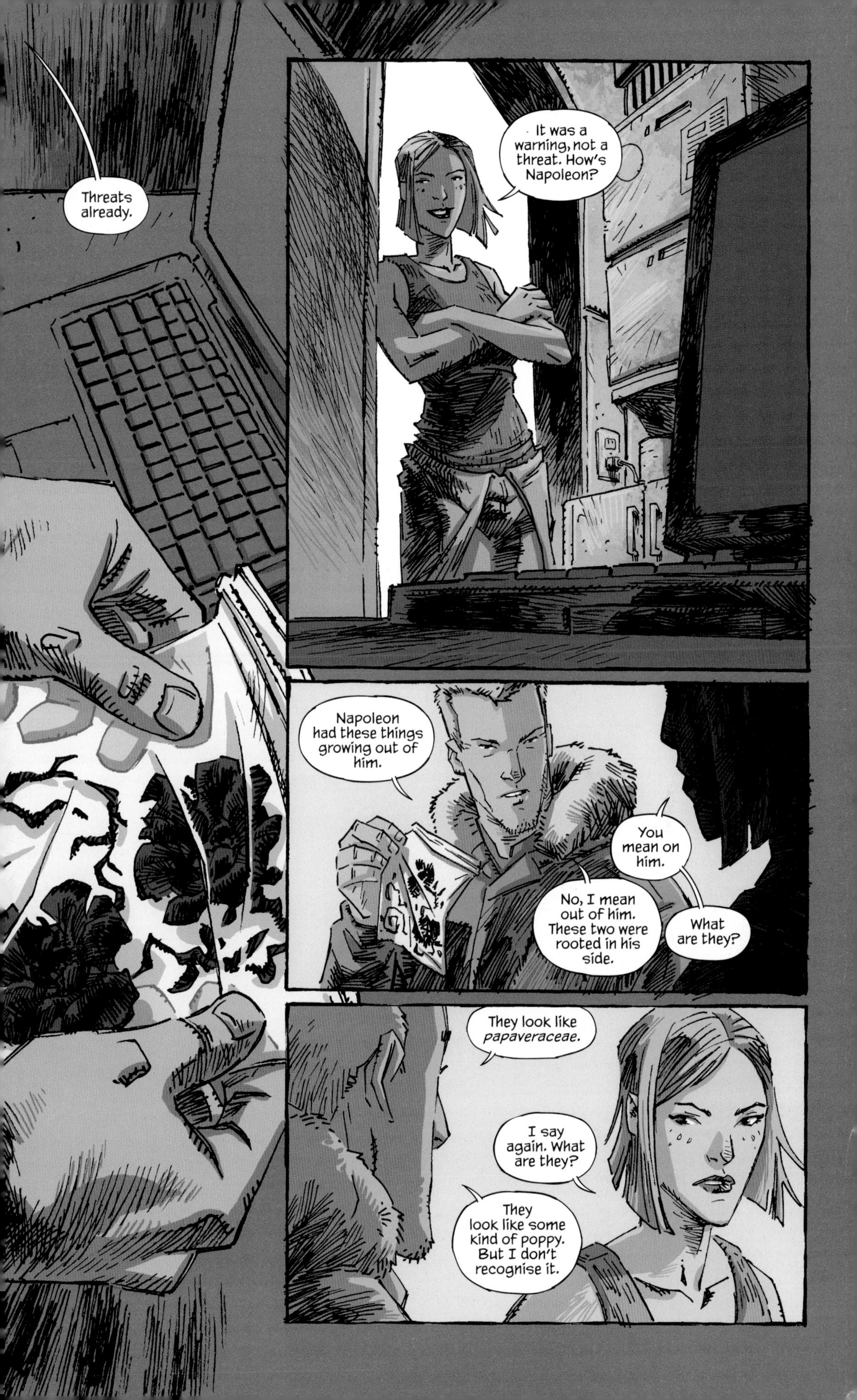
Threats already.
It was a warning, not a threat. How's Napoleon?
Napoleon had these things growing out of him.
You mean on him.
No, I mean out of him. These two were rooted in his side.
What are they?
They look like *papaveraceae.*
I say again. What are they?
They look like some kind of poppy. But I don't recognise it.

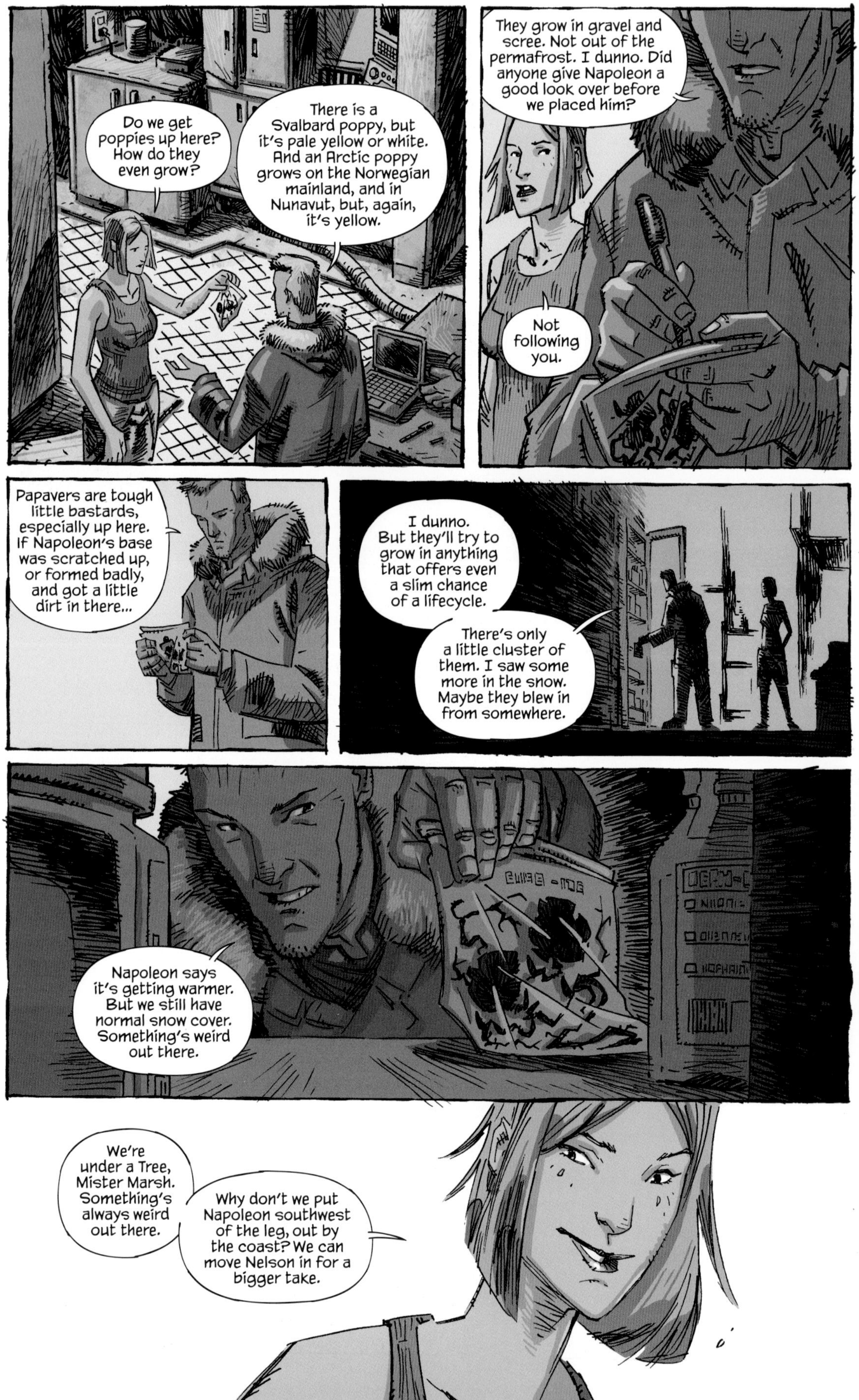
Do we get poppies up here? How do they even grow?
There is a Svalbard poppy, but it's pale yellow or white. And an Arctic poppy grows on the Norwegian mainland, and in Nunavut, but, again, it's yellow.
They grow in gravel and scree. Not out of the permafrost. I dunno. Did anyone give Napoleon a good look over before we placed him?
Not following you.
Papavers are tough little bastards, especially up here. If Napoleon's base was scratched up, or formed badly, and got a little dirt in there...
I dunno. But they'll try to grow in anything that offers even a slim chance of a lifecycle.
There's only a little cluster of them. I saw some more in the snow. Maybe they blew in from somewhere.
Napoleon says it's getting warmer. But we still have normal snow cover. Something's weird out there.
We're under a Tree, Mister Marsh. Something's always weird out there.
Why don't we put Napoleon southwest of the leg, out by the coast? We can move Nelson in for a bigger take.

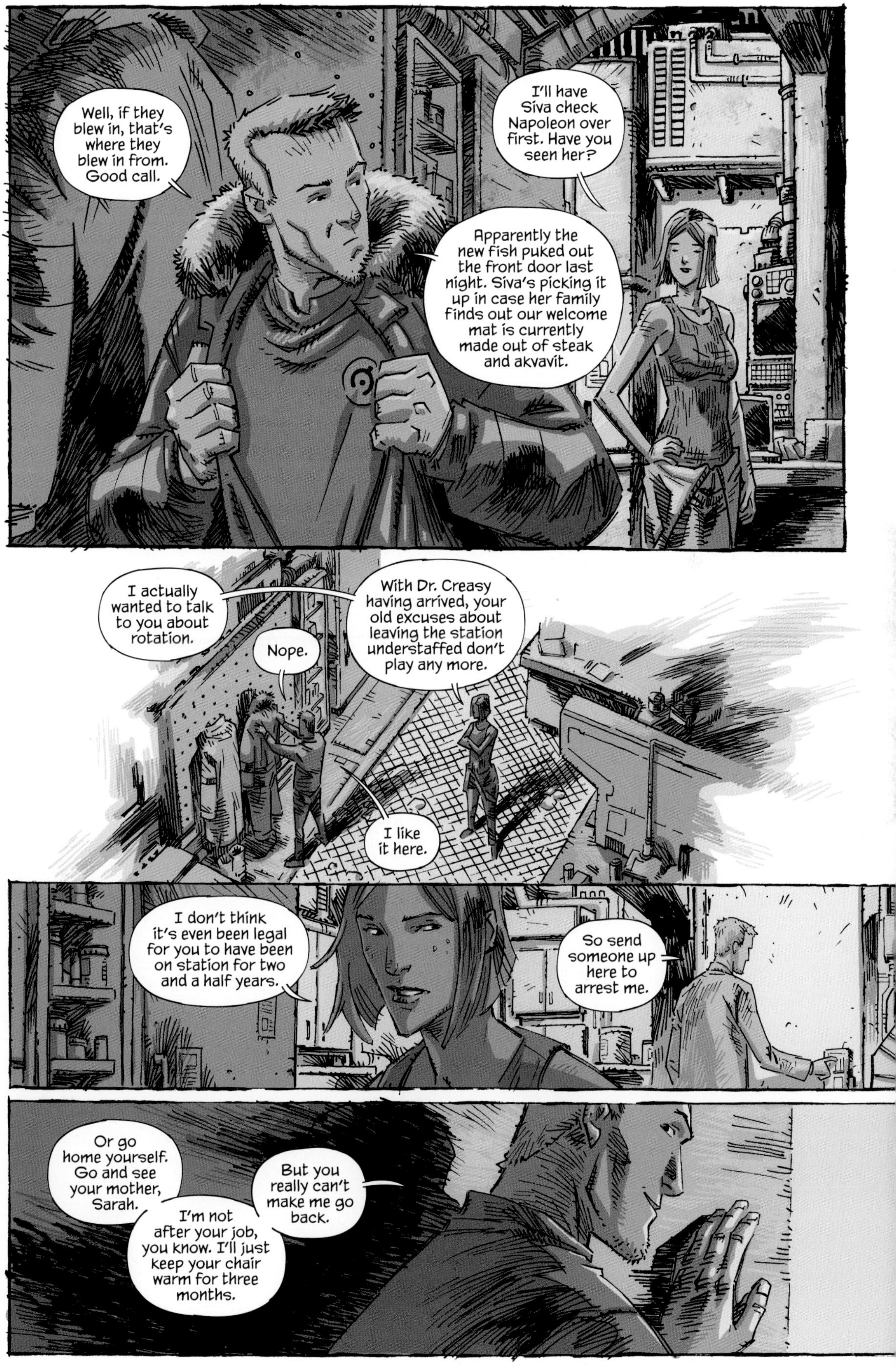
Well, if they blew in, that's where they blew in from. Good call.
I'll have Siva check Napoleon over first. Have you seen her?
Apparently the new fish puked out the front door last night. Siva's picking it up in case her family finds out our welcome mat is currently made out of steak and akvavit.
I actually wanted to talk to you about rotation.
Nope.
With Dr. Creasy having arrived, your old excuses about leaving the station understaffed don't play any more.
I like it here.
I don't think it's even been legal for you to have been on station for two and a half years.
So send someone up here to arrest me.
Or go home yourself. Go and see your mother, Sarah.
I'm not after your job, you know. I'll just keep your chair warm for three months.
But you really can't make me go back.

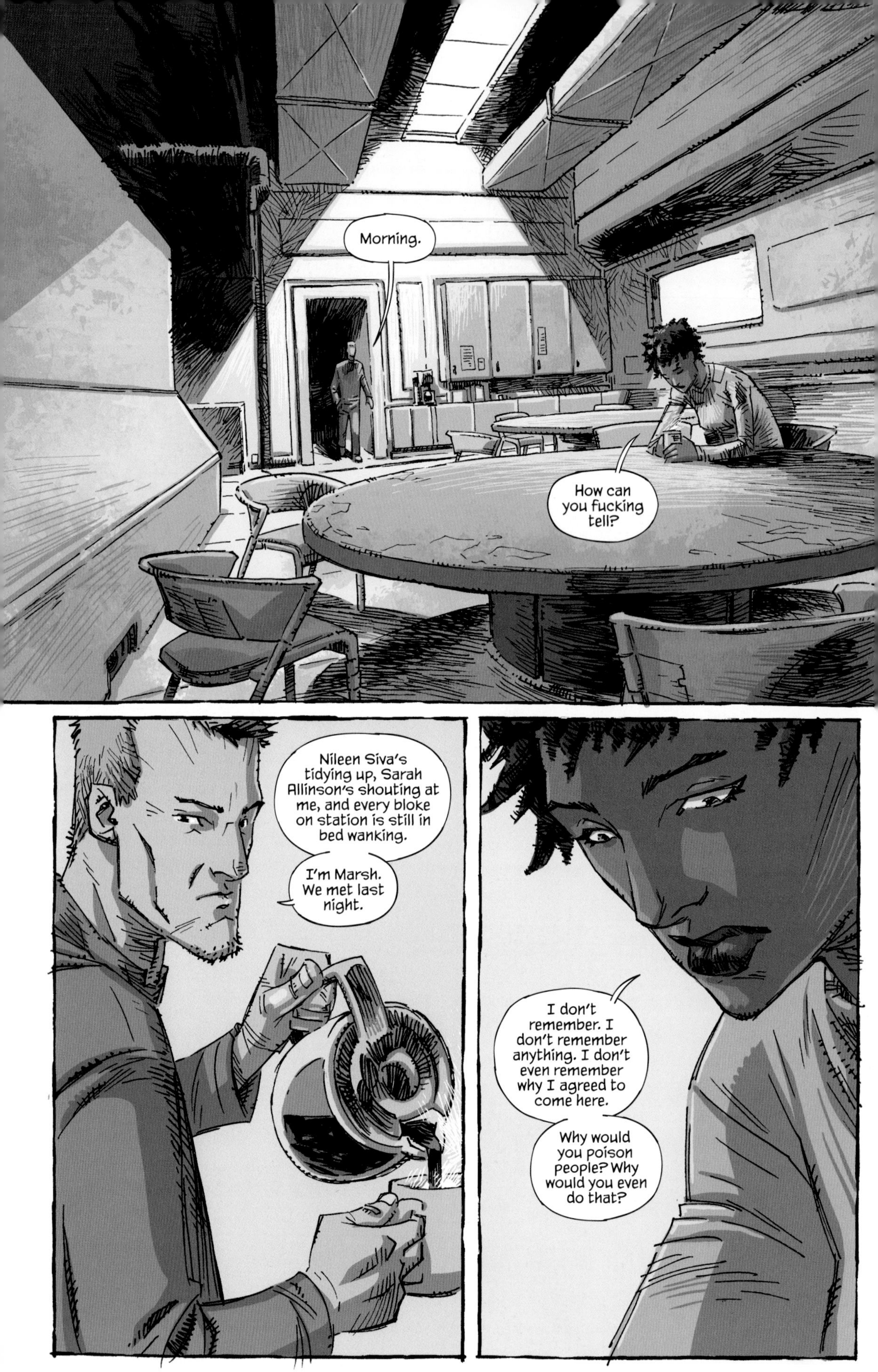
Morning.
How can you fucking tell?
Nileen Siva's tidying up, Sarah Allinson's shouting at me, and every bloke on station is still in bed wanking.
I'm Marsh. We met last night.
I don't remember. I don't remember anything. I don't even remember why I agreed to come here.
Why would you poison people? Why would you even do that?

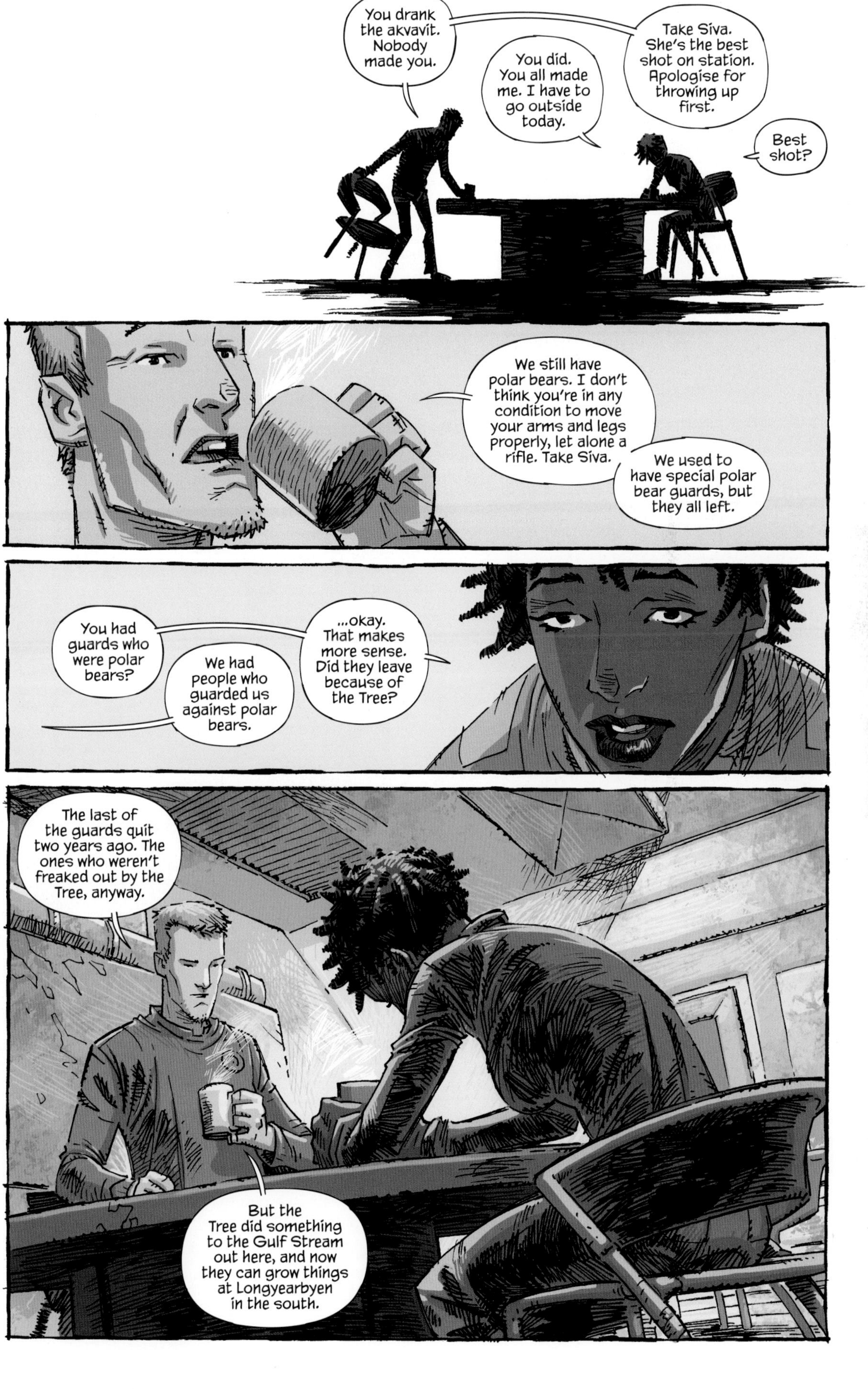
You drank the akvavit. Nobody made you.
You did. You all made me. I have to go outside today.
Take Siva. She's the best shot on station. Apologise for throwing up first.
Best shot?
We still have polar bears. I don't think you're in any condition to move your arms and legs properly, let alone a rifle. Take Siva.
We used to have special polar bear guards, but they all left.
You had guards who were polar bears?
We had people who guarded us against polar bears.
...okay. That makes more sense. Did they leave because of the Tree?
The last of the guards quit two years ago. The ones who weren't freaked out by the Tree, anyway.
But the Tree did something to the Gulf Stream out here, and now they can grow things at Longyearbyen in the south.

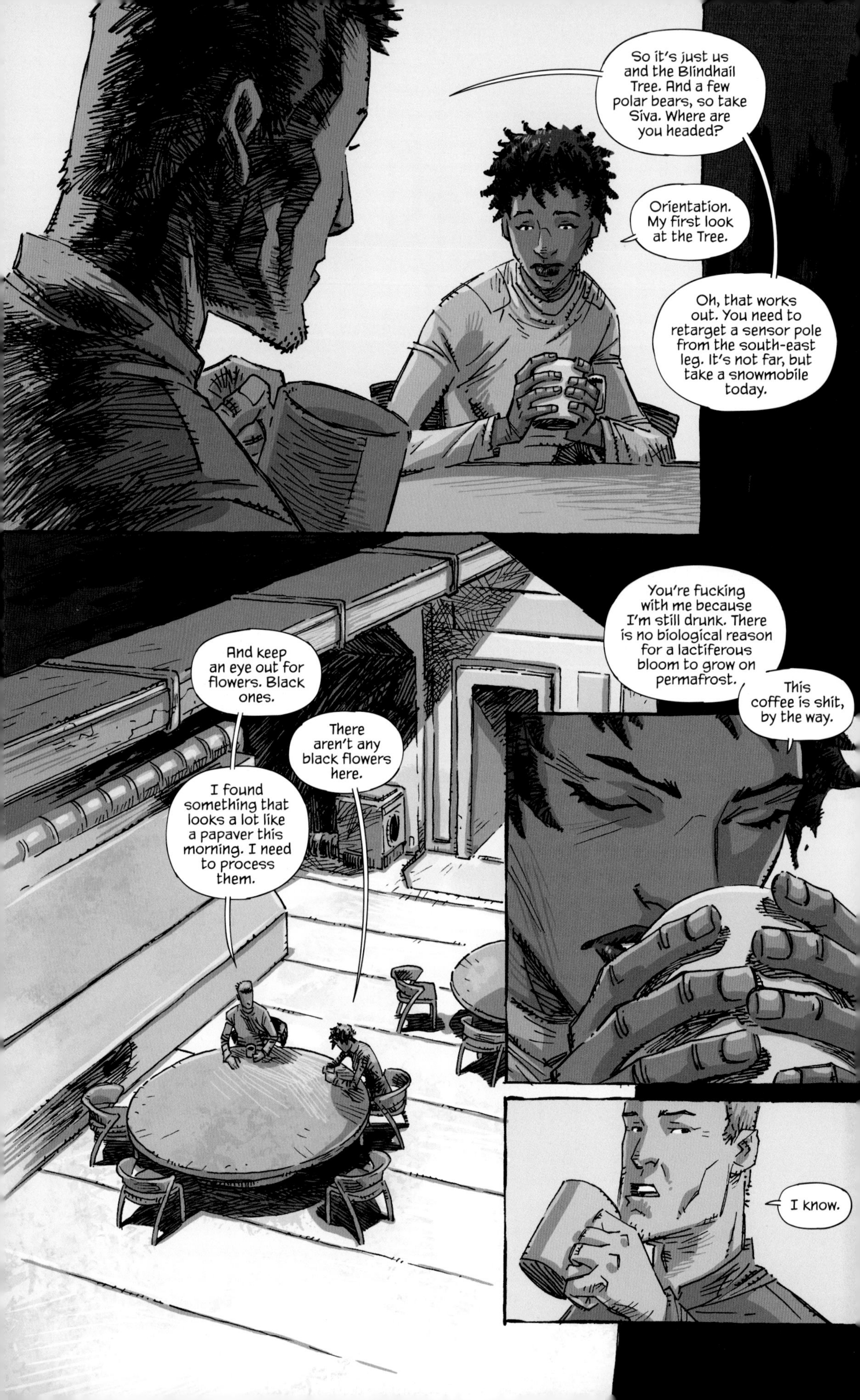
So it's just us and the Blindhail Tree. And a few polar bears, so take Siva. Where are you headed?
Orientation. My first look at the Tree.
Oh, that works out. You need to retarget a sensor pole from the south-east leg. It's not far, but take a snowmobile today.
And keep an eye out for flowers. Black ones.
There aren't any black flowers here.
I found something that looks a lot like a papaver this morning. I need to process them.
You're fucking with me because I'm still drunk. There is no biological reason for a lactiferous bloom to grow on permafrost.
This coffee is shit, by the way.
I know.

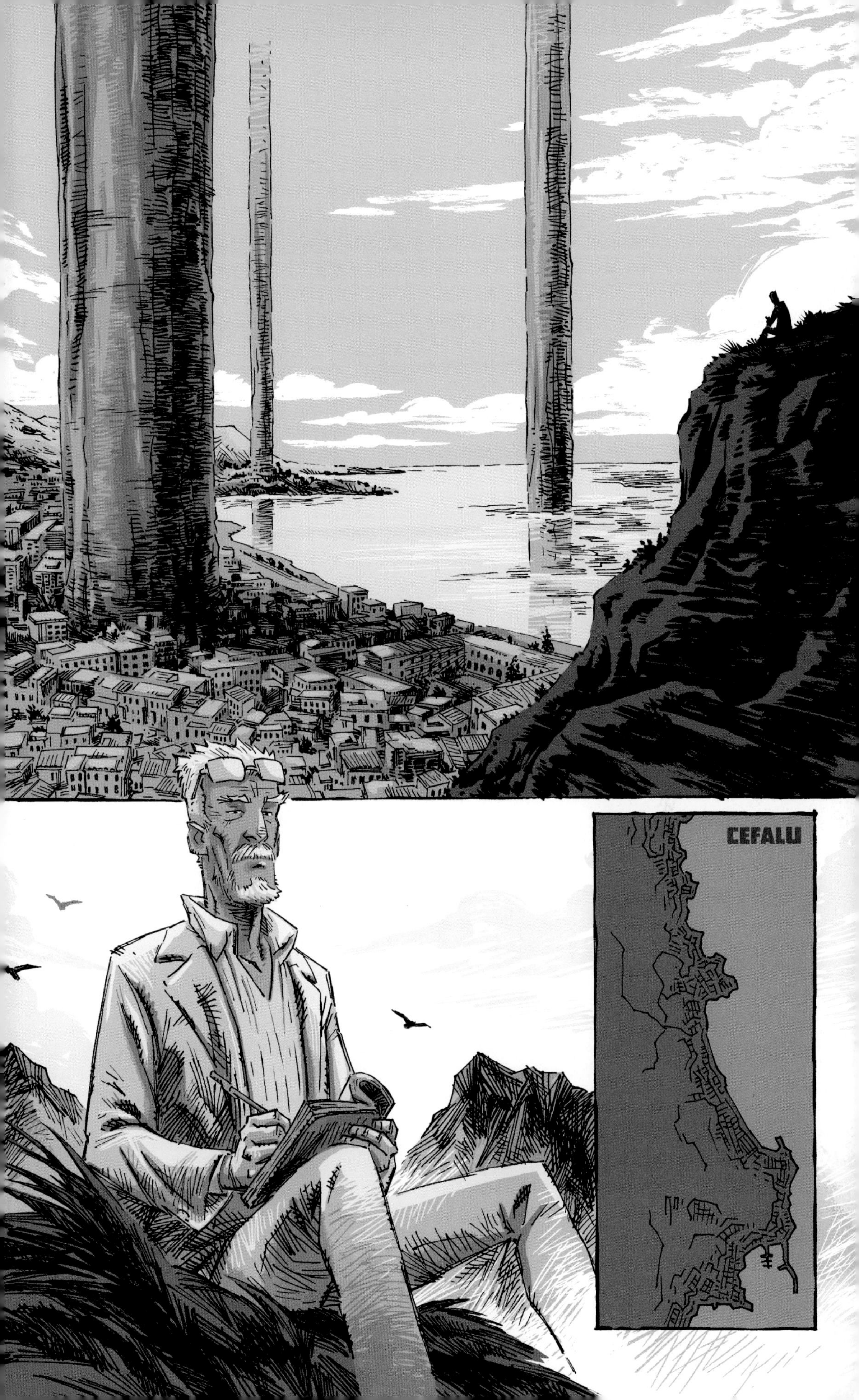
CEFALU

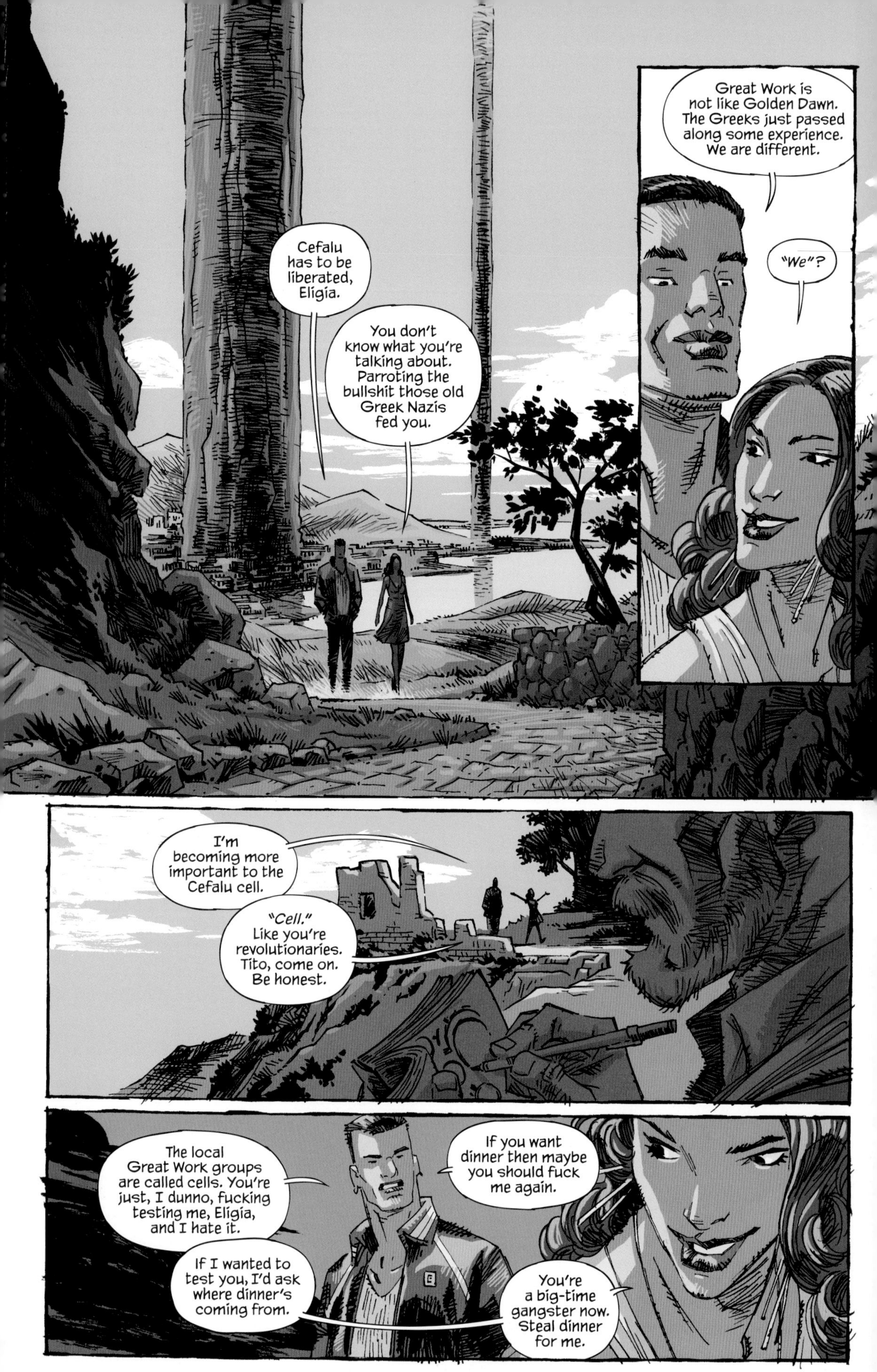
Cefalu has to be liberated, Eligia.
You don't know what you're talking about. Parroting the bullshit those old Greek Nazis fed you.
Great Work is not like Golden Dawn. The Greeks just passed along some experience. We are different.
"We"?
I'm becoming more important to the Cefalu cell.
"Cell." Like you're revolutionaries. Tito, come on. Be honest.
The local Great Work groups are called cells. You're just, I dunno, fucking testing me, Eligia, and I hate it.
If you want dinner then maybe you should fuck me again.
If I wanted to test you, I'd ask where dinner's coming from.
You're a big-time gangster now. Steal dinner for me.

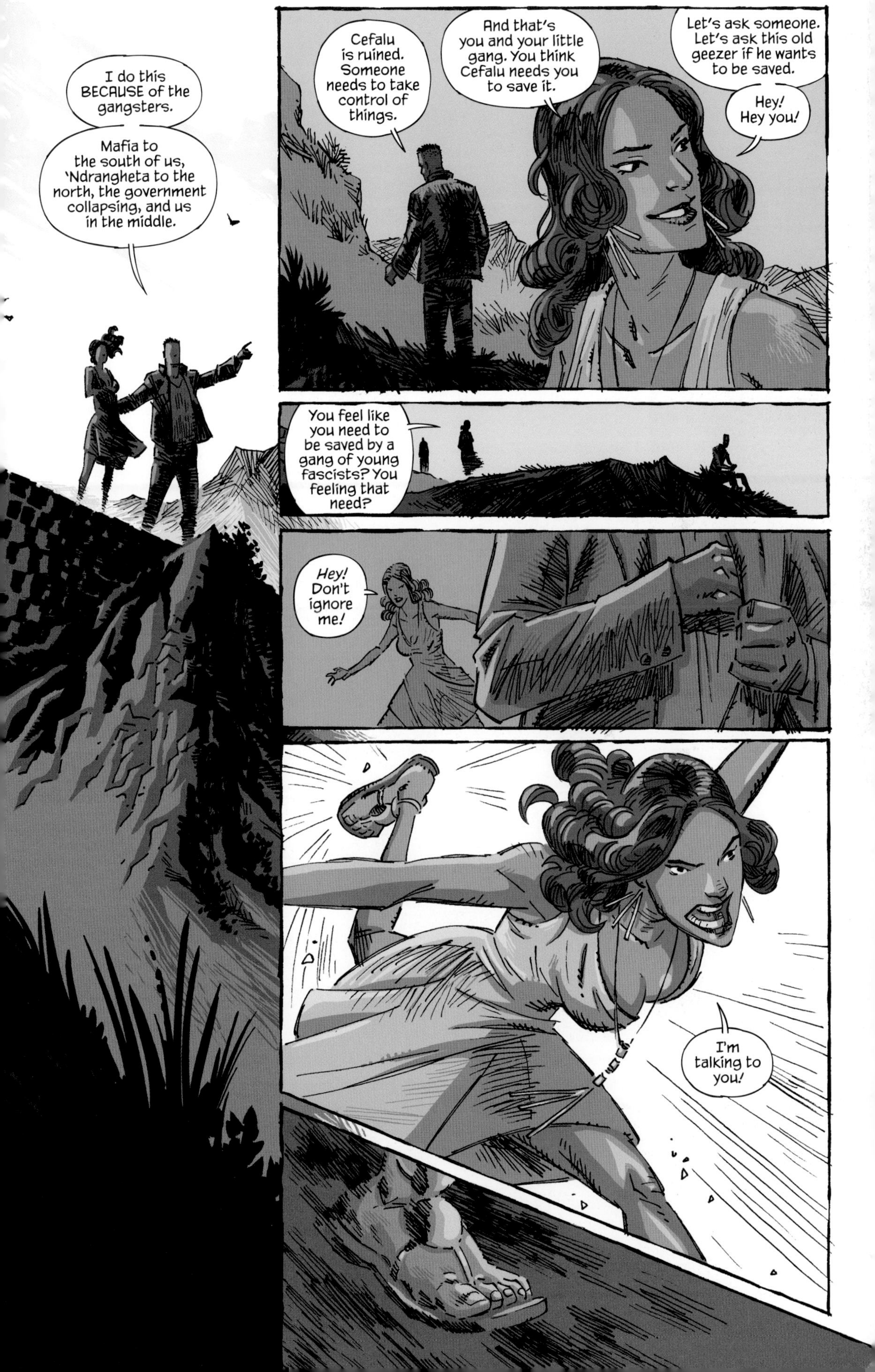
I do this BECAUSE of the gangsters.
Mafia to the south of us, 'Ndrangheta to the north, the government collapsing, and us in the middle.
Cefalu is ruined. Someone needs to take control of things.
And that's you and your little gang. You think Cefalu needs you to save it.
Let's ask someone. Let's ask this old geezer if he wants to be saved.
Hey! Hey you!
You feel like you need to be saved by a gang of young fascists? You feeling that need?
Hey! Don't ignore me!
I'm talking to you!

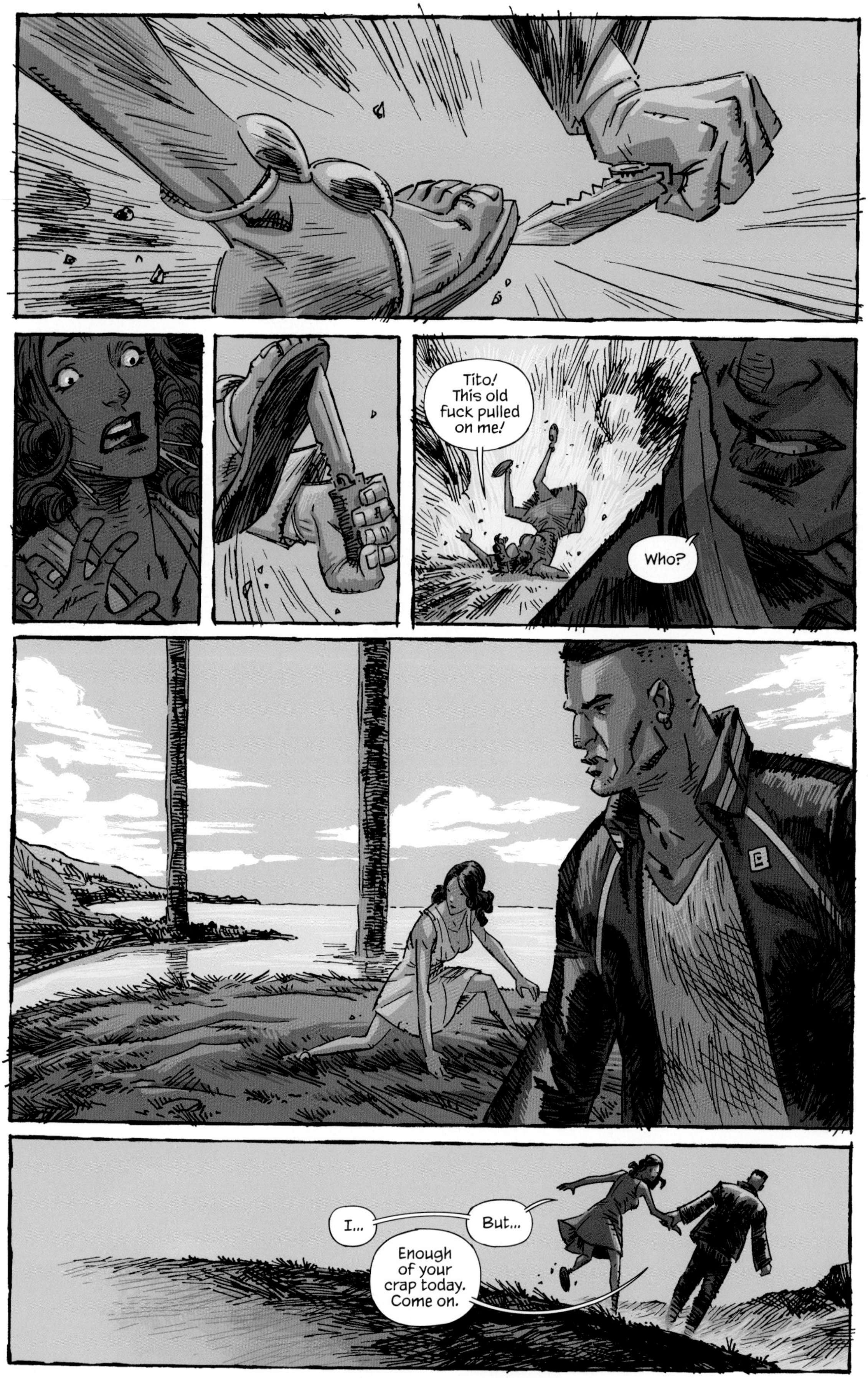
Tito! This old fuck pulled on me!
Who?
I...
But...
Enough of your crap today. Come on.

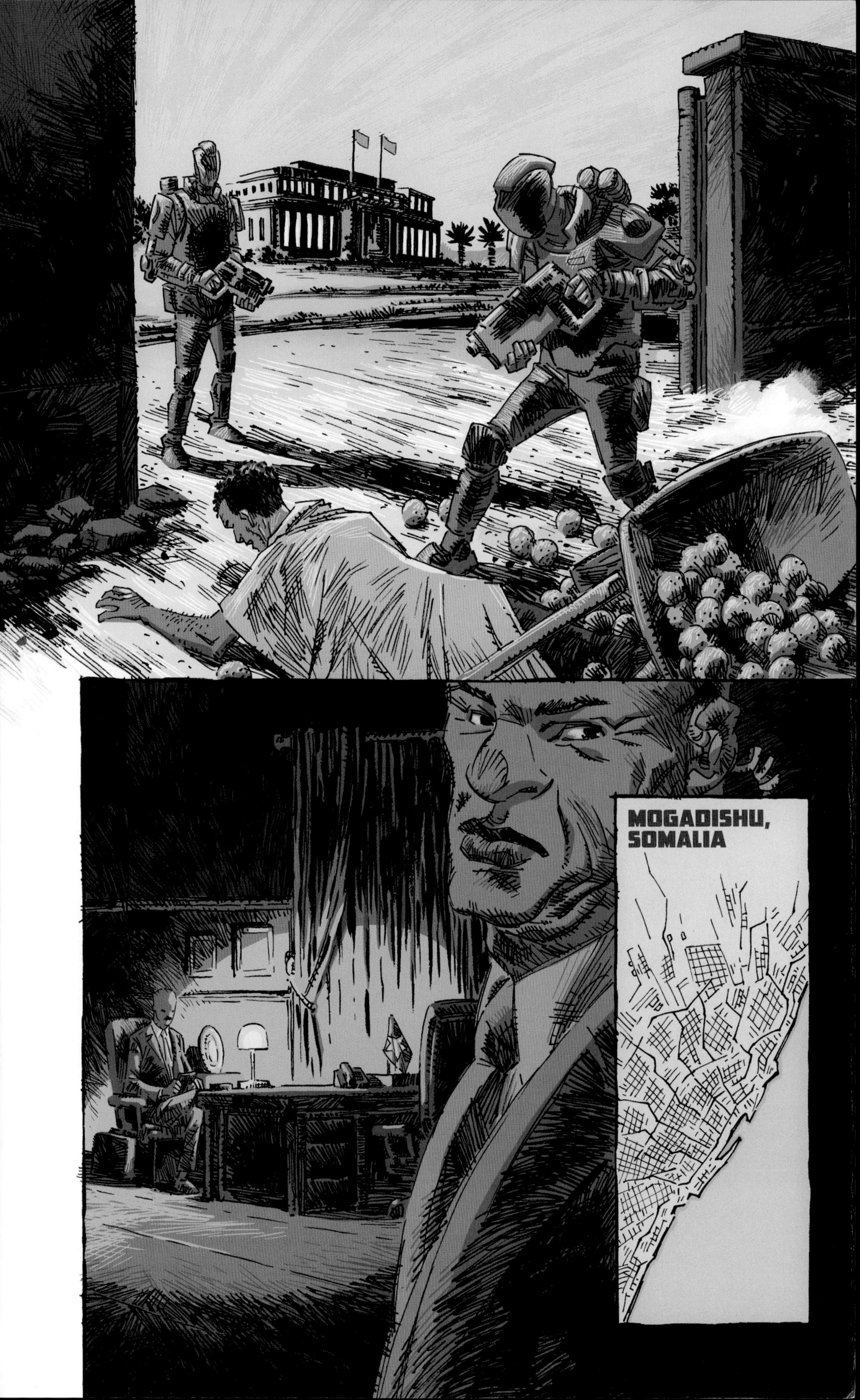
MOGADISHU, SOMALIA

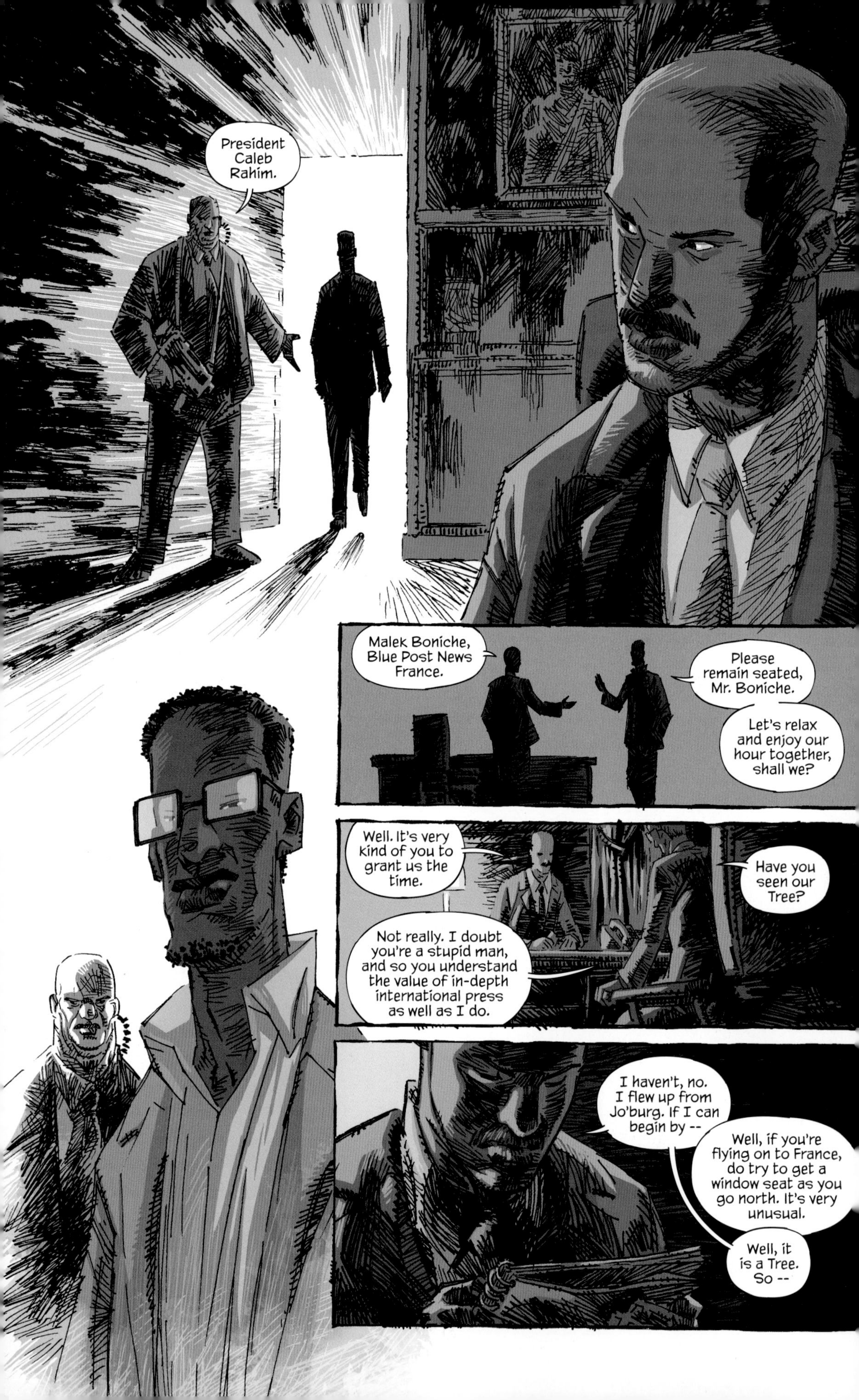
President Caleb Rahim.
Malek Boniche, Blue Post News France.
Please remain seated, Mr. Boniche.
Let's relax and enjoy our hour together, shall we?
Well. It's very kind of you to grant us the time.
Not really. I doubt you're a stupid man, and so you understand the value of in-depth international press as well as I do.
Have you seen our Tree?
I haven't, no. I flew up from Jo'burg. If I can begin by --
Well, if you're flying on to France, do try to get a window seat as you go north. It's very unusual.
Well, it is a Tree. So --

Oh, no, no, it's more than that. We believe it to be the shortest Tree in the world.

It may, in fact, be the only strategic Tree in the world.

I did want to talk a little about strategy, but...

Forgive me. Our Tree is something of a hobby of mine. Not everyone is as fascinated, believe me.

I just, I have questions I need to get to, but--

--but you've kind of hooked me now. How do you mean, strategic?

It's low. Low enough to be accessible by helicopter. And it straddles federated Somali territory and Puntland.

The Puntland Tree, strategically speaking, is a stage.

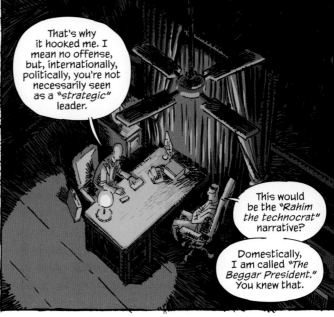

That's why it hooked me. I mean no offense, but, internationally, politically, you're not necessarily seen as a "strategic" leader.

This would be the "Rahim the technocrat" narrative?

Domestically, I am called "The Beggar President." You knew that.

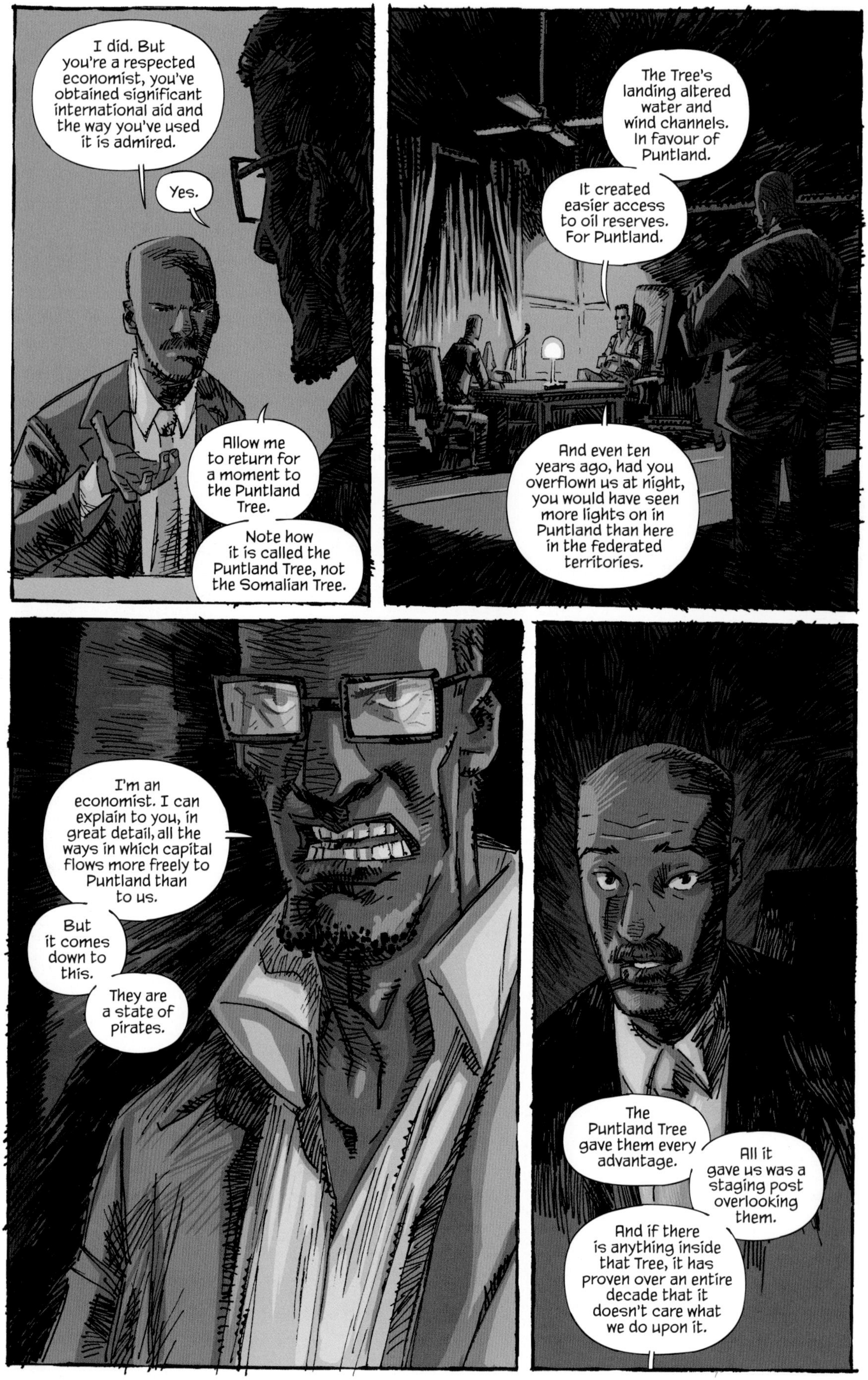
I did. But you're a respected economist, you've obtained significant international aid and the way you've used it is admired.
Yes.
Allow me to return for a moment to the Puntland Tree.
Note how it is called the Puntland Tree, not the Somalian Tree.
The Tree's landing altered water and wind channels. In favour of Puntland.
It created easier access to oil reserves. For Puntland.
And even ten years ago, had you overflown us at night, you would have seen more lights on in Puntland than here in the federated territories.
I'm an economist. I can explain to you, in great detail, all the ways in which capital flows more freely to Puntland than to us.
But it comes down to this.
They are a state of pirates.
The Puntland Tree gave them every advantage.
All it gave us was a staging post overlooking them.
And if there is anything inside that Tree, it has proven over an entire decade that it doesn't care what we do upon it.

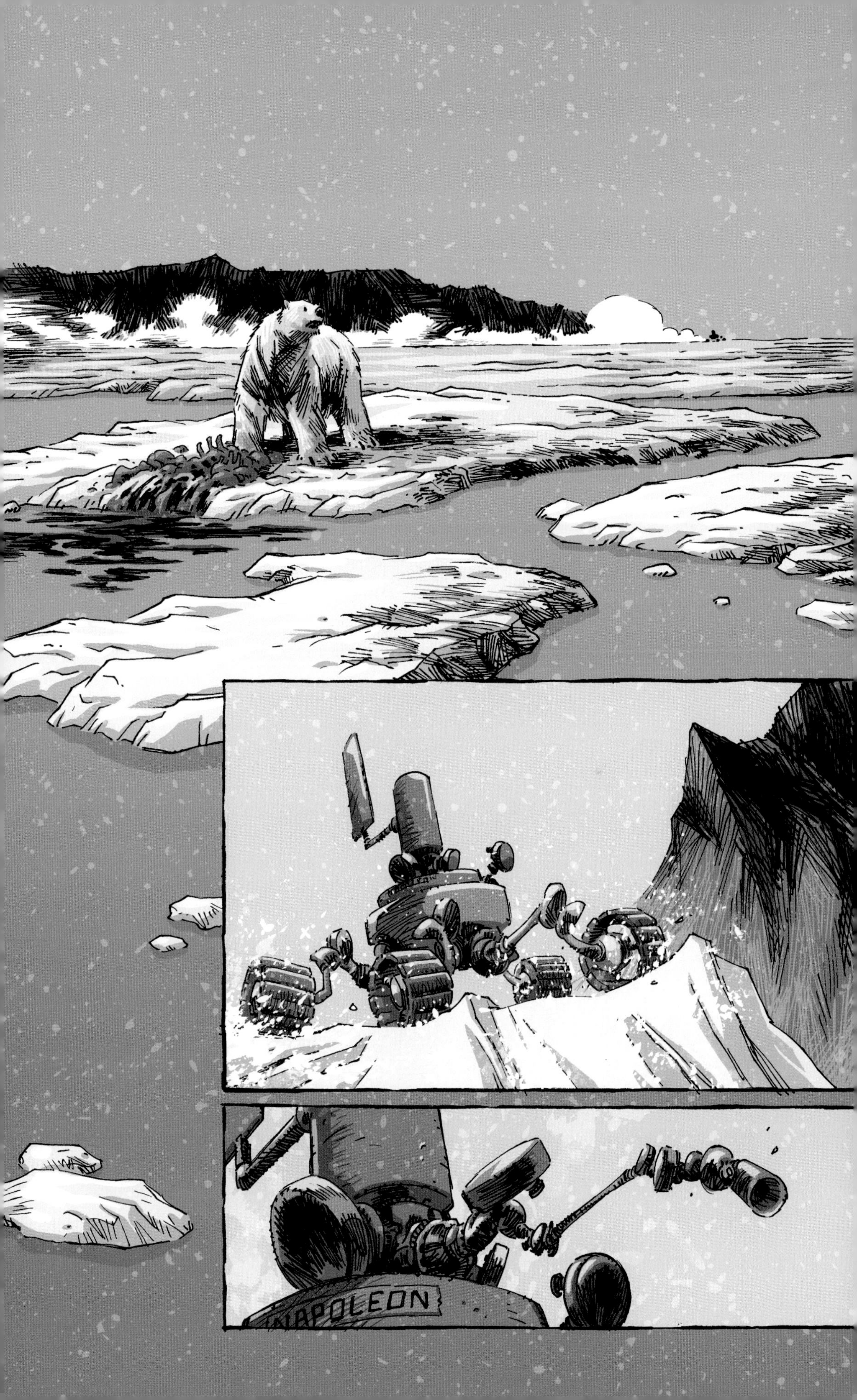
NAPOLEON

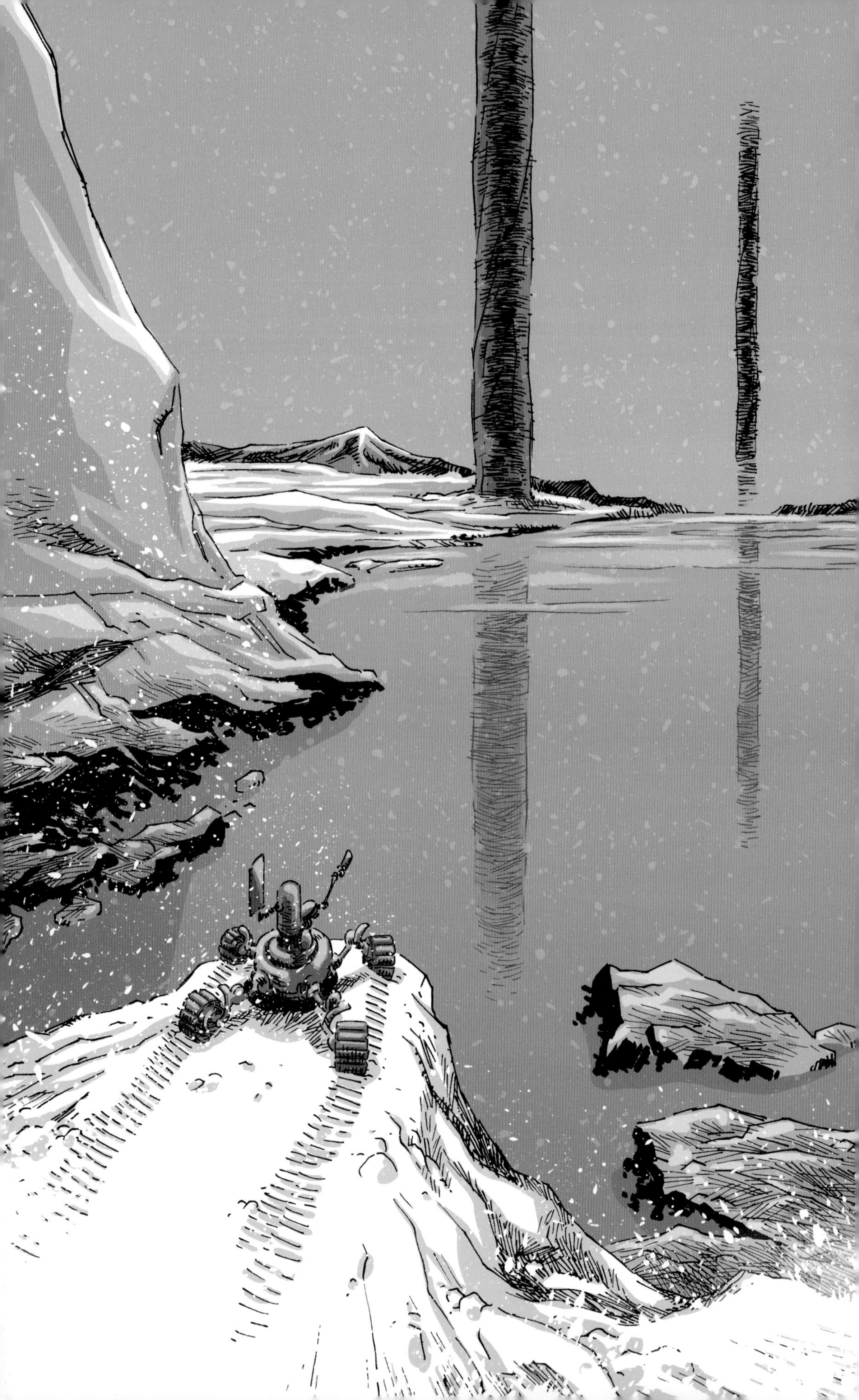

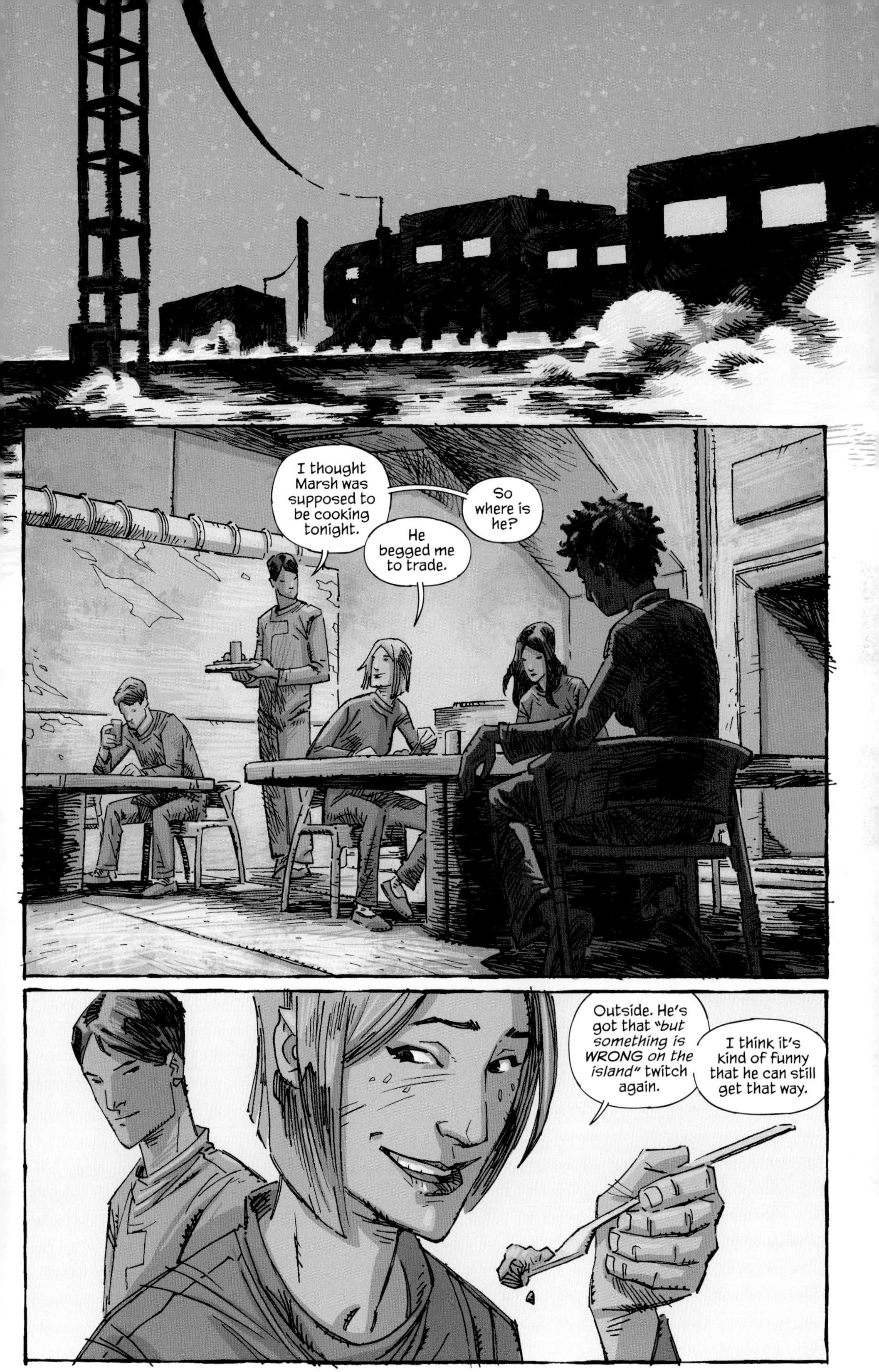
I thought Marsh was supposed to be cooking tonight.
So where is he?
He begged me to trade.
Outside. He's got that "but something is WRONG on the island" twitch again.
I think it's kind of funny that he can still get that way.

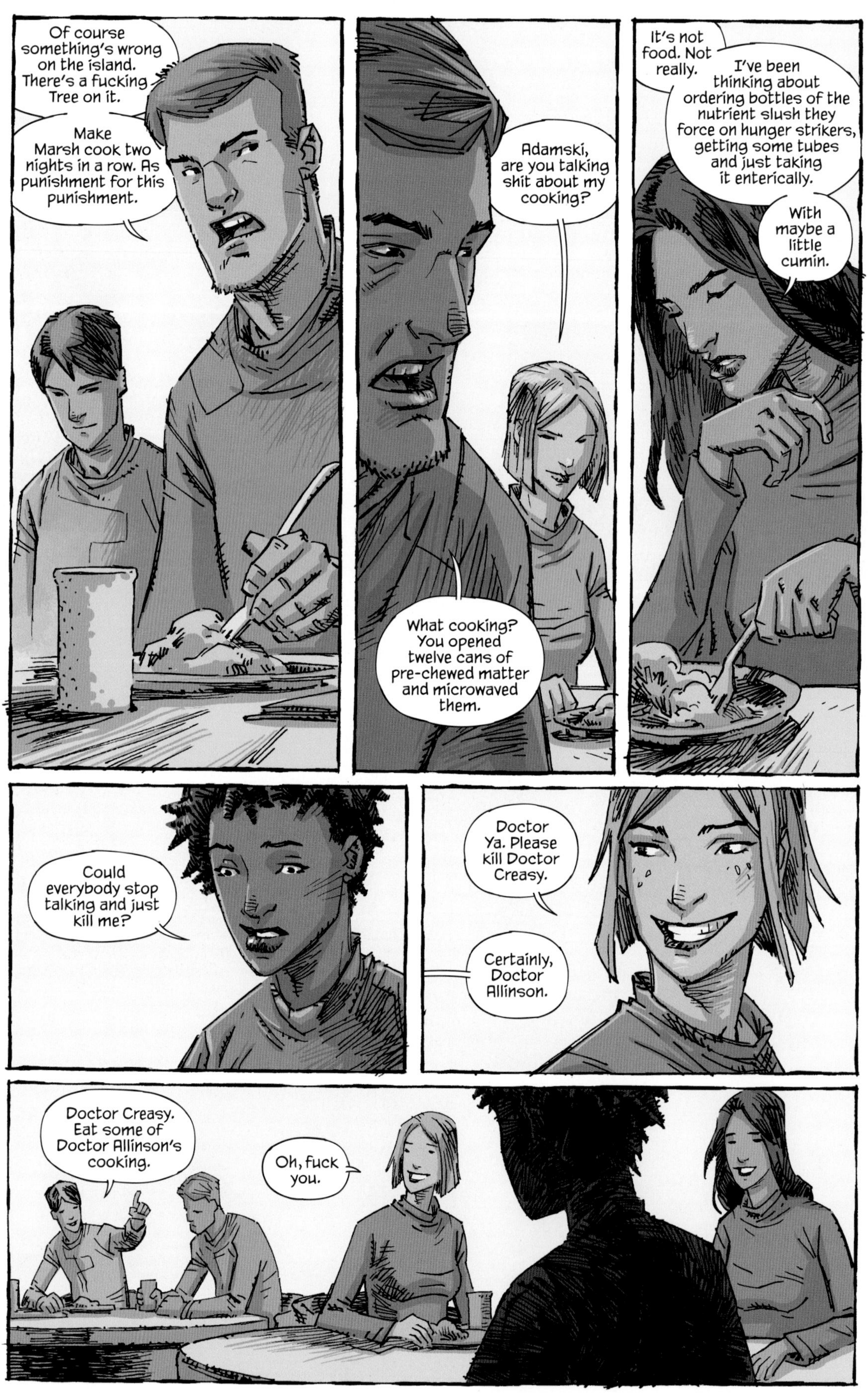
Of course something's wrong on the island. There's a fucking Tree on it.
Make Marsh cook two nights in a row. As punishment for this punishment.
Adamski, are you talking shit about my cooking?
What cooking? You opened twelve cans of pre-chewed matter and microwaved them.
It's not food. Not really.
I've been thinking about ordering bottles of the nutrient slush they force on hunger strikers, getting some tubes and just taking it enterically.
With maybe a little cumin.
Could everybody stop talking and just kill me?
Doctor Ya. Please kill Doctor Creasy.
Certainly, Doctor Allinson.
Doctor Creasy. Eat some of Doctor Allinson's cooking.
Oh, fuck you.

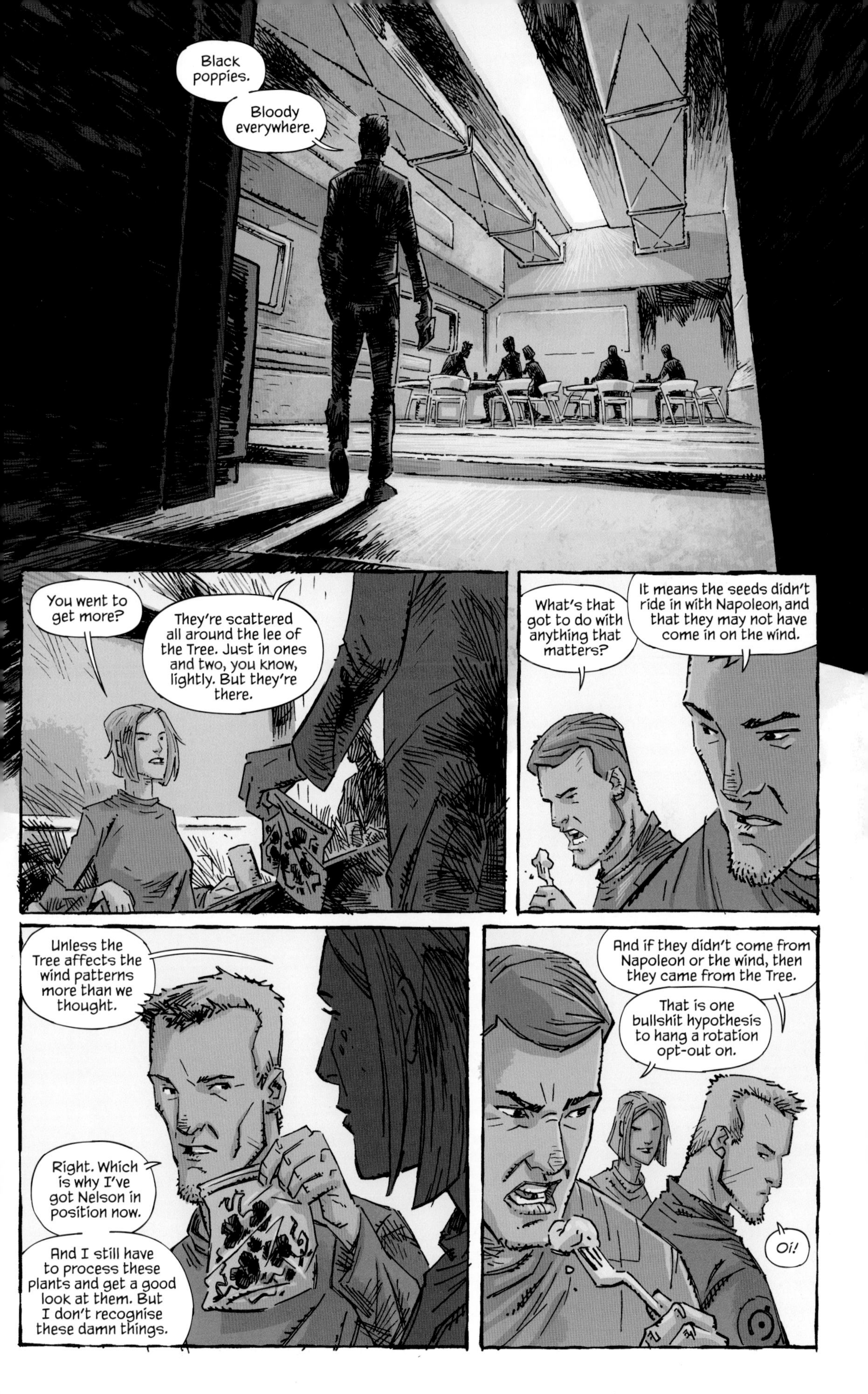
Black poppies.
Bloody everywhere.
You went to get more?
They're scattered all around the lee of the Tree. Just in ones and two, you know, lightly. But they're there.
What's that got to do with anything that matters?
It means the seeds didn't ride in with Napoleon, and that they may not have come in on the wind.
Unless the Tree affects the wind patterns more than we thought.
Right. Which is why I've got Nelson in position now.
And I still have to process these plants and get a good look at them. But I don't recognise these damn things.
And if they didn't come from Napoleon or the wind, then they came from the Tree.
That is one bullshit hypothesis to hang a rotation opt-out on.
Oi!

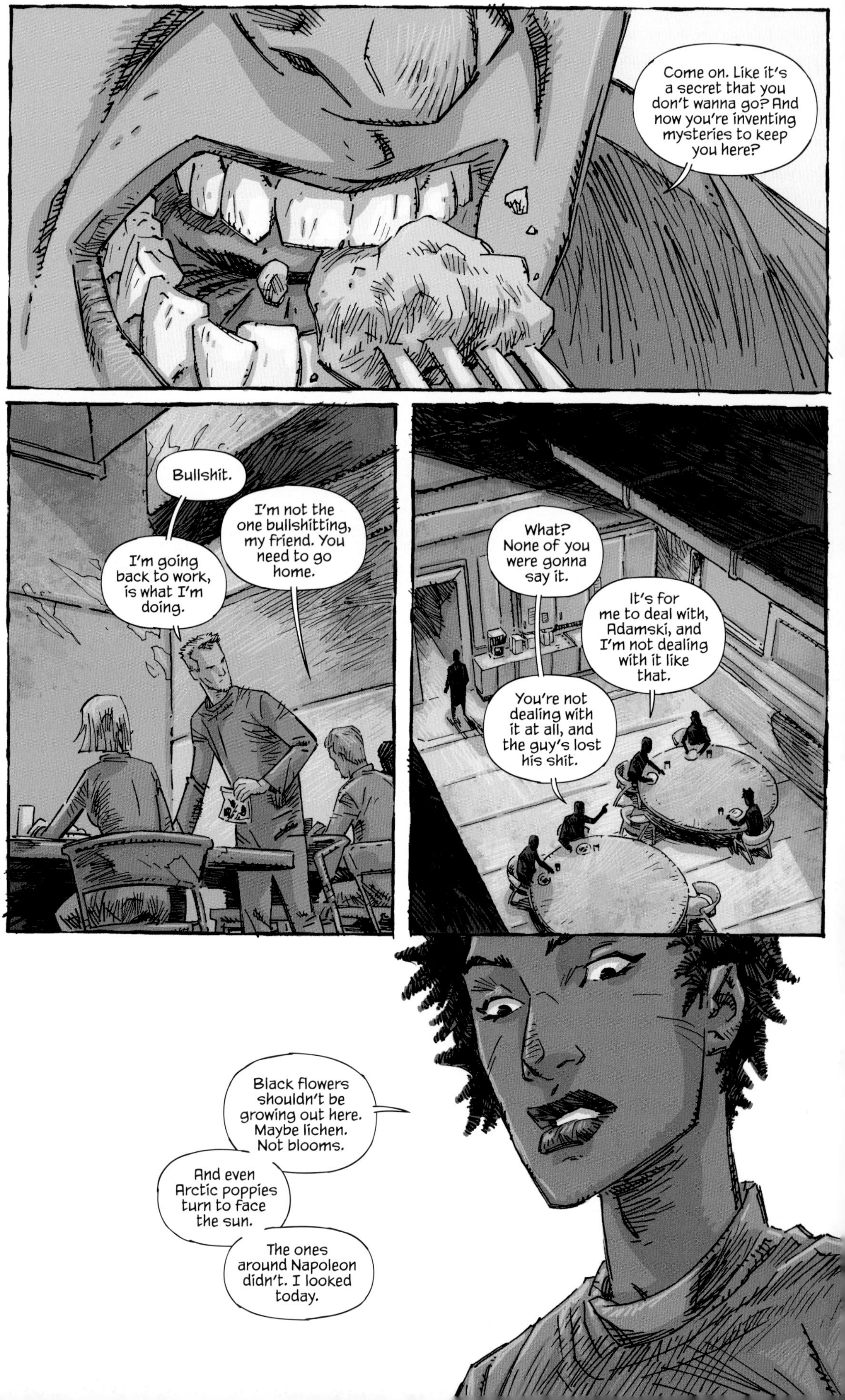
Come on. Like it's a secret that you don't wanna go? And now you're inventing mysteries to keep you here?
Bullshit.
I'm going back to work, is what I'm doing.
I'm not the one bullshitting, my friend. You need to go home.
What? None of you were gonna say it.
You're not dealing with it at all, and the guy's lost his shit.
It's for me to deal with, Adamski, and I'm not dealing with it like that.
Black flowers shouldn't be growing out here. Maybe lichen. Not blooms.
And even Arctic poppies turn to face the sun.
The ones around Napoleon didn't. I looked today.

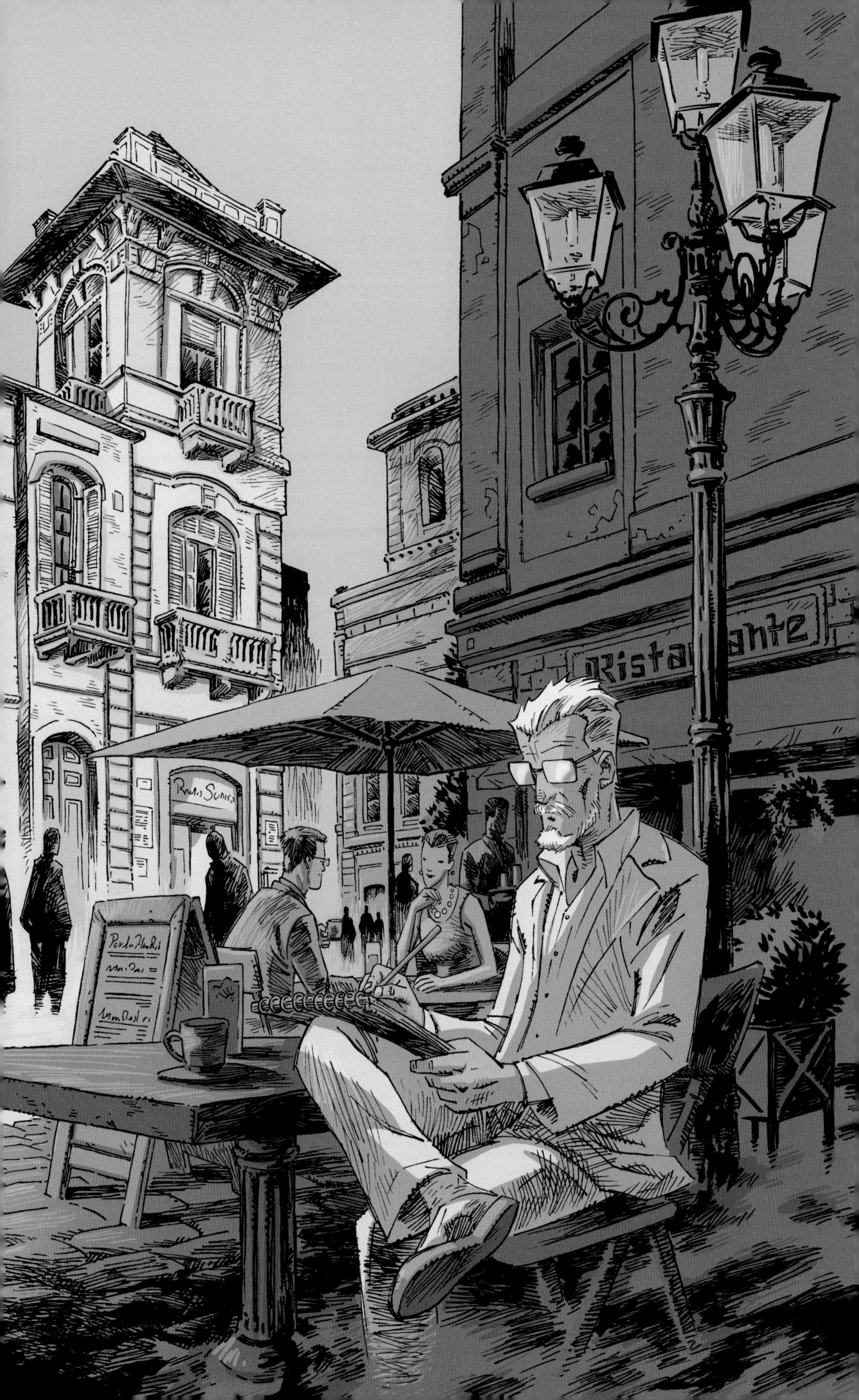

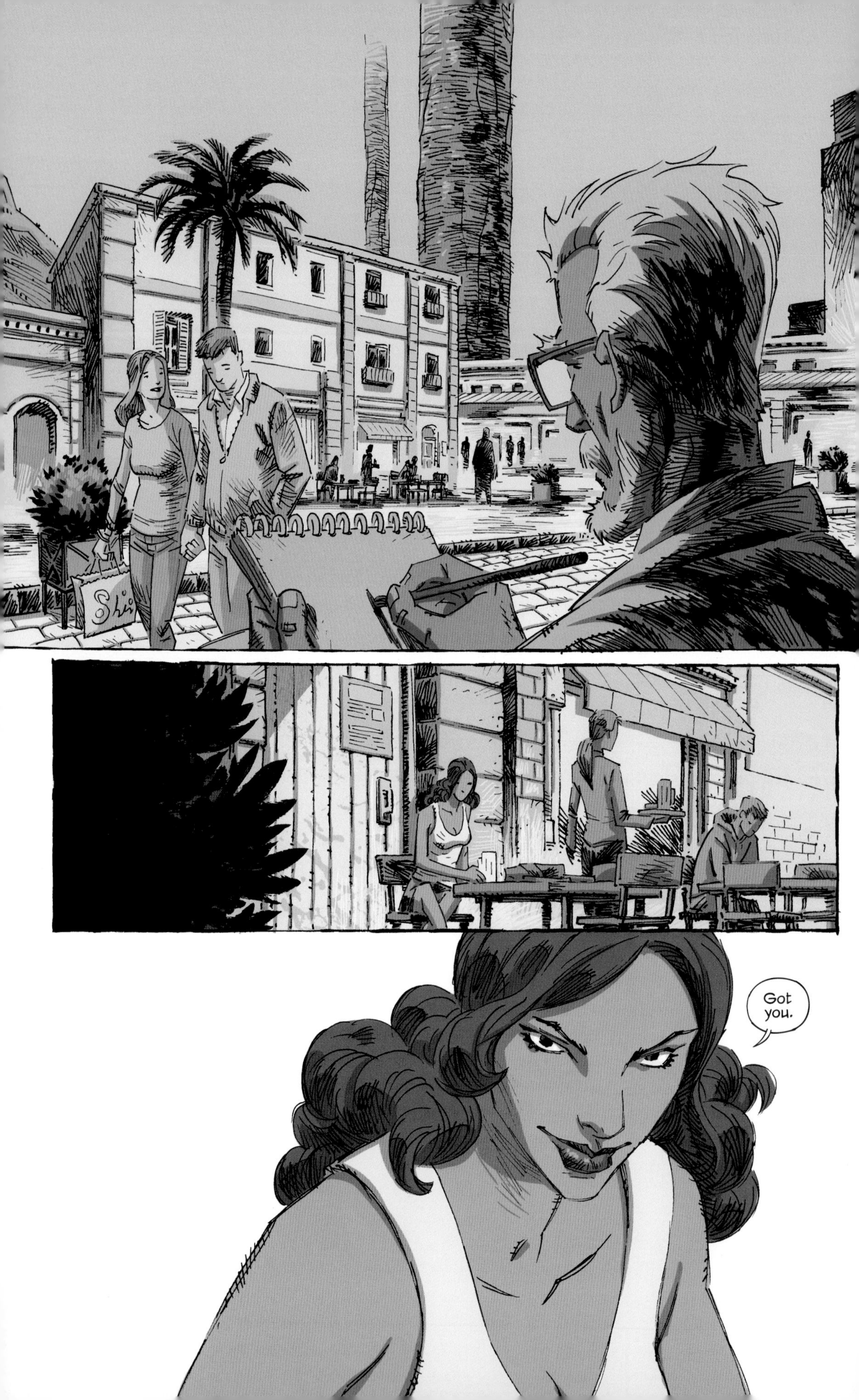
Got you.

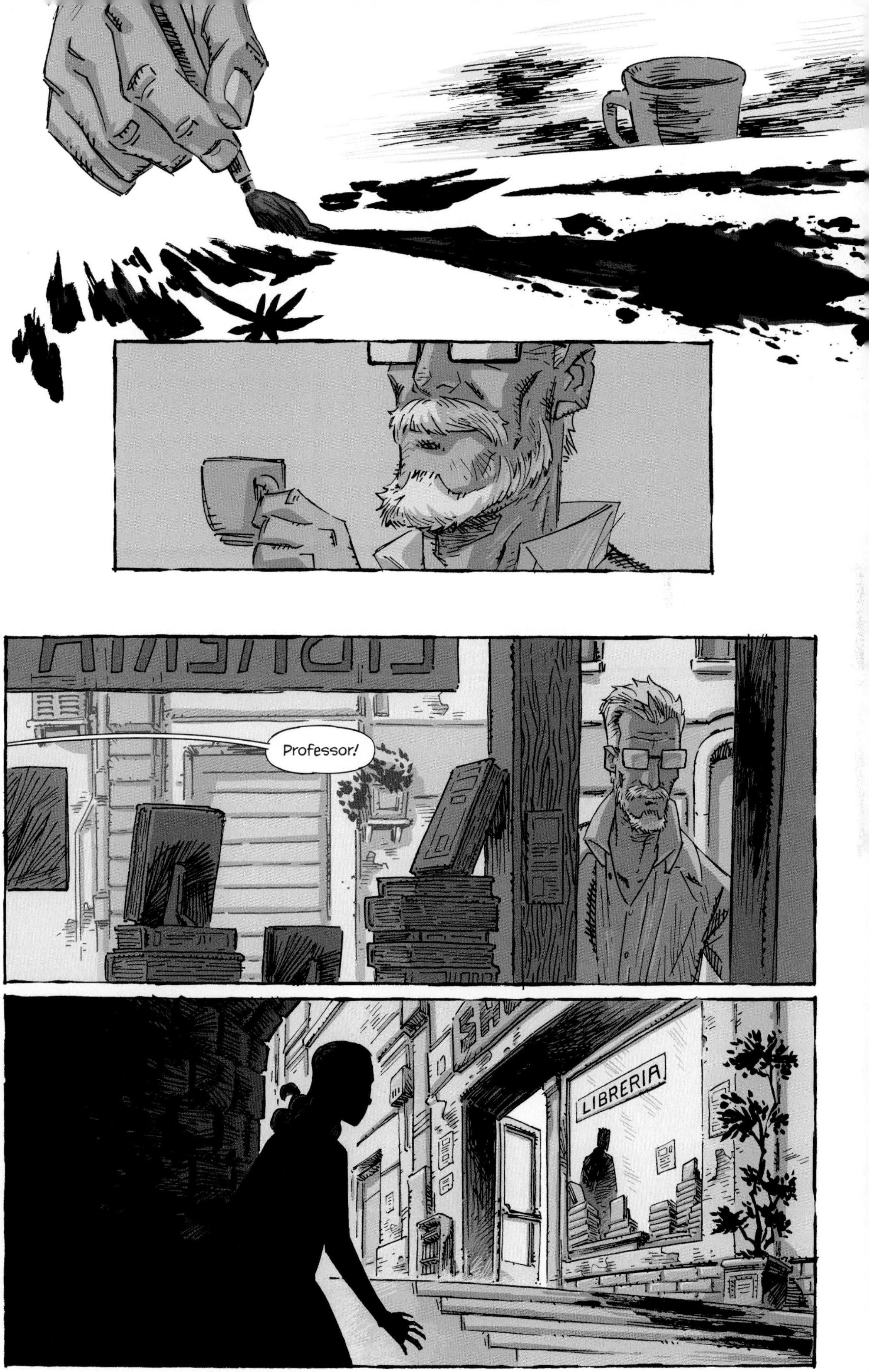
Professor!
LIBRERIA

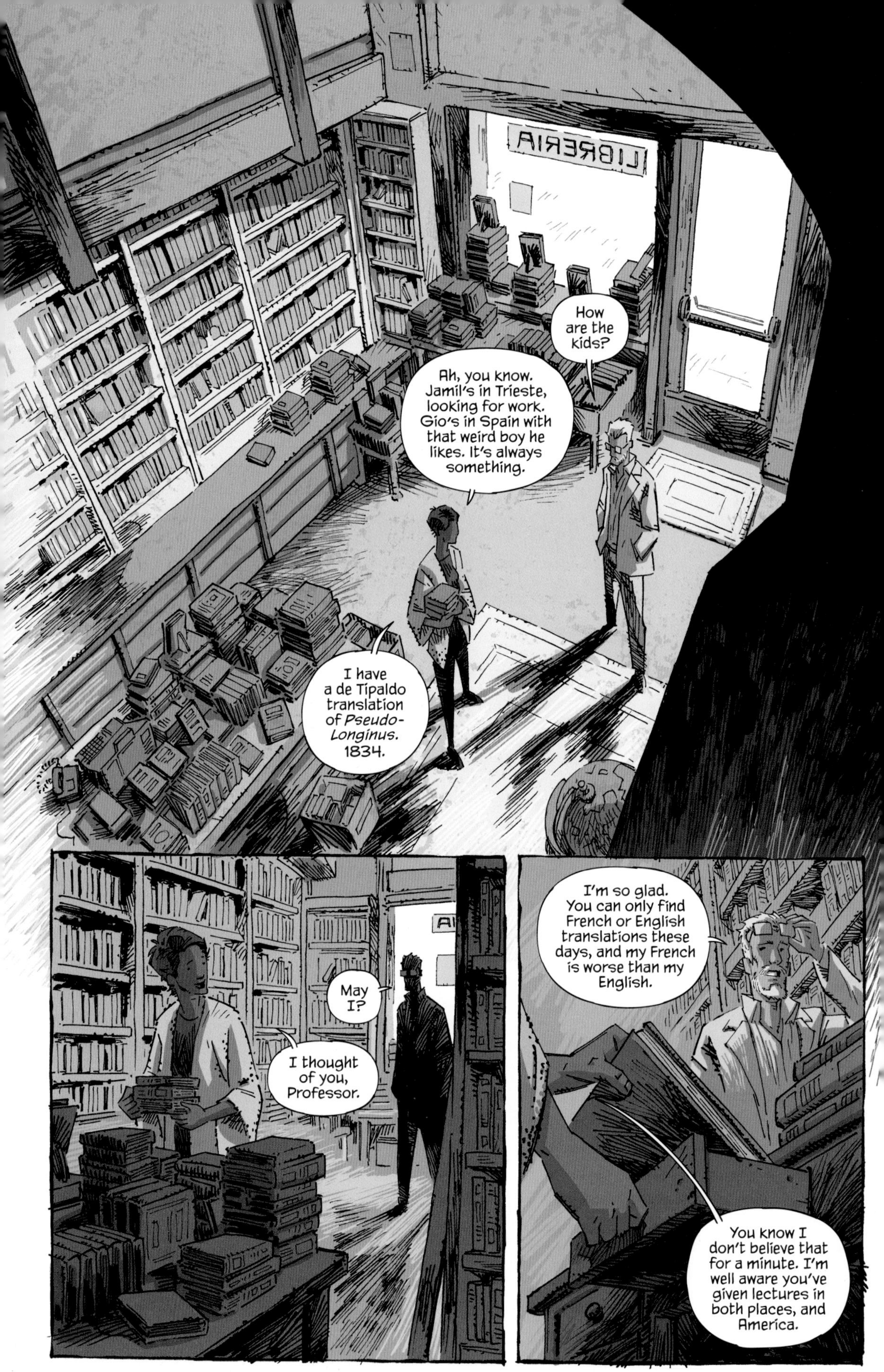
LIBRERIA
How are the kids?
Ah, you know. Jamil's in Trieste, looking for work. Gio's in Spain with that weird boy he likes. It's always something.
I have a de Tipaldo translation of *Pseudo-Longinus.* 1834.
May I?
I thought of you, Professor.
I'm so glad. You can only find French or English translations these days, and my French is worse than my English.
You know I don't believe that for a minute. I'm well aware you've given lectures in both places, and America.

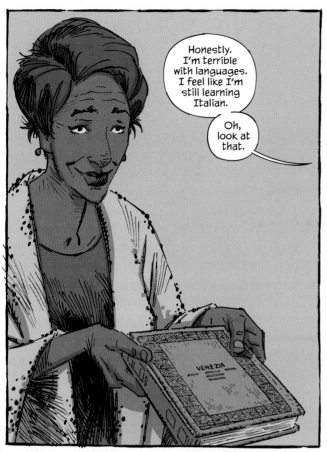

Honestly. I'm terrible with languages. I feel like I'm still learning Italian.
Oh, look at that.
VENEZIA
Wonderful.
Messages about beauty from deep time.
DEL SUBLIME
TRATTATO
"Many barbarians, in the poverty and meagreness of their art, call hills, and motionless trees, and unmarked stones by the name of gods, though in no way nearer to gods than is their form."

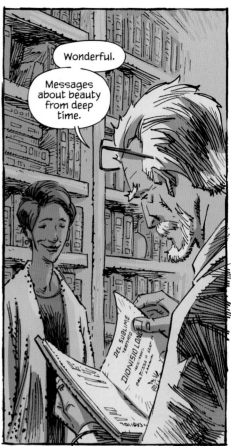

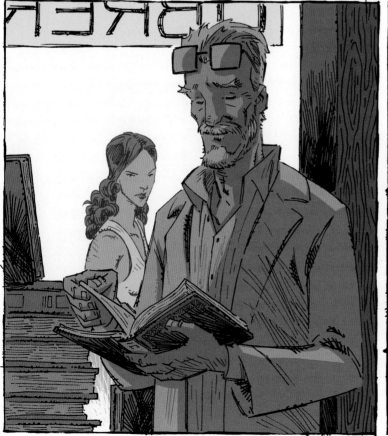

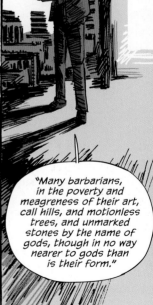

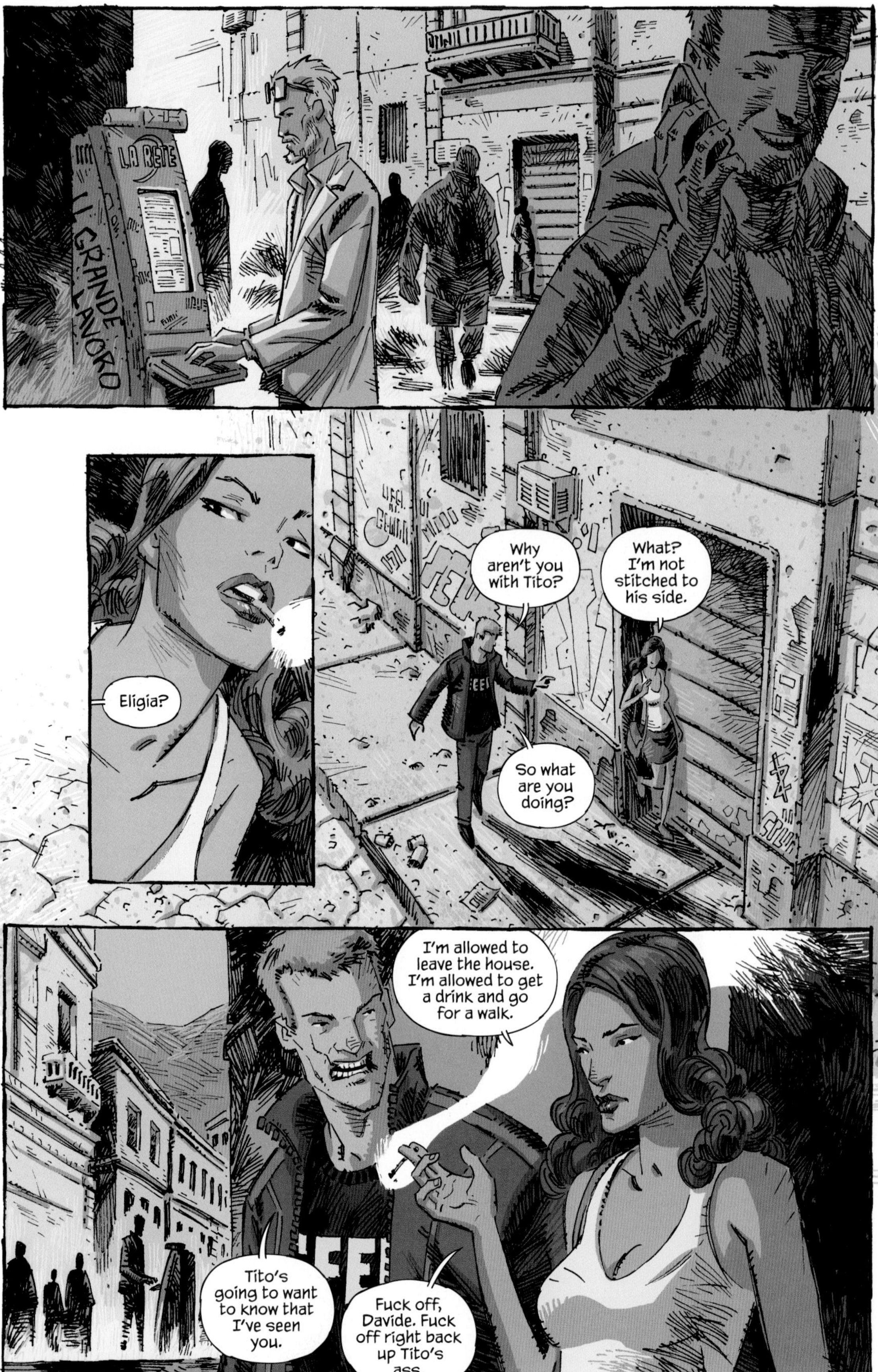
LA RETE
IL GRANDE LAVORO
Eligia?
Why aren't you with Tito?
What? I'm not stitched to his side.
So what are you doing?
I'm allowed to leave the house. I'm allowed to get a drink and go for a walk.
Tito's going to want to know that I've seen you.
Fuck off, Davide. Fuck off right back up Tito's ass.

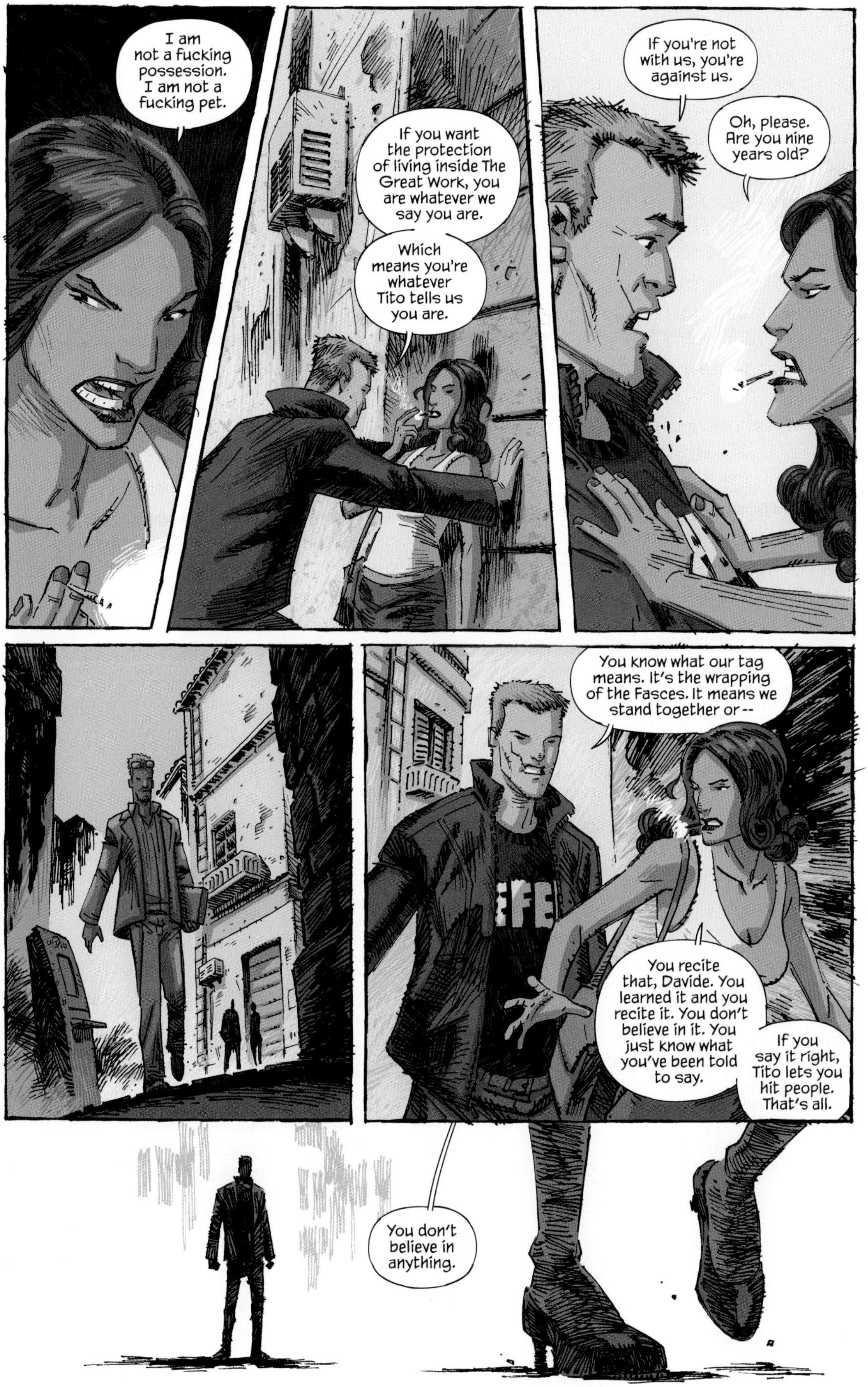
I am not a fucking possession. I am not a fucking pet.
If you want the protection of living inside The Great Work, you are whatever we say you are.
Which means you're whatever Tito tells us you are.
If you're not with us, you're against us.
Oh, please. Are you nine years old?
You know what our tag means. It's the wrapping of the Fasces. It means we stand together or --
You recite that, Davide. You learned it and you recite it. You don't believe in it. You just know what you've been told to say.
If you say it right, Tito lets you hit people. That's all.
You don't believe in anything.

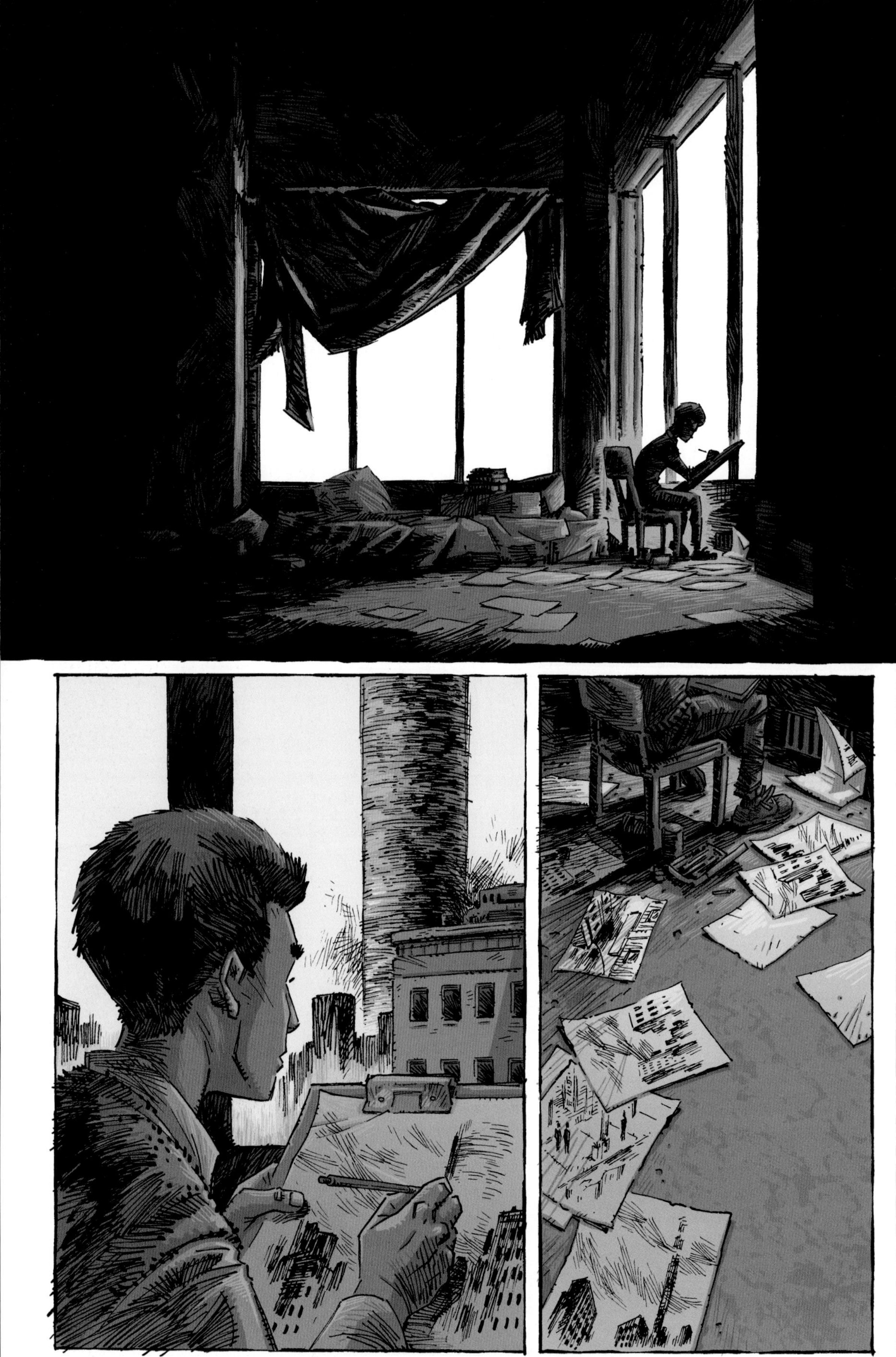

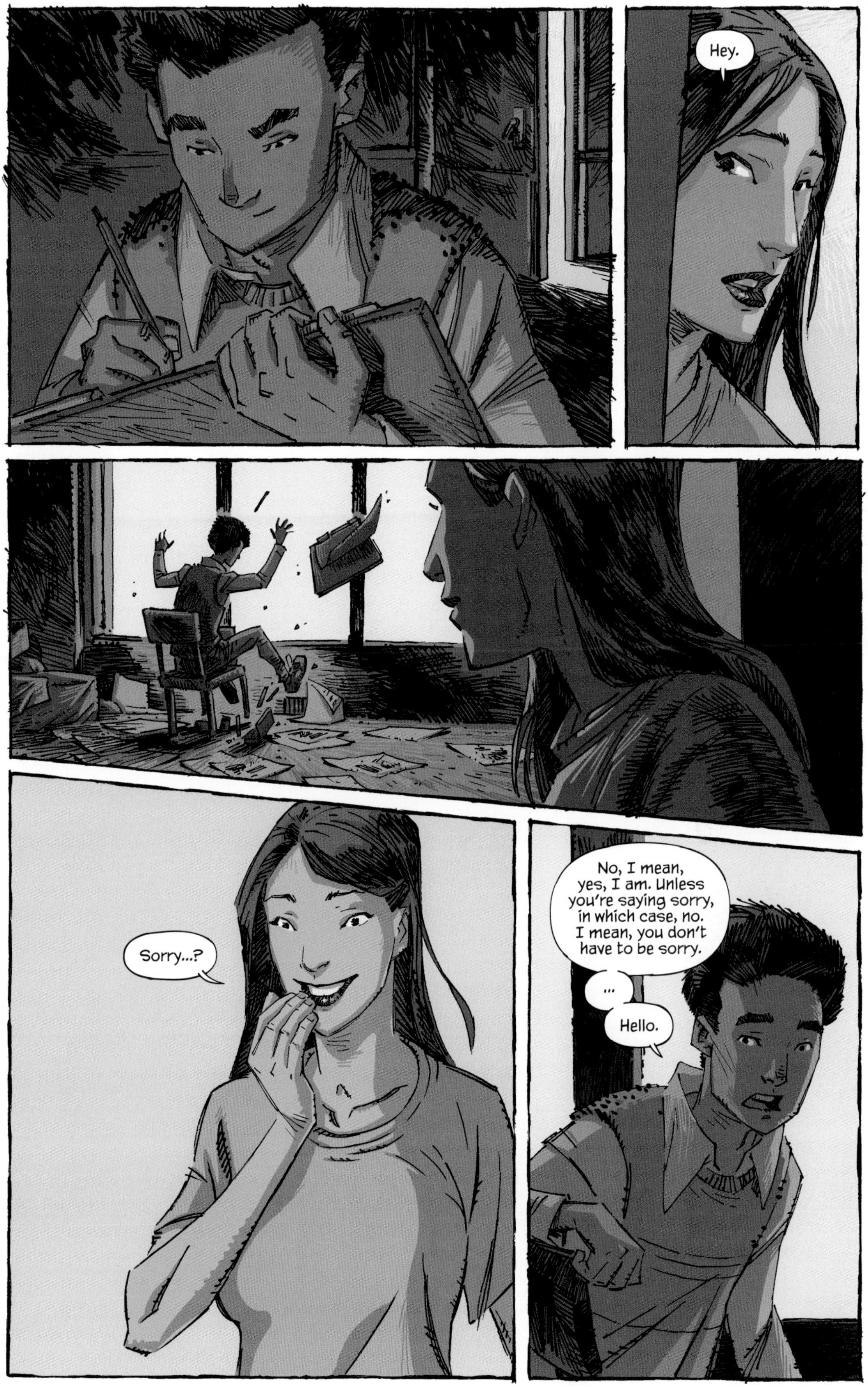
Hey.
Sorry...?
No, I mean, yes, I am. Unless you're saying sorry, in which case, no. I mean, you don't have to be sorry.
...
Hello.

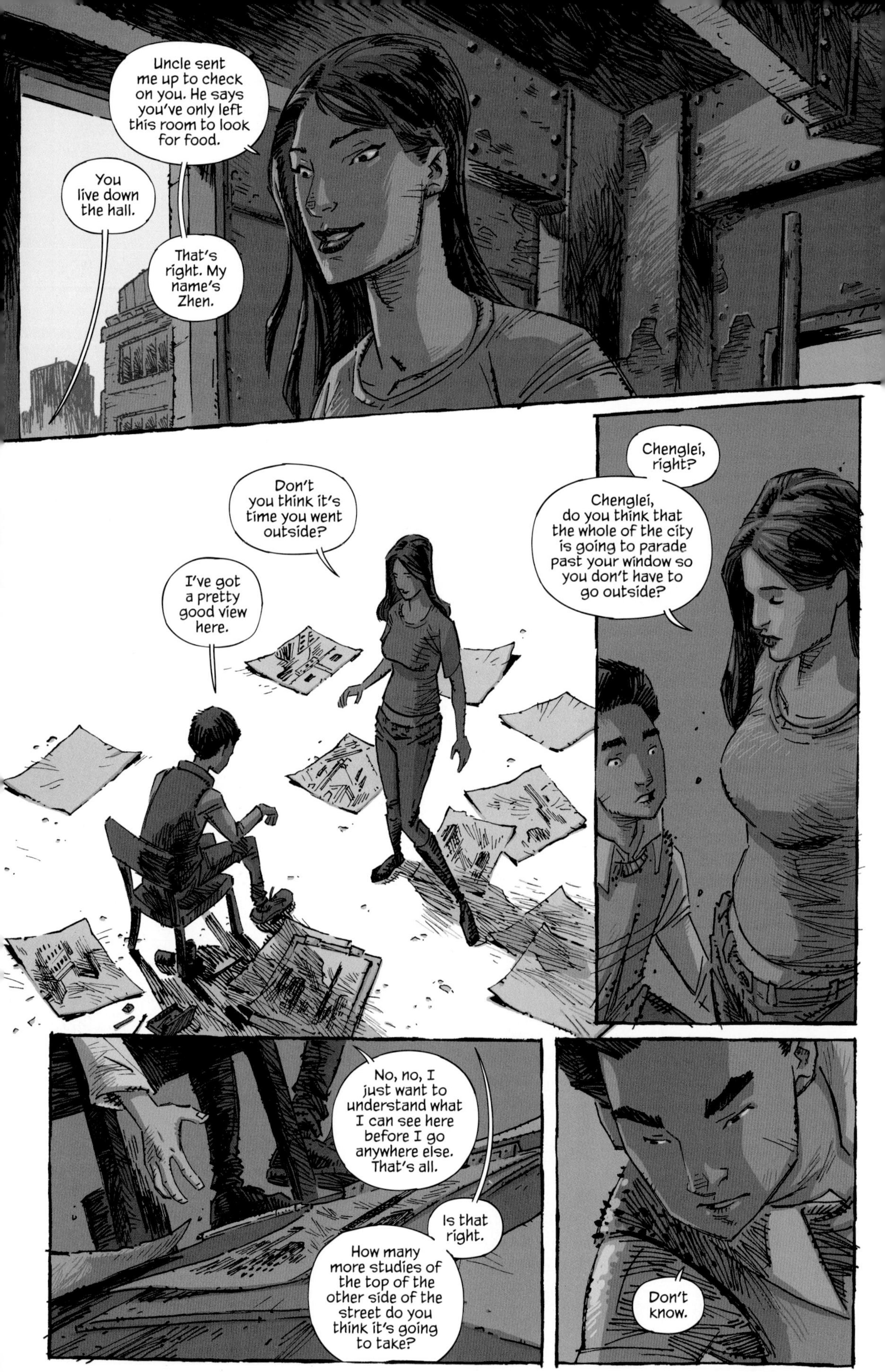
Uncle sent me up to check on you. He says you've only left this room to look for food.
You live down the hall.
That's right. My name's Zhen.
Don't you think it's time you went outside?
I've got a pretty good view here.
Chenglei, right?
Chenglei, do you think that the whole of the city is going to parade past your window so you don't have to go outside?
No, no, I just want to understand what I can see here before I go anywhere else. That's all.
Is that right.
How many more studies of the top of the other side of the street do you think it's going to take?
Don't know.

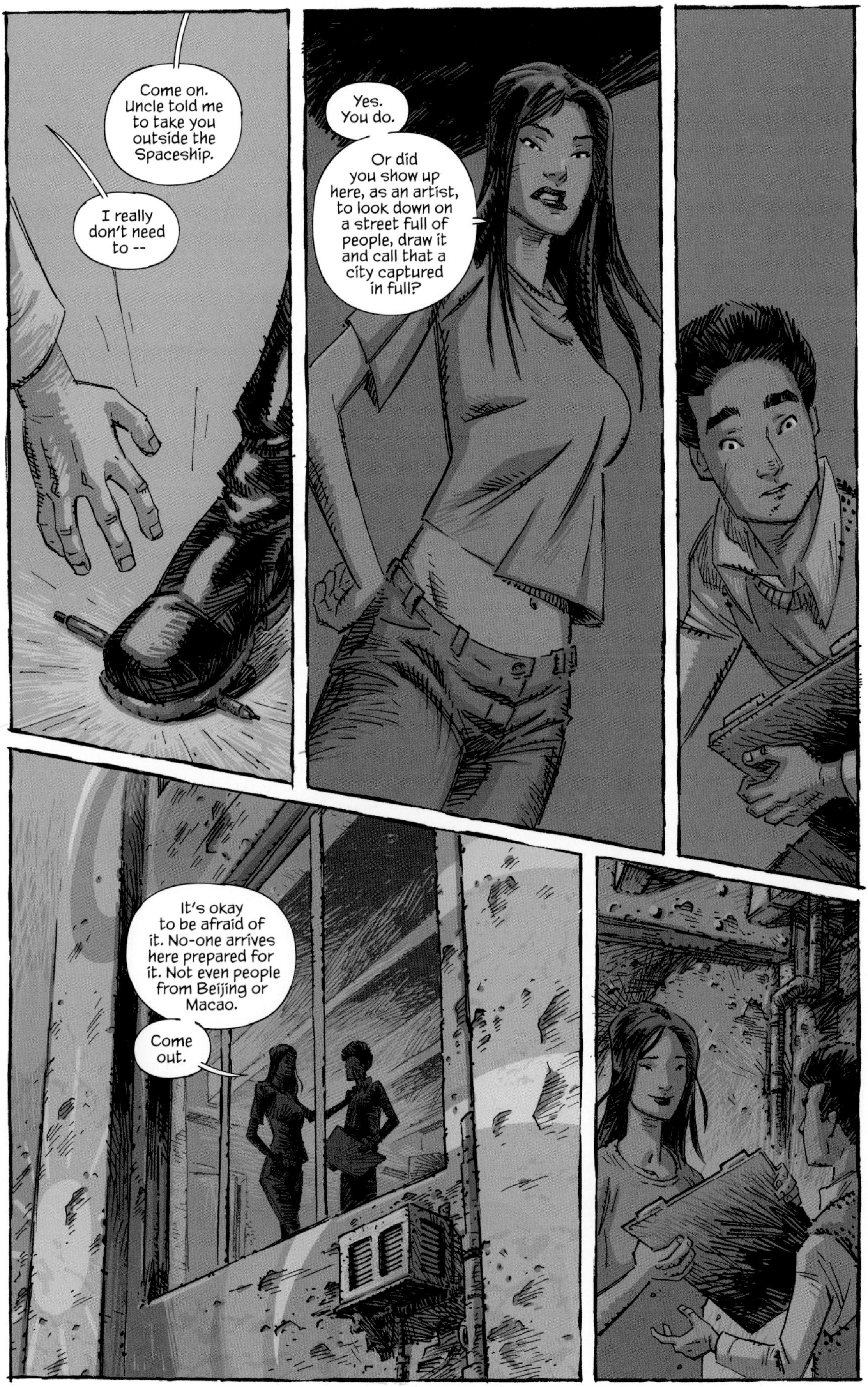
Come on. Uncle told me to take you outside the Spaceship.
I really don't need to --
Yes. You do.
Or did you show up here, as an artist, to look down on a street full of people, draw it and call that a city captured in full?
It's okay to be afraid of it. No-one arrives here prepared for it. Not even people from Beijing or Macao.
Come out.

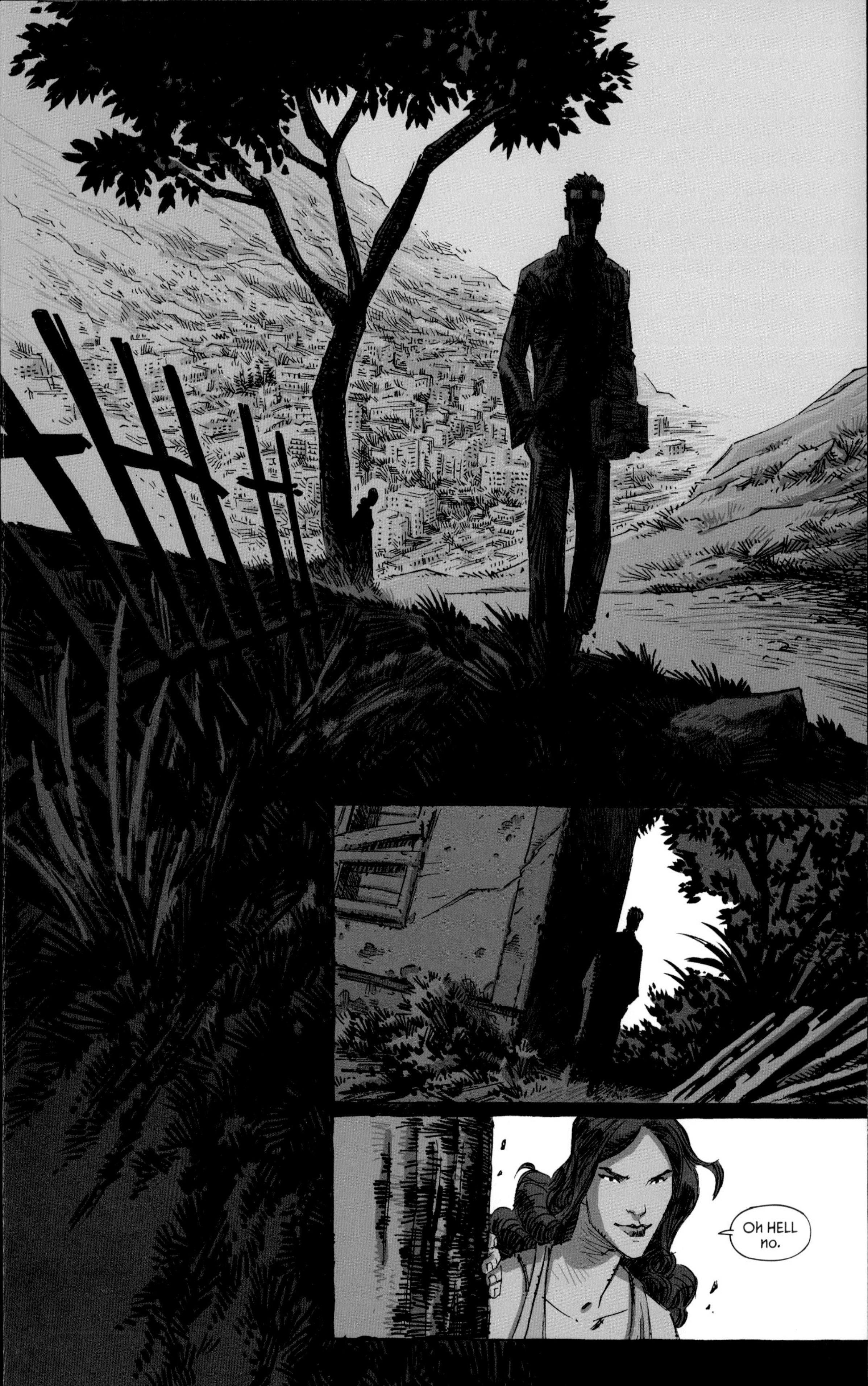
Oh HELL no.

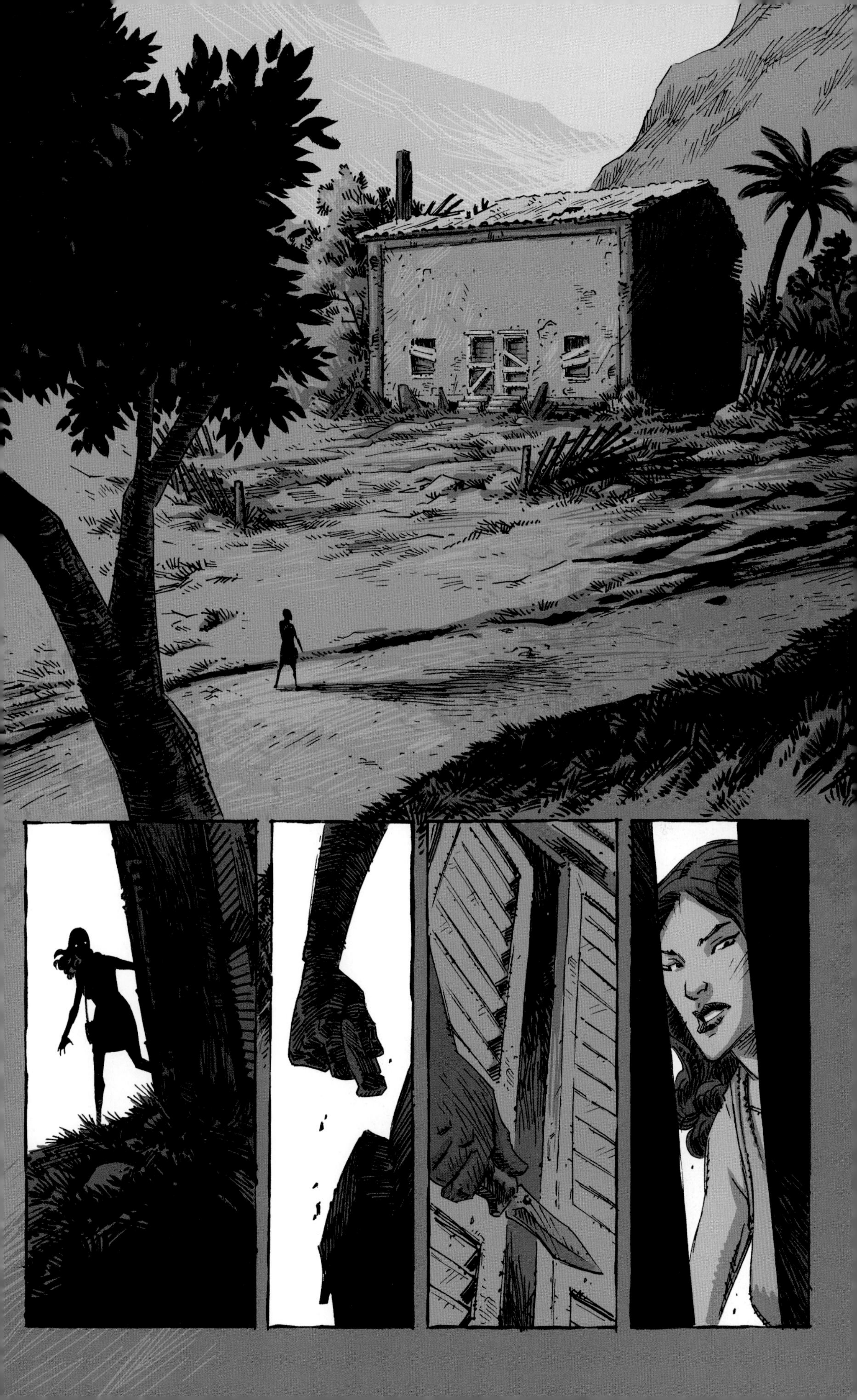

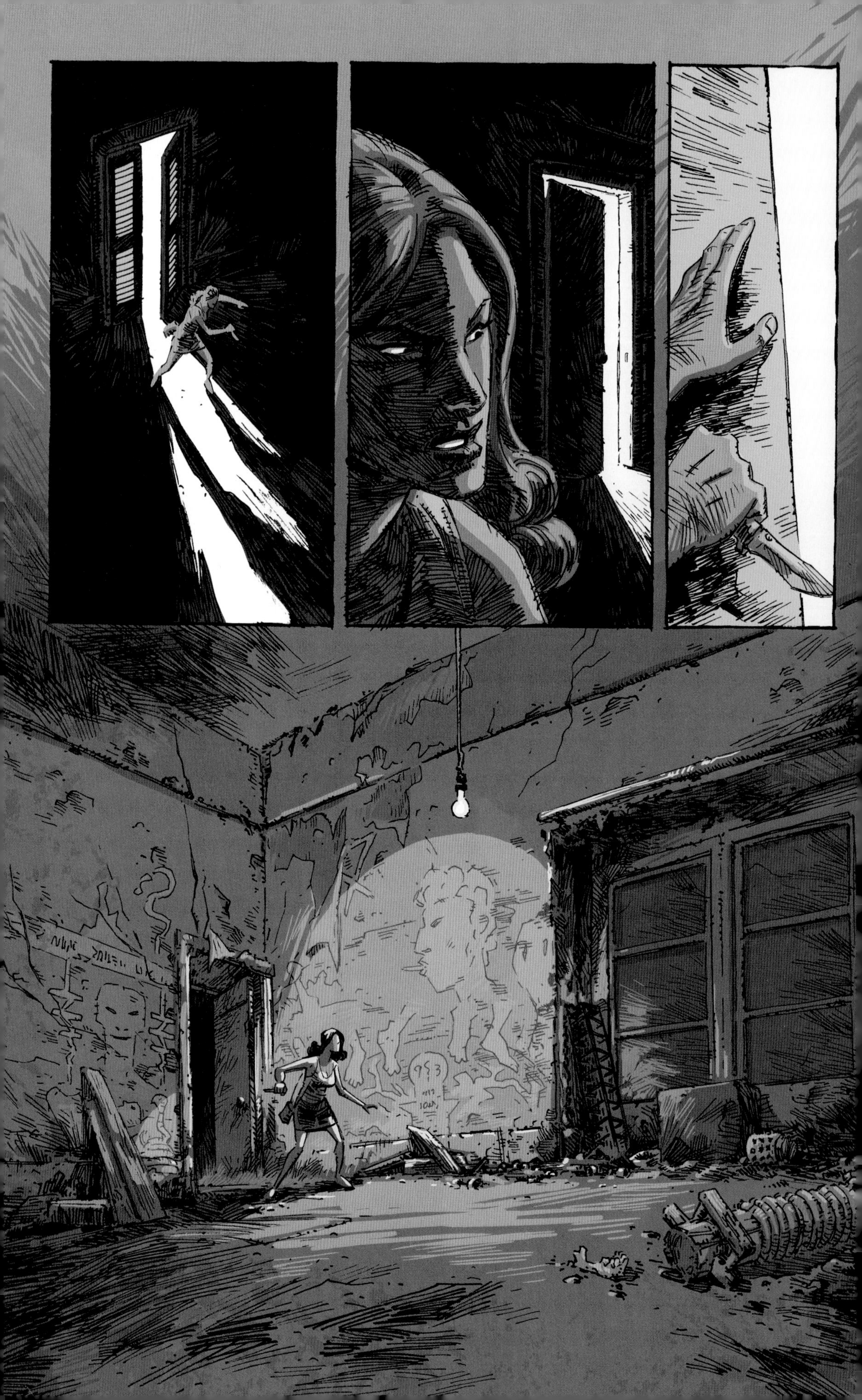

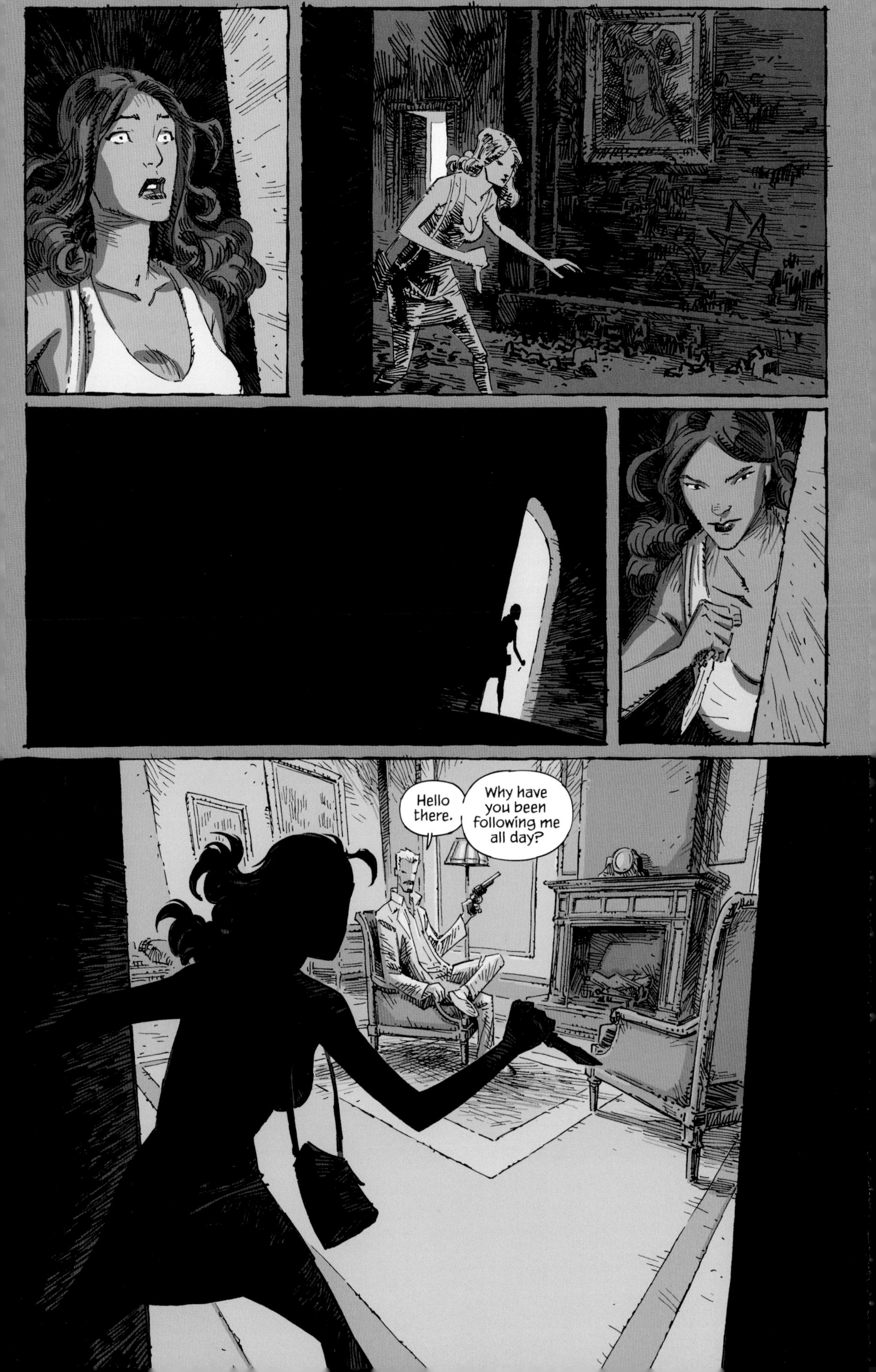
Hello there.
Why have you been following me all day?

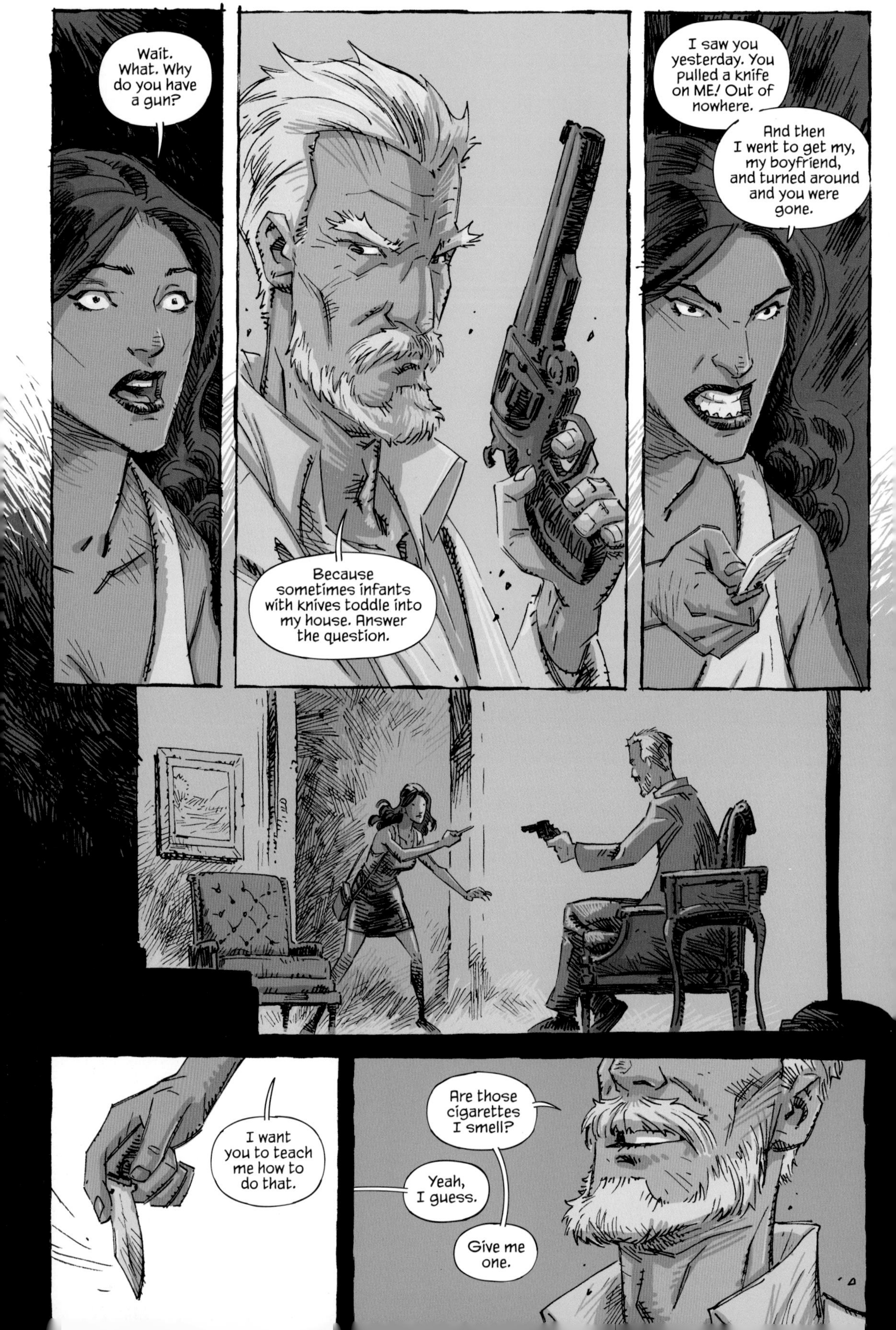
Wait. What. Why do you have a gun?
Because sometimes infants with knives toddle into my house. Answer the question.
I saw you yesterday. You pulled a knife on ME! Out of nowhere.
And then I went to get my, my boyfriend, and turned around and you were gone.
I want you to teach me how to do that.
Are those cigarettes I smell?
Yeah, I guess.
Give me one.

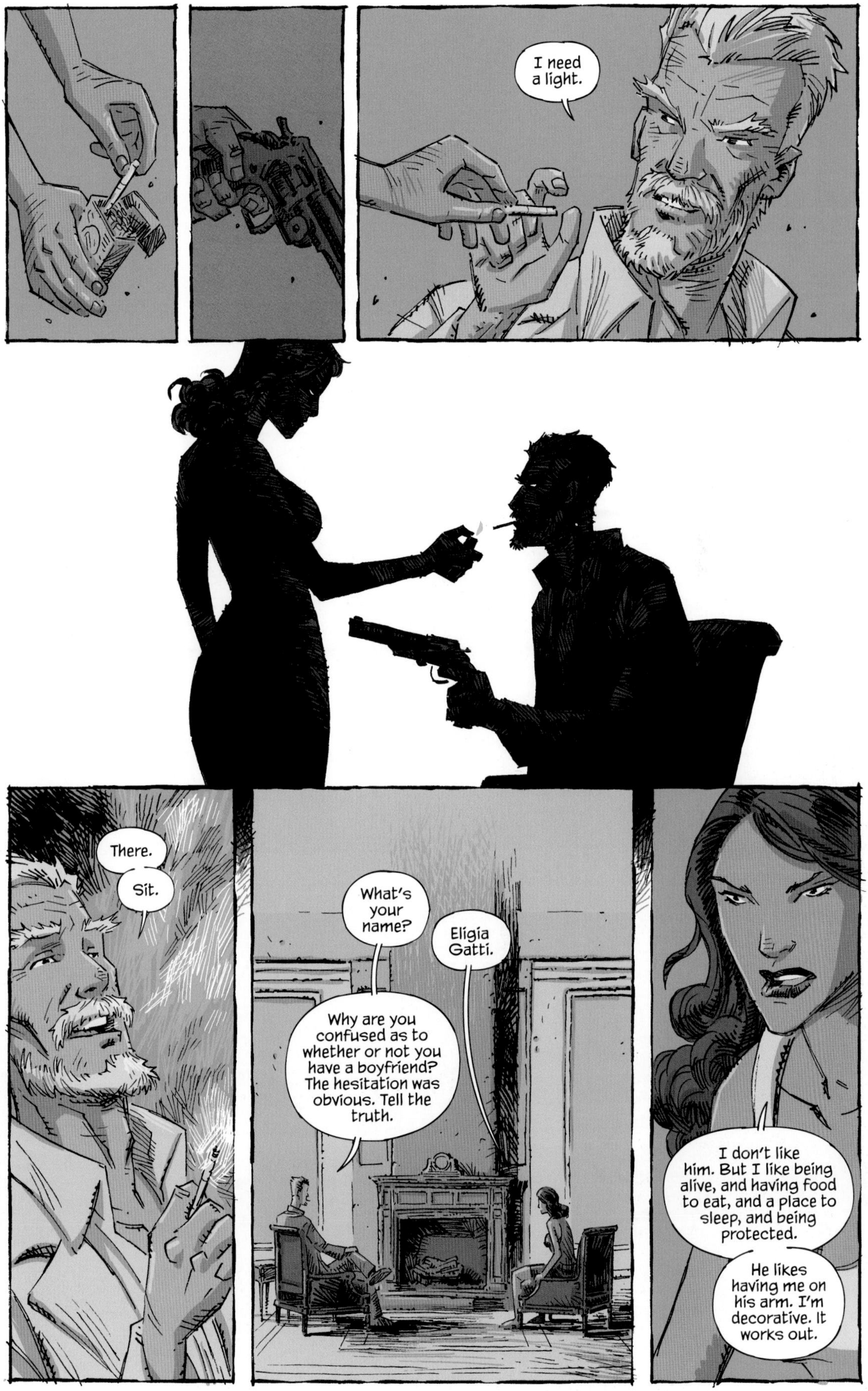

I need a light.
There.
Sit.
What's your name?
Eligia Gatti.
Why are you confused as to whether or not you have a boyfriend? The hesitation was obvious. Tell the truth.
I don't like him. But I like being alive, and having food to eat, and a place to sleep, and being protected.
He likes having me on his arm. I'm decorative. It works out.

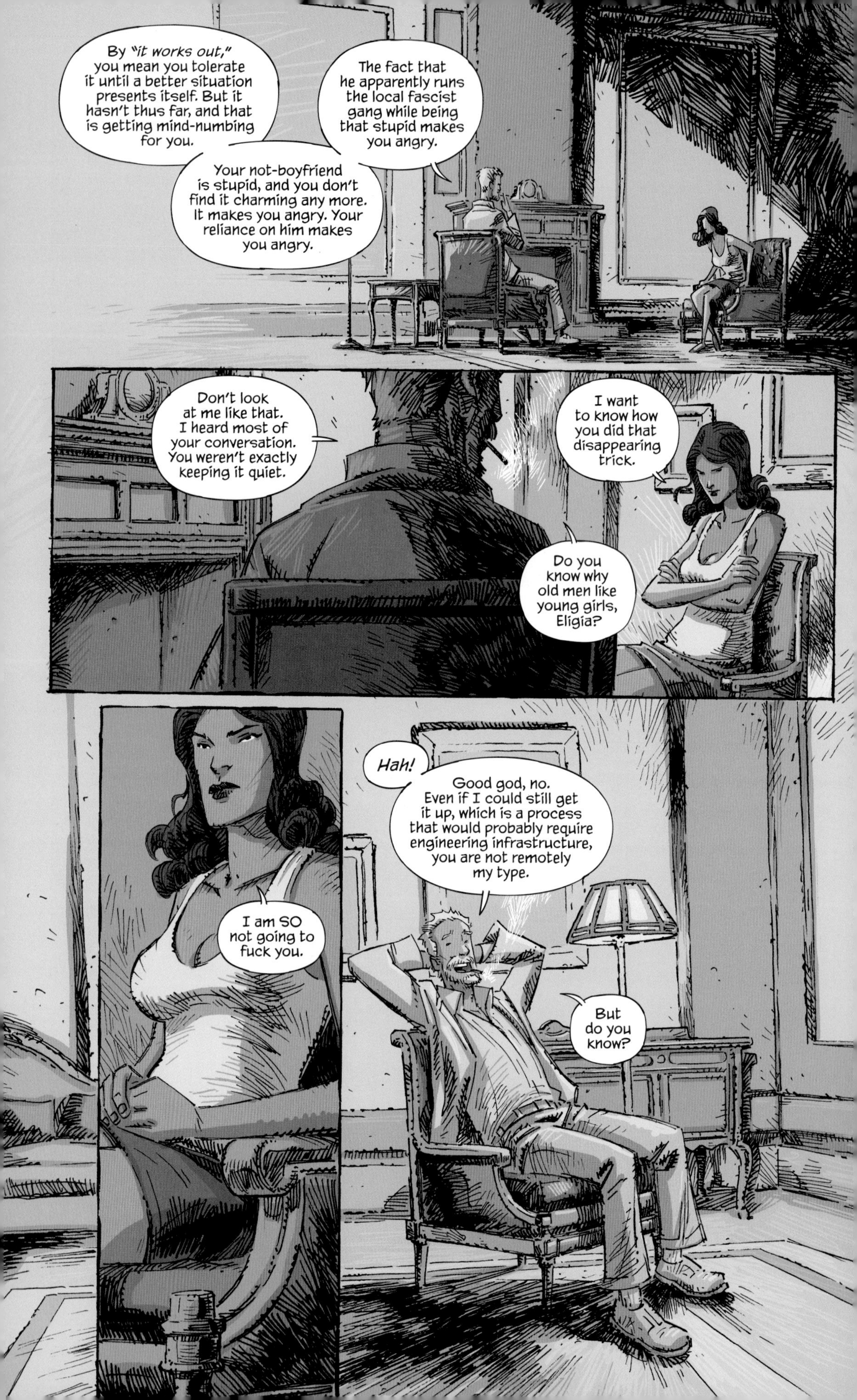
By *"it works out,"* you mean you tolerate it until a better situation presents itself. But it hasn't thus far, and that is getting mind-numbing for you.
The fact that he apparently runs the local fascist gang while being that stupid makes you angry.
Your not-boyfriend is stupid, and you don't find it charming any more. It makes you angry. Your reliance on him makes you angry.
Don't look at me like that. I heard most of your conversation. You weren't exactly keeping it quiet.
I want to know how you did that disappearing trick.
Do you know why old men like young girls, Eligia?
I am SO not going to fuck you.
Hah!
Good god, no. Even if I could still get it up, which is a process that would probably require engineering infrastructure, you are not remotely my type.
But do you know?

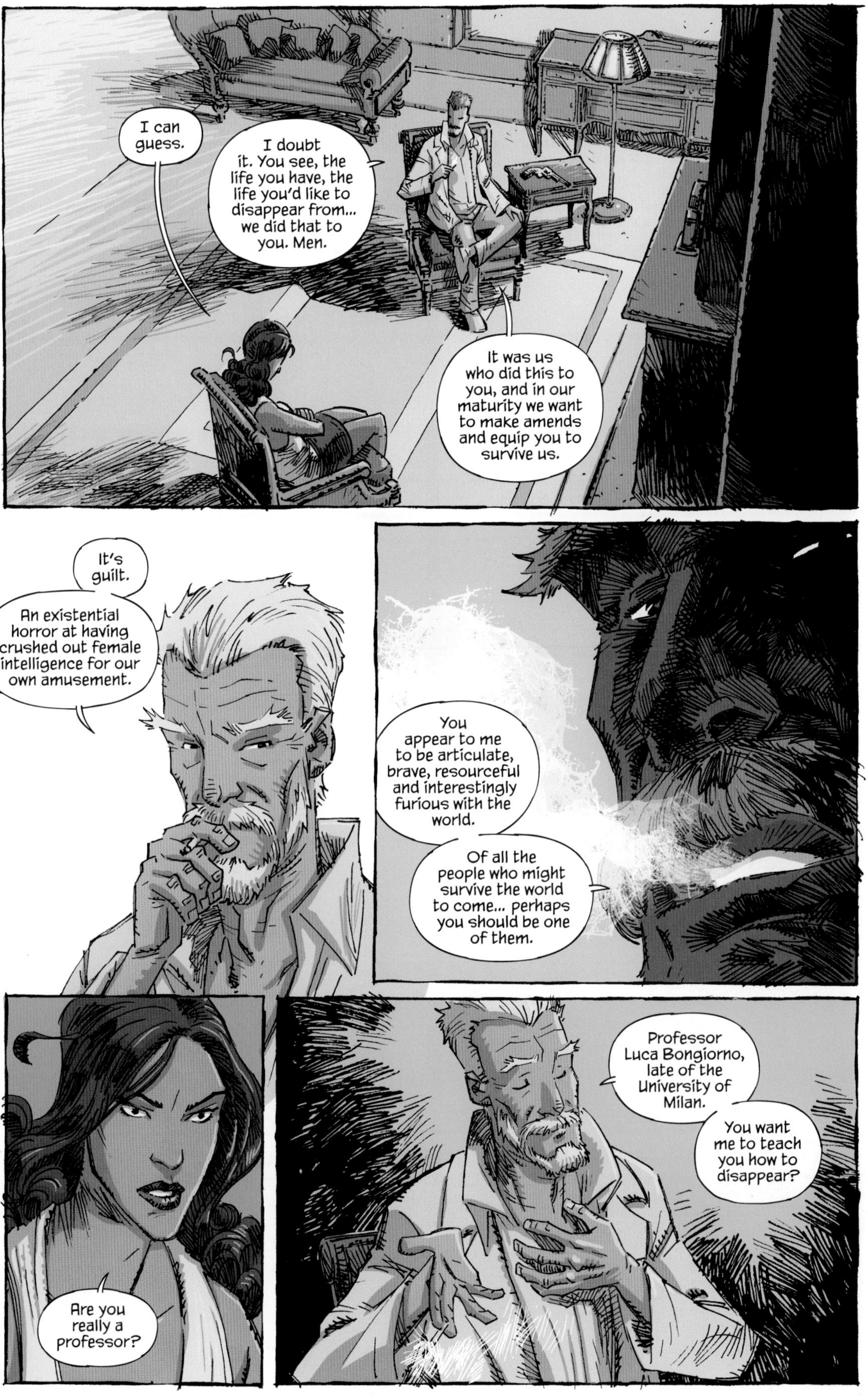
I can guess.
I doubt it. You see, the life you have, the life you'd like to disappear from... we did that to you. Men.
It was us who did this to you, and in our maturity we want to make amends and equip you to survive us.
It's guilt.
An existential horror at having crushed out female intelligence for our own amusement.
You appear to me to be articulate, brave, resourceful and interestingly furious with the world.
Of all the people who might survive the world to come... perhaps you should be one of them.
Are you really a professor?
Professor Luca Bongiorno, late of the University of Milan.
You want me to teach you how to disappear?

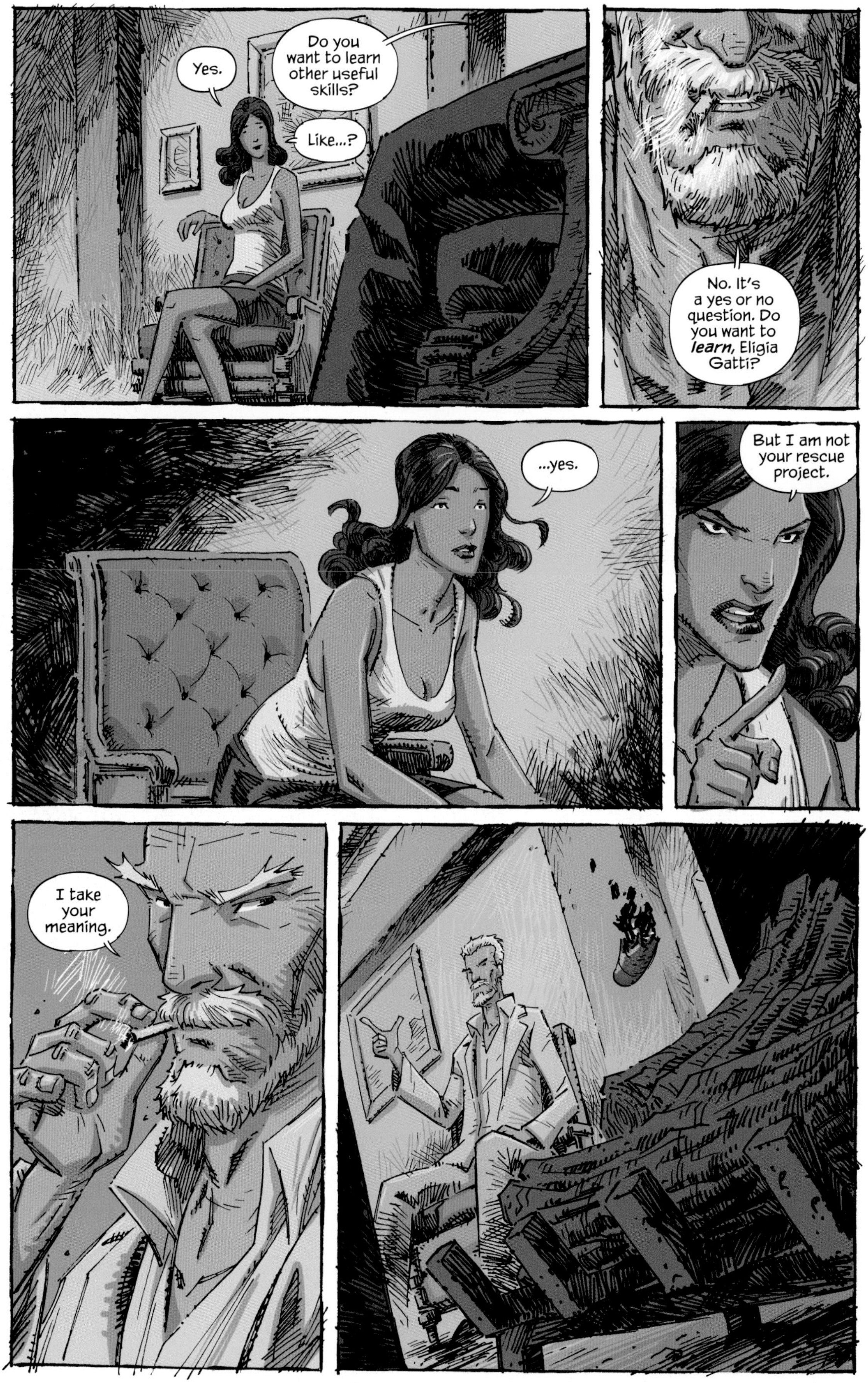
Yes.
Do you want to learn other useful skills?
Like...?
No. It's a yes or no question. Do you want to *learn*, Eligia Gatti?
...yes.
But I am not your rescue project.
I take your meaning.

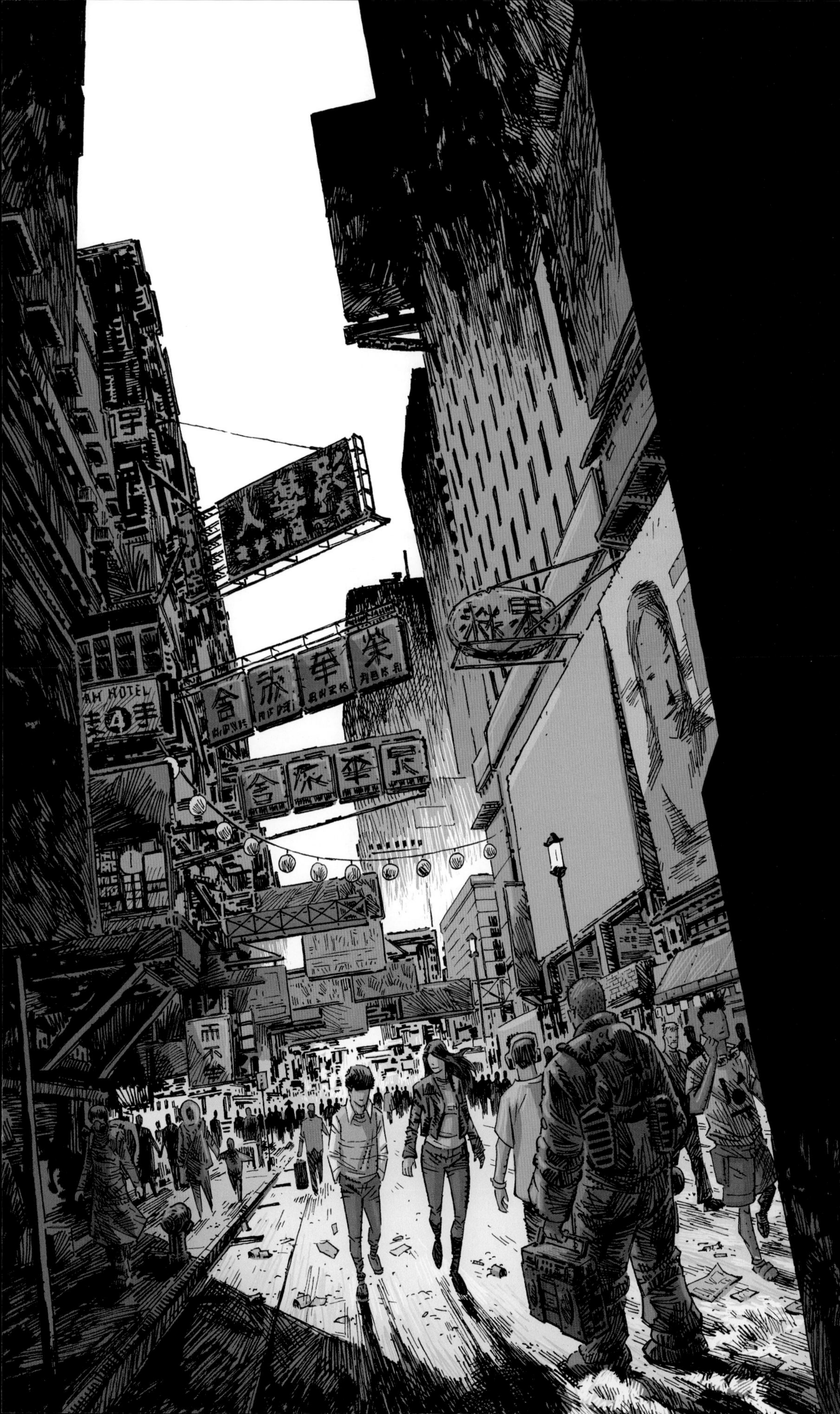
AH HOTEL

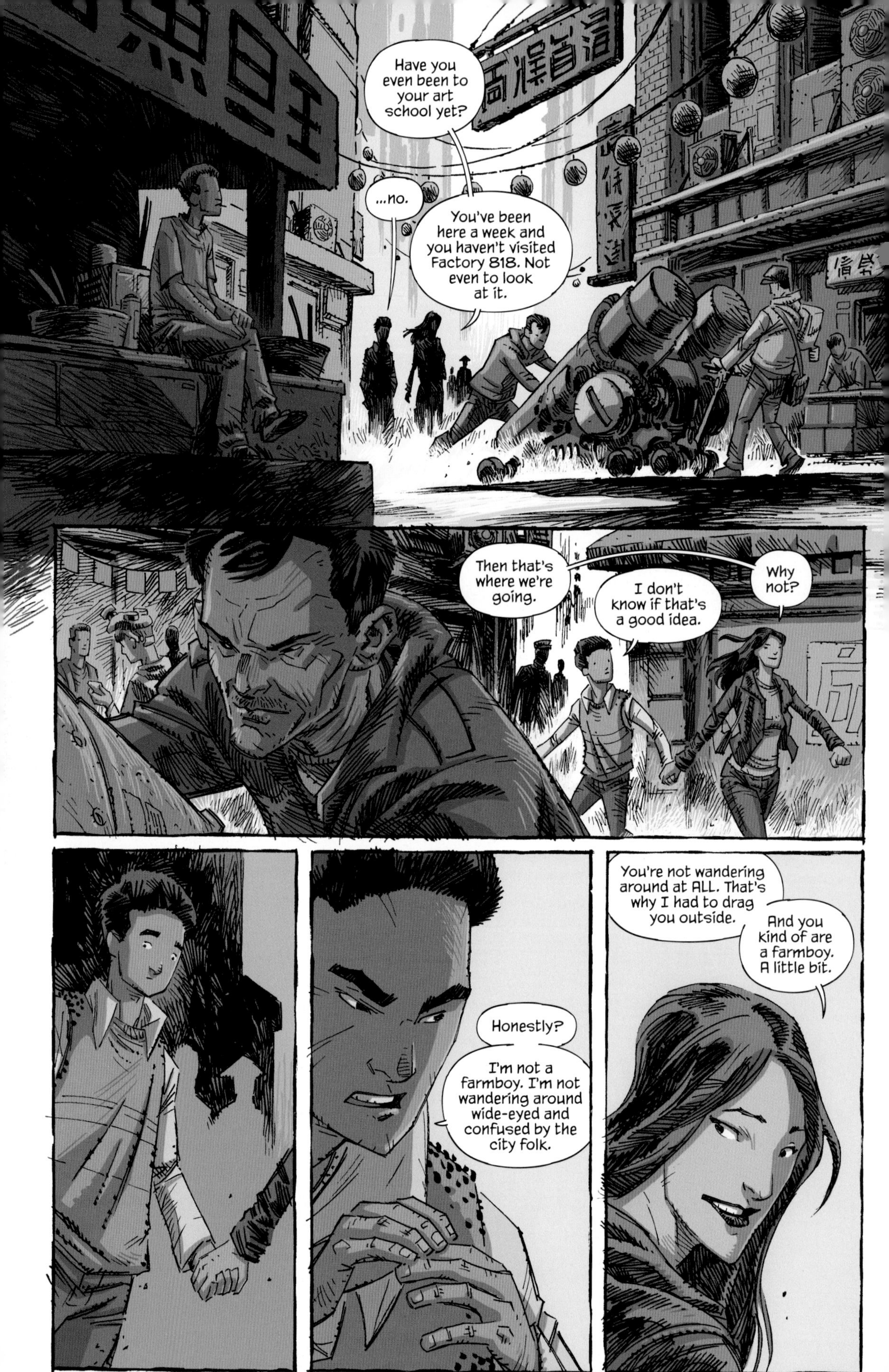
Have you even been to your art school yet?
...no.
You've been here a week and you haven't visited Factory 818. Not even to look at it.
Then that's where we're going.
I don't know if that's a good idea.
Why not?
Honestly?
I'm not a farmboy. I'm not wandering around wide-eyed and confused by the city folk.
You're not wandering around at ALL. That's why I had to drag you outside.
And you kind of are a farmboy. A little bit.

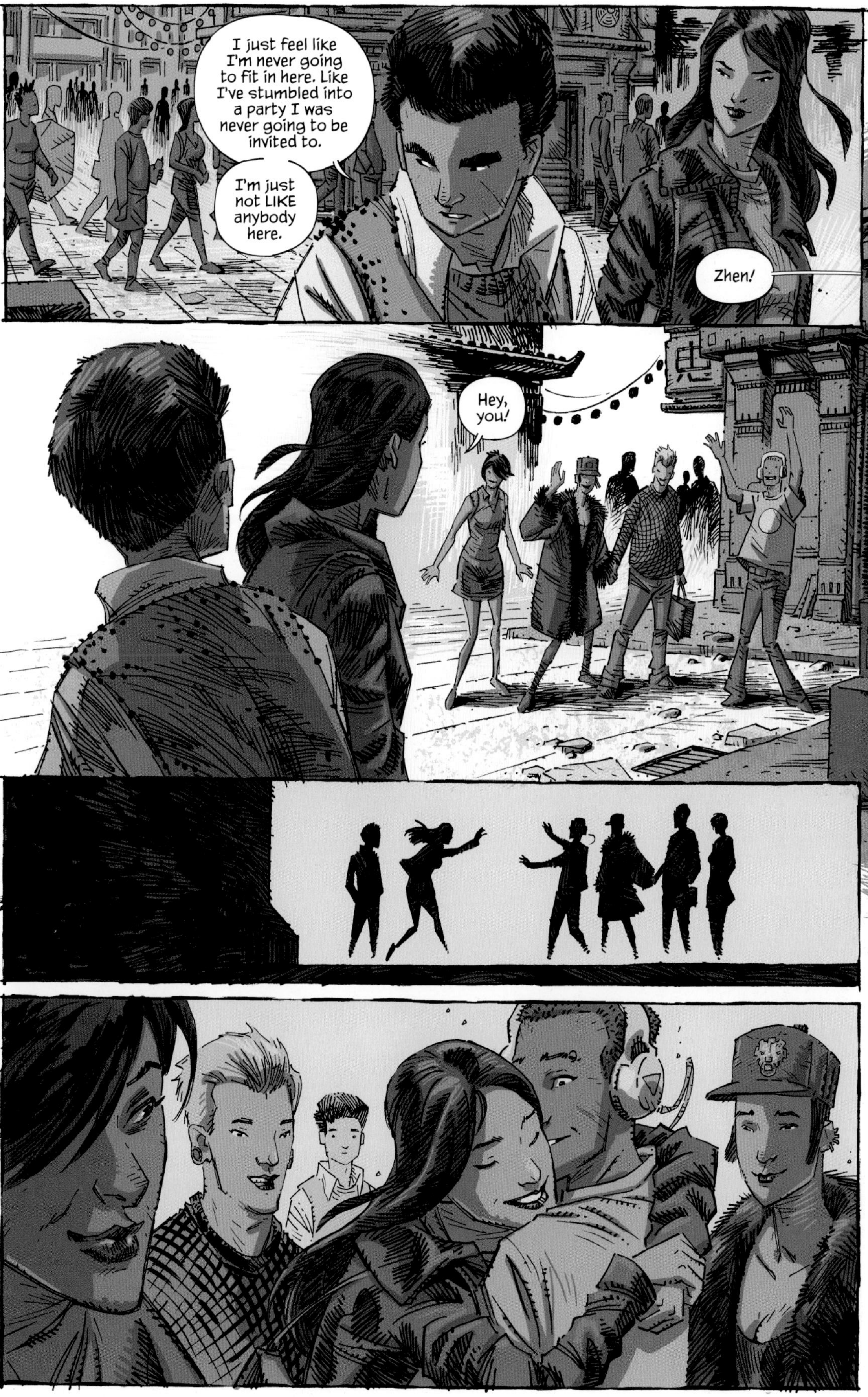
I just feel like I'm never going to fit in here. Like I've stumbled into a party I was never going to be invited to.
I'm just not LIKE anybody here.
Zhen!
Hey, you!

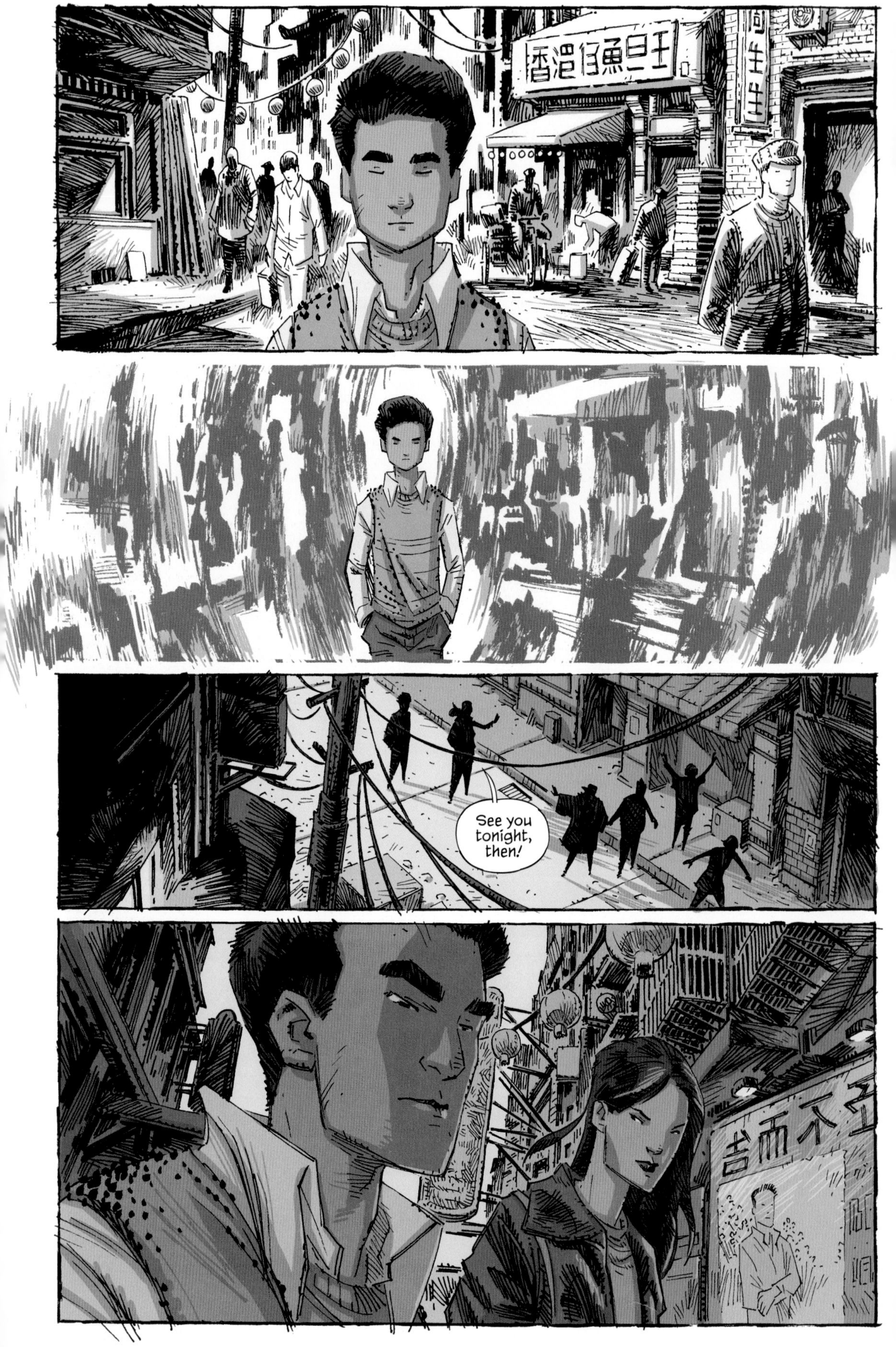
See you tonight, then!

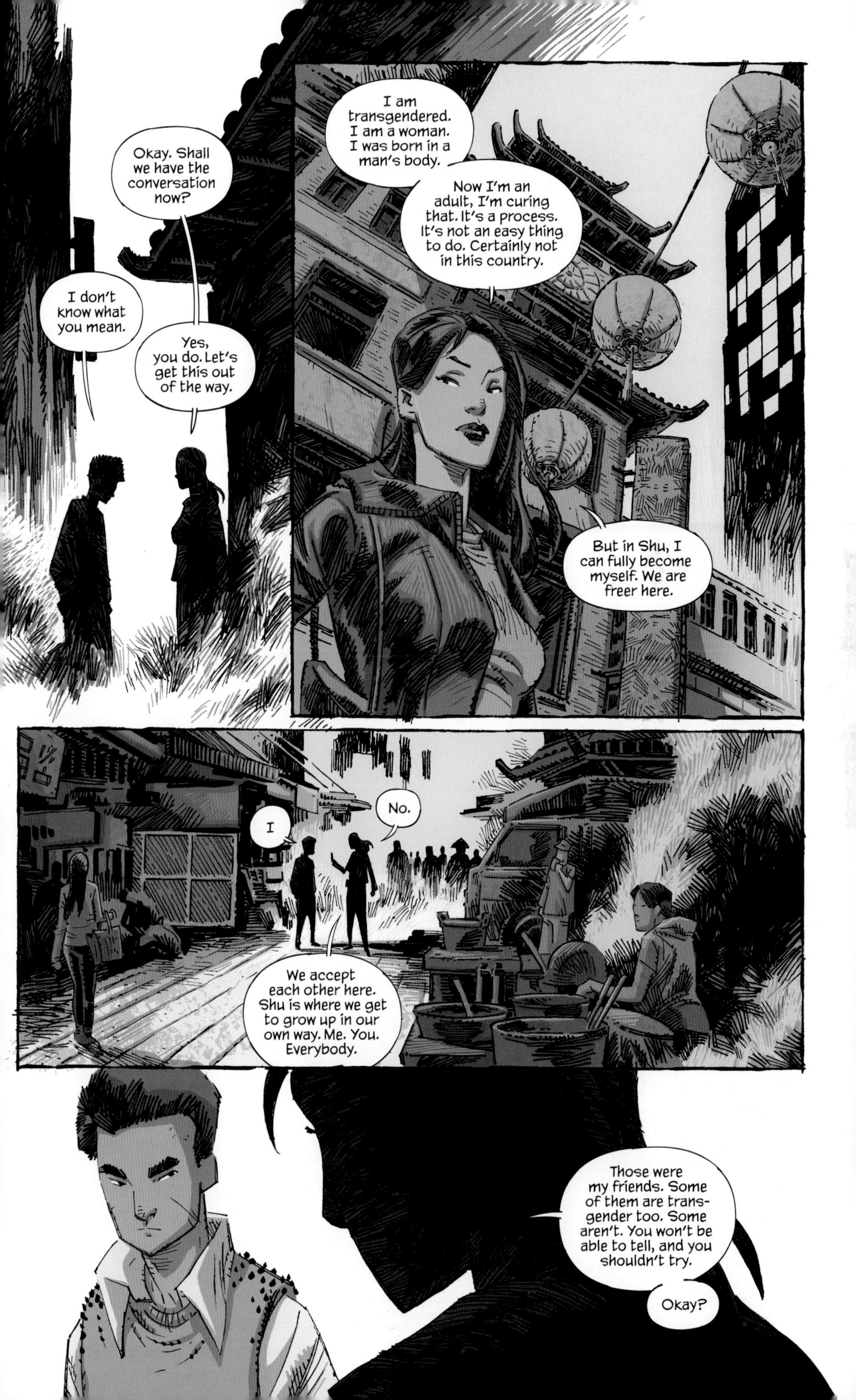
Okay. Shall we have the conversation now?
I don't know what you mean.
Yes, you do. Let's get this out of the way.
I am transgendered. I am a woman. I was born in a man's body.
Now I'm an adult, I'm curing that. It's a process. It's not an easy thing to do. Certainly not in this country.
But in Shu, I can fully become myself. We are freer here.
I
No.
We accept each other here. Shu is where we get to grow up in our own way. Me. You. Everybody.
Those were my friends. Some of them are transgender too. Some aren't. You won't be able to tell, and you shouldn't try.
Okay?

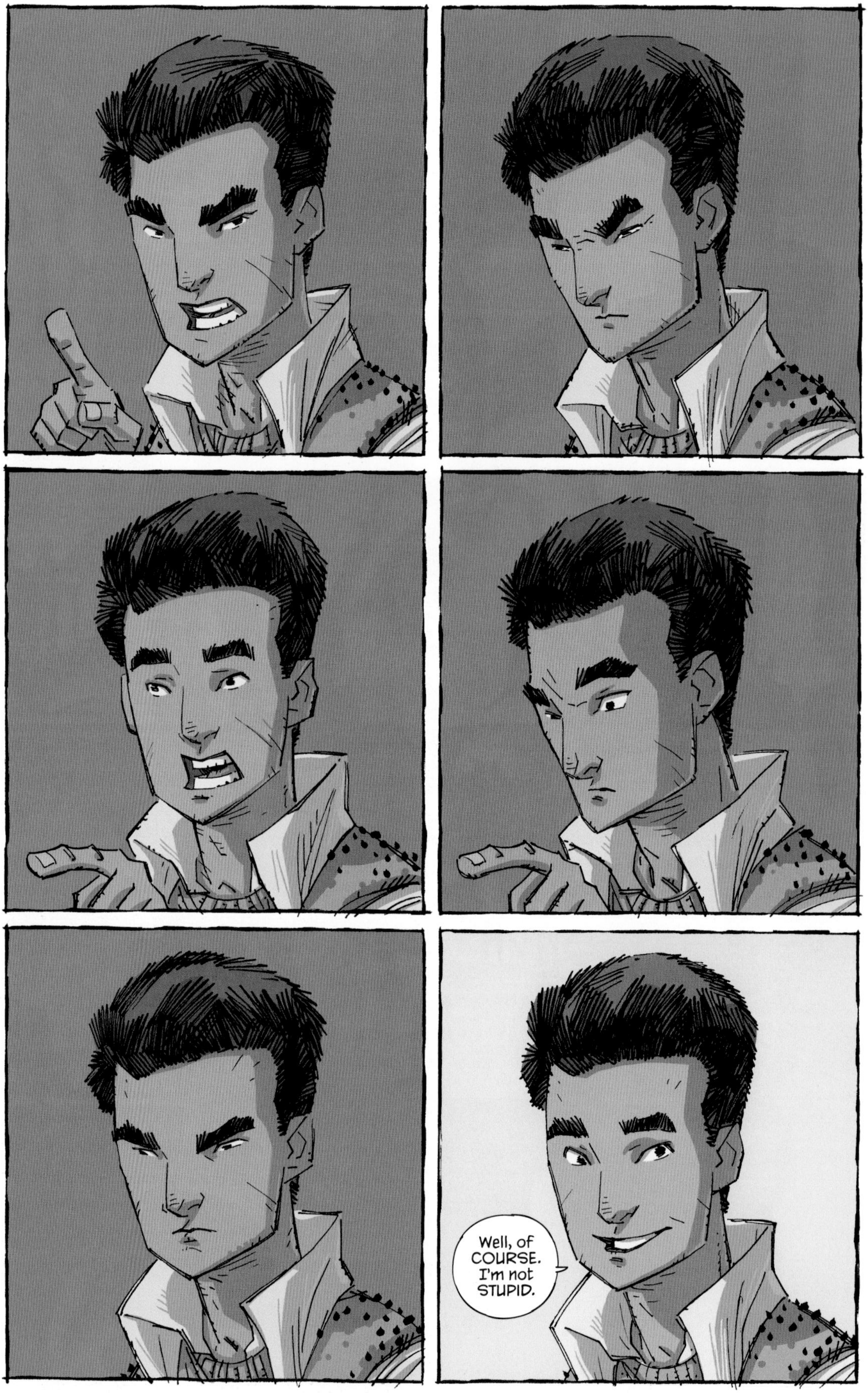
Well, of COURSE. I'm not STUPID.

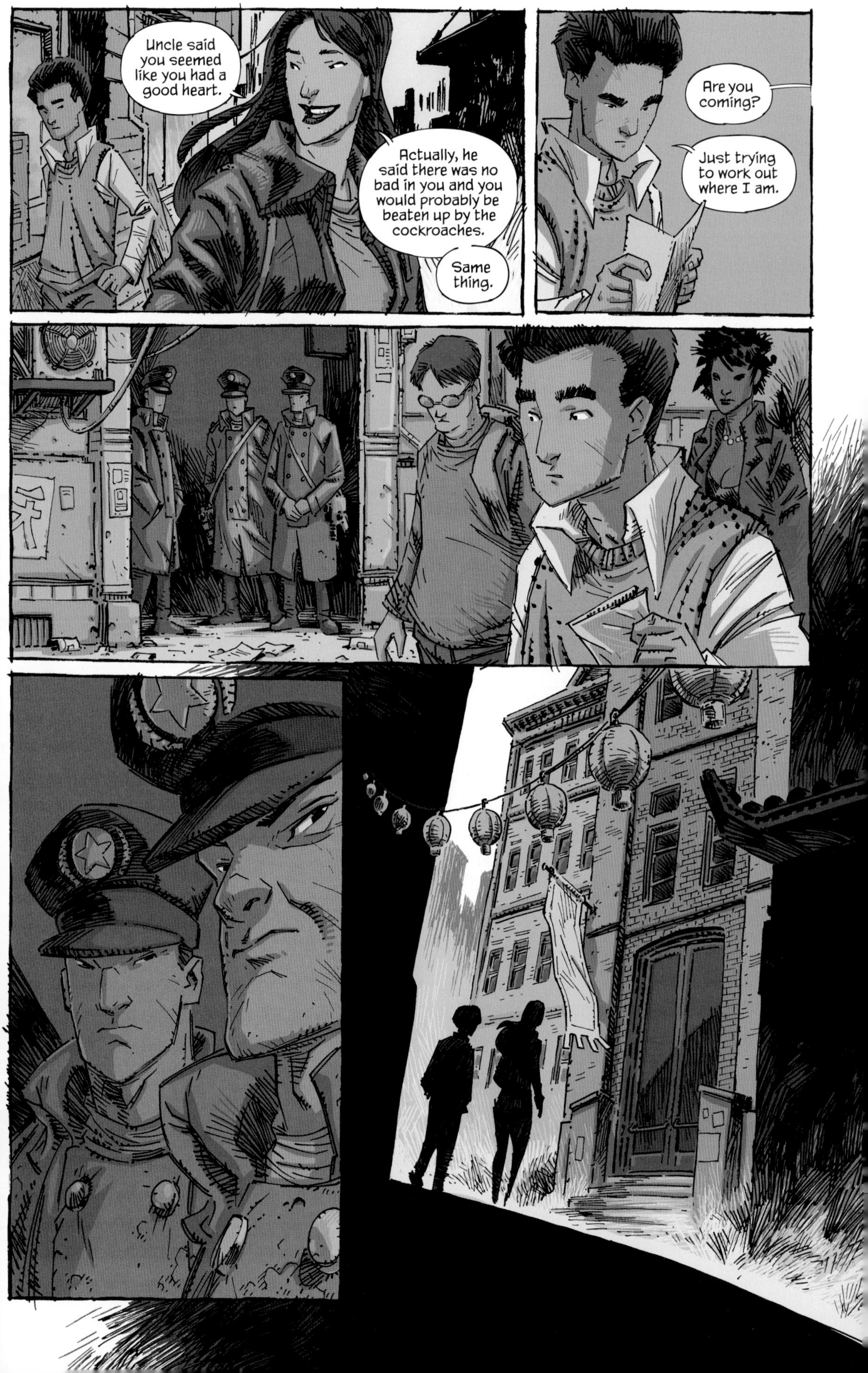
Uncle said you seemed like you had a good heart.
Actually, he said there was no bad in you and you would probably be beaten up by the cockroaches.
Same thing.
Are you coming?
Just trying to work out where I am.

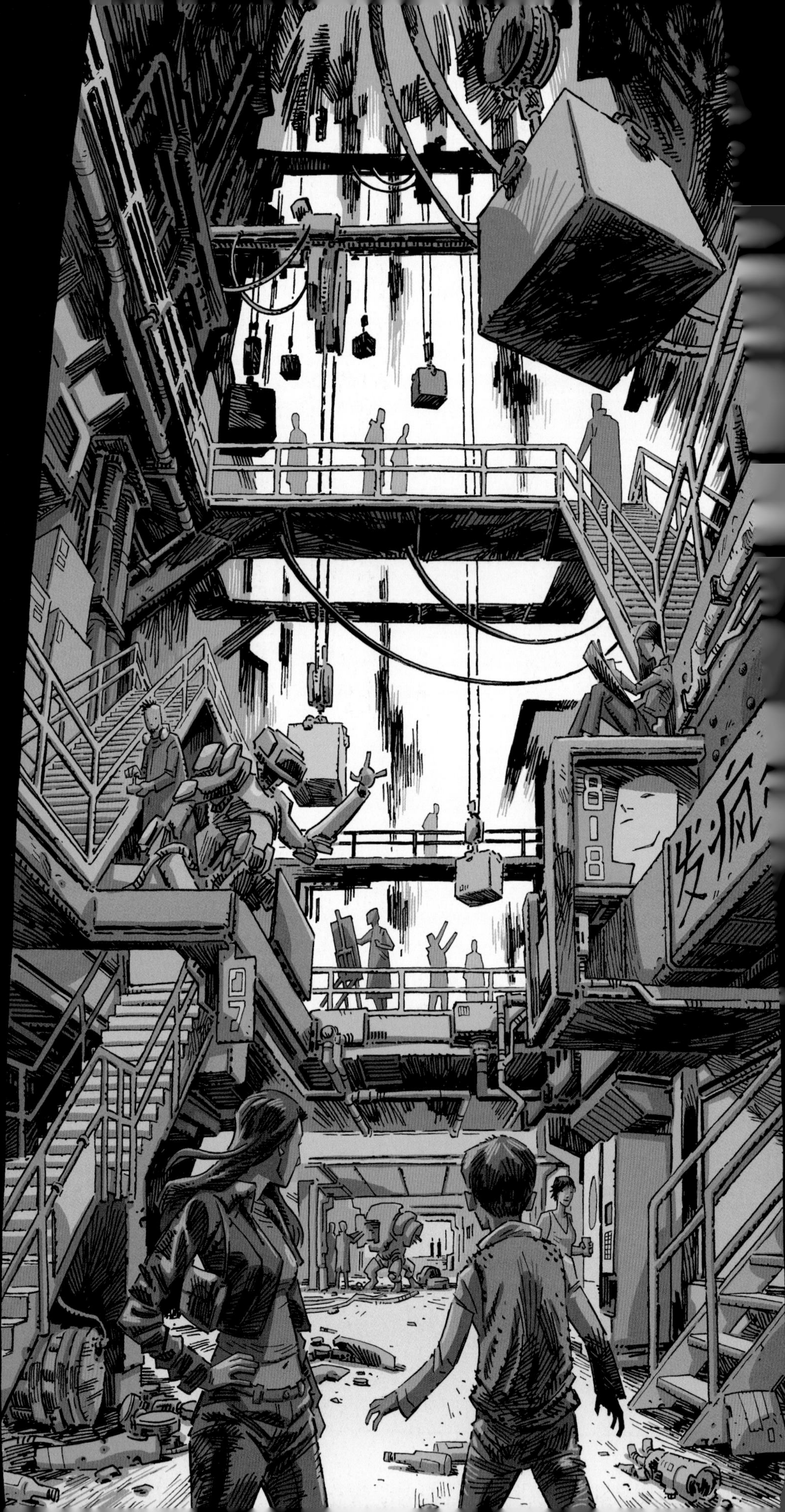
818
发疯
07

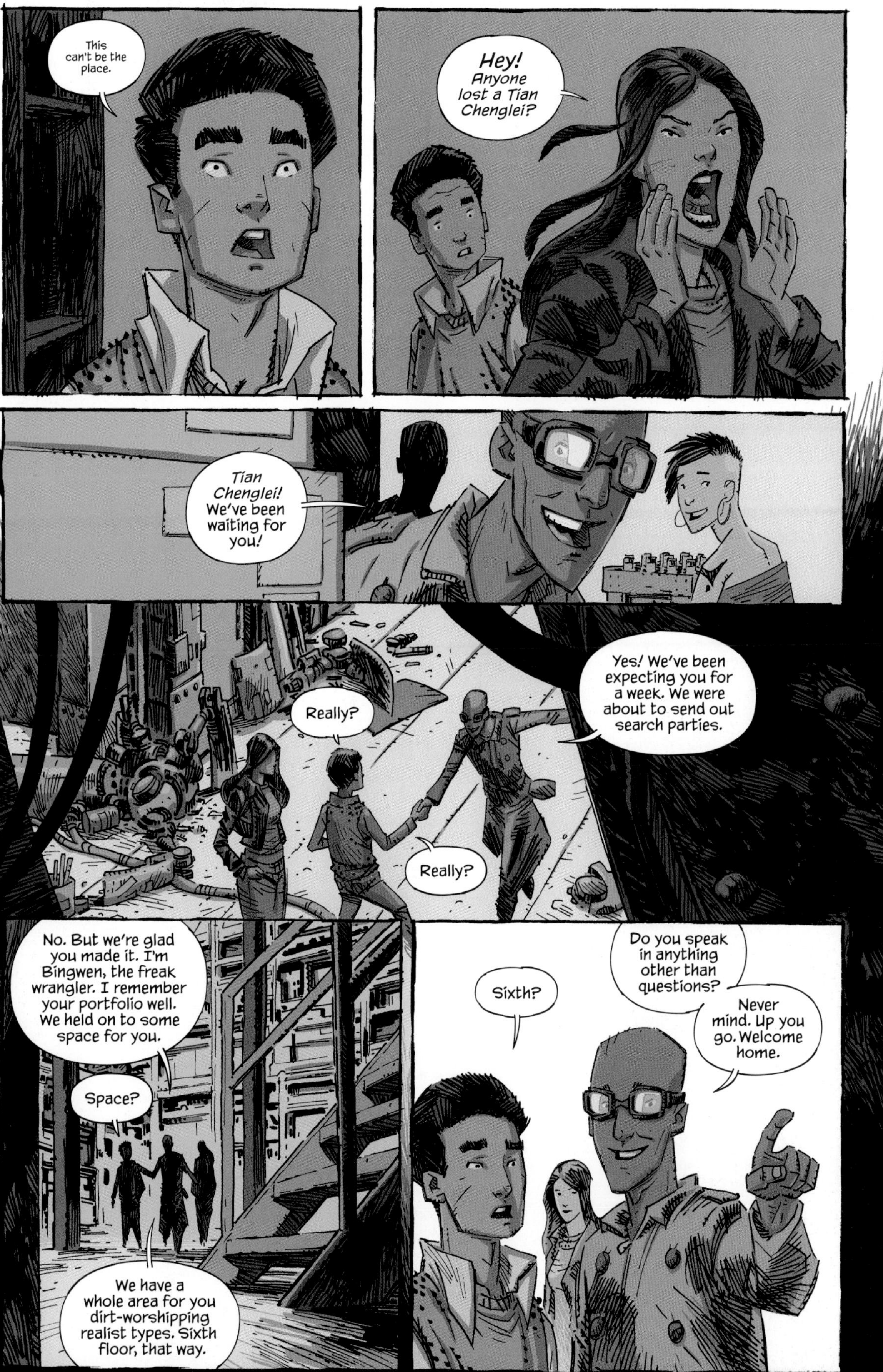
This can't be the place.
Hey! Anyone lost a Tian Chenglei?
Tian Chenglei! We've been waiting for you!
Really?
Yes! We've been expecting you for a week. We were about to send out search parties.
Really?
No. But we're glad you made it. I'm Bingwen, the freak wrangler. I remember your portfolio well. We held on to some space for you.
Space?
We have a whole area for you dirt-worshipping realist types. Sixth floor, that way.
Sixth?
Do you speak in anything other than questions?
Never mind. Up you go. Welcome home.

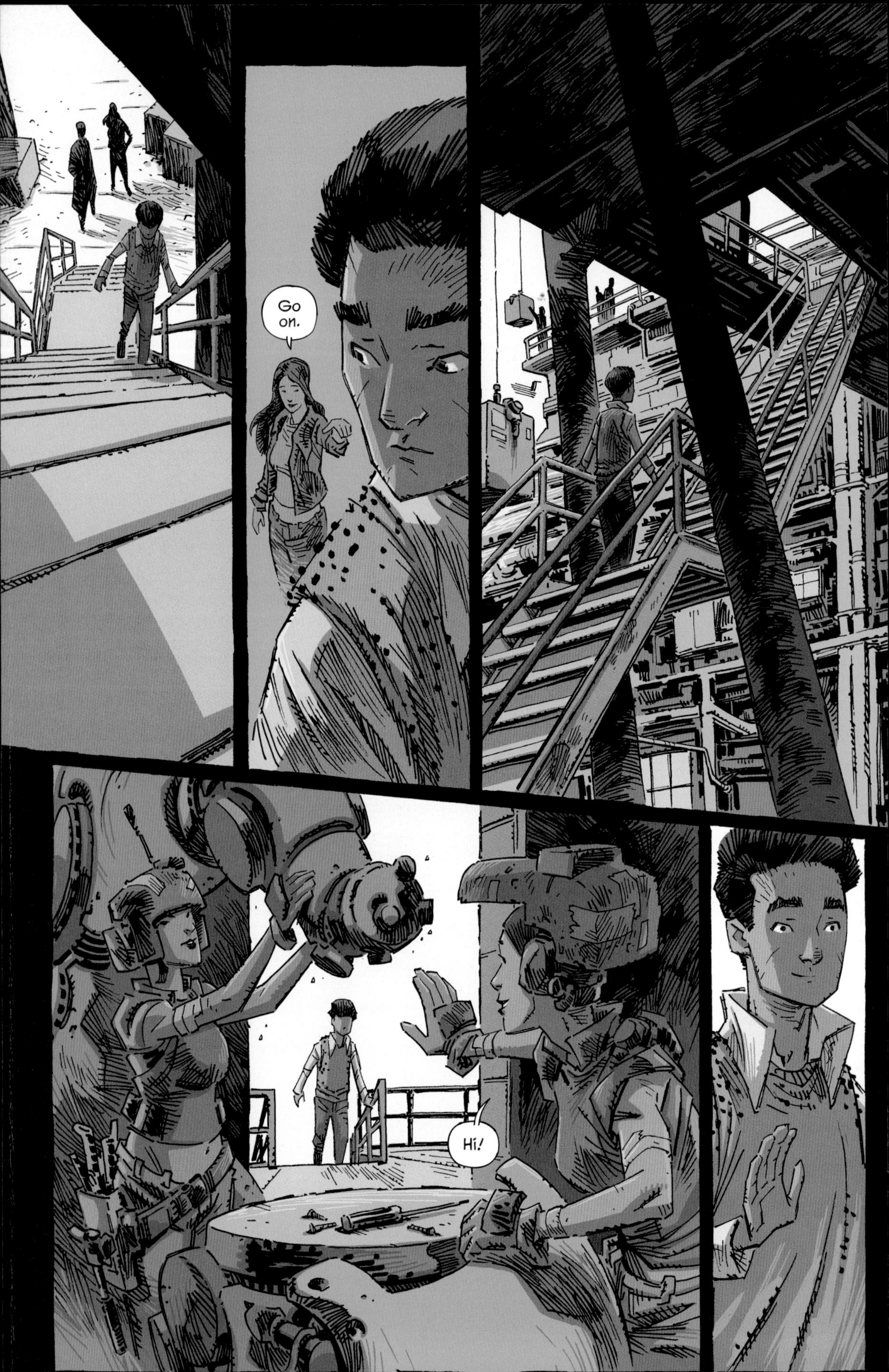
Go on.
Hi!

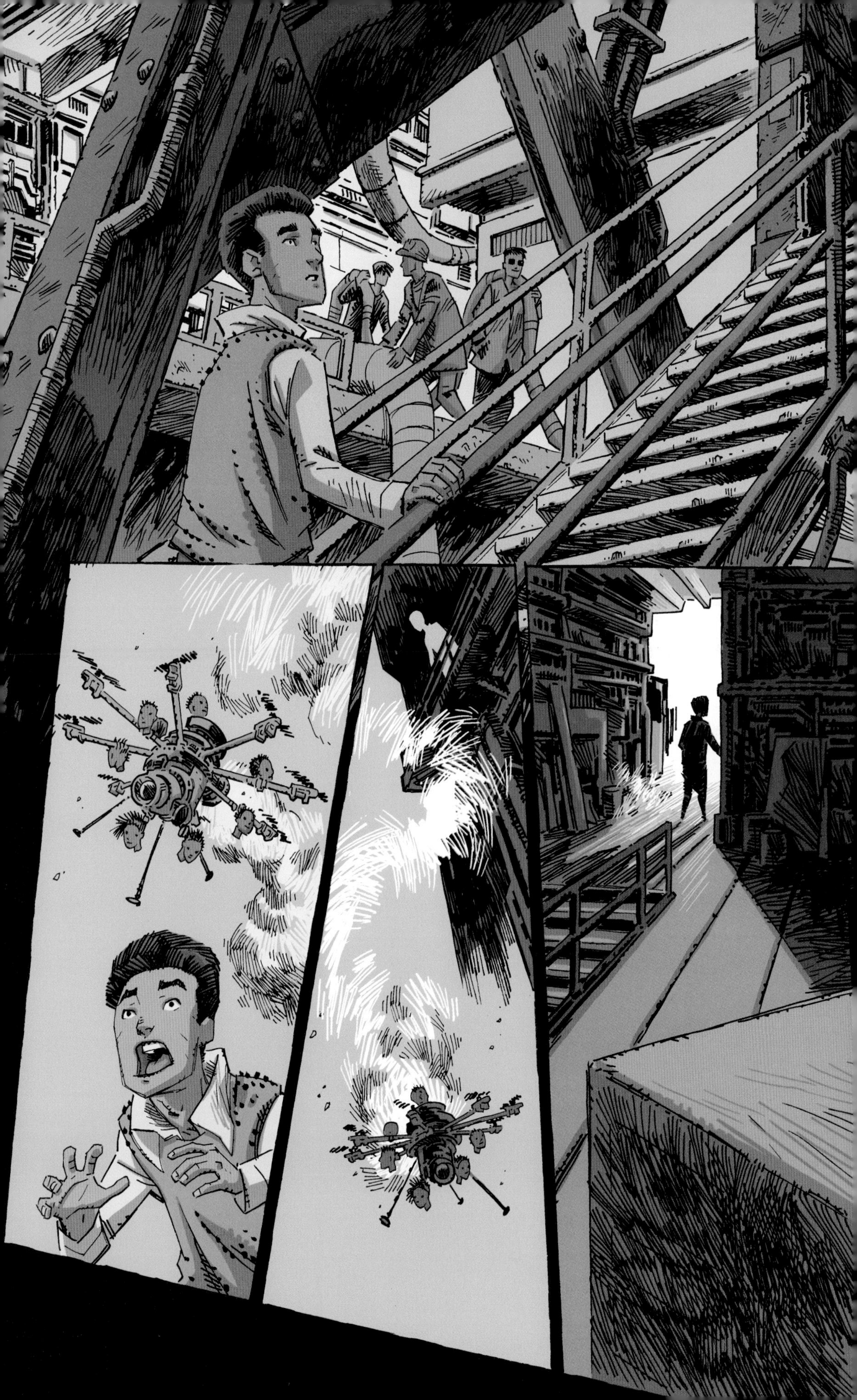

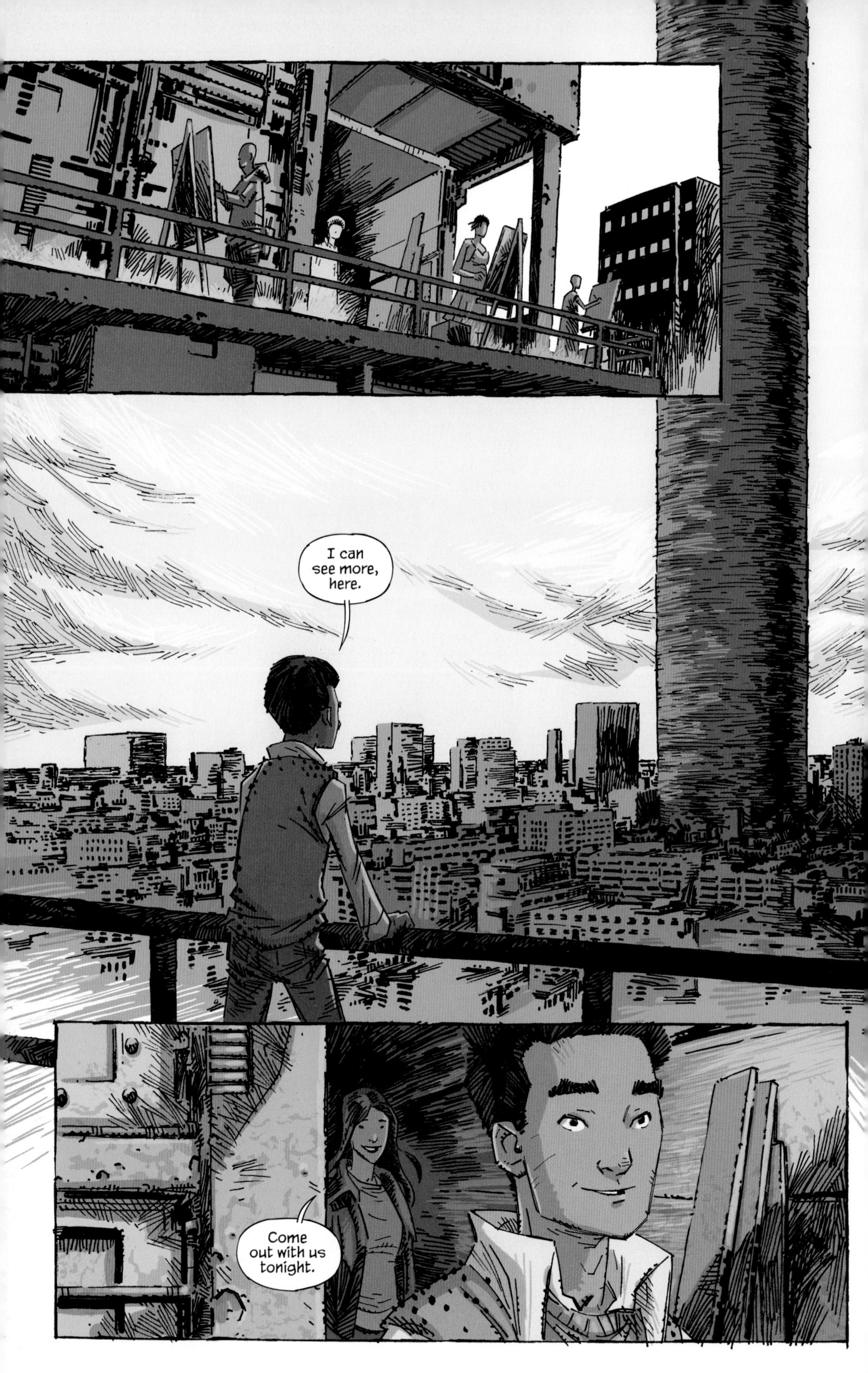
I can see more, here.
Come out with us tonight.

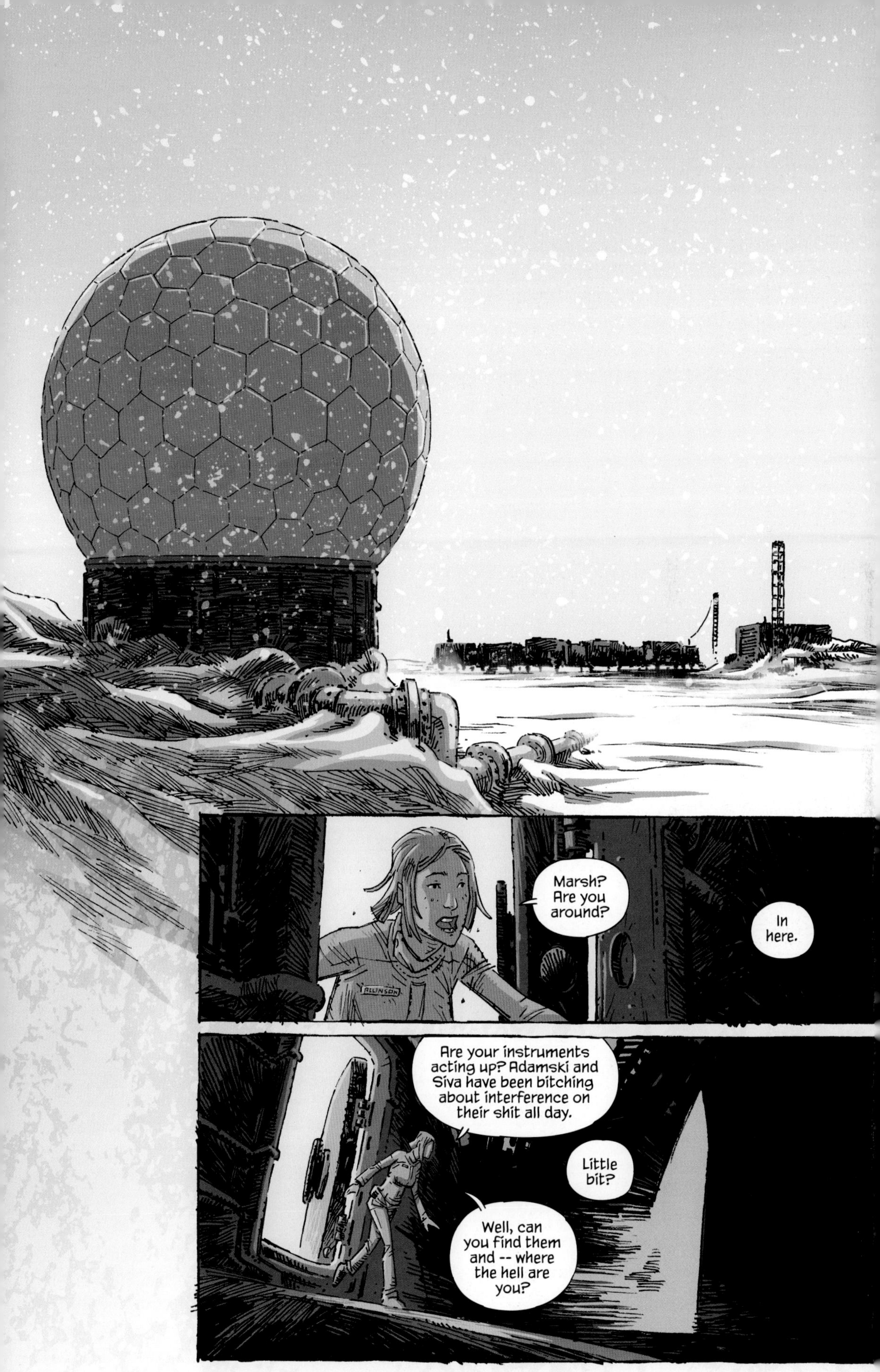
Marsh? Are you around?
In here.
Are your instruments acting up? Adamski and Siva have been bitching about interference on their shit all day.
Little bit?
Well, can you find them and -- where the hell are you?

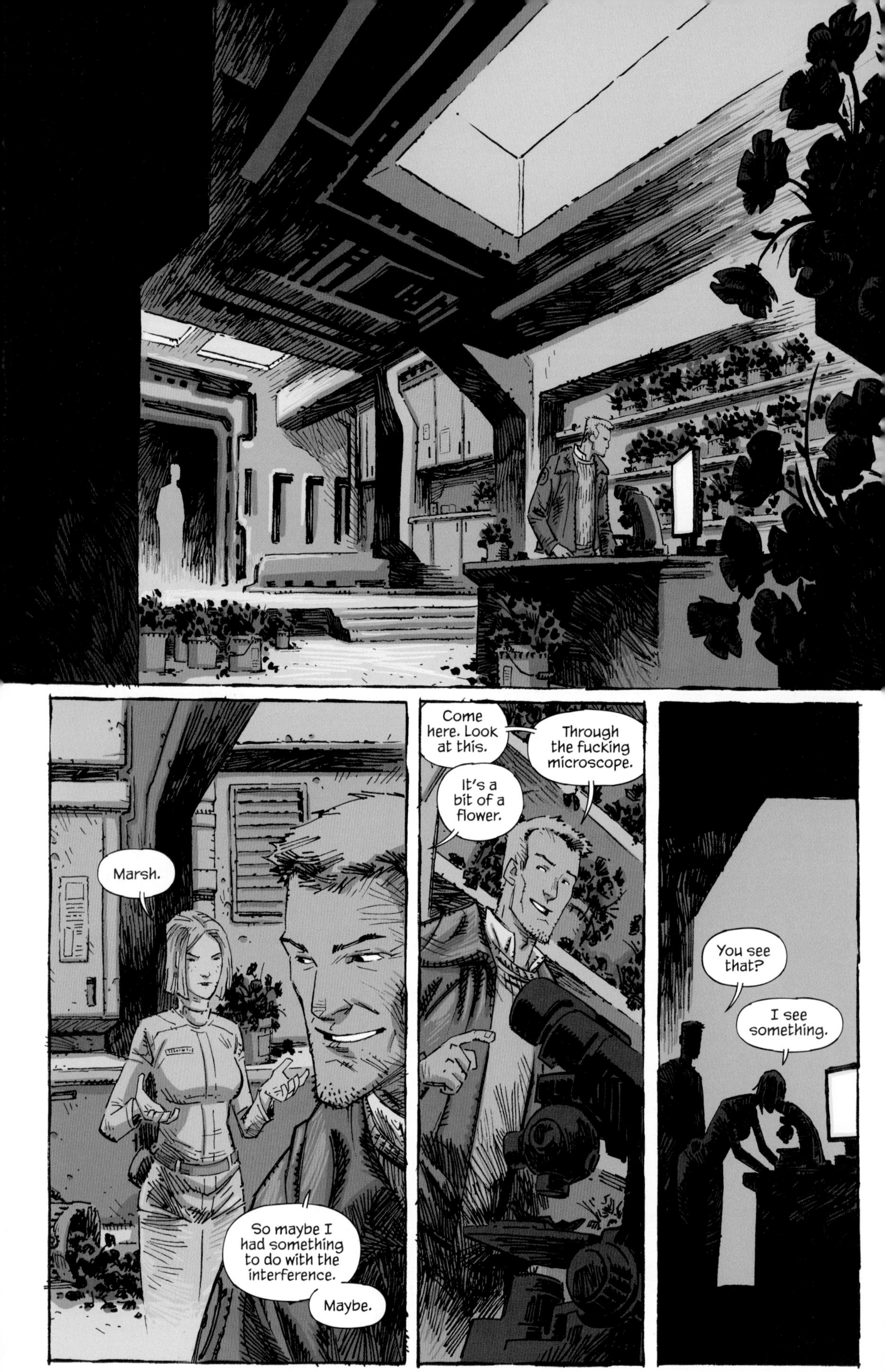
Marsh.
So maybe I had something to do with the interference.
Maybe.
Come here. Look at this.
Through the fucking microscope.
It's a bit of a flower.
You see that?
I see something.

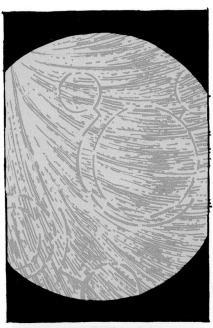

Those are wires, Sarah.

Okay then. Metal filaments.

Bullshit.

Tainted sample. Metal shavings off Napoleon.

No. I took samples from every growth site I could find. We never even put robots in some of those places.

These petals have micrometer wires. They're growing a mineral structure on a biological substrate.

And I started getting noise on the radio and crap on my instruments after I collected... well, a bit less than what you see now.

So why did you keep collecting them?

Oh, come on.

I needed the samples. I needed to be sure what was happening. I just needed more of them. Why wouldn't I? Who wouldn't do that?

I see. And what is your plan?

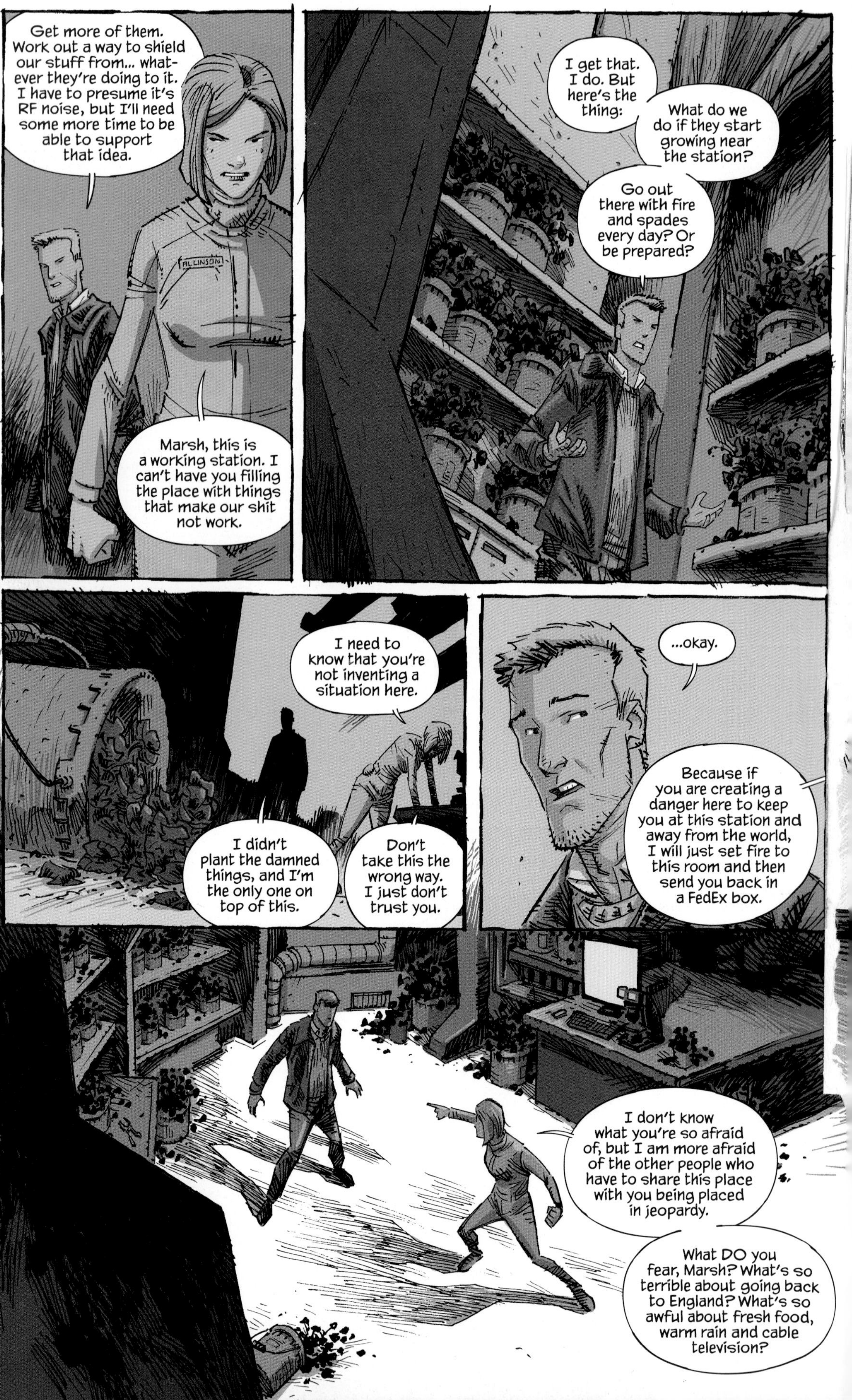
Get more of them. Work out a way to shield our stuff from... whatever they're doing to it. I have to presume it's RF noise, but I'll need some more time to be able to support that idea.
ALLINSON
Marsh, this is a working station. I can't have you filling the place with things that make our shit not work.
I get that. I do. But here's the thing:
What do we do if they start growing near the station?
Go out there with fire and spades every day? Or be prepared?
I need to know that you're not inventing a situation here.
I didn't plant the damned things, and I'm the only one on top of this.
Don't take this the wrong way. I just don't trust you.
...okay.
Because if you are creating a danger here to keep you at this station and away from the world, I will just set fire to this room and then send you back in a FedEx box.
I don't know what you're so afraid of, but I am more afraid of the other people who have to share this place with you being placed in jeopardy.
What DO you fear, Marsh? What's so terrible about going back to England? What's so awful about fresh food, warm rain and cable television?

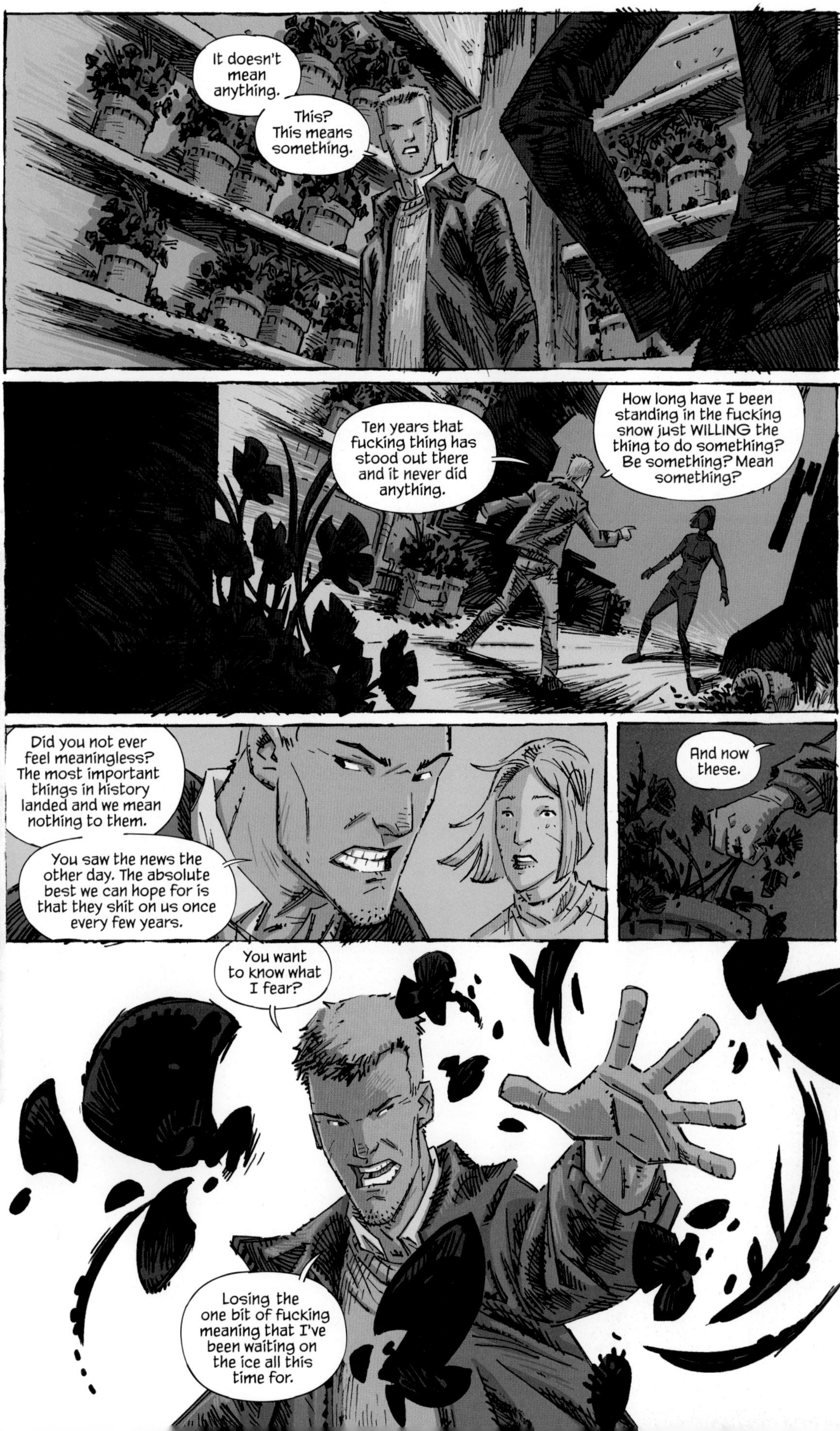
It doesn't mean anything.
This? This means something.
Ten years that fucking thing has stood out there and it never did anything.
How long have I been standing in the fucking snow just WILLING the thing to do something? Be something? Mean something?
Did you not ever feel meaningless? The most important things in history landed and we mean nothing to them.
You saw the news the other day. The absolute best we can hope for is that they shit on us once every few years.
And now these.
You want to know what I fear?
Losing the one bit of fucking meaning that I've been waiting on the ice all this time for.

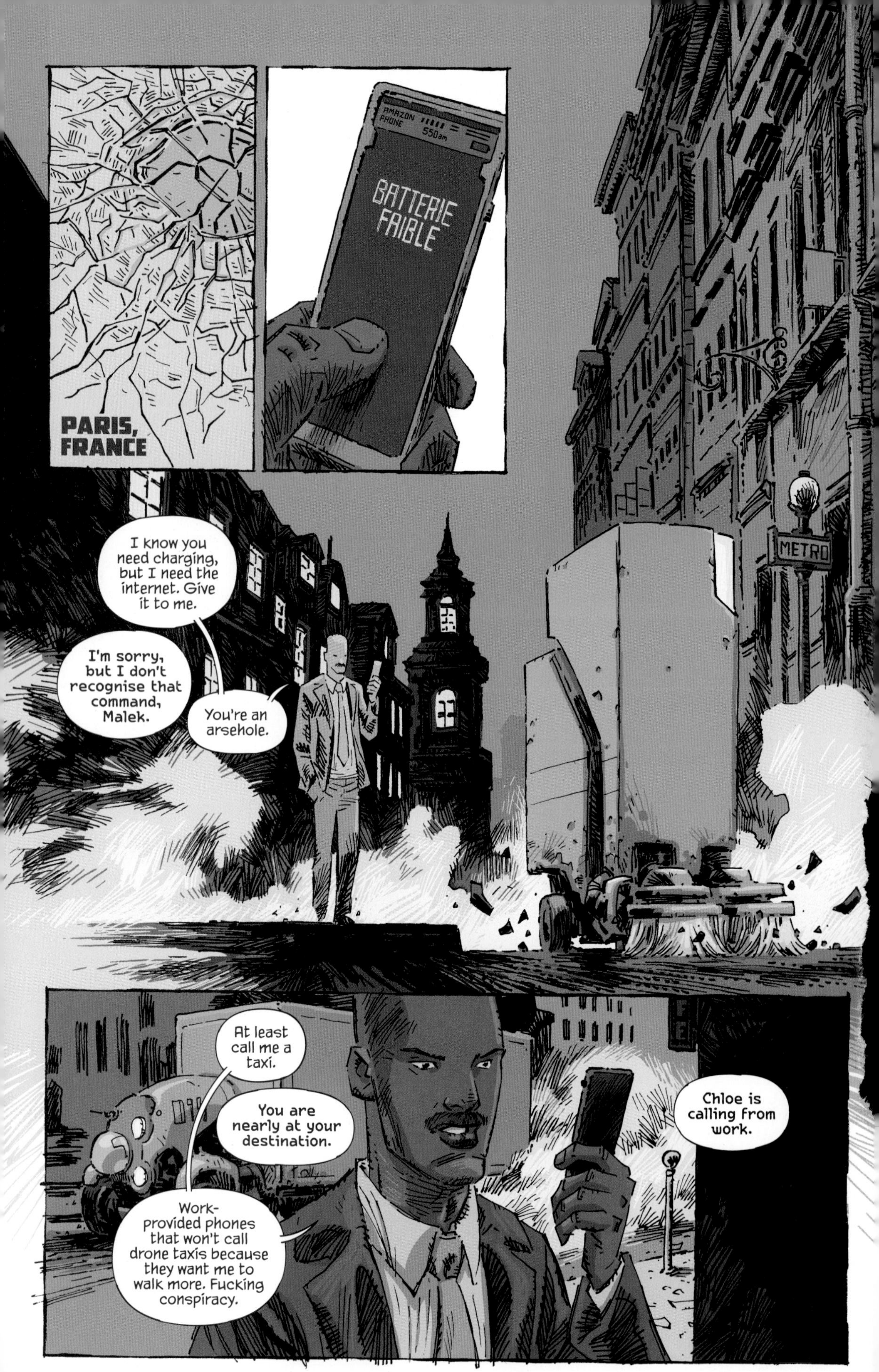
PARIS, FRANCE
AMAZON PHONE
5:50am
BATTERIE FAIBLE
I know you need charging, but I need the internet. Give it to me.
I'm sorry, but I don't recognise that command, Malek.
You're an arsehole.
METRO
At least call me a taxi.
You are nearly at your destination.
Work-provided phones that won't call drone taxis because they want me to walk more. Fucking conspiracy.
Chloe is calling from work.

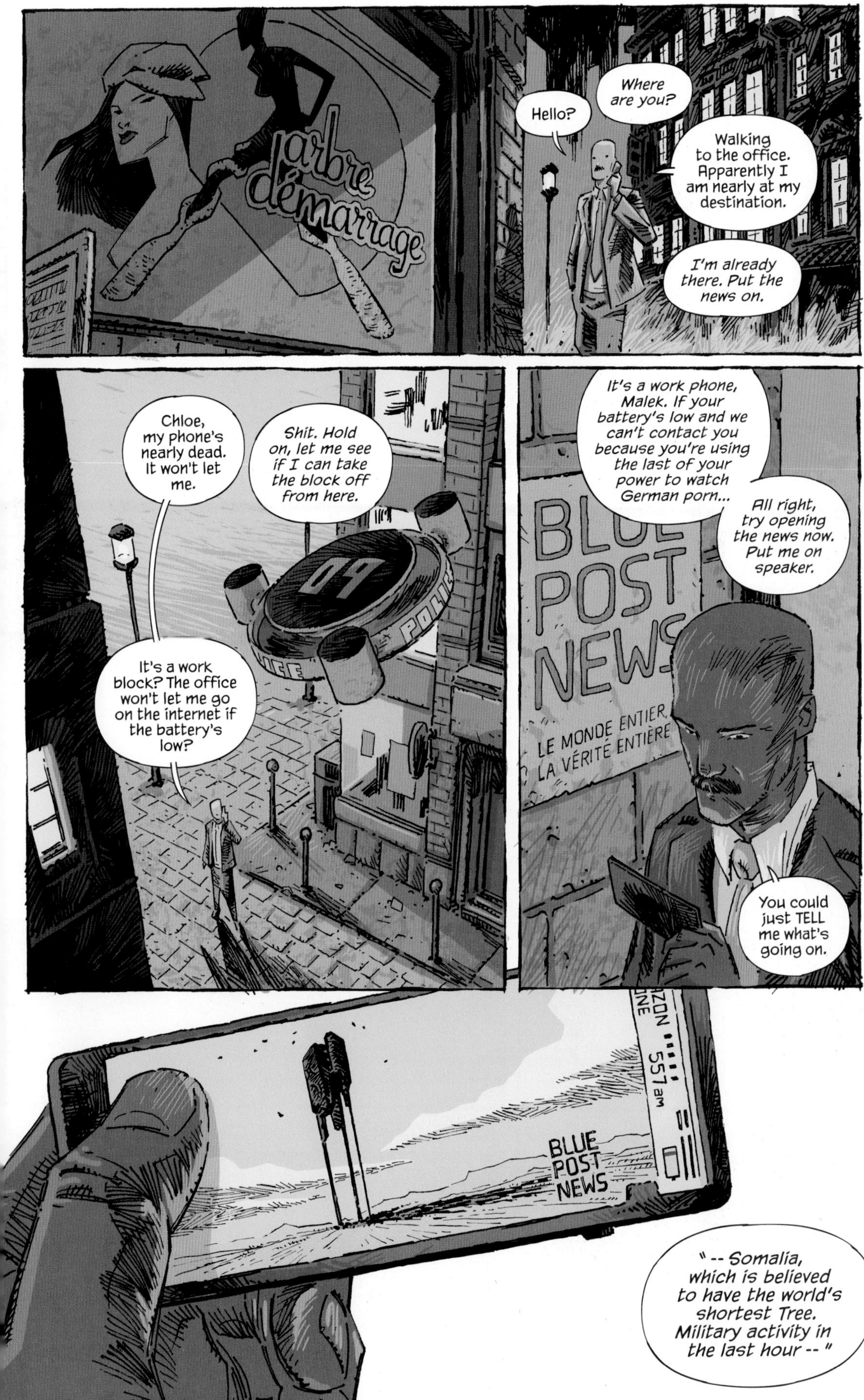
arbre démarrage
Hello?
Where are you?
Walking to the office. Apparently I am nearly at my destination.
I'm already there. Put the news on.
Chloe, my phone's nearly dead. It won't let me.
Shit. Hold on, let me see if I can take the block off from here.
It's a work block? The office won't let me go on the internet if the battery's low?
PD
POLICE
It's a work phone, Malek. If your battery's low and we can't contact you because you're using the last of your power to watch German porn...
All right, try opening the news now. Put me on speaker.
BLUE POST NEWS
LE MONDE ENTIER, LA VÉRITÉ ENTIÈRE
You could just TELL me what's going on.
557 am
BLUE POST NEWS
" -- Somalia, which is believed to have the world's shortest Tree. Military activity in the last hour -- "

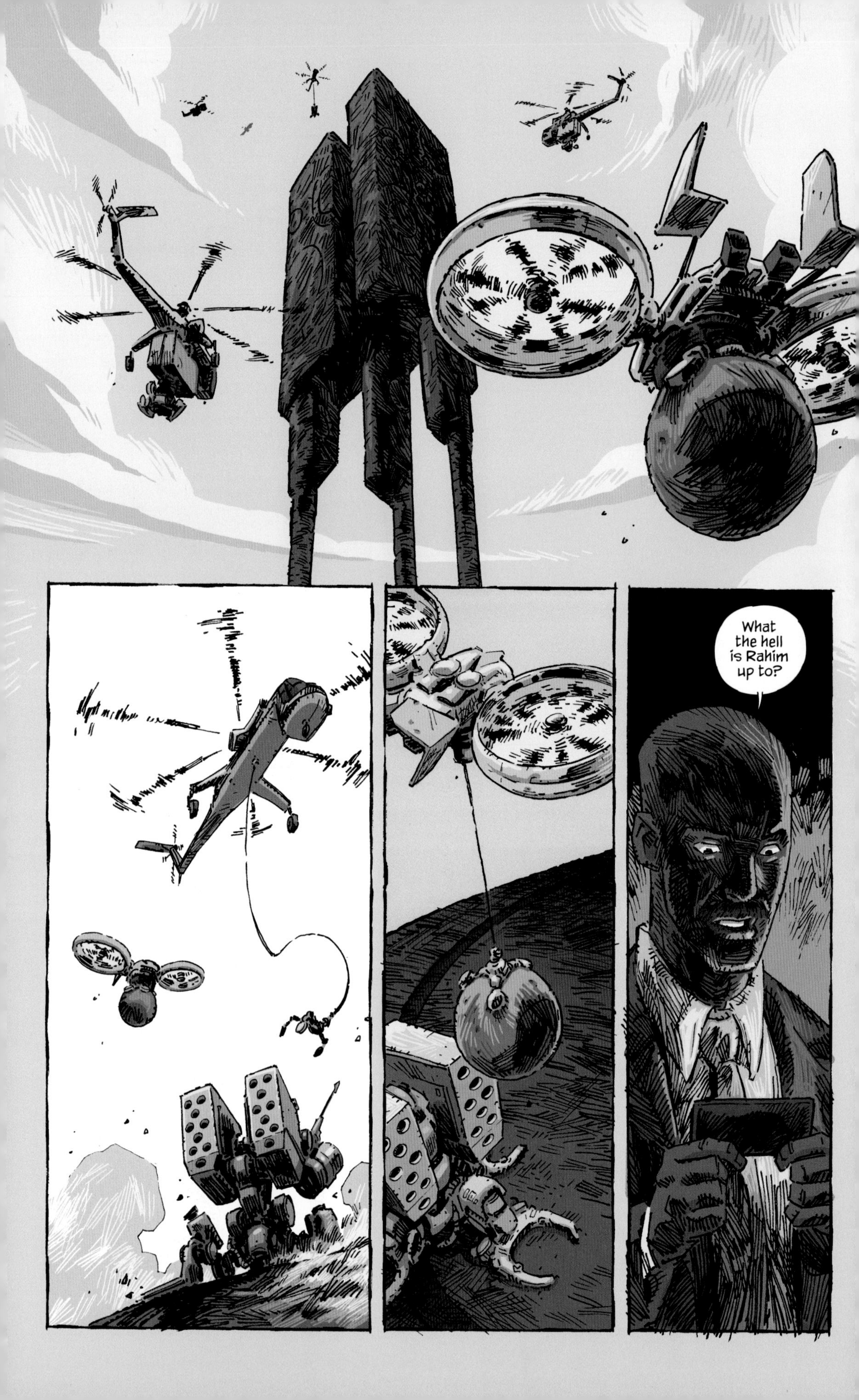
What the hell is Rahim up to?

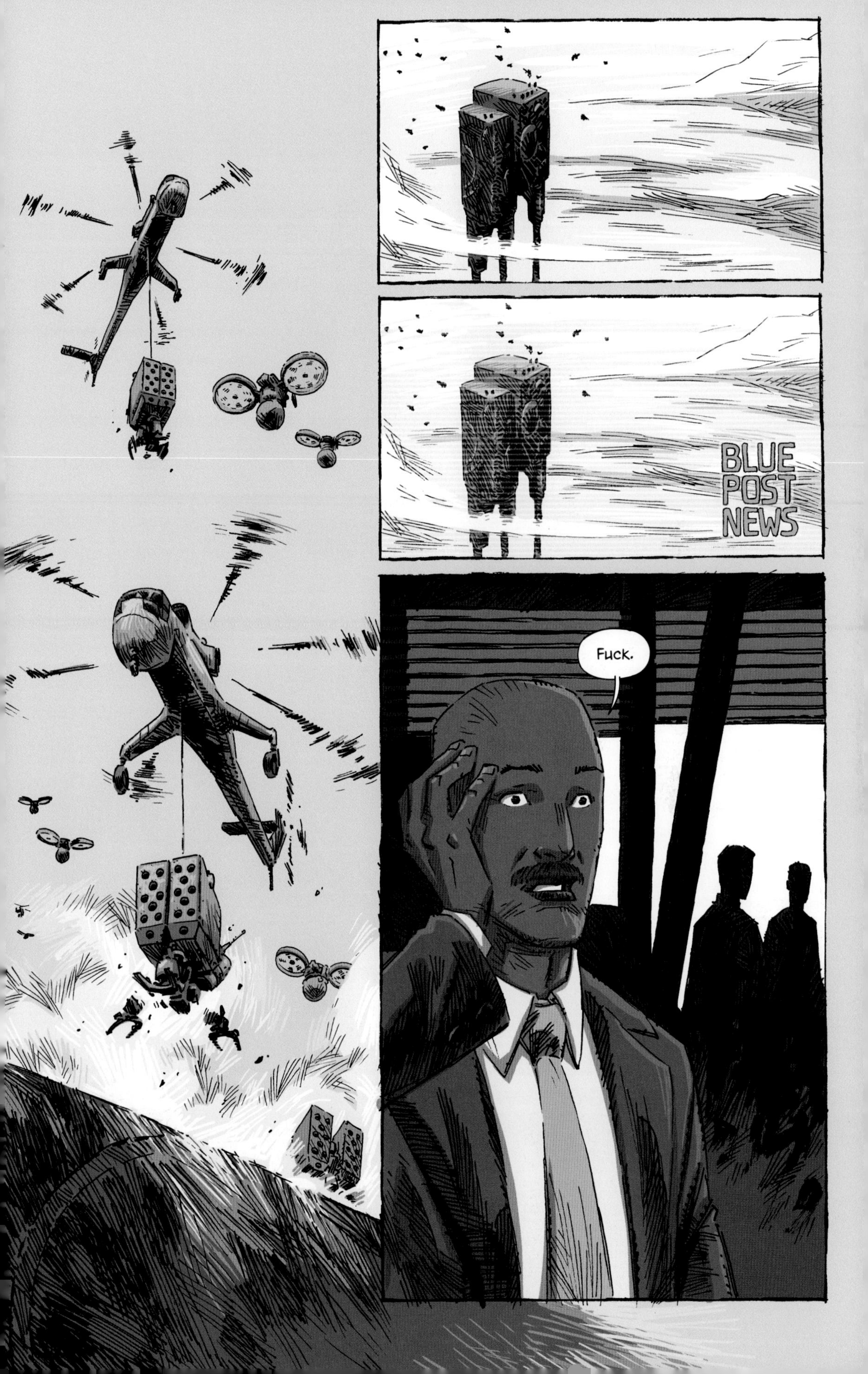
BLUE POST NEWS
Fuck.

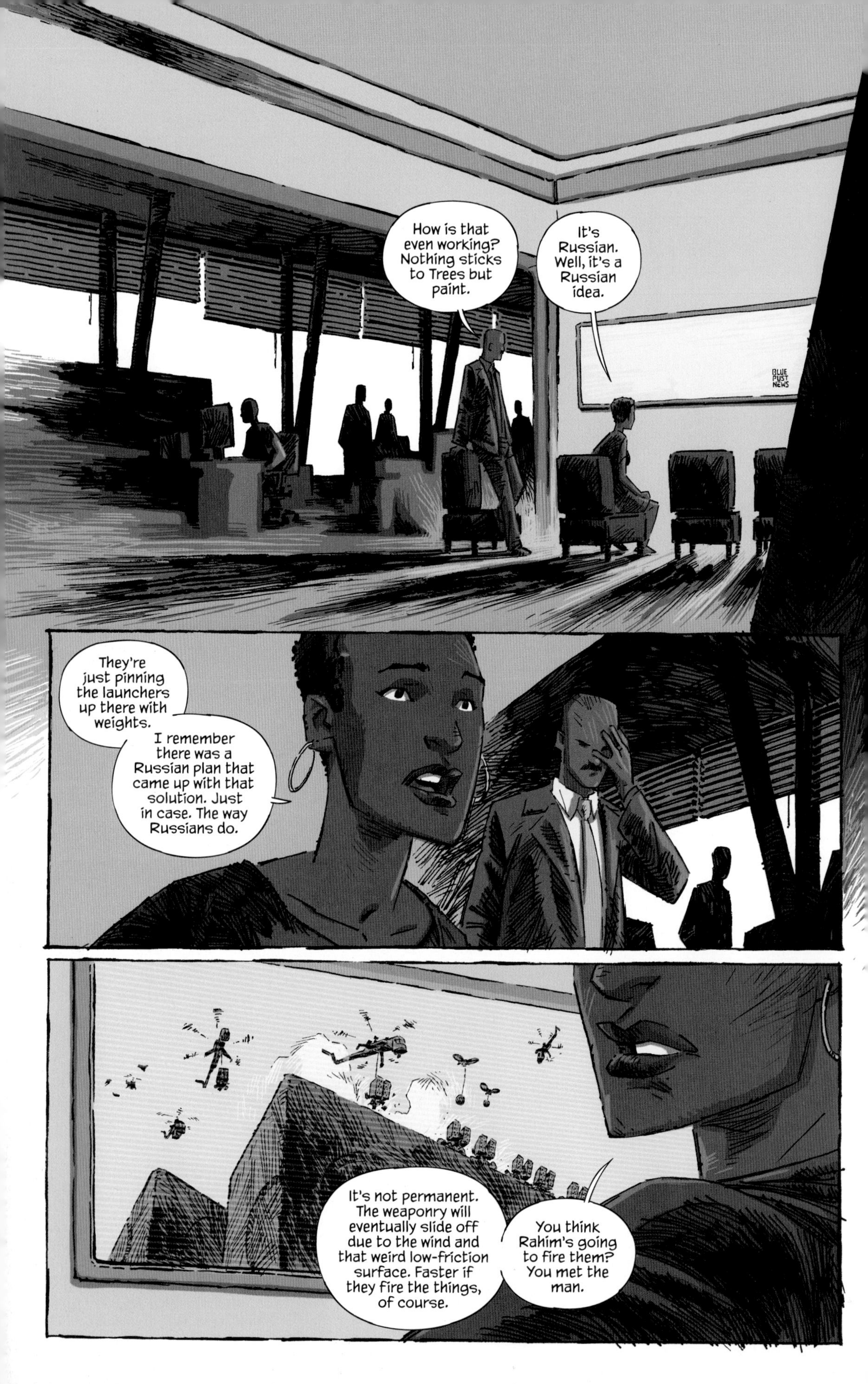
How is that even working? Nothing sticks to Trees but paint.
It's Russian. Well, it's a Russian idea.
BLUE PUST NEWS
They're just pinning the launchers up there with weights.
I remember there was a Russian plan that came up with that solution. Just in case. The way Russians do.
It's not permanent. The weaponry will eventually slide off due to the wind and that weird low-friction surface. Faster if they fire the things, of course.
You think Rahim's going to fire them? You met the man.

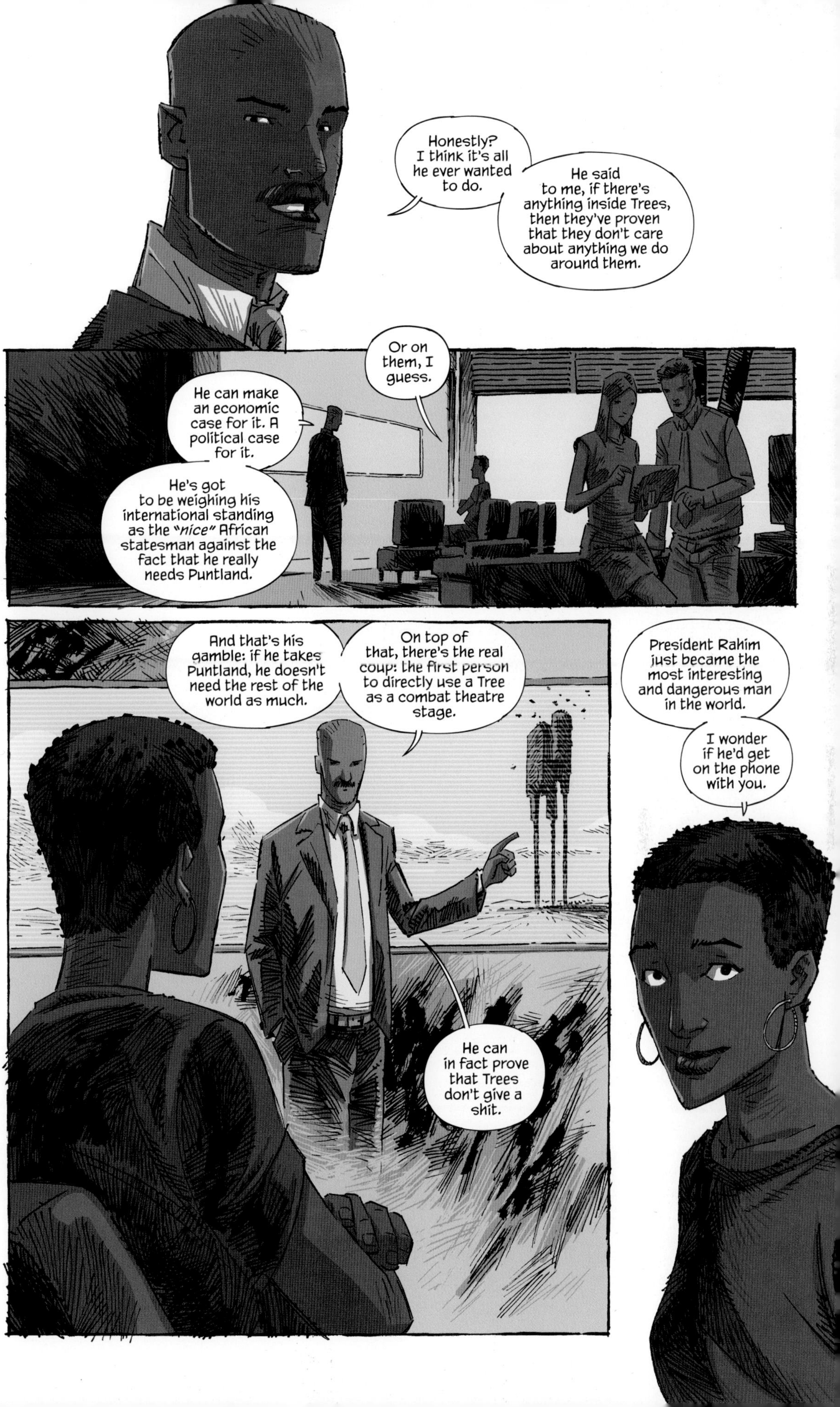
Honestly? I think it's all he ever wanted to do.
He said to me, if there's anything inside Trees, then they've proven that they don't care about anything we do around them.
Or on them, I guess.
He can make an economic case for it. A political case for it.
He's got to be weighing his international standing as the *"nice"* African statesman against the fact that he really needs Puntland.
And that's his gamble: if he takes Puntland, he doesn't need the rest of the world as much.
On top of that, there's the real coup: the first person to directly use a Tree as a combat theatre stage.
He can in fact prove that Trees don't give a shit.
President Rahim just became the most interesting and dangerous man in the world.
I wonder if he'd get on the phone with you.

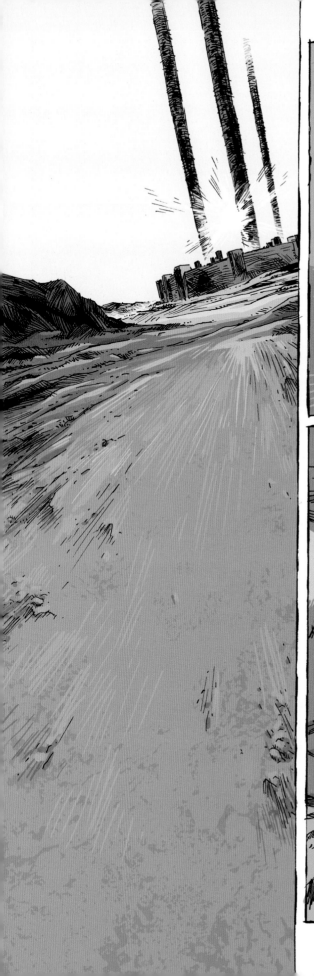

I don't know what happened.

There was a party that Zhen talked me into.

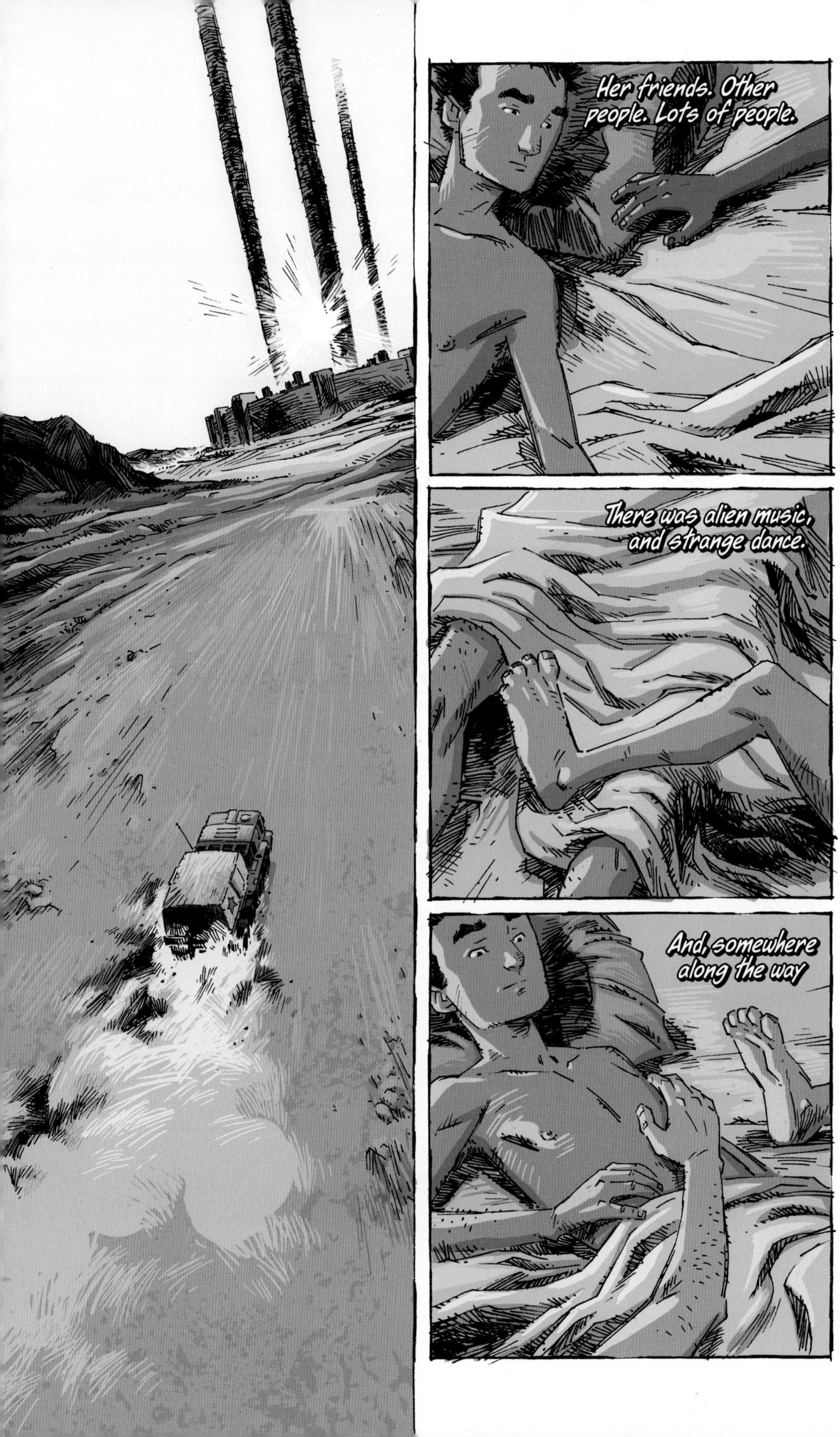
Her friends. Other people. Lots of people.
There was alien music, and strange dance.
And, somewhere along the way

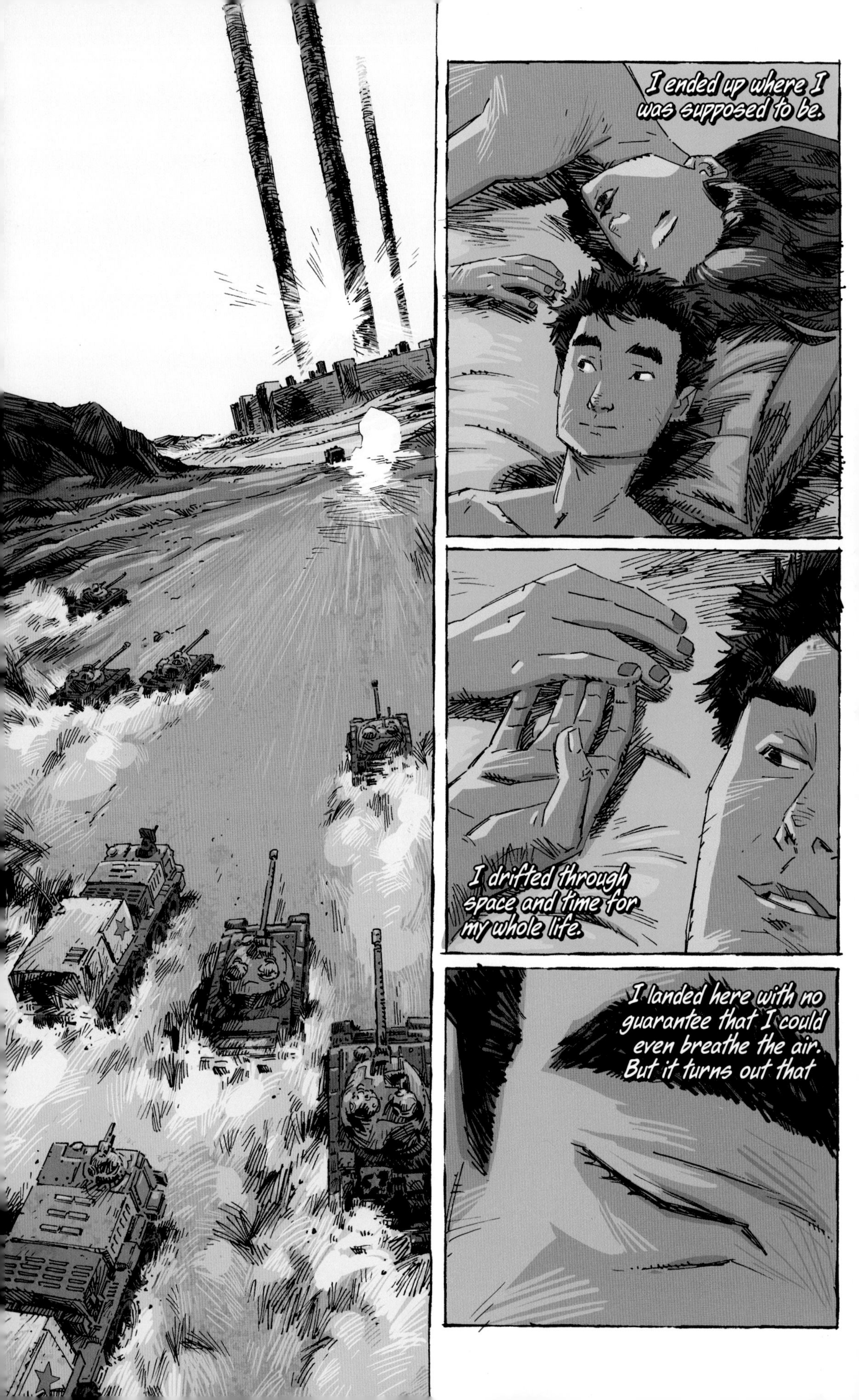
I ended up where I was supposed to be.
I drifted through space and time for my whole life.
I landed here with no guarantee that I could even breathe the air. But it turns out that

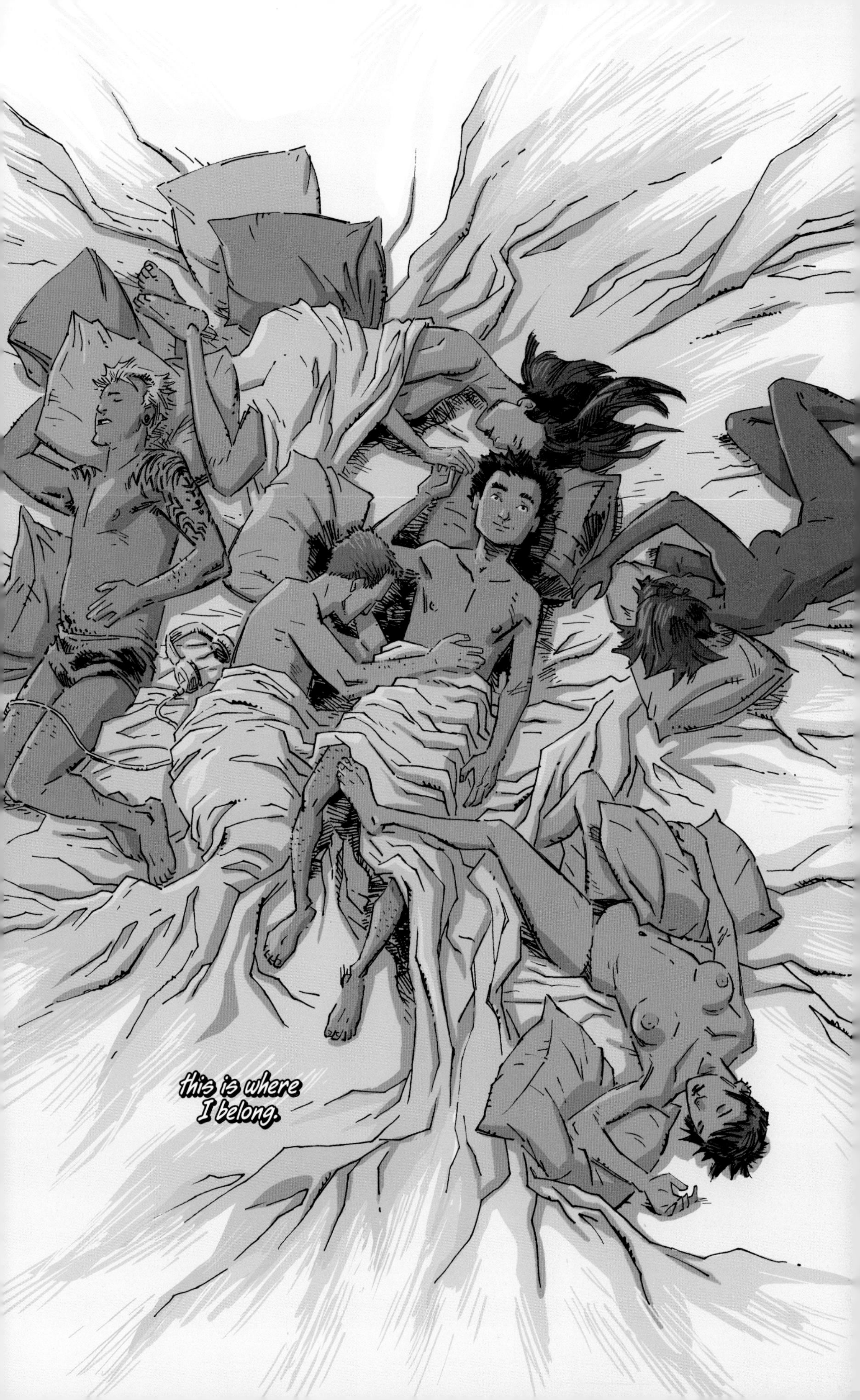
this is where I belong.

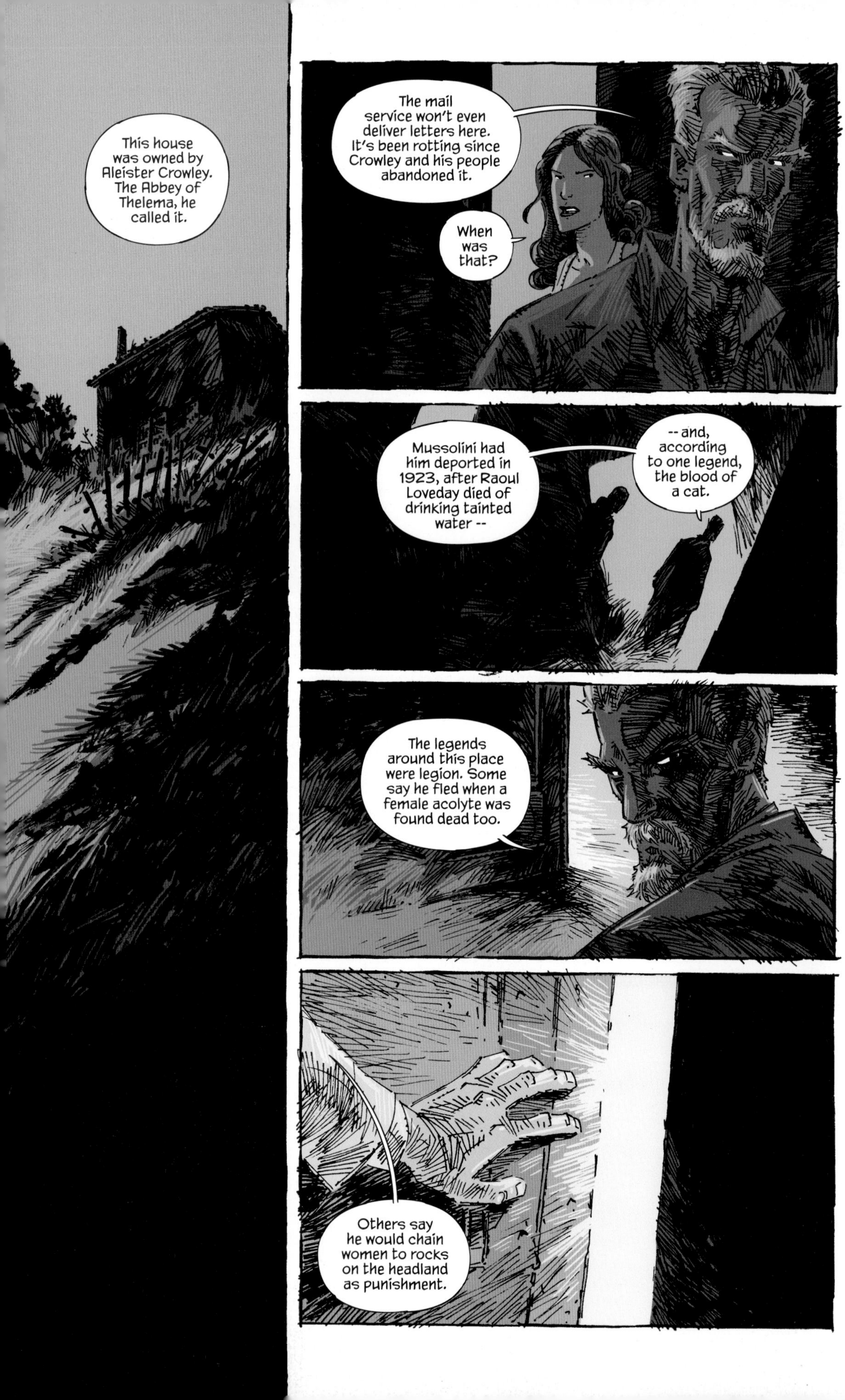
This house was owned by Aleister Crowley. The Abbey of Thelema, he called it.
The mail service won't even deliver letters here. It's been rotting since Crowley and his people abandoned it.
When was that?
Mussolini had him deported in 1923, after Raoul Loveday died of drinking tainted water --
-- and, according to one legend, the blood of a cat.
The legends around this place were legion. Some say he fled when a female acolyte was found dead too.
Others say he would chain women to rocks on the headland as punishment.

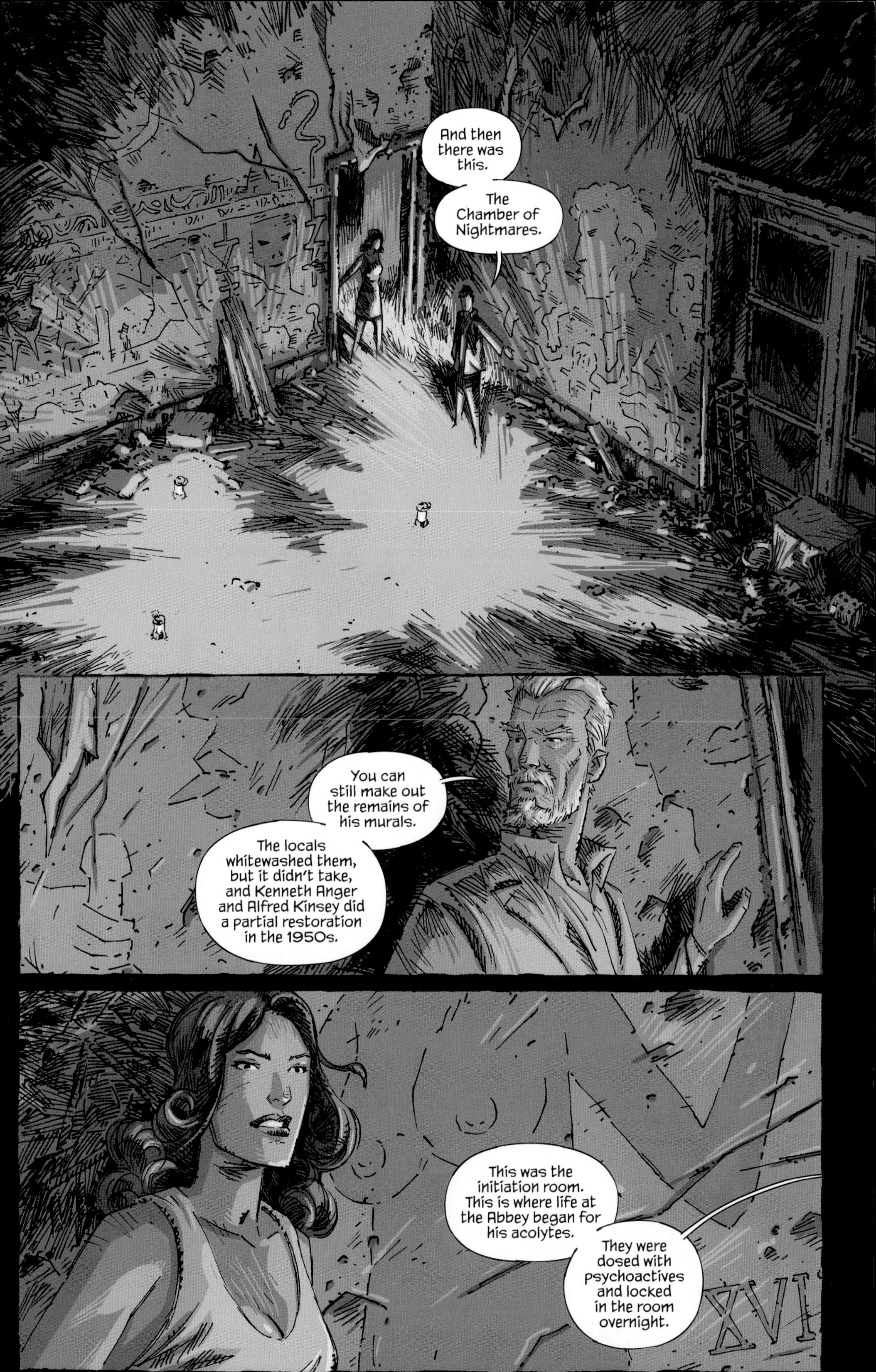
And then there was this.
The Chamber of Nightmares.
You can still make out the remains of his murals.
The locals whitewashed them, but it didn't take, and Kenneth Anger and Alfred Kinsey did a partial restoration in the 1950s.
This was the initiation room. This is where life at the Abbey began for his acolytes.
They were dosed with psychoactives and locked in the room overnight.
XVI

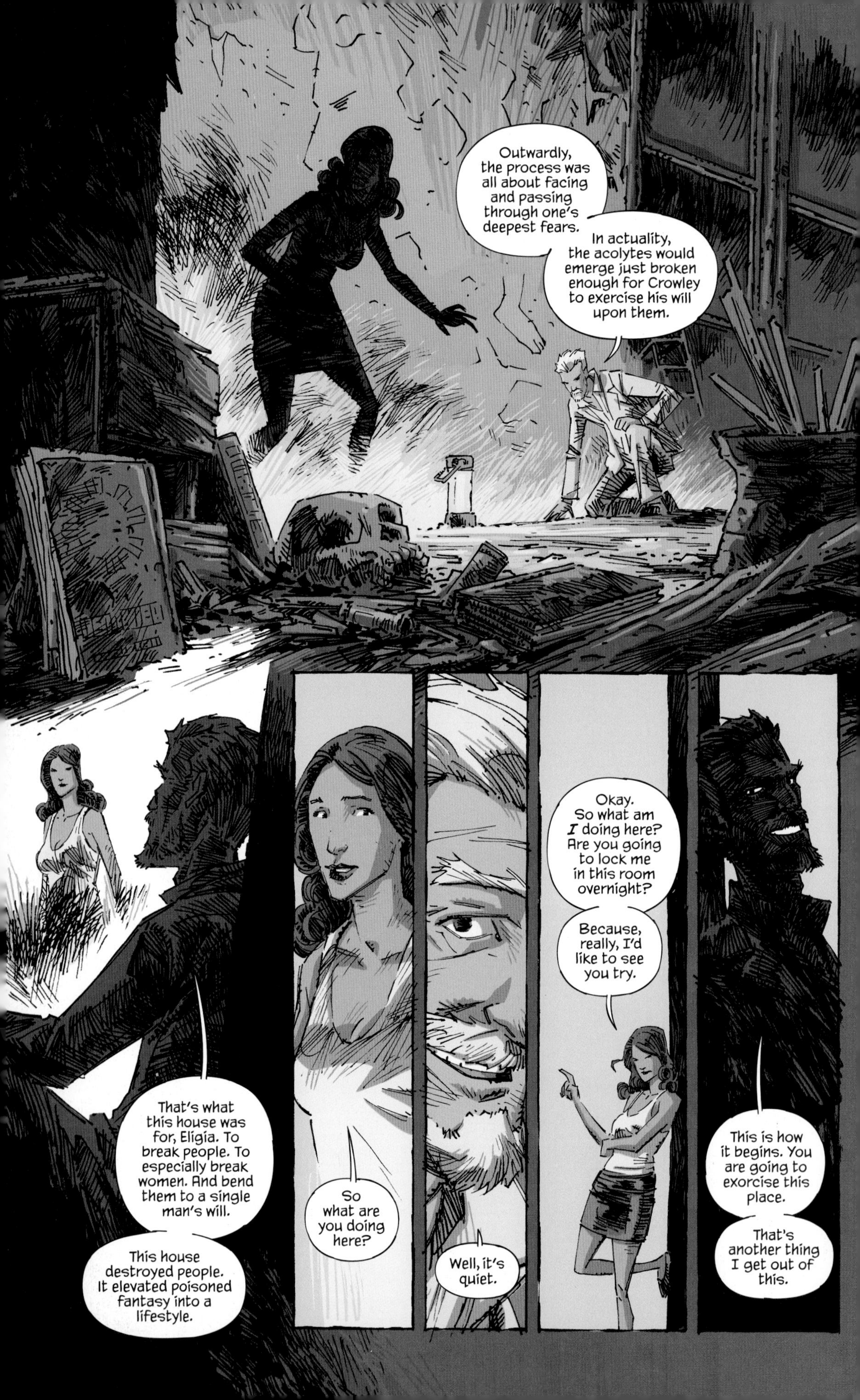

Outwardly, the process was all about facing and passing through one's deepest fears.
In actuality, the acolytes would emerge just broken enough for Crowley to exercise his will upon them.
That's what this house was for, Eligia. To break people. To especially break women. And bend them to a single man's will.
This house destroyed people. It elevated poisoned fantasy into a lifestyle.
So what are you doing here?
Well, it's quiet.
Okay. So what am *I* doing here? Are you going to lock me in this room overnight?
Because, really, I'd like to see you try.
This is how it begins. You are going to exorcise this place.
That's another thing I get out of this.

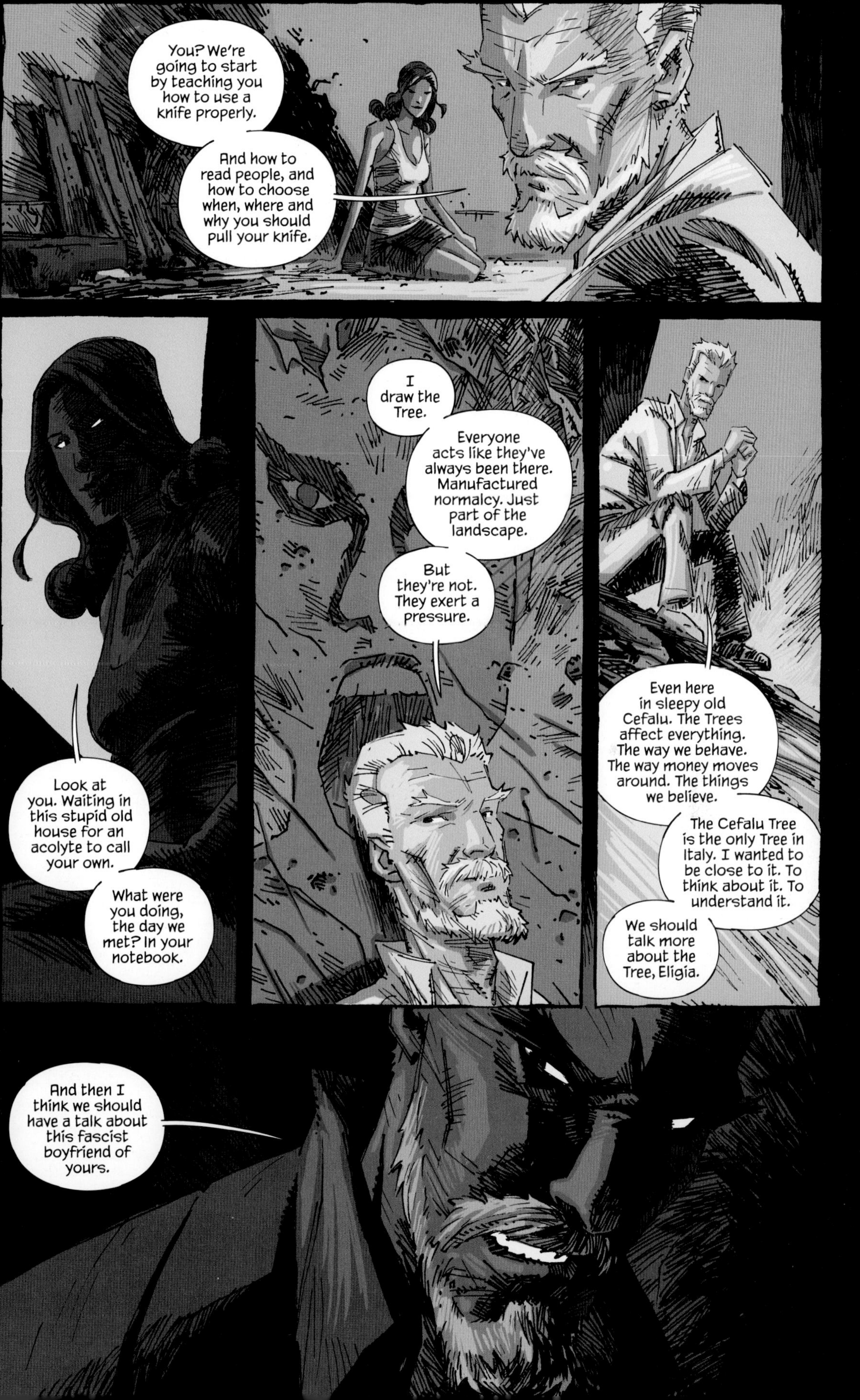

You? We're going to start by teaching you how to use a knife properly.
And how to read people, and how to choose when, where and why you should pull your knife.
Look at you. Waiting in this stupid old house for an acolyte to call your own.
What were you doing, the day we met? In your notebook.
I draw the Tree.
Everyone acts like they've always been there. Manufactured normalcy. Just part of the landscape.
But they're not. They exert a pressure.
Even here in sleepy old Cefalu. The Trees affect everything. The way we behave. The way money moves around. The things we believe.
The Cefalu Tree is the only Tree in Italy. I wanted to be close to it. To think about it. To understand it.
We should talk more about the Tree, Eligia.
And then I think we should have a talk about this fascist boyfriend of yours.

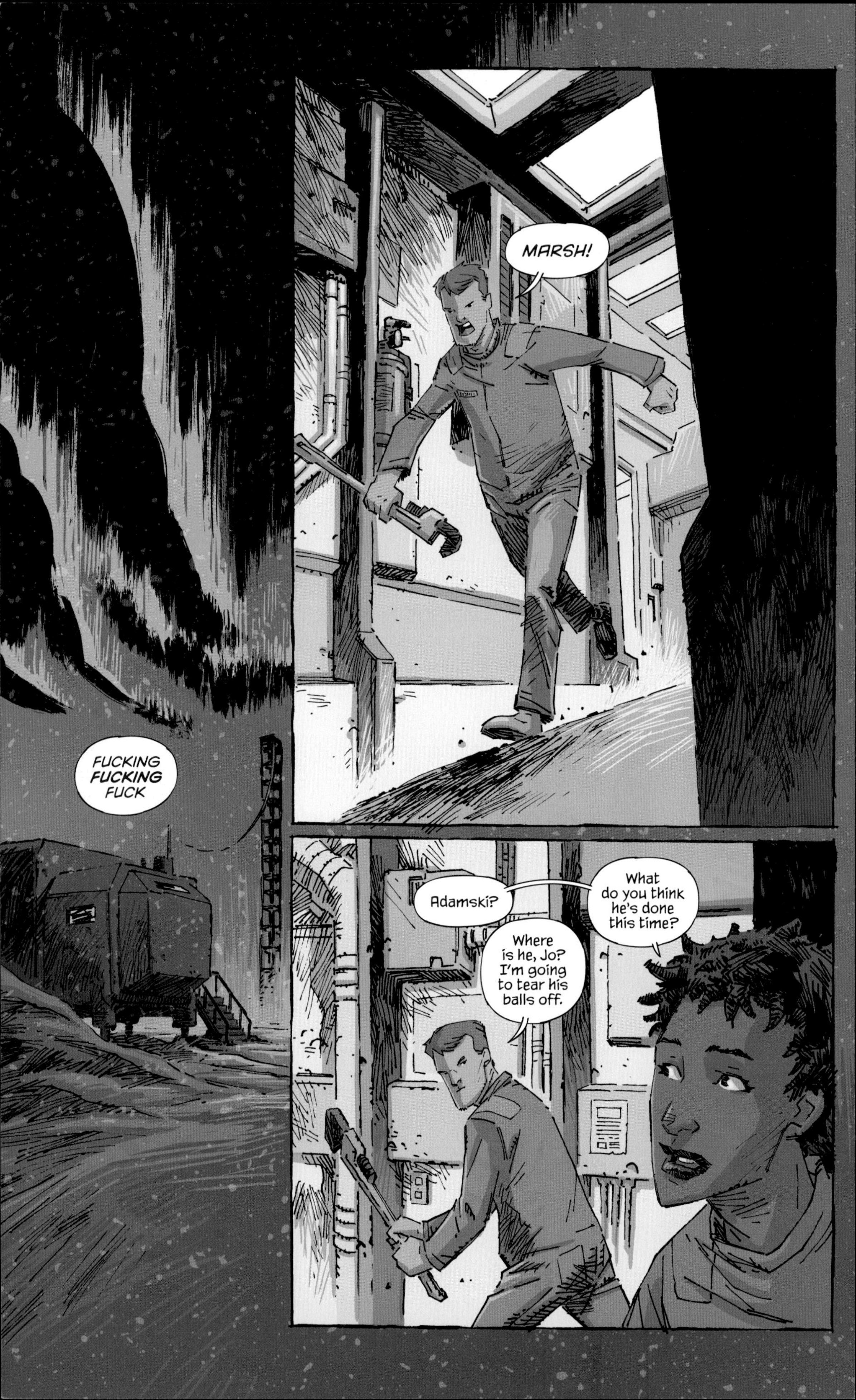
MARSH!
FUCKING FUCKING FUCK
Adamski?
What do you think he's done this time?
Where is he, Jo? I'm going to tear his balls off.

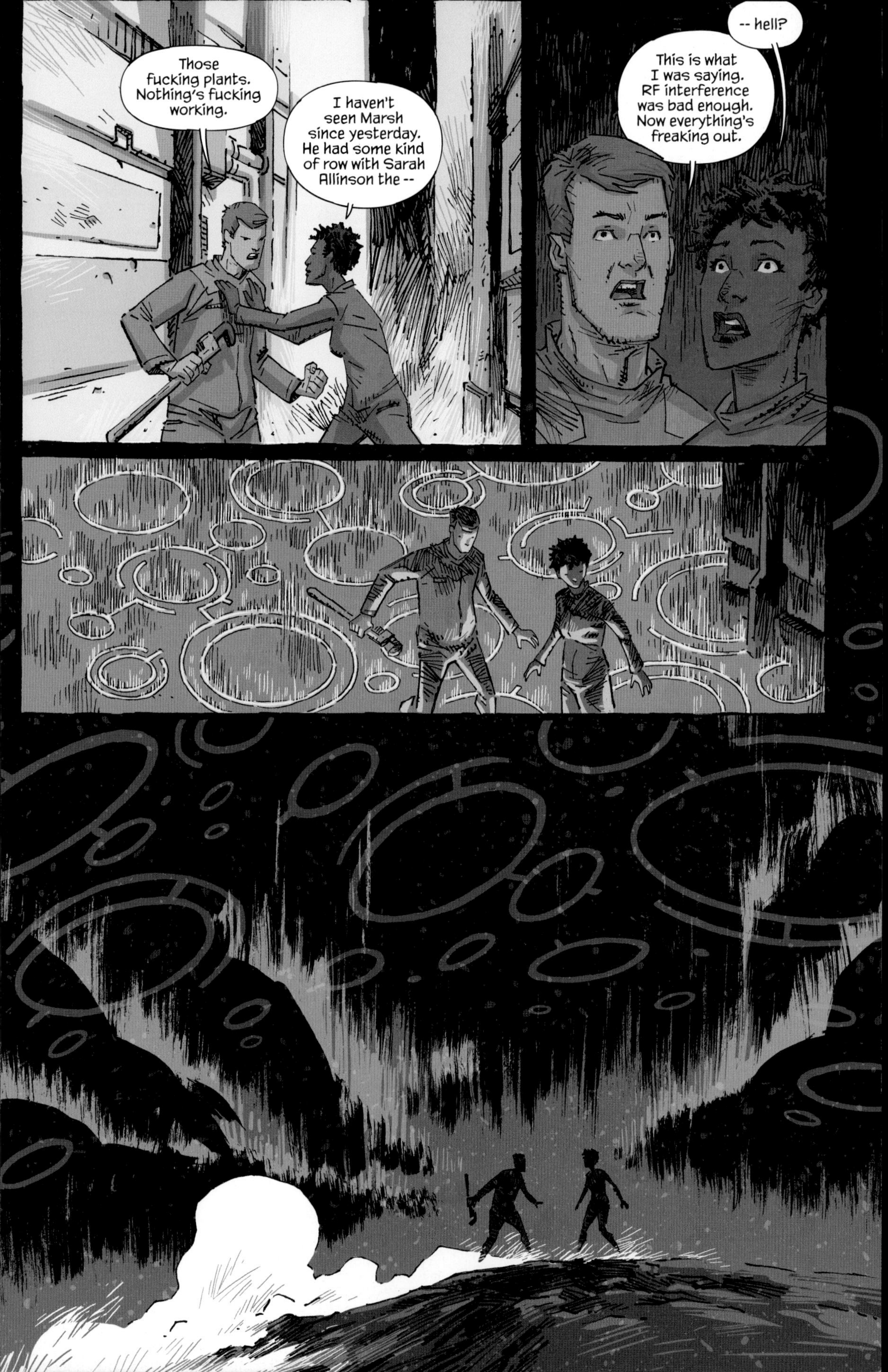
Those fucking plants. Nothing's fucking working.
I haven't seen Marsh since yesterday. He had some kind of row with Sarah Allinson the --
This is what I was saying. RF interference was bad enough. Now everything's freaking out.
-- hell?

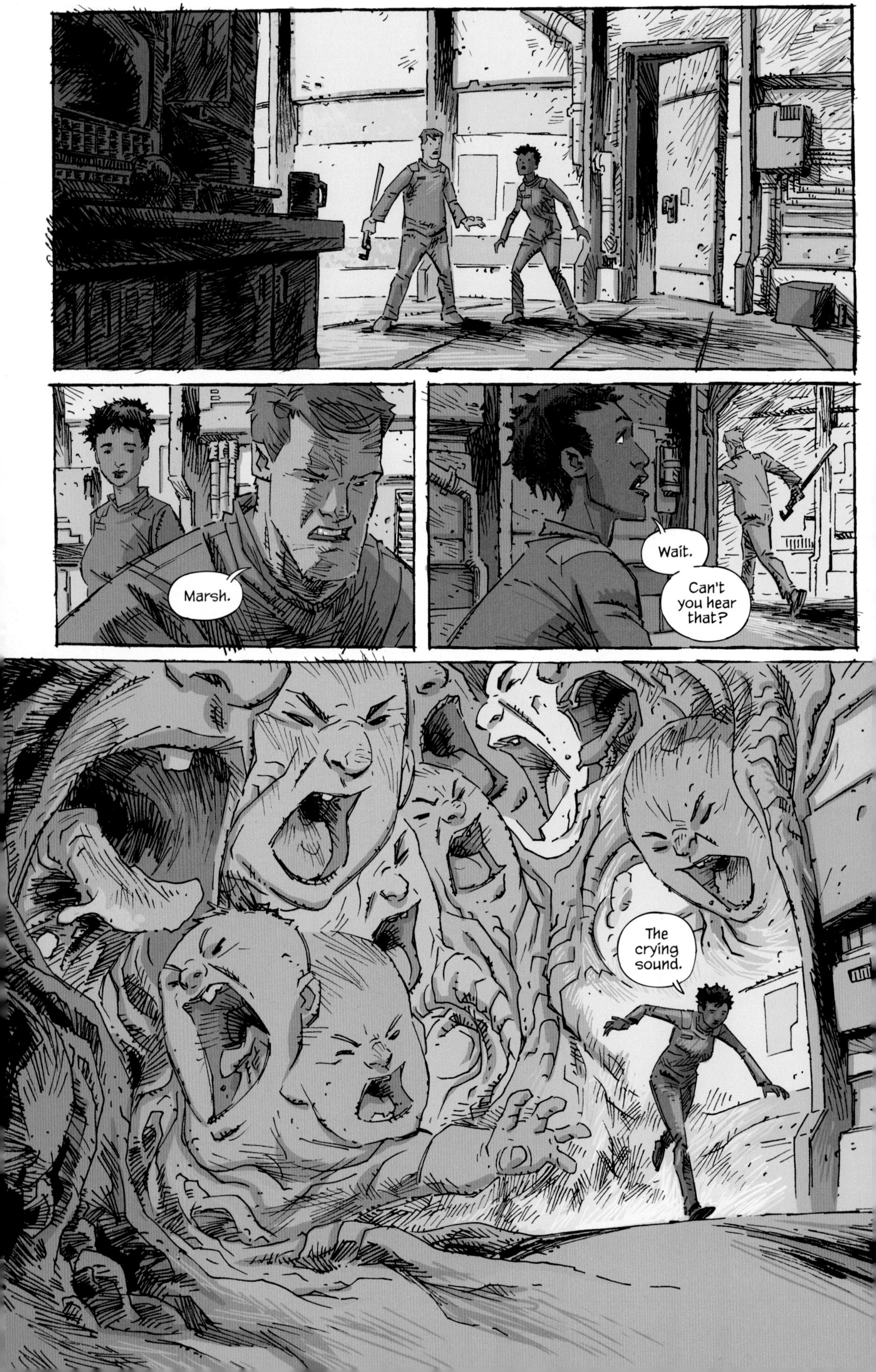
Marsh.
Wait.
Can't you hear that?
The crying sound.

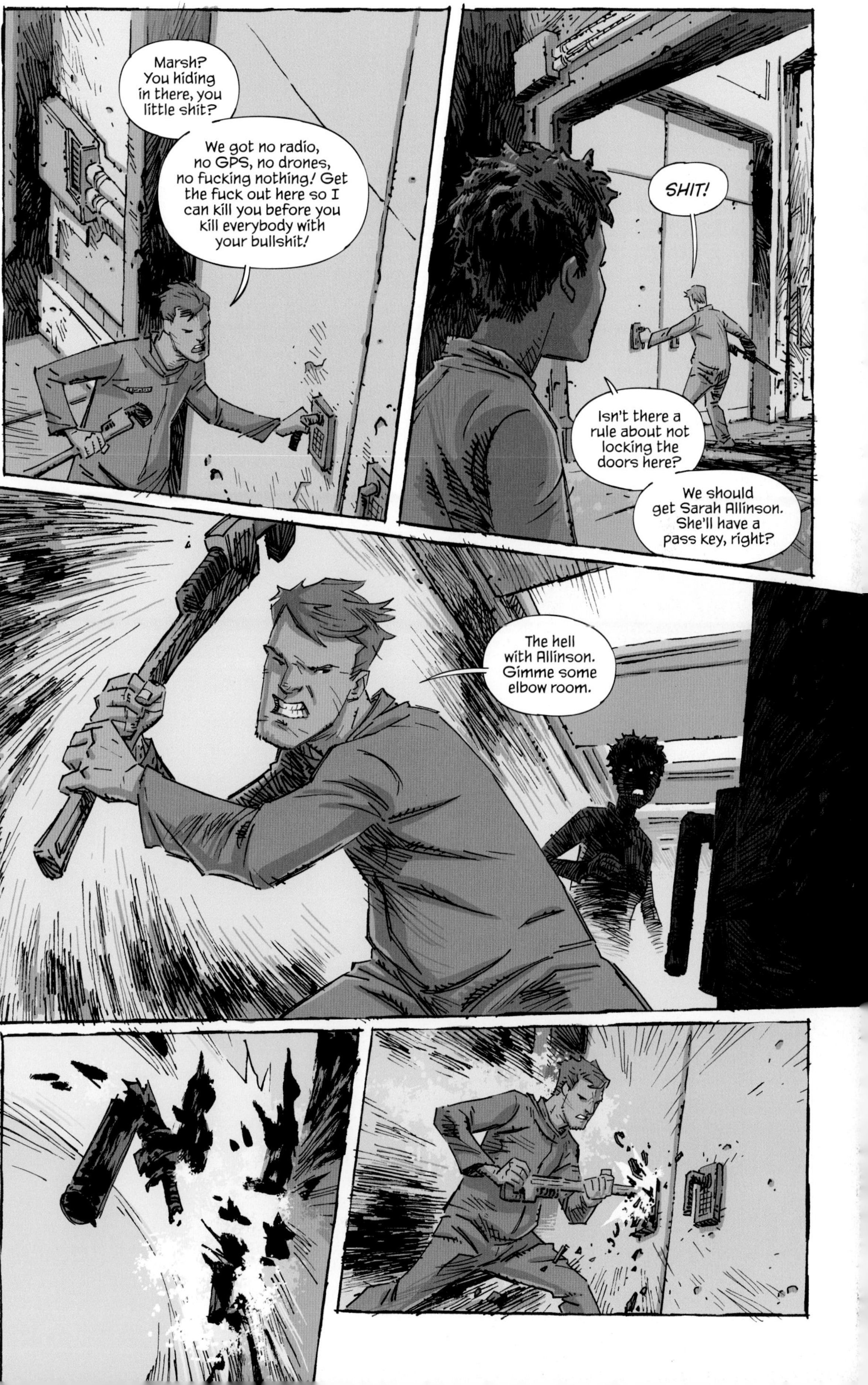
Marsh? You hiding in there, you little shit?
We got no radio, no GPS, no drones, no fucking nothing! Get the fuck out here so I can kill you before you kill everybody with your bullshit!
SHIT!
Isn't there a rule about not locking the doors here?
We should get Sarah Allinson. She'll have a pass key, right?
The hell with Allinson. Gimme some elbow room.

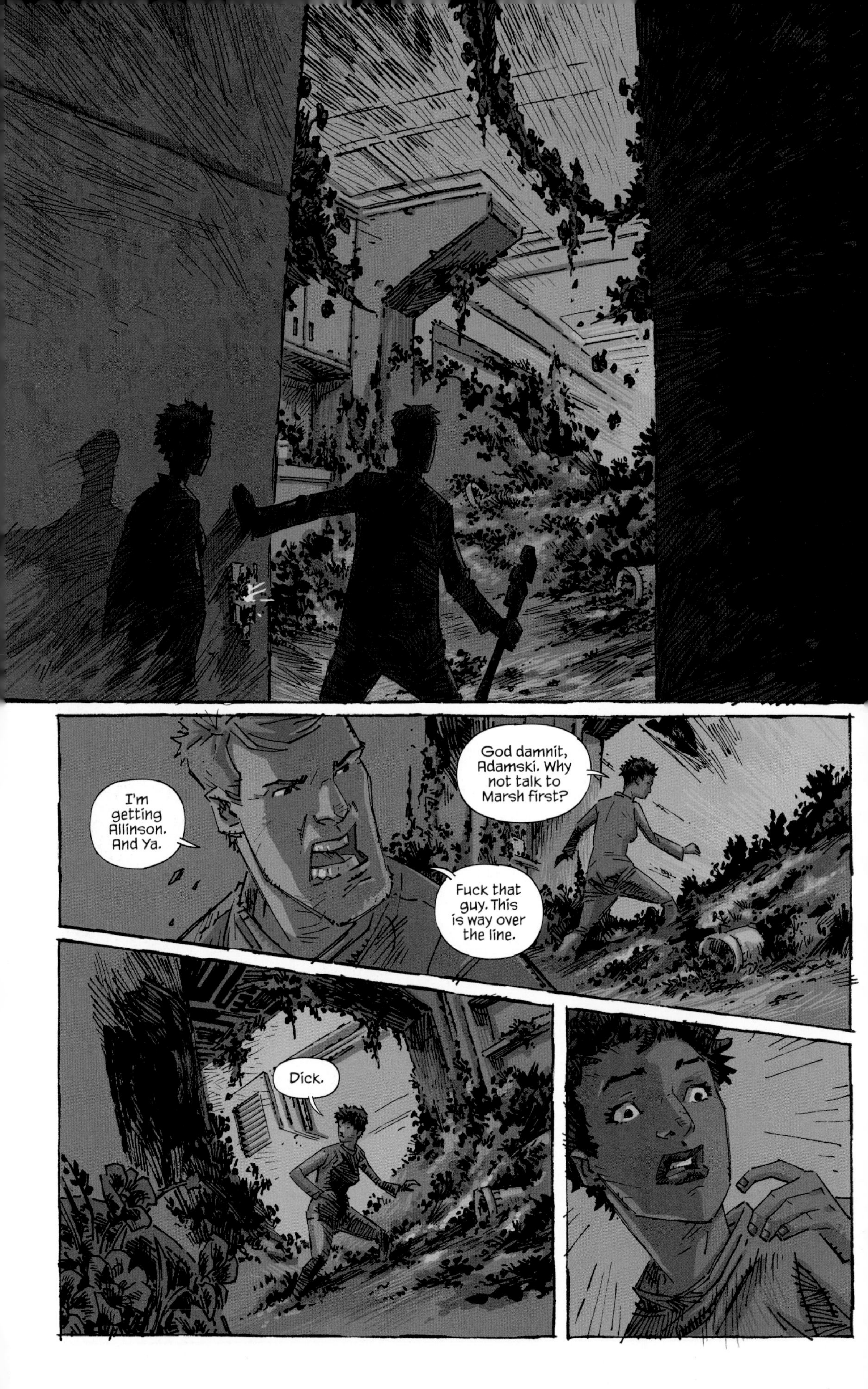
I'm getting Allinson. And Ya.
Fuck that guy. This is way over the line.
God damnit, Adamski. Why not talk to Marsh first?
Dick.

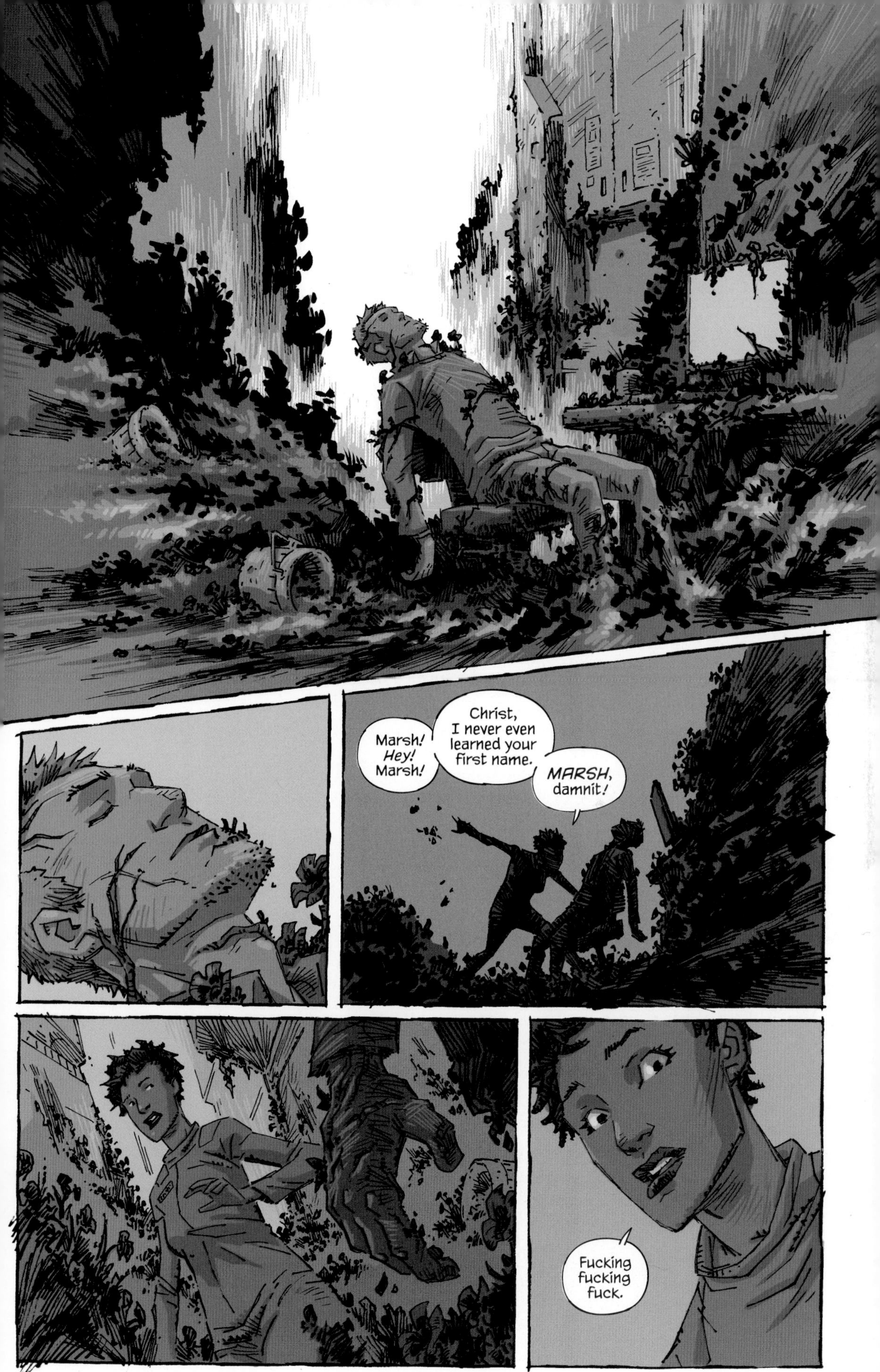
Marsh! Hey! Marsh!
Christ, I never even learned your first name.
MARSH, damnit!
Fucking fucking fuck.

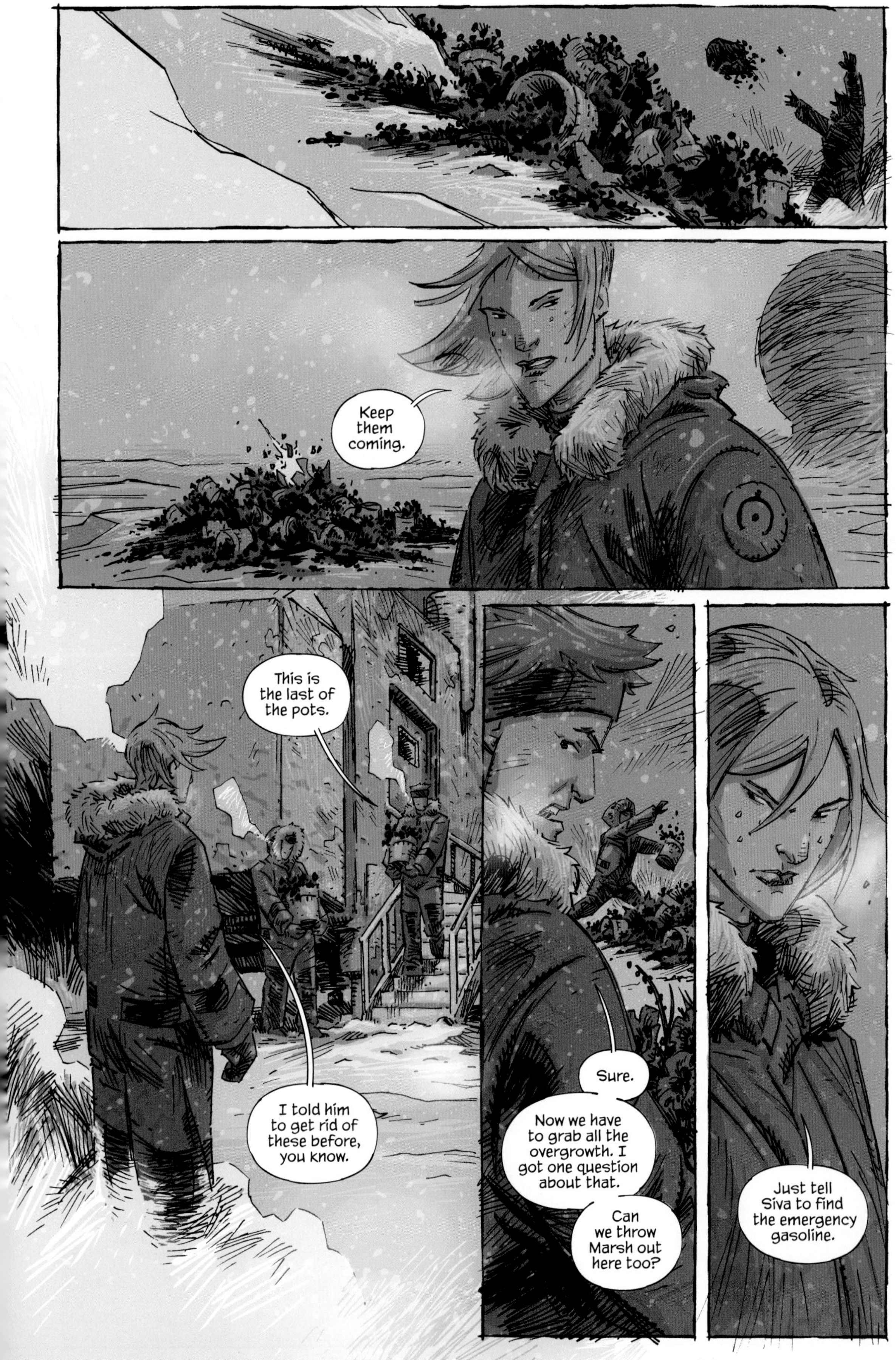
Keep them coming.
This is the last of the pots.
I told him to get rid of these before, you know.
Sure.
Now we have to grab all the overgrowth. I got one question about that.
Can we throw Marsh out here too?
Just tell Siva to find the emergency gasoline.

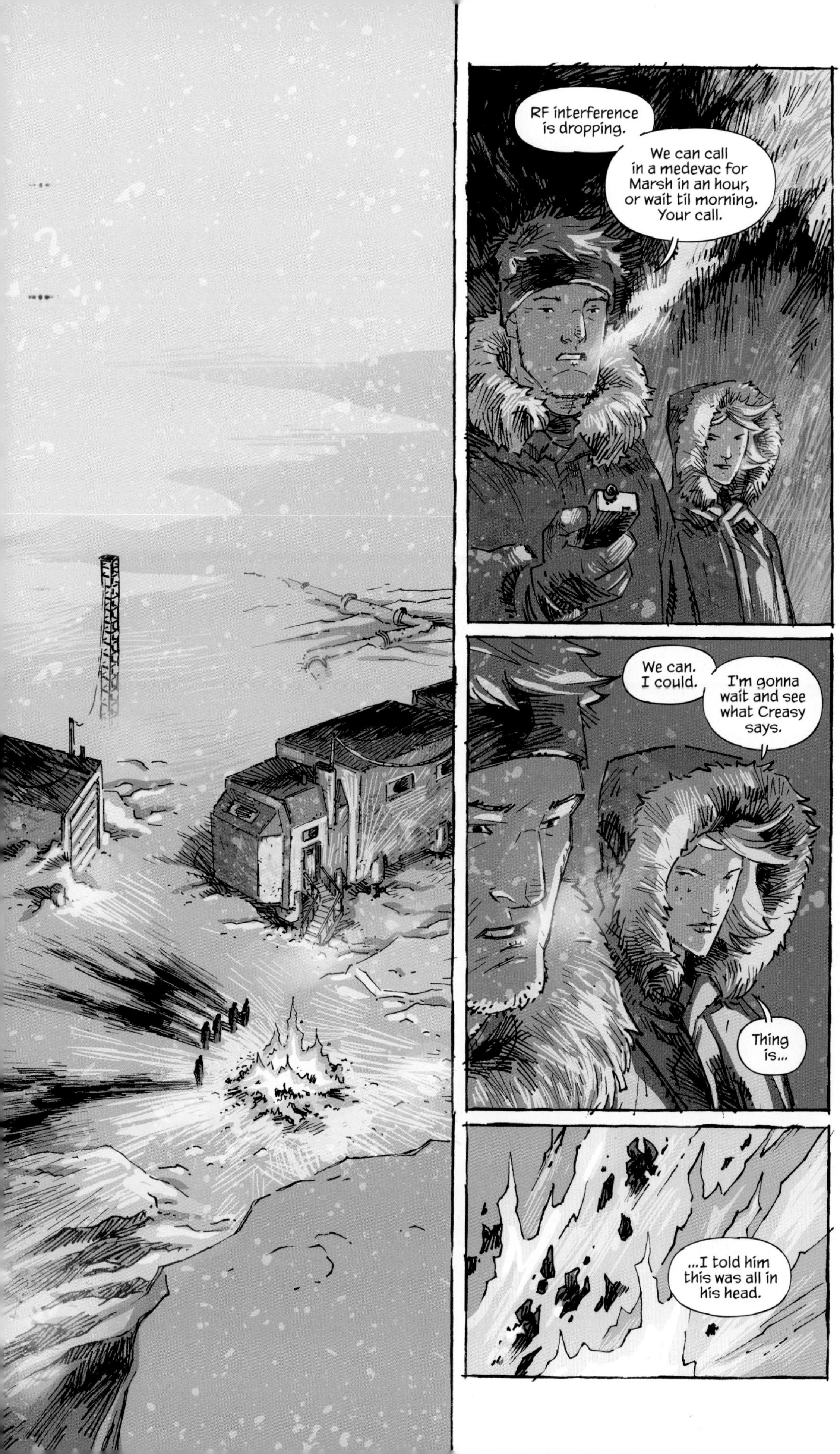
RF interference is dropping.
We can call in a medevac for Marsh in an hour, or wait til morning. Your call.
We can. I could.
I'm gonna wait and see what Creasy says.
Thing is...
...I told him this was all in his head.

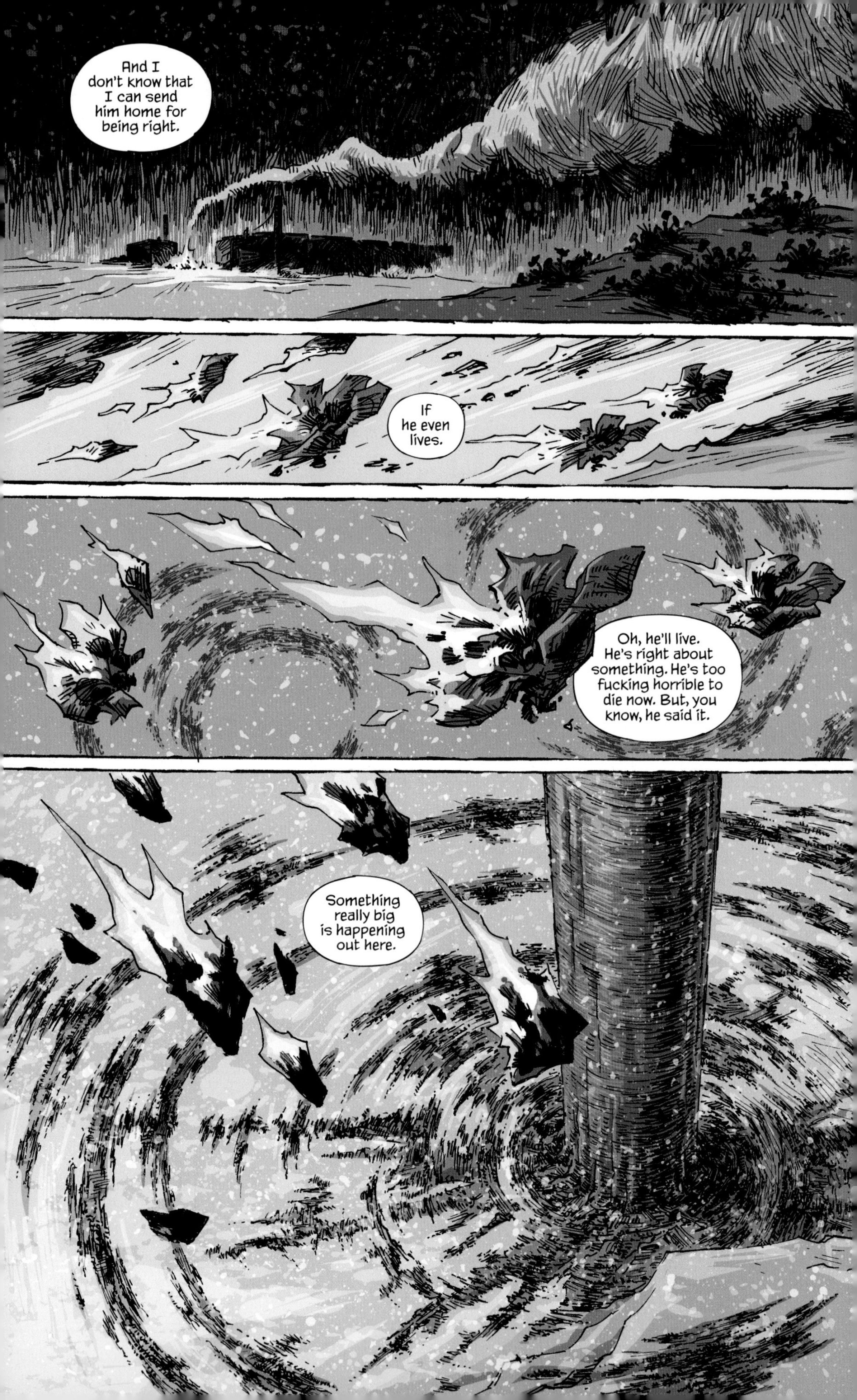
And I don't know that I can send him home for being right.
If he even lives.
Oh, he'll live. He's right about something. He's too fucking horrible to die now. But, you know, he said it.
Something really big is happening out here.

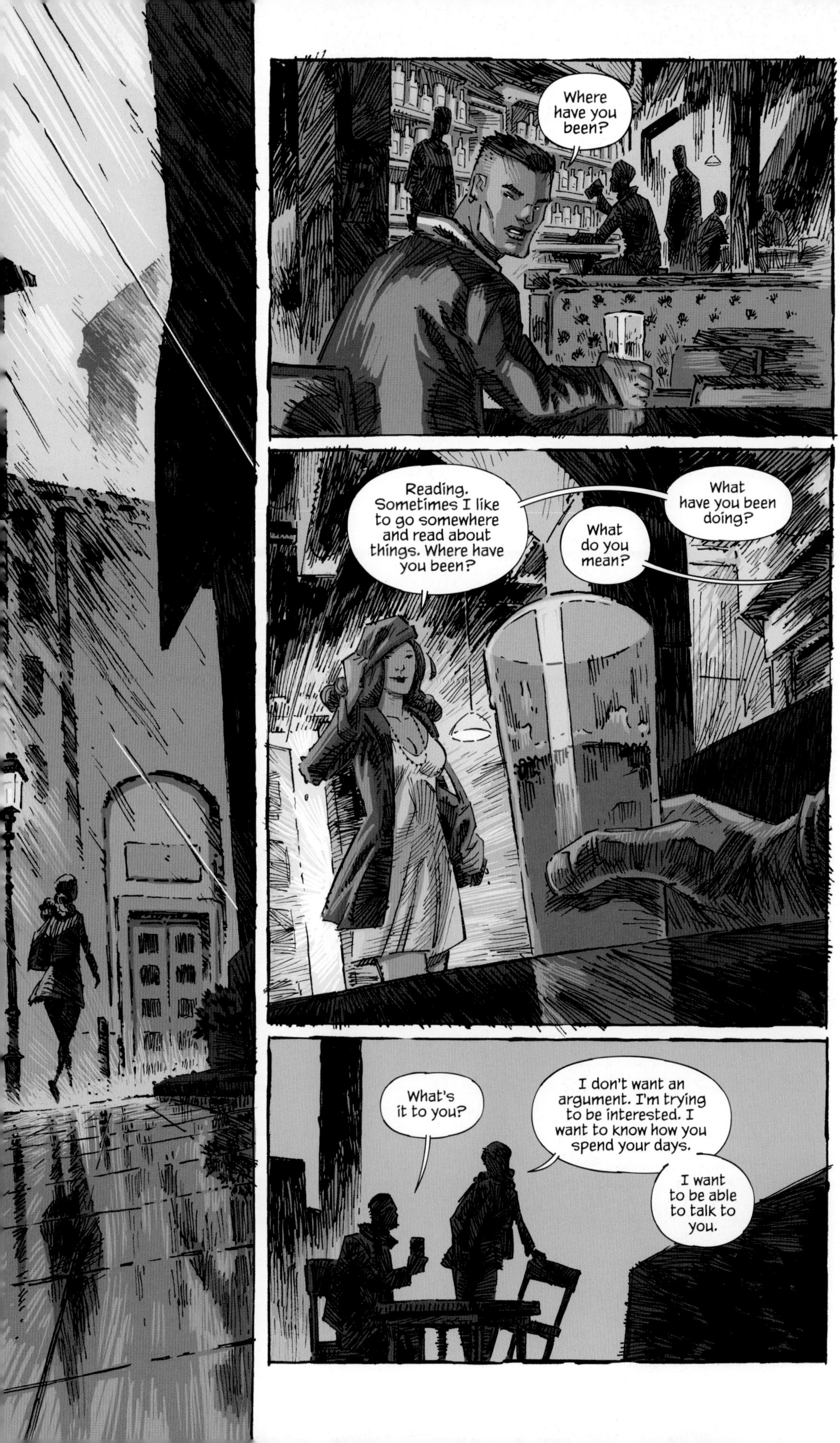
Where have you been?
Reading. Sometimes I like to go somewhere and read about things. Where have you been?
What have you been doing?
What do you mean?
What's it to you?
I don't want an argument. I'm trying to be interested. I want to know how you spend your days.
I want to be able to talk to you.

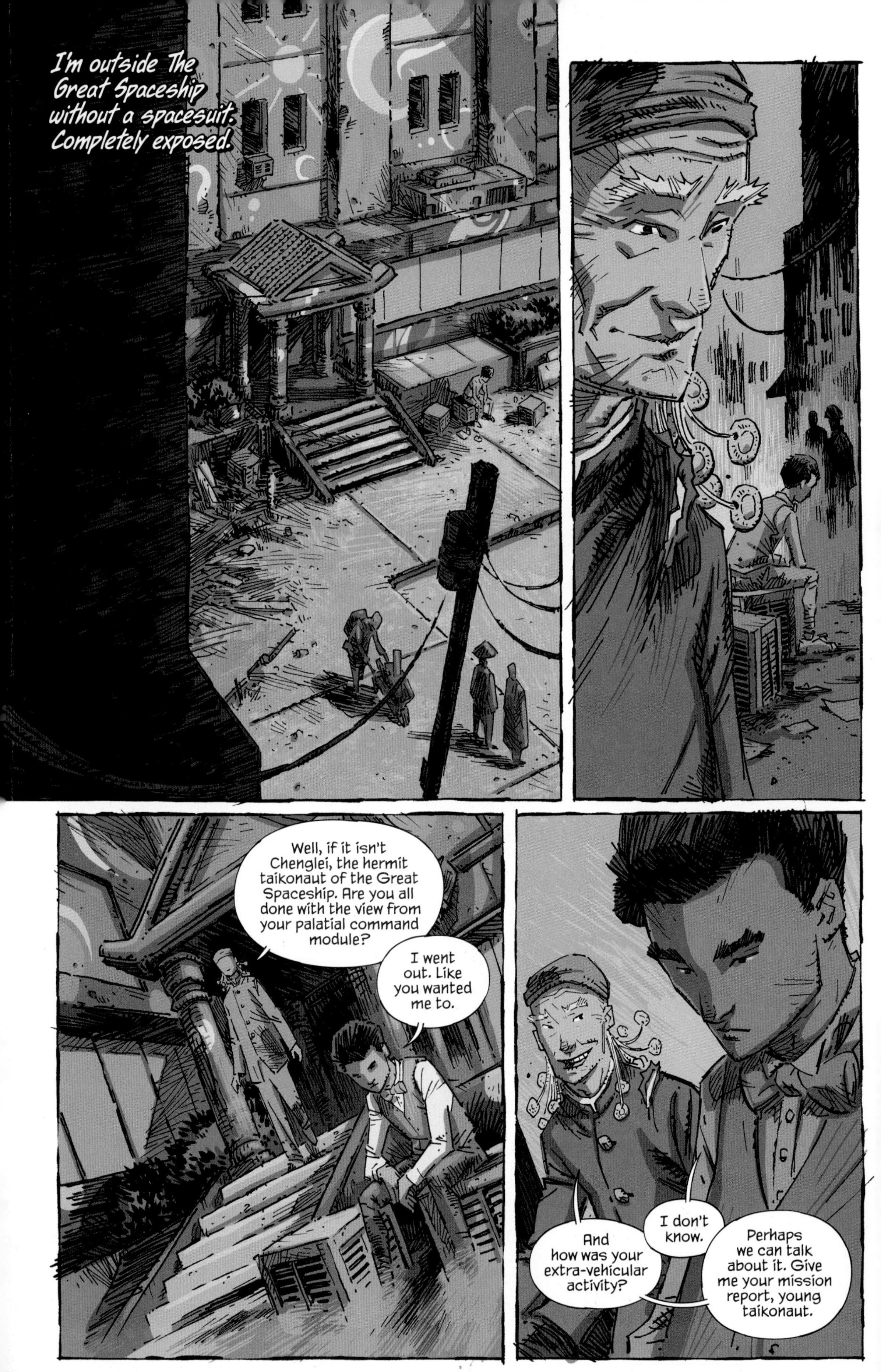
I'm outside The Great Spaceship without a spacesuit. Completely exposed.
Well, if it isn't Chenglei, the hermit taikonaut of the Great Spaceship. Are you all done with the view from your palatial command module?
I went out. Like you wanted me to.
And how was your extra-vehicular activity?
I don't know.
Perhaps we can talk about it. Give me your mission report, young taikonaut.

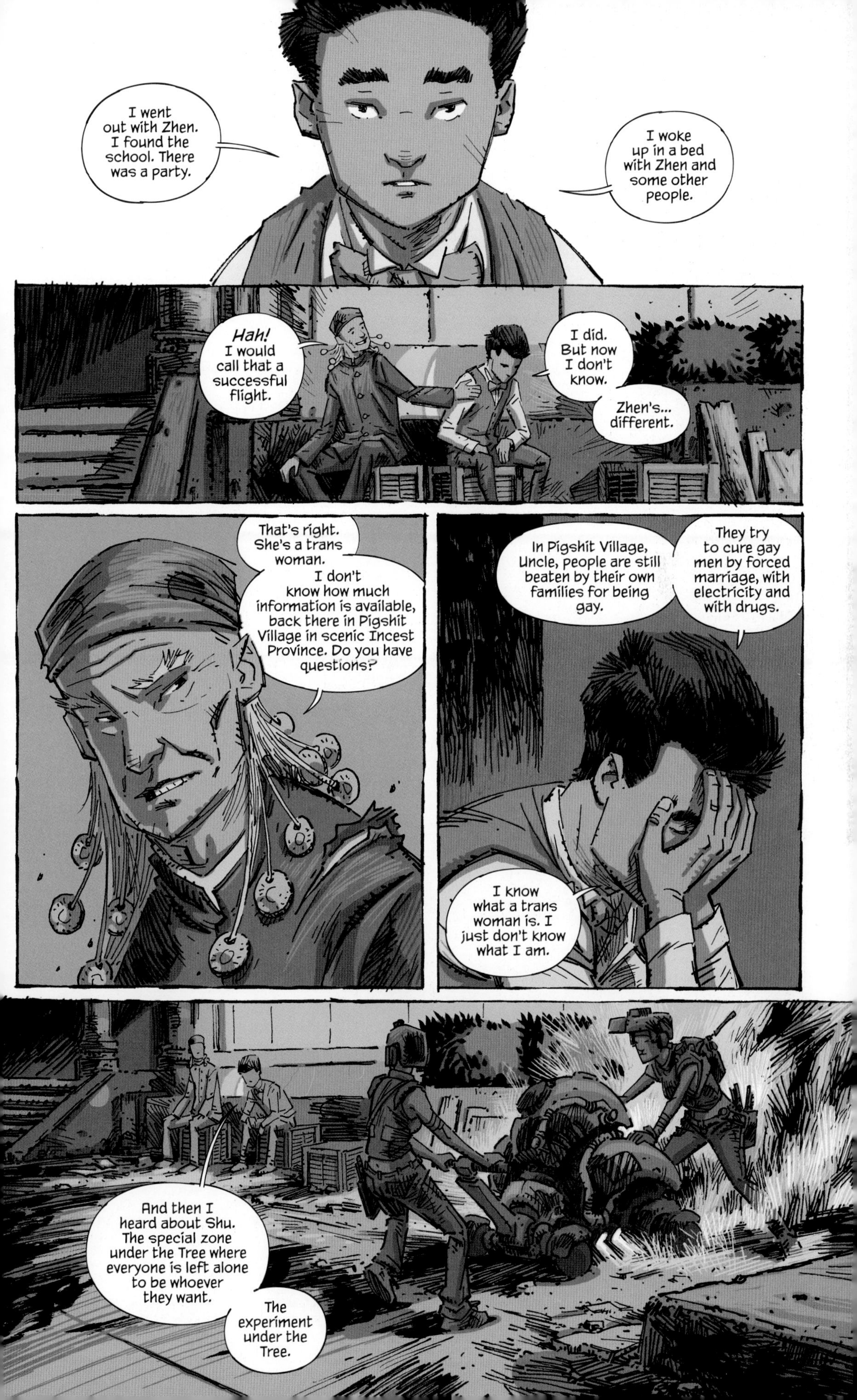
I went out with Zhen. I found the school. There was a party.
I woke up in a bed with Zhen and some other people.
Hah! I would call that a successful flight.
I did. But now I don't know.
Zhen's... different.
That's right. She's a trans woman.
I don't know how much information is available, back there in Pigshit Village in scenic Incest Province. Do you have questions?
In Pigshit Village, Uncle, people are still beaten by their own families for being gay.
They try to cure gay men by forced marriage, with electricity and with drugs.
I know what a trans woman is. I just don't know what I am.
And then I heard about Shu. The special zone under the Tree where everyone is left alone to be whoever they want.
The experiment under the Tree.

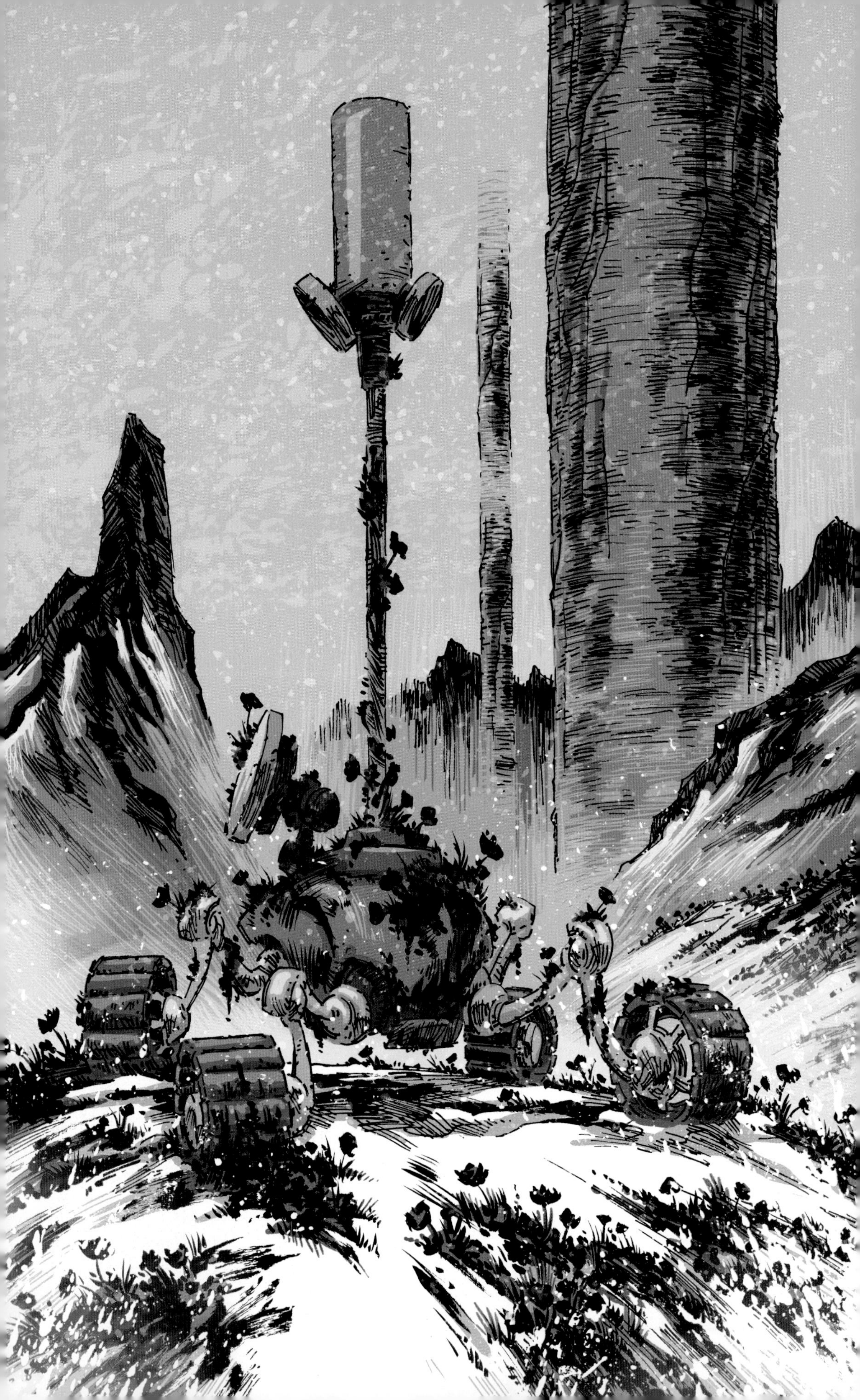

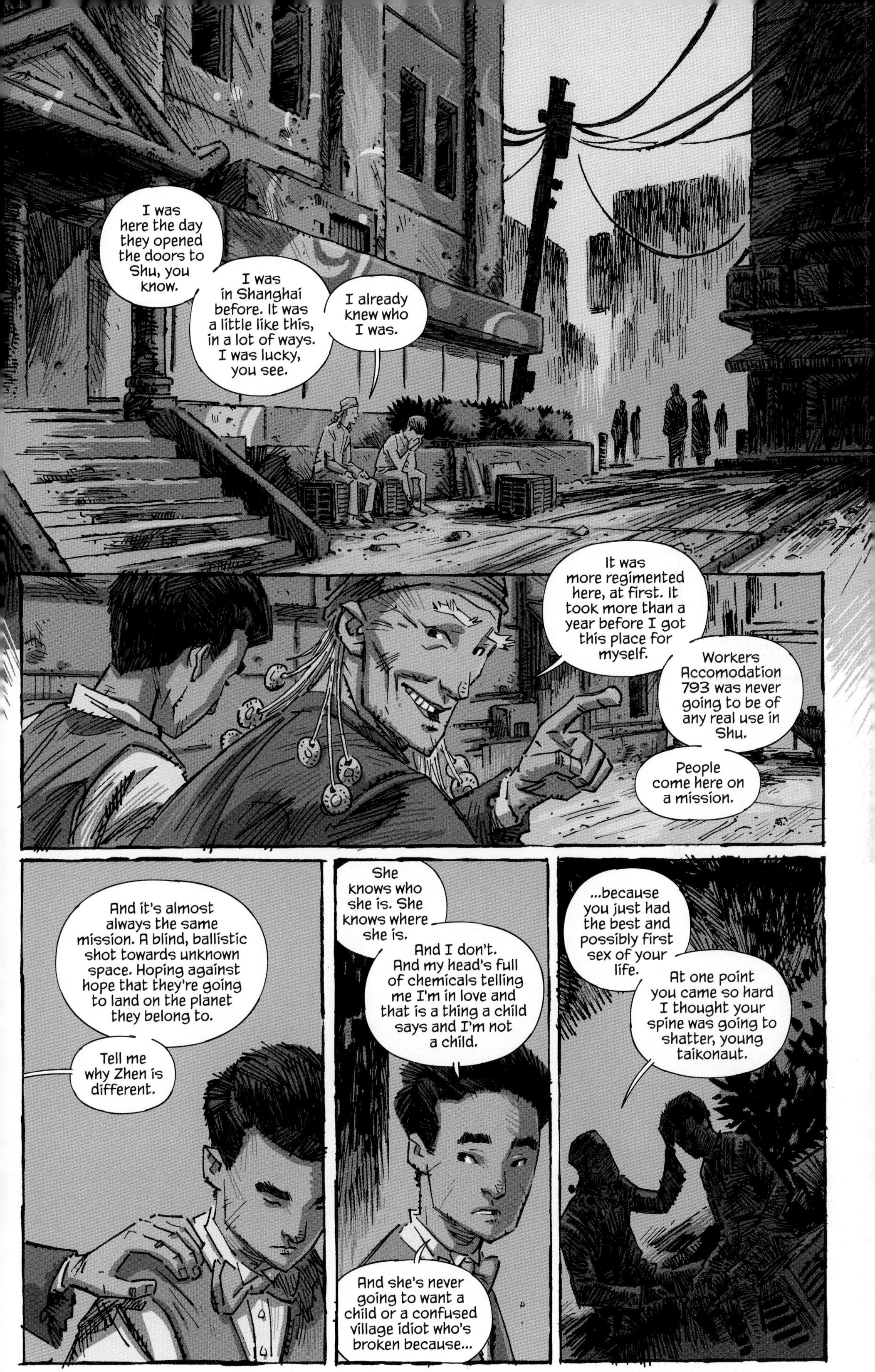
I was here the day they opened the doors to Shu, you know.
I was in Shanghai before. It was a little like this, in a lot of ways. I was lucky, you see.
I already knew who I was.
It was more regimented here, at first. It took more than a year before I got this place for myself.
Workers Accomodation 793 was never going to be of any real use in Shu.
People come here on a mission.
And it's almost always the same mission. A blind, ballistic shot towards unknown space. Hoping against hope that they're going to land on the planet they belong to.
Tell me why Zhen is different.
She knows who she is. She knows where she is.
And I don't. And my head's full of chemicals telling me I'm in love and that is a thing a child says and I'm not a child.
And she's never going to want a child or a confused village idiot who's broken because...
...because you just had the best and possibly first sex of your life.
At one point you came so hard I thought your spine was going to shatter, young taikonaut.

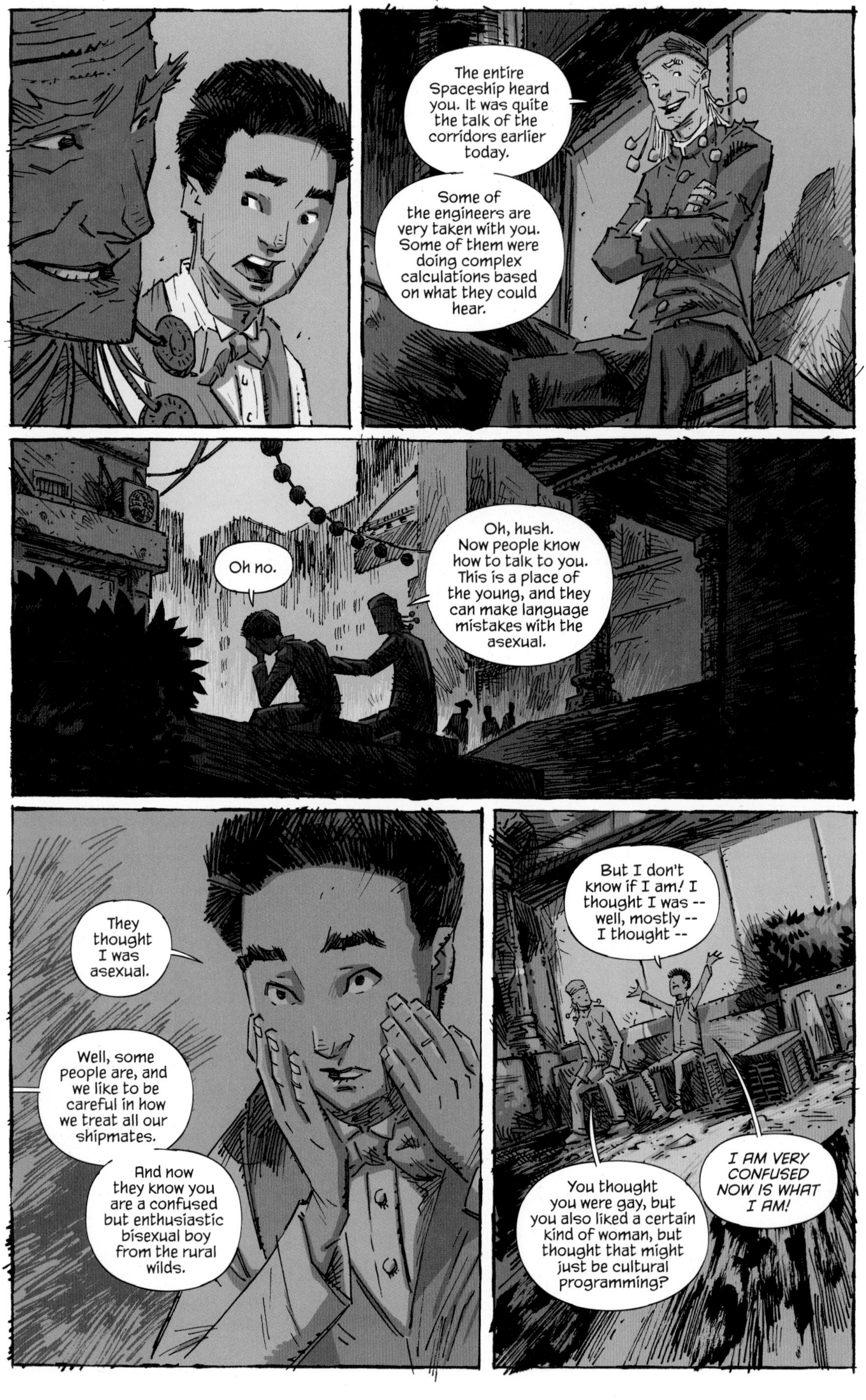
The entire Spaceship heard you. It was quite the talk of the corridors earlier today.
Some of the engineers are very taken with you. Some of them were doing complex calculations based on what they could hear.
Oh no.
Oh, hush. Now people know how to talk to you. This is a place of the young, and they can make language mistakes with the asexual.
They thought I was asexual.
Well, some people are, and we like to be careful in how we treat all our shipmates.
And now they know you are a confused but enthusiastic bisexual boy from the rural wilds.
But I don't know if I am! I thought I was -- well, mostly -- I thought --
You thought you were gay, but you also liked a certain kind of woman, but thought that might just be cultural programming?
I AM VERY CONFUSED NOW IS WHAT I AM!

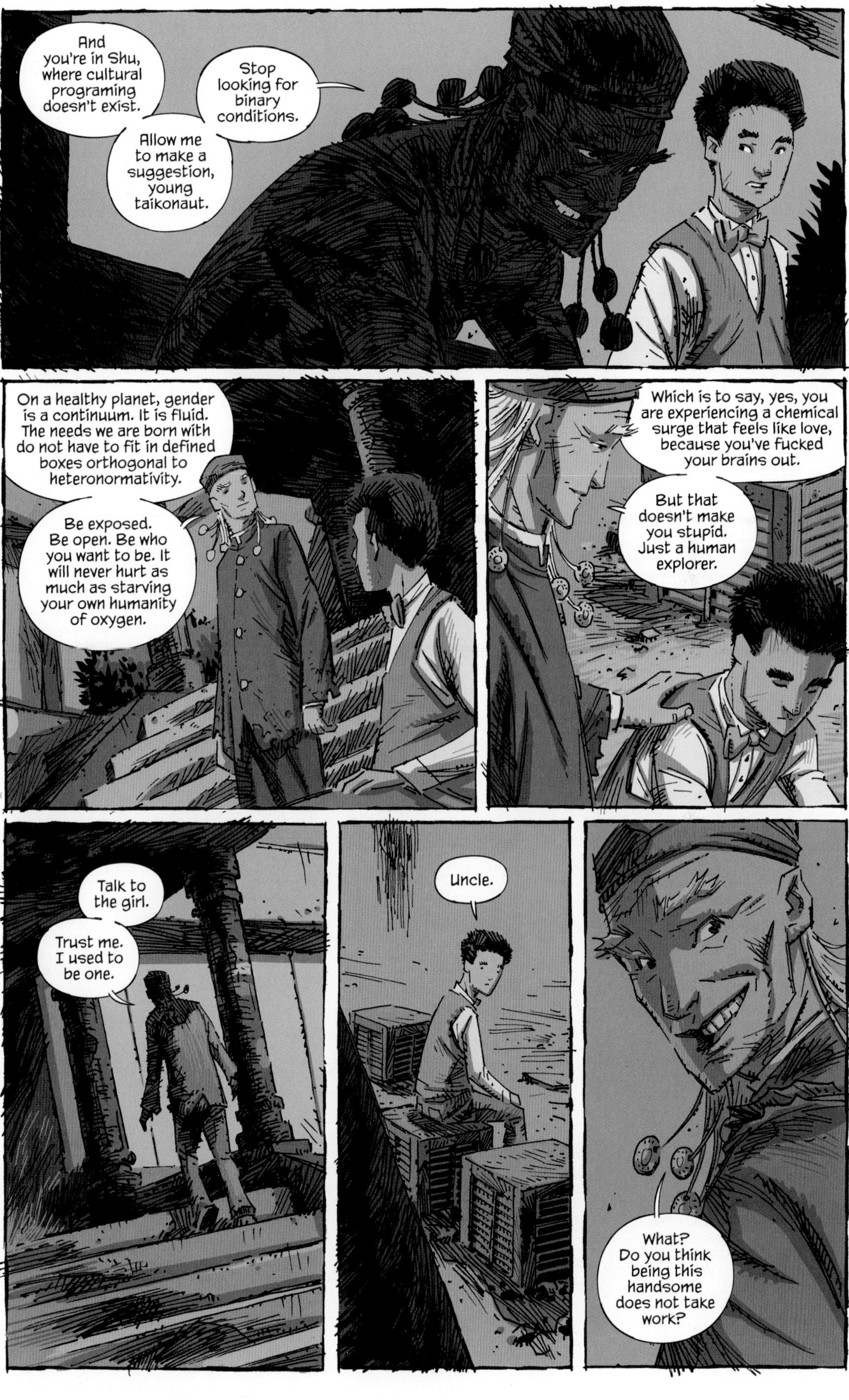
And you're in Shu, where cultural programing doesn't exist.
Allow me to make a suggestion, young taikonaut.
Stop looking for binary conditions.
On a healthy planet, gender is a continuum. It is fluid. The needs we are born with do not have to fit in defined boxes orthogonal to heteronormativity.
Be exposed. Be open. Be who you want to be. It will never hurt as much as starving your own humanity of oxygen.
Which is to say, yes, you are experiencing a chemical surge that feels like love, because you've fucked your brains out.
But that doesn't make you stupid. Just a human explorer.
Talk to the girl.
Trust me. I used to be one.
Uncle.
What? Do you think being this handsome does not take work?

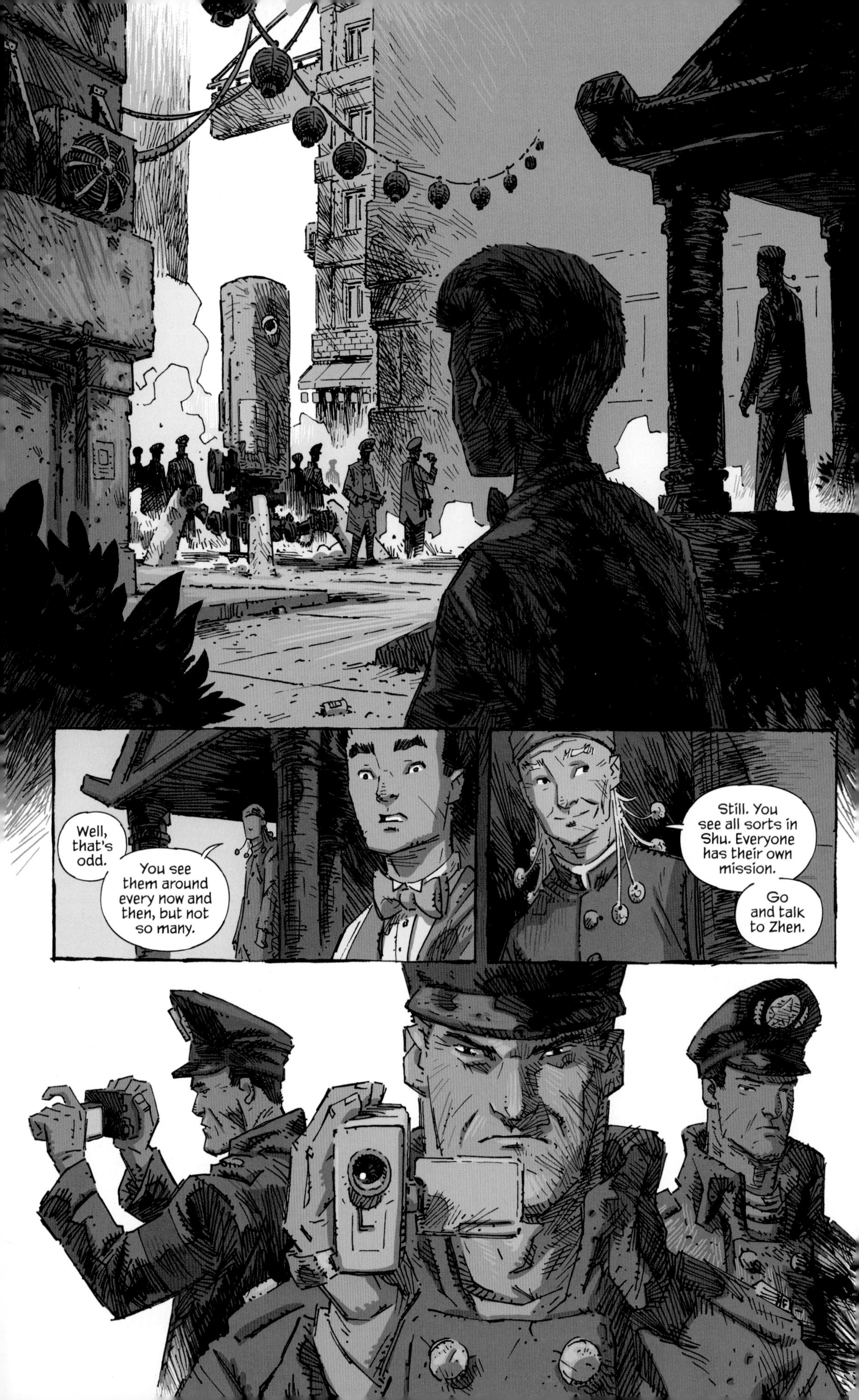
Well, that's odd.
You see them around every now and then, but not so many.
Still. You see all sorts in Shu. Everyone has their own mission.
Go and talk to Zhen.

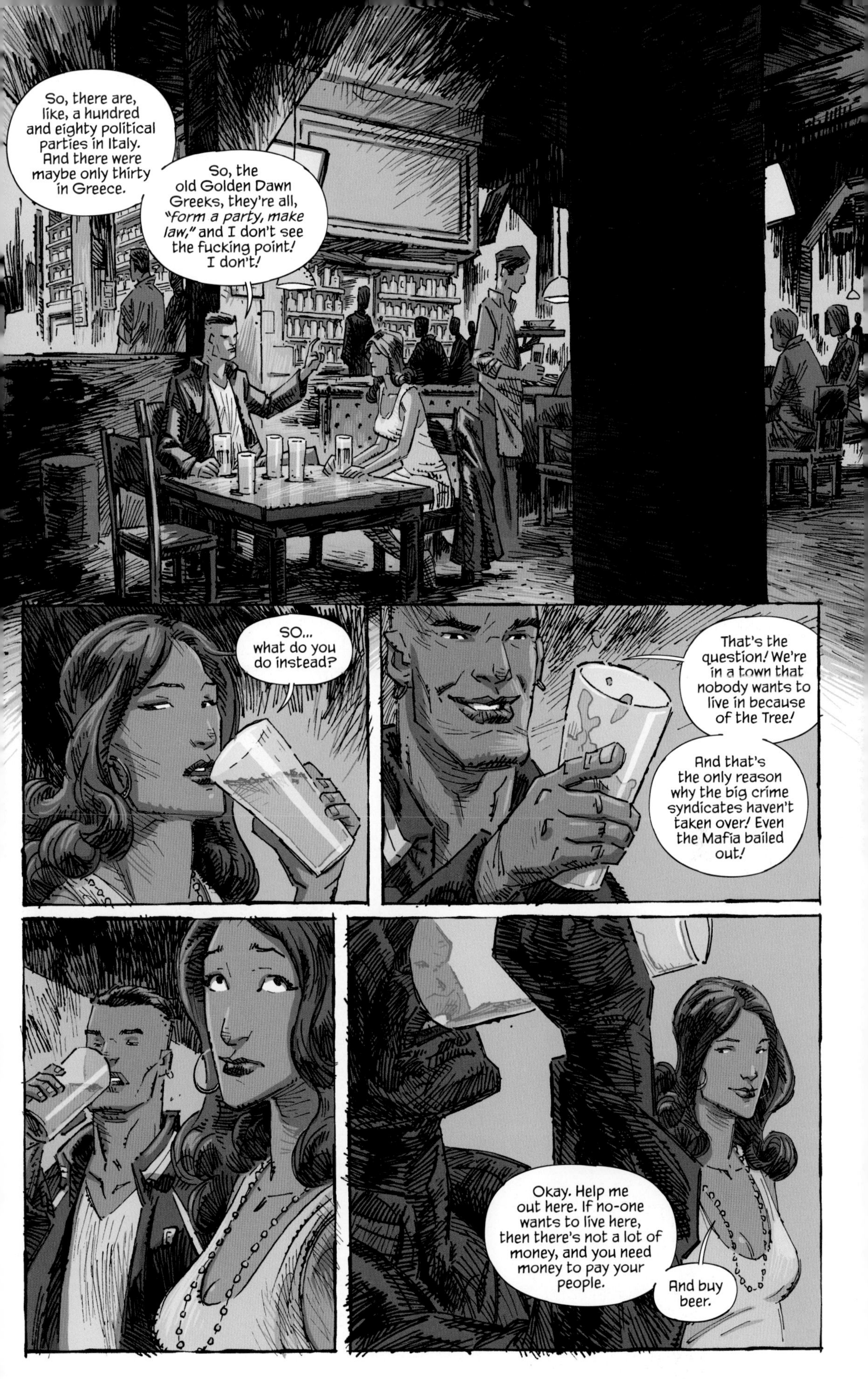
So, there are, like, a hundred and eighty political parties in Italy. And there were maybe only thirty in Greece.
So, the old Golden Dawn Greeks, they're all, *"form a party, make law,"* and I don't see the fucking point! I don't!
SO... what do you do instead?
That's the question! We're in a town that nobody wants to live in because of the Tree!
And that's the only reason why the big crime syndicates haven't taken over! Even the Mafia bailed out!
Okay. Help me out here. If no-one wants to live here, then there's not a lot of money, and you need money to pay your people.
And buy beer.

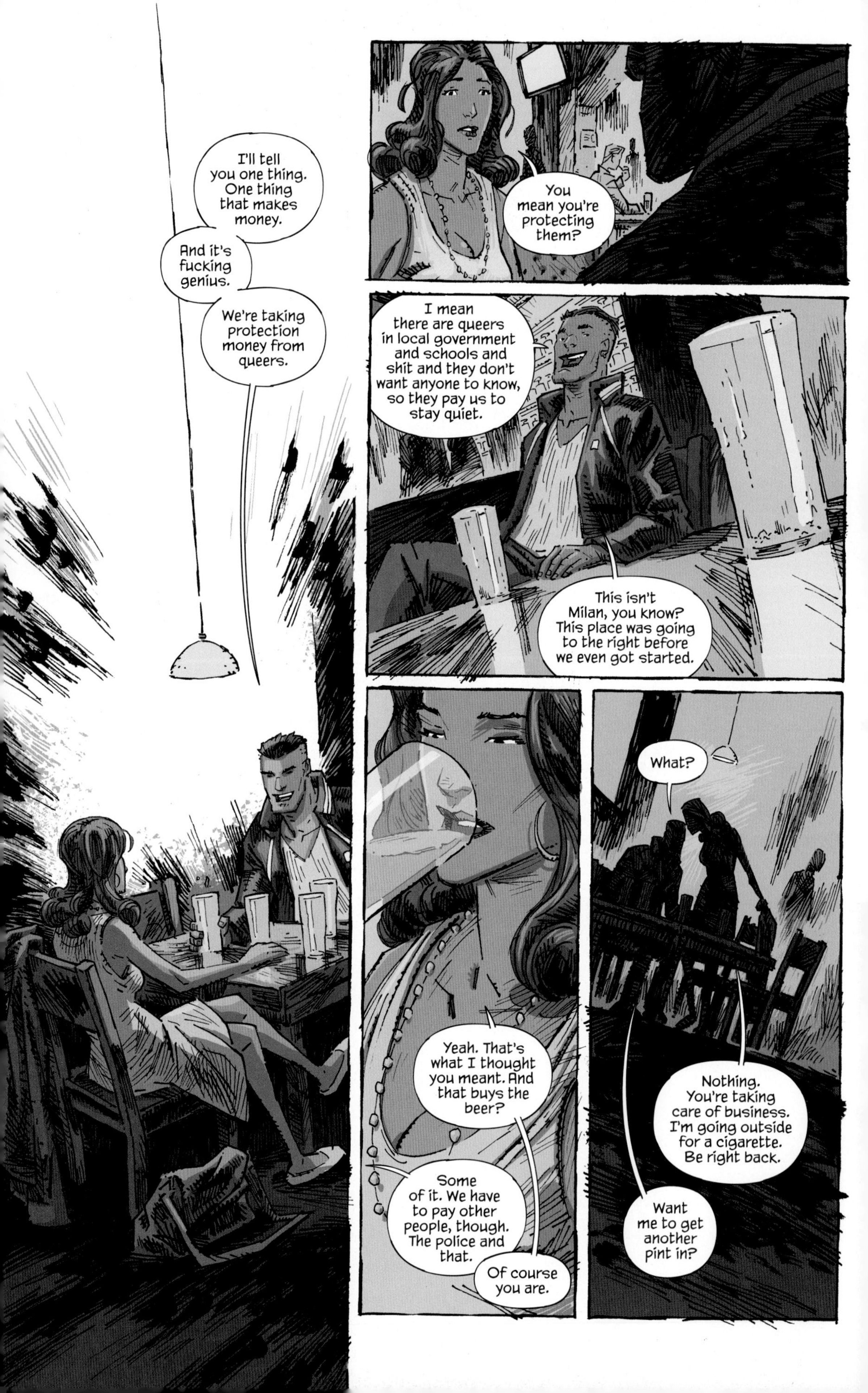
I'll tell you one thing. One thing that makes money.
And it's fucking genius.
We're taking protection money from queers.
You mean you're protecting them?
I mean there are queers in local government and schools and shit and they don't want anyone to know, so they pay us to stay quiet.
This isn't Milan, you know? This place was going to the right before we even got started.
Yeah. That's what I thought you meant. And that buys the beer?
Some of it. We have to pay other people, though. The police and that.
Of course you are.
What?
Nothing. You're taking care of business. I'm going outside for a cigarette. Be right back.
Want me to get another pint in?

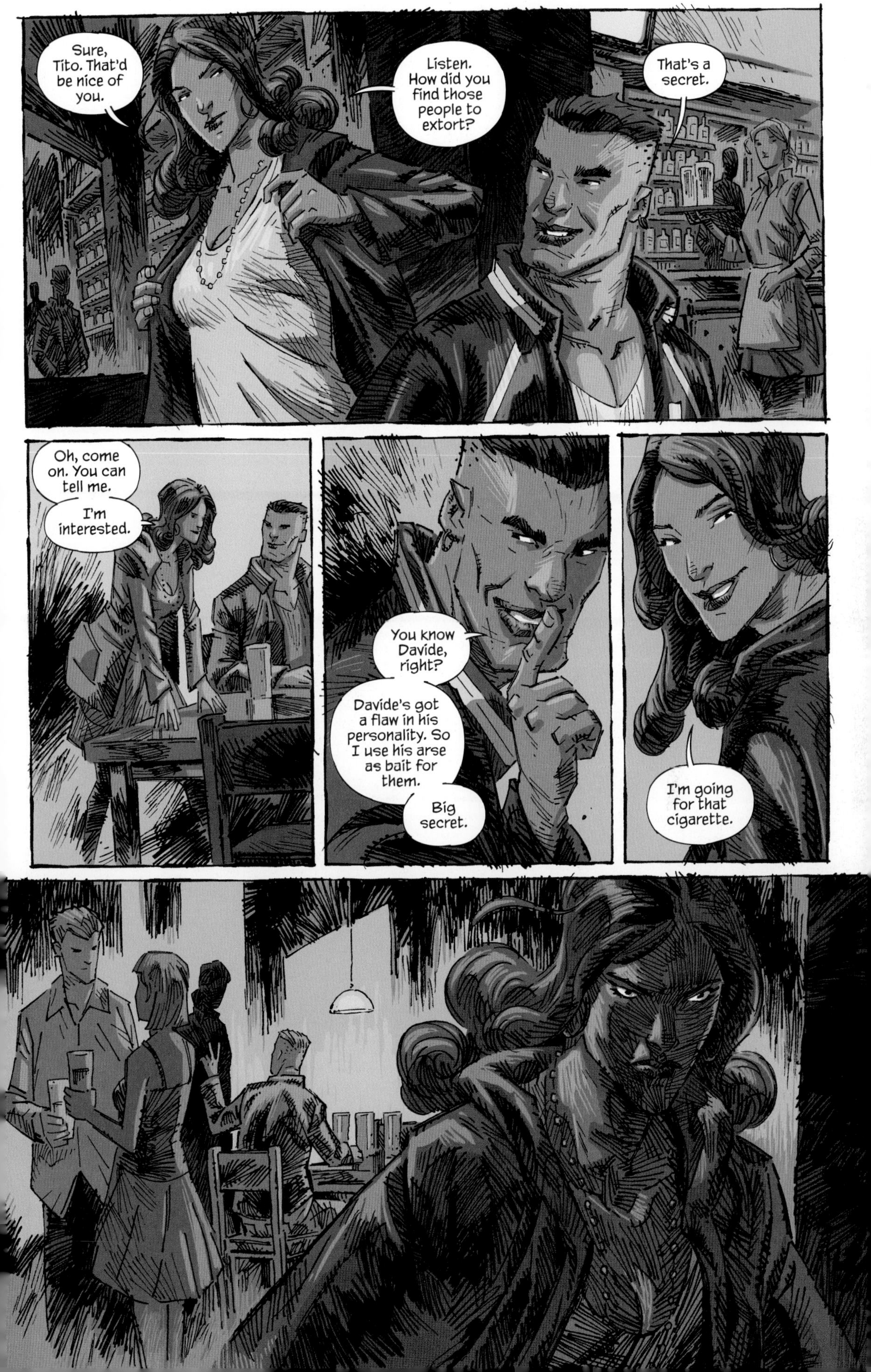

Sure, Tito. That'd be nice of you.
Listen. How did you find those people to extort?
That's a secret.
Oh, come on. You can tell me.
I'm interested.
You know Davide, right?
Davide's got a flaw in his personality. So I use his arse as bait for them.
Big secret.
I'm going for that cigarette.

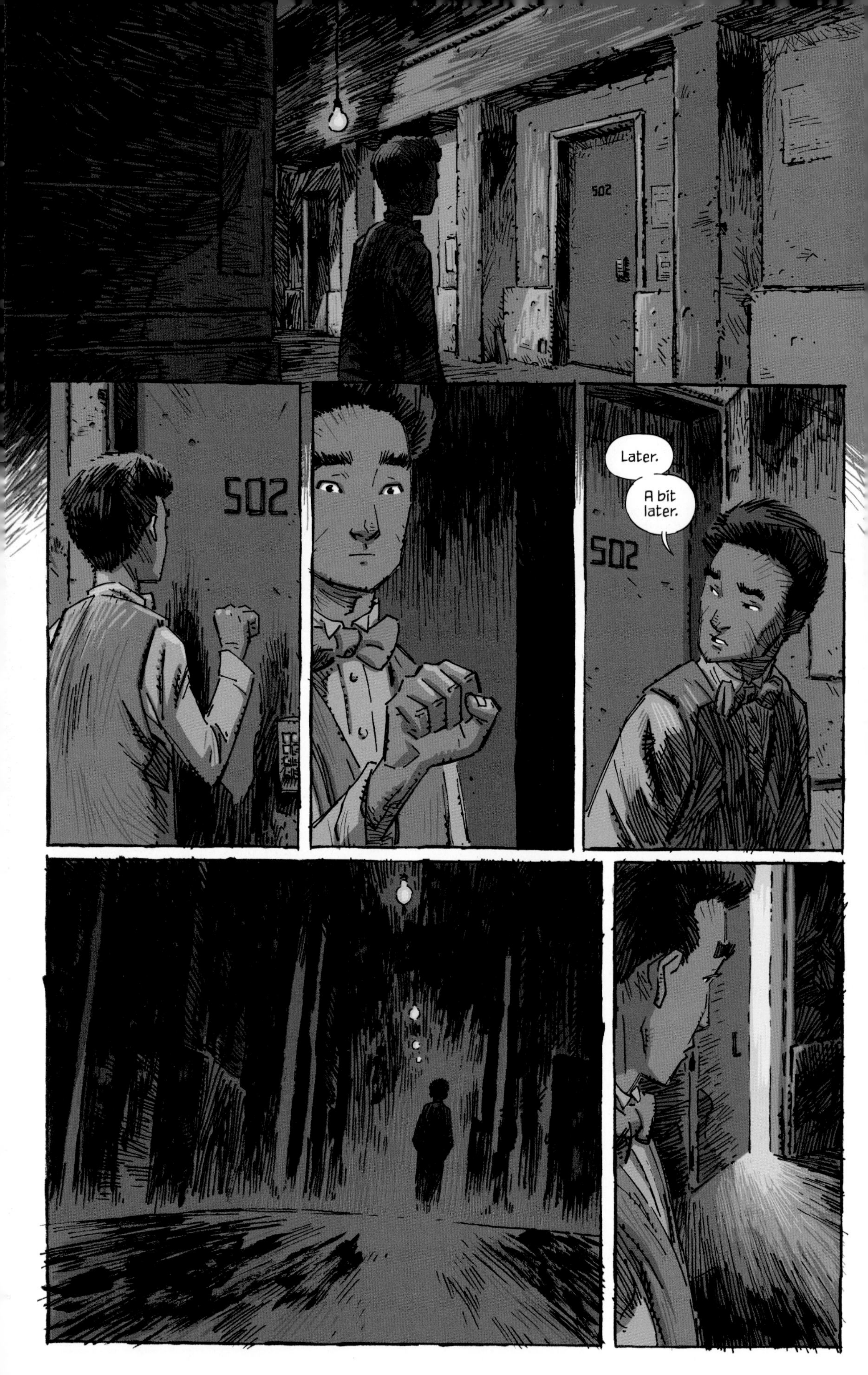

502
502
Later.
A bit later.

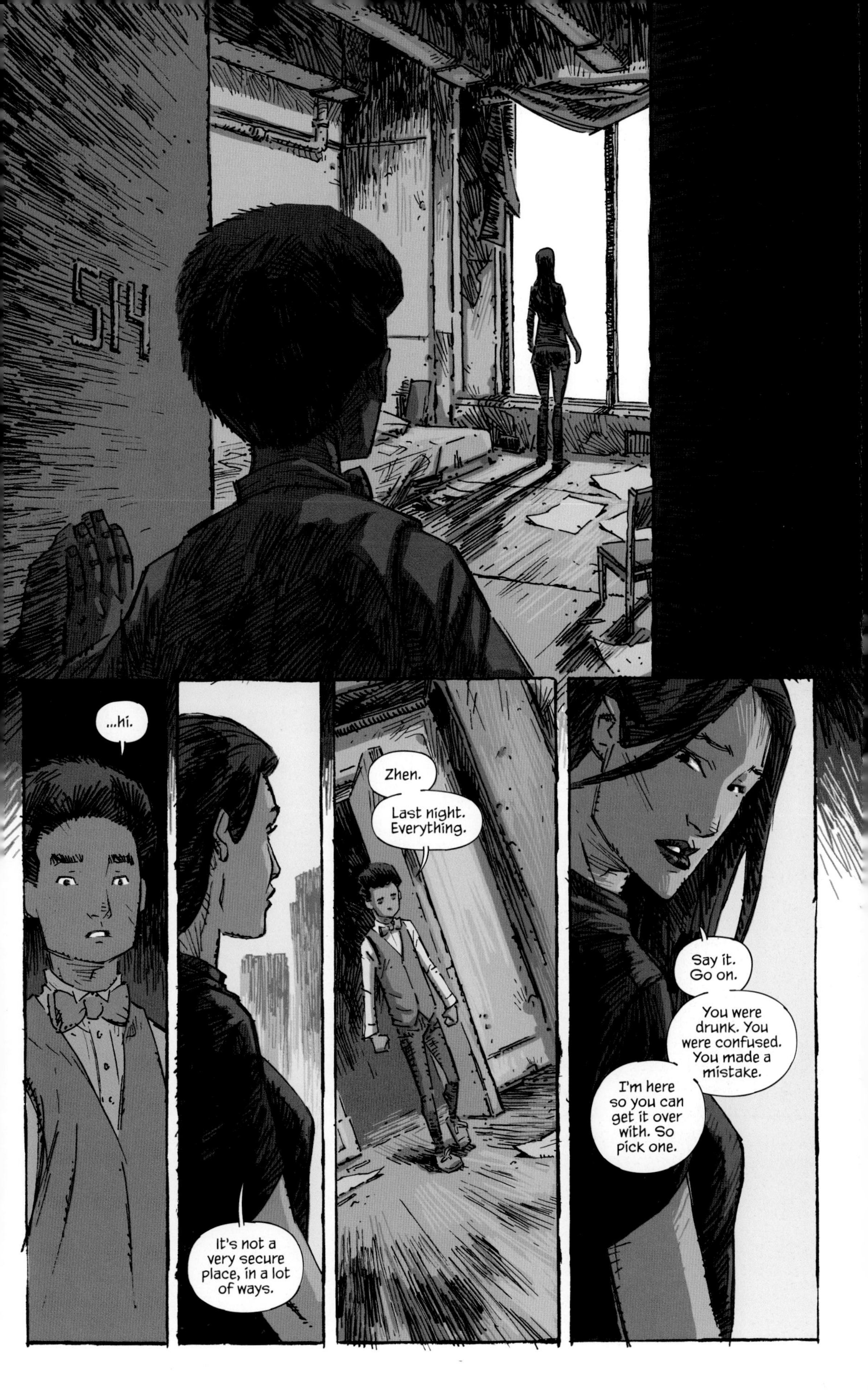
514
...hi.
It's not a very secure place, in a lot of ways.
Zhen.
Last night. Everything.
Say it. Go on.
You were drunk. You were confused. You made a mistake.
I'm here so you can get it over with. So pick one.

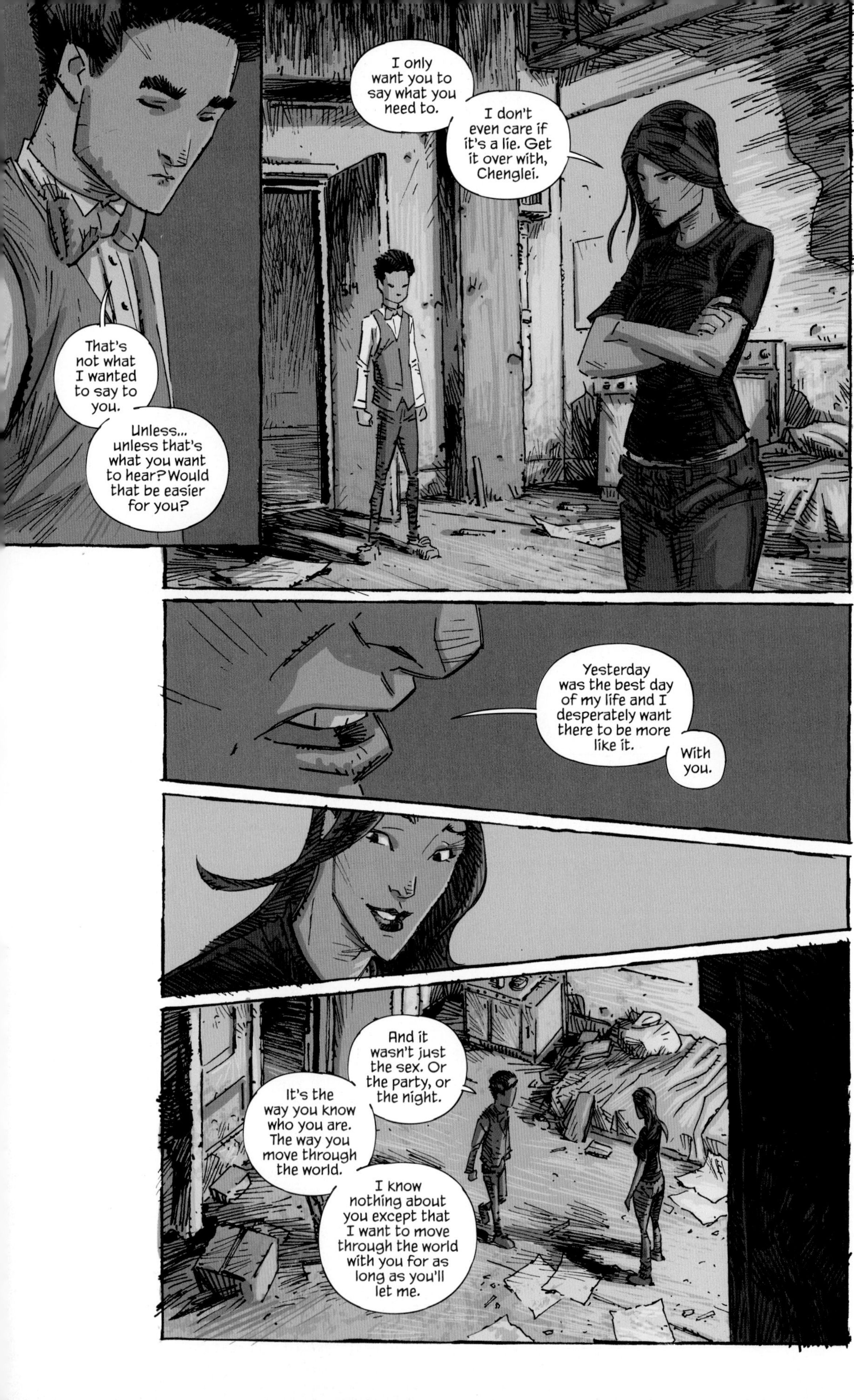
I only want you to say what you need to.
I don't even care if it's a lie. Get it over with, Chenglei.
That's not what I wanted to say to you.
Unless... unless that's what you want to hear? Would that be easier for you?
Yesterday was the best day of my life and I desperately want there to be more like it.
With you.
And it wasn't just the sex. Or the party, or the night.
It's the way you know who you are. The way you move through the world.
I know nothing about you except that I want to move through the world with you for as long as you'll let me.

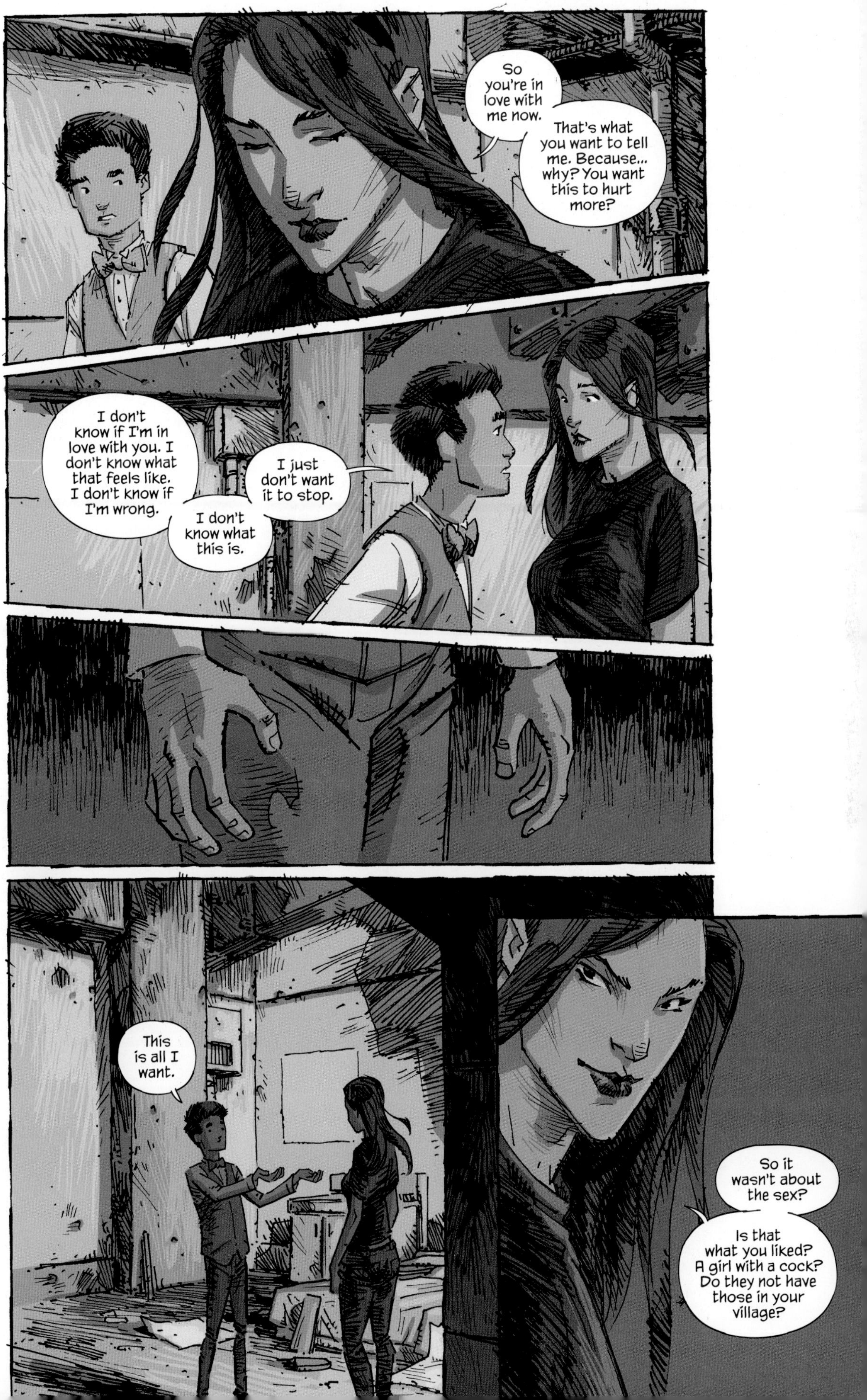
So you're in love with me now.
That's what you want to tell me. Because... why? You want this to hurt more?
I don't know if I'm in love with you. I don't know what that feels like. I don't know if I'm wrong.
I don't know what this is.
I just don't want it to stop.
This is all I want.
So it wasn't about the sex?
Is that what you liked? A girl with a cock? Do they not have those in your village?

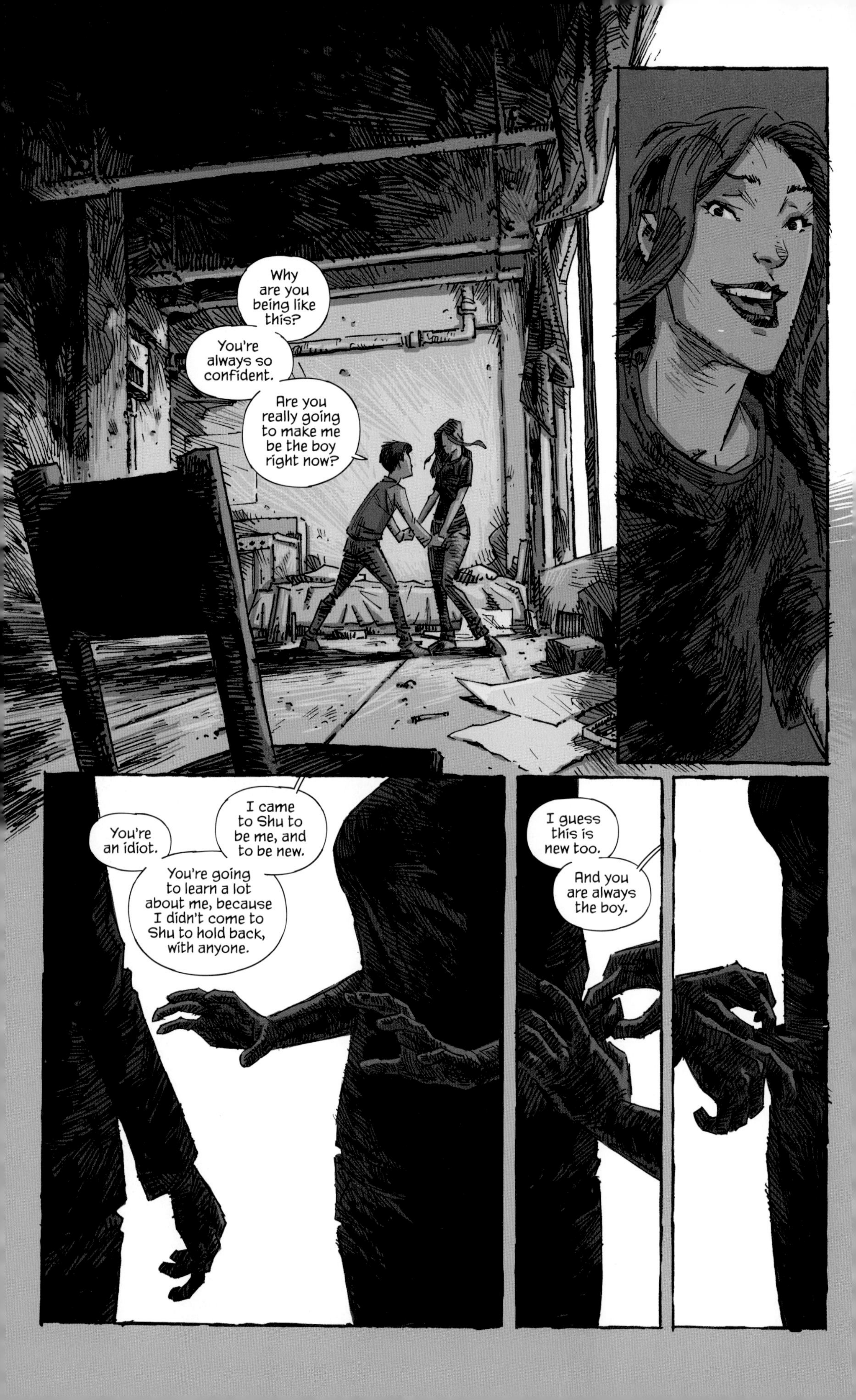
Why are you being like this?
You're always so confident.
Are you really going to make me be the boy right now?
You're an idiot.
I came to Shu to be me, and to be new.
You're going to learn a lot about me, because I didn't come to Shu to hold back, with anyone.
I guess this is new too.
And you are always the boy.

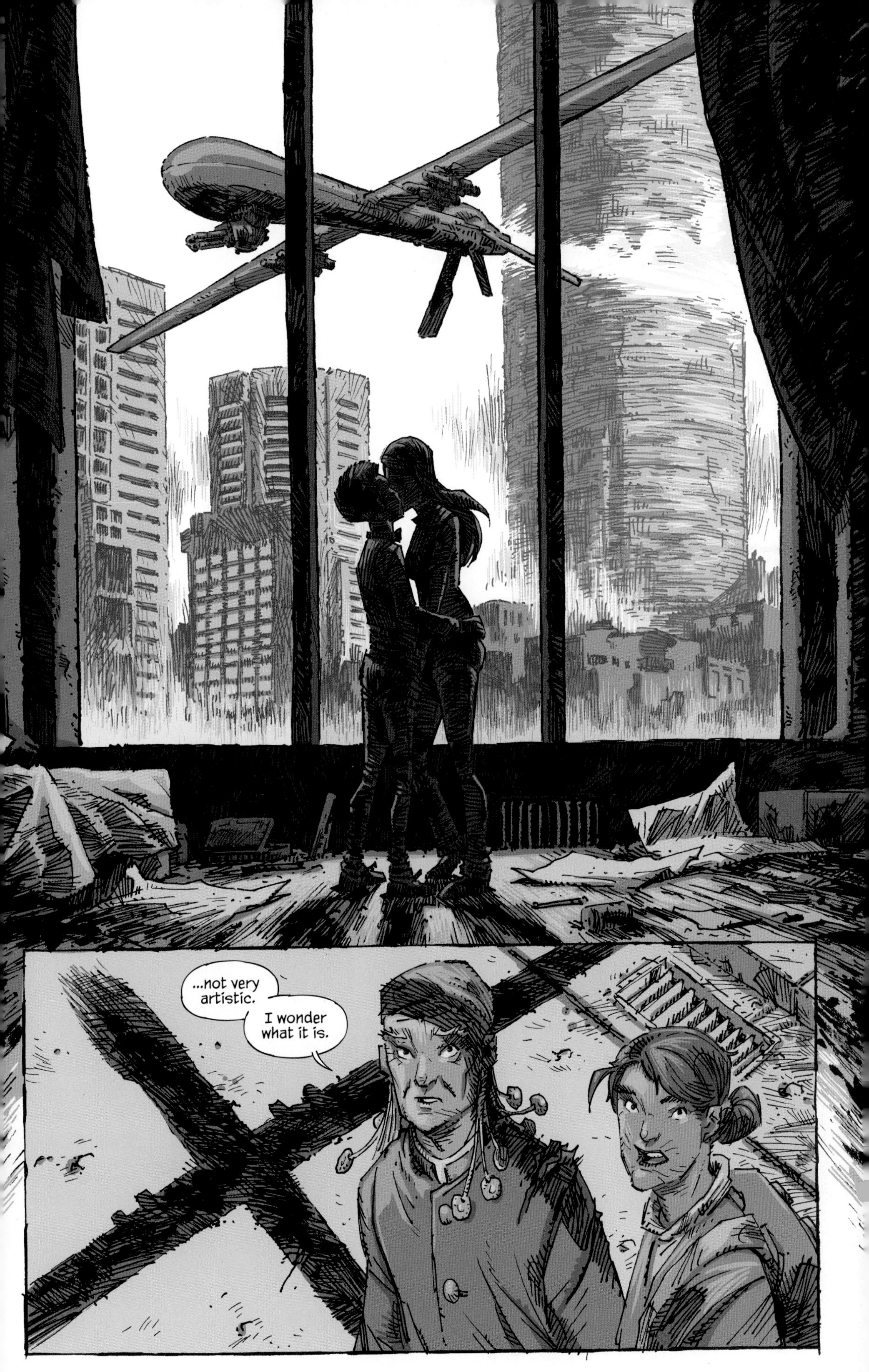
...not very artistic.
I wonder what it is.

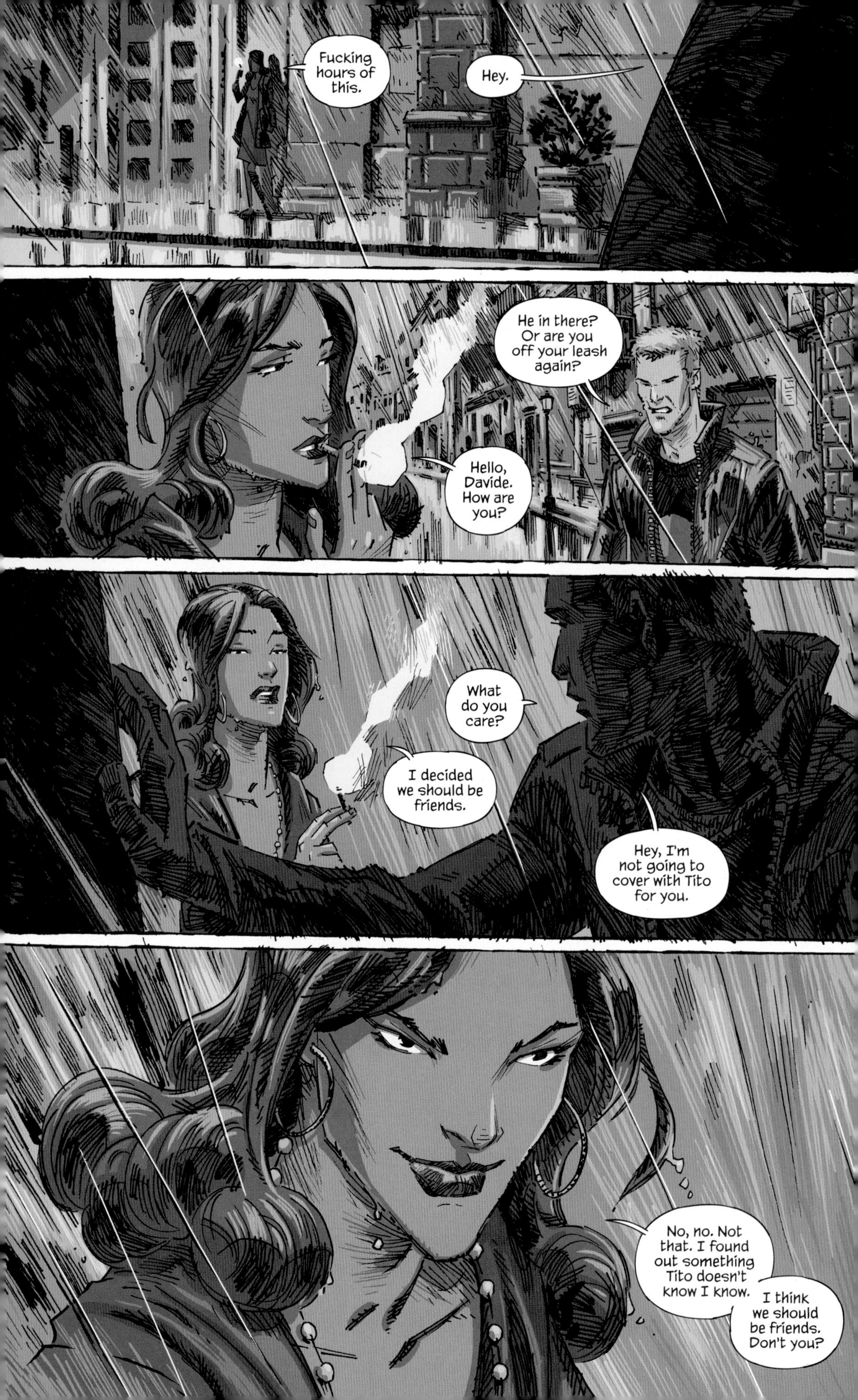
Fucking hours of this.
Hey.
He in there? Or are you off your leash again?
Hello, Davide. How are you?
What do you care?
I decided we should be friends.
Hey, I'm not going to cover with Tito for you.
No, no. Not that. I found out something Tito doesn't know I know.
I think we should be friends. Don't you?

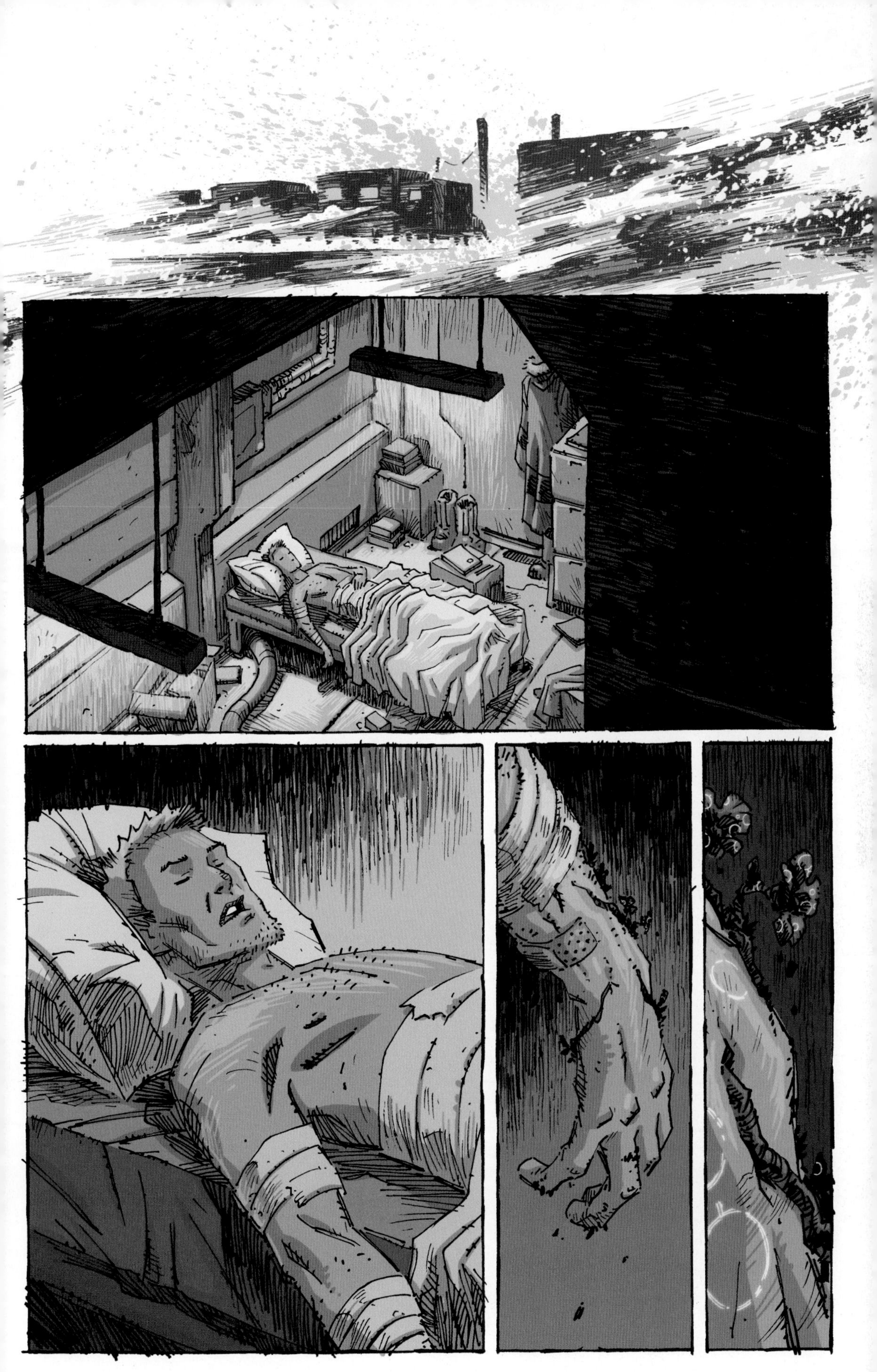

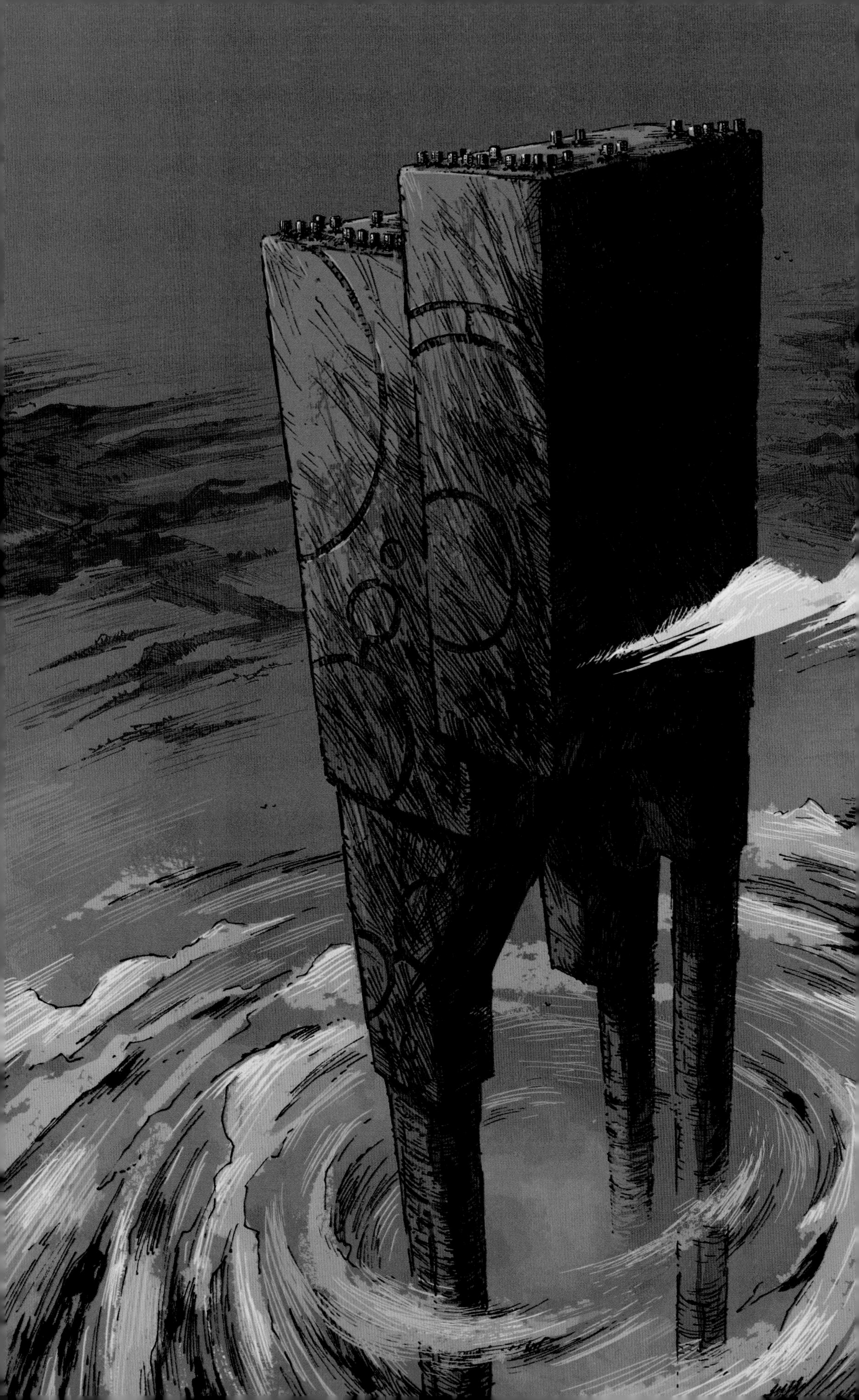

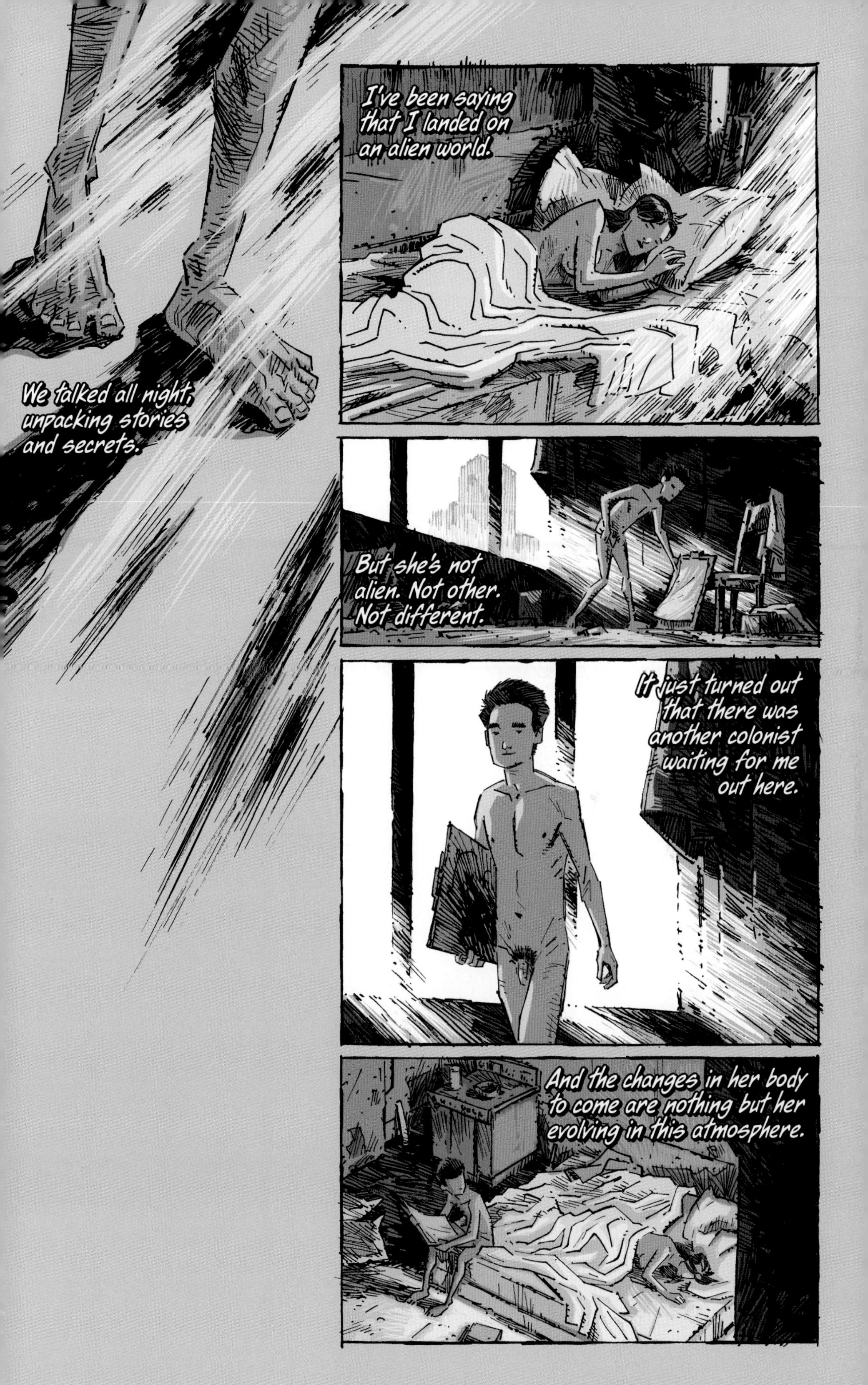
We talked all night, unpacking stories and secrets.
I've been saying that I landed on an alien world.
But she's not alien. Not other. Not different.
It just turned out that there was another colonist waiting for me out here.
And the changes in her body to come are nothing but her evolving in this atmosphere.

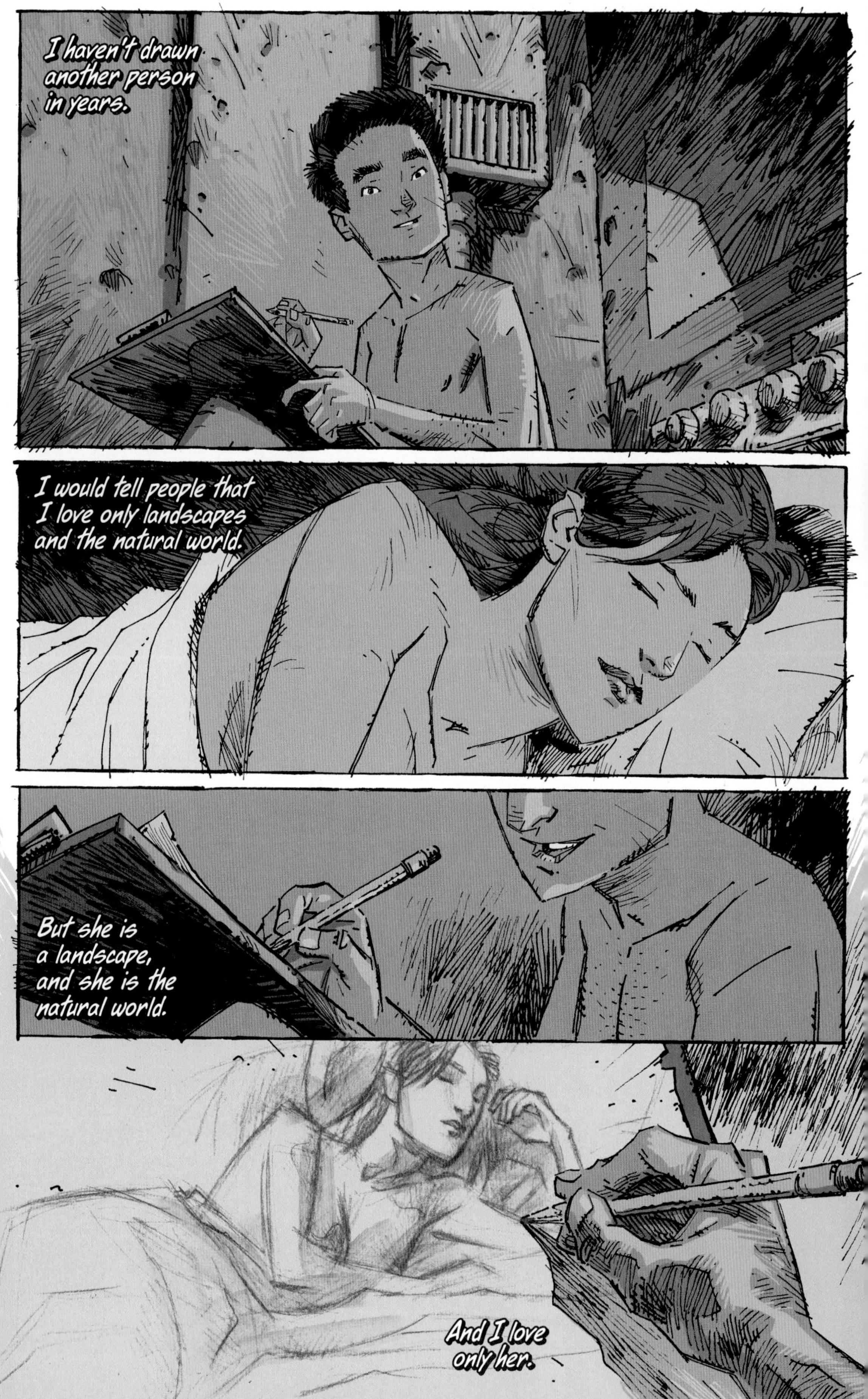
I haven't drawn another person in years.
I would tell people that I love only landscapes and the natural world.
But she is a landscape, and she is the natural world.
And I love only her.

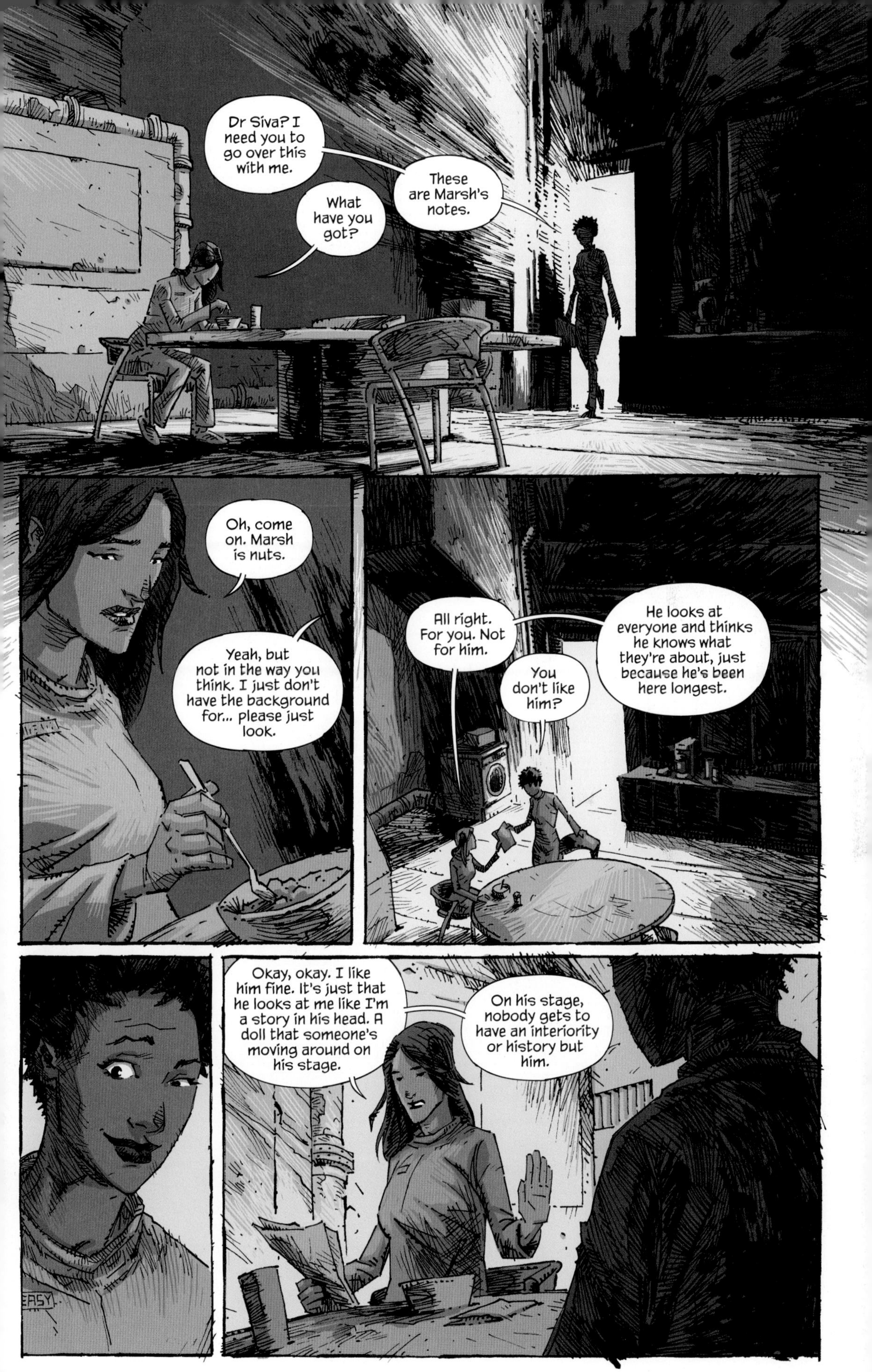
Dr Siva? I need you to go over this with me.
These are Marsh's notes.
What have you got?
Oh, come on. Marsh is nuts.
Yeah, but not in the way you think. I just don't have the background for... please just look.
All right. For you. Not for him.
You don't like him?
He looks at everyone and thinks he knows what they're about, just because he's been here longest.
Okay, okay. I like him fine. It's just that he looks at me like I'm a story in his head. A doll that someone's moving around on his stage.
On his stage, nobody gets to have an interiority or history but him.
EASY

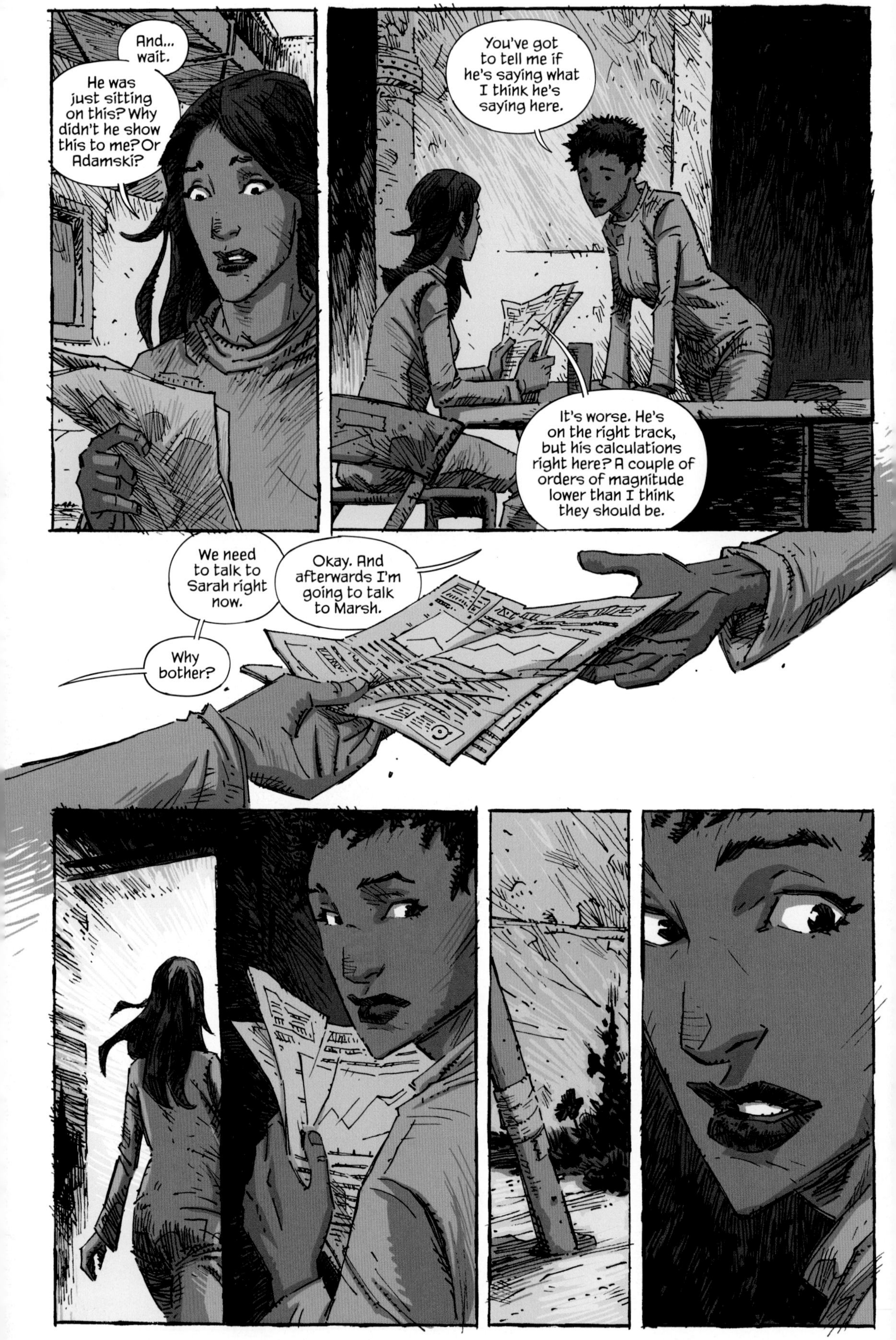
And... wait.
He was just sitting on this? Why didn't he show this to me? Or Adamski?
You've got to tell me if he's saying what I think he's saying here.
It's worse. He's on the right track, but his calculations right here? A couple of orders of magnitude lower than I think they should be.
We need to talk to Sarah right now.
Okay. And afterwards I'm going to talk to Marsh.
Why bother?

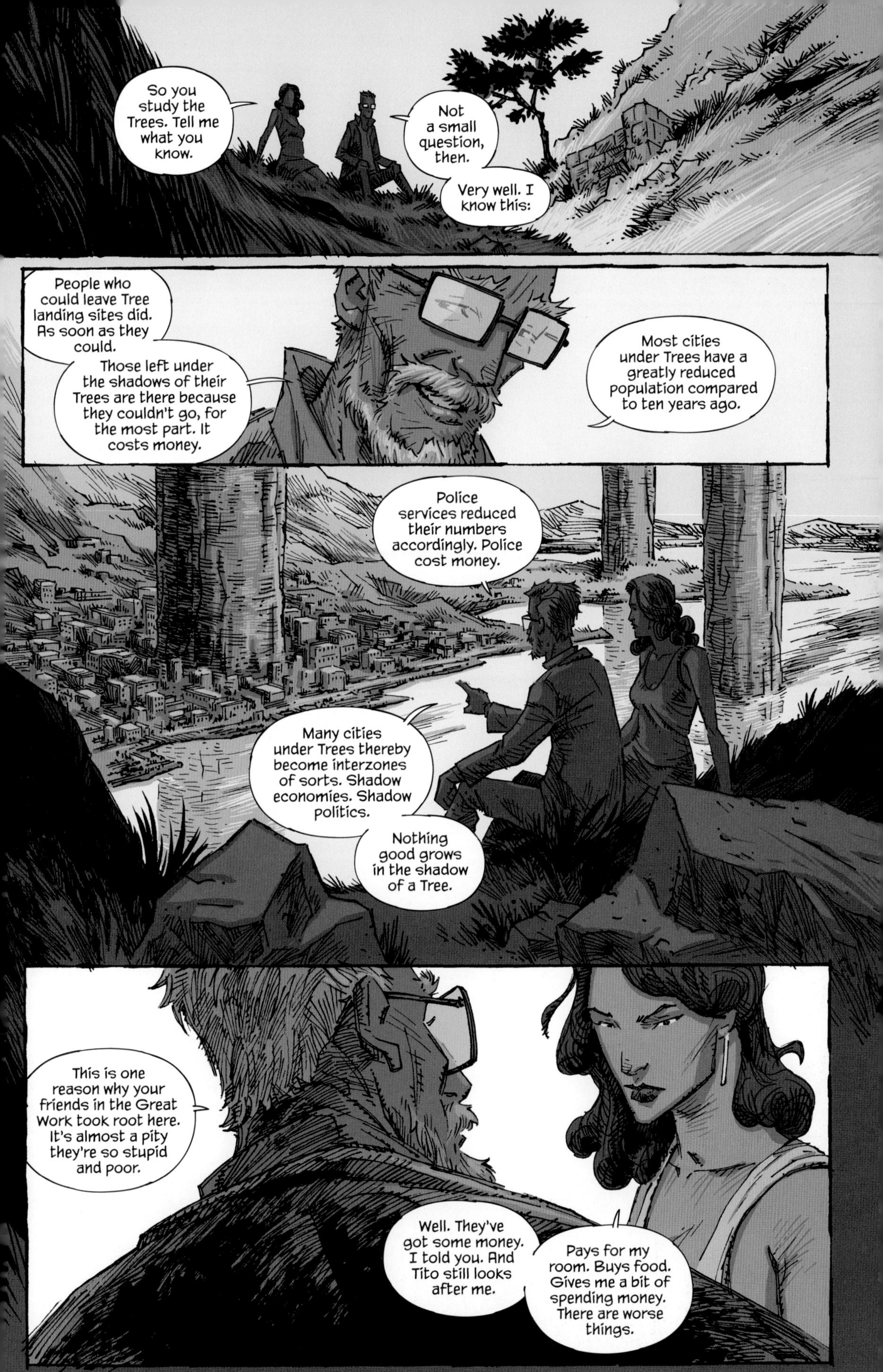

So you study the Trees. Tell me what you know.
Not a small question, then.
Very well. I know this:
People who could leave Tree landing sites did. As soon as they could.
Those left under the shadows of their Trees are there because they couldn't go, for the most part. It costs money.
Most cities under Trees have a greatly reduced population compared to ten years ago.
Police services reduced their numbers accordingly. Police cost money.
Many cities under Trees thereby become interzones of sorts. Shadow economies. Shadow politics.
Nothing good grows in the shadow of a Tree.
This is one reason why your friends in the Great Work took root here. It's almost a pity they're so stupid and poor.
Well. They've got some money. I told you. And Tito still looks after me.
Pays for my room. Buys food. Gives me a bit of spending money. There are worse things.

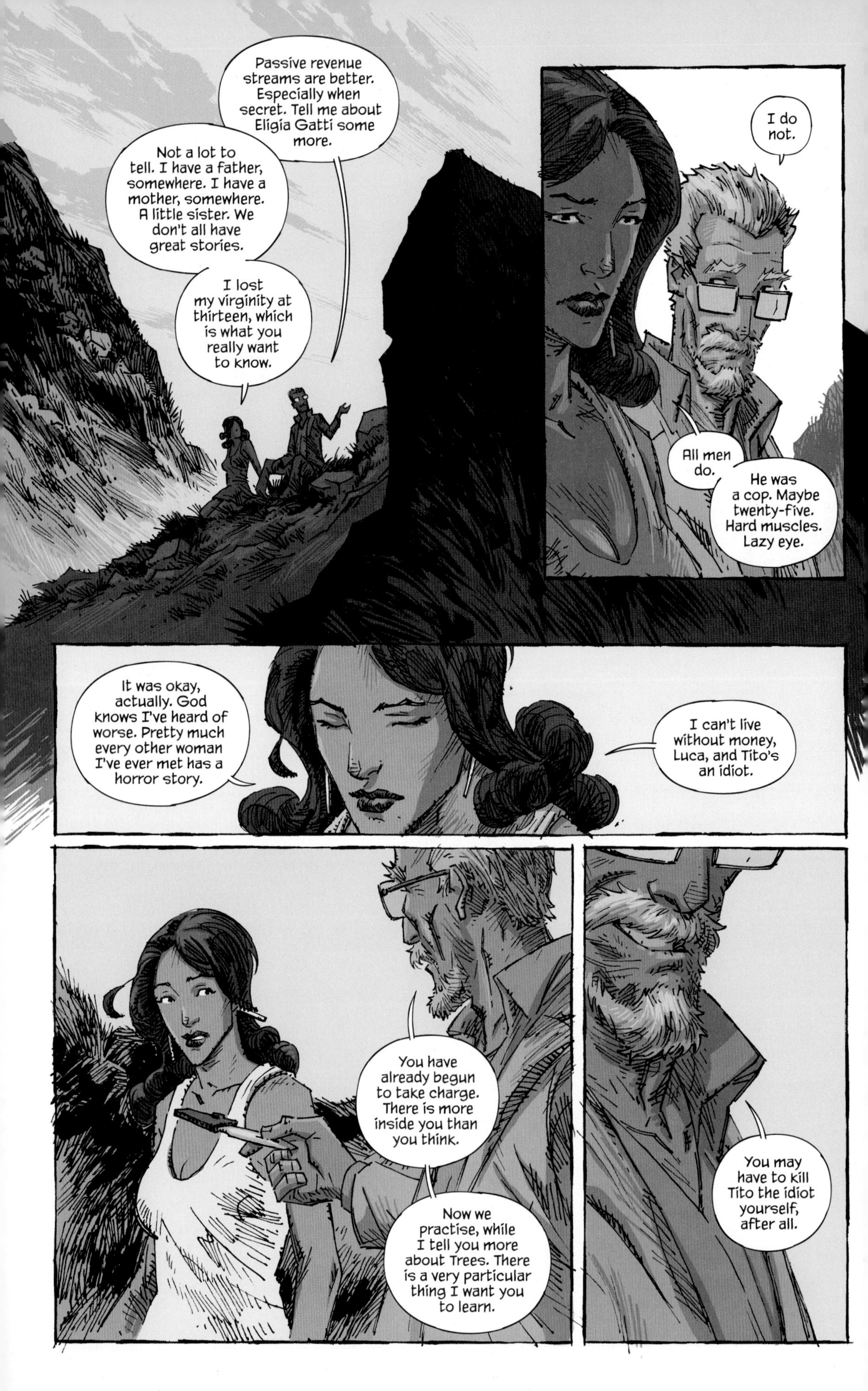
Passive revenue streams are better. Especially when secret. Tell me about Eligia Gatti some more.
Not a lot to tell. I have a father, somewhere. I have a mother, somewhere. A little sister. We don't all have great stories.
I lost my virginity at thirteen, which is what you really want to know.
I do not.
All men do.
He was a cop. Maybe twenty-five. Hard muscles. Lazy eye.
It was okay, actually. God knows I've heard of worse. Pretty much every other woman I've ever met has a horror story.
I can't live without money, Luca, and Tito's an idiot.
You have already begun to take charge. There is more inside you than you think.
Now we practise, while I tell you more about Trees. There is a very particular thing I want you to learn.
You may have to kill Tito the idiot yourself, after all.

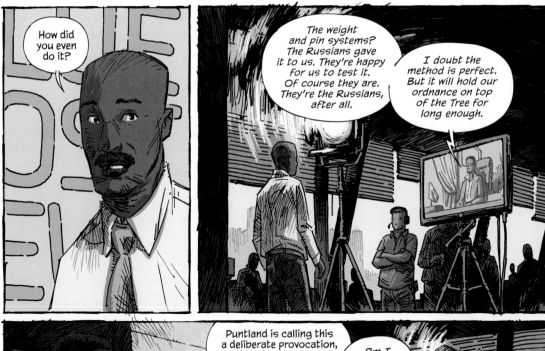

How did you even do it?

The weight and pin systems? The Russians gave it to us. They're happy for us to test it. Of course they are. They're the Russians, after all.

I doubt the method is perfect. But it will hold our ordnance on top of the Tree for long enough.

Puntland is calling this a deliberate provocation, and saying they'll meet it in kind. What do you say to that?

Am I supposed to be surprised?

I have played the internationalist game.

I have played the diplomatic game.

I have played the beggar game.

And now, if I must, I will play the tyrant's game.

Or, at least, be in service of the tyranny of numbers.

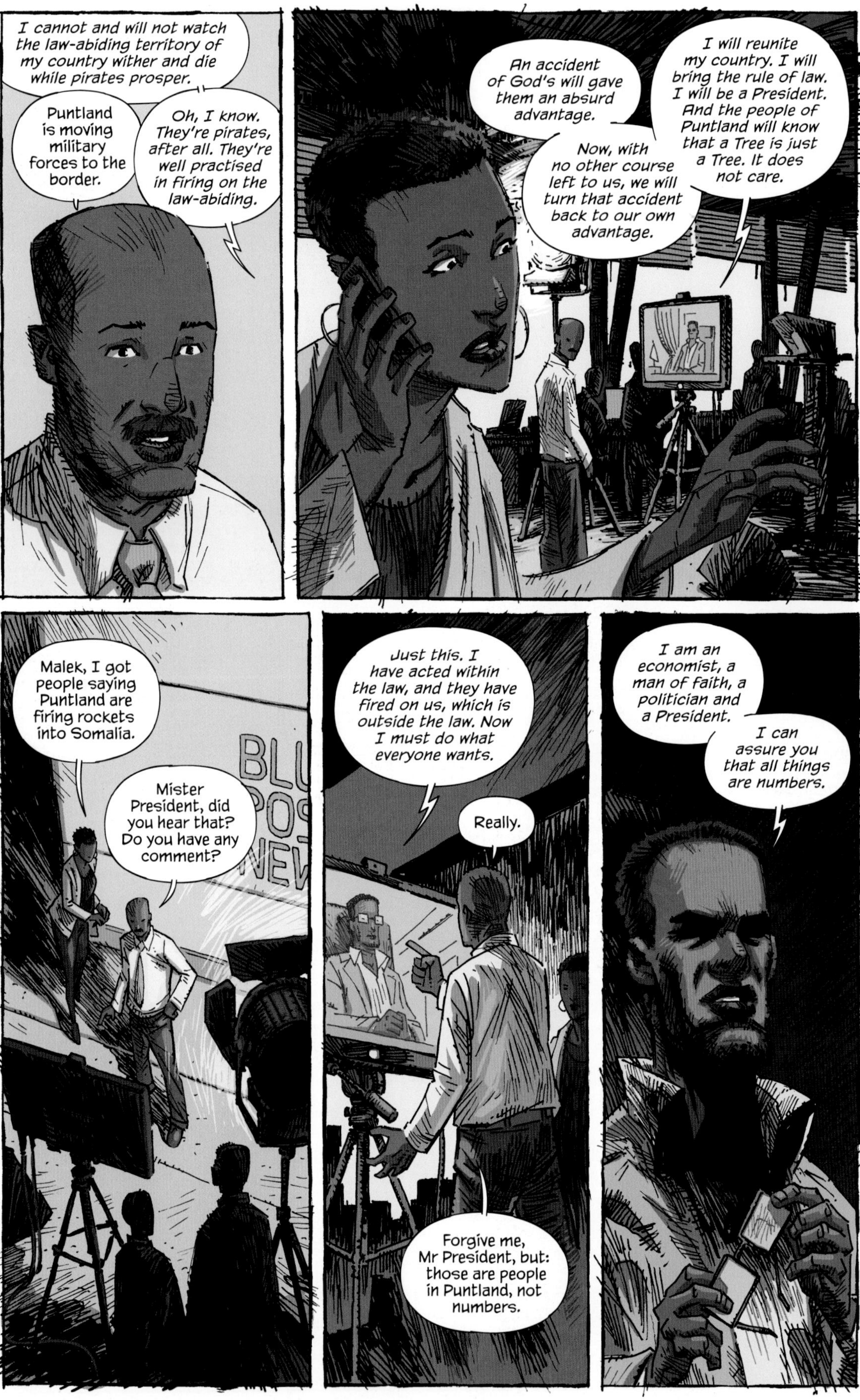
I cannot and will not watch the law-abiding territory of my country wither and die while pirates prosper.
Puntland is moving military forces to the border.
Oh, I know. They're pirates, after all. They're well practised in firing on the law-abiding.
An accident of God's will gave them an absurd advantage.
Now, with no other course left to us, we will turn that accident back to our own advantage.
I will reunite my country. I will bring the rule of law. I will be a President. And the people of Puntland will know that a Tree is just a Tree. It does not care.
Malek, I got people saying Puntland are firing rockets into Somalia.
Mister President, did you hear that? Do you have any comment?
Just this. I have acted within the law, and they have fired on us, which is outside the law. Now I must do what everyone wants.
Really.
Forgive me, Mr President, but: those are people in Puntland, not numbers.
I am an economist, a man of faith, a politician and a President.
I can assure you that all things are numbers.

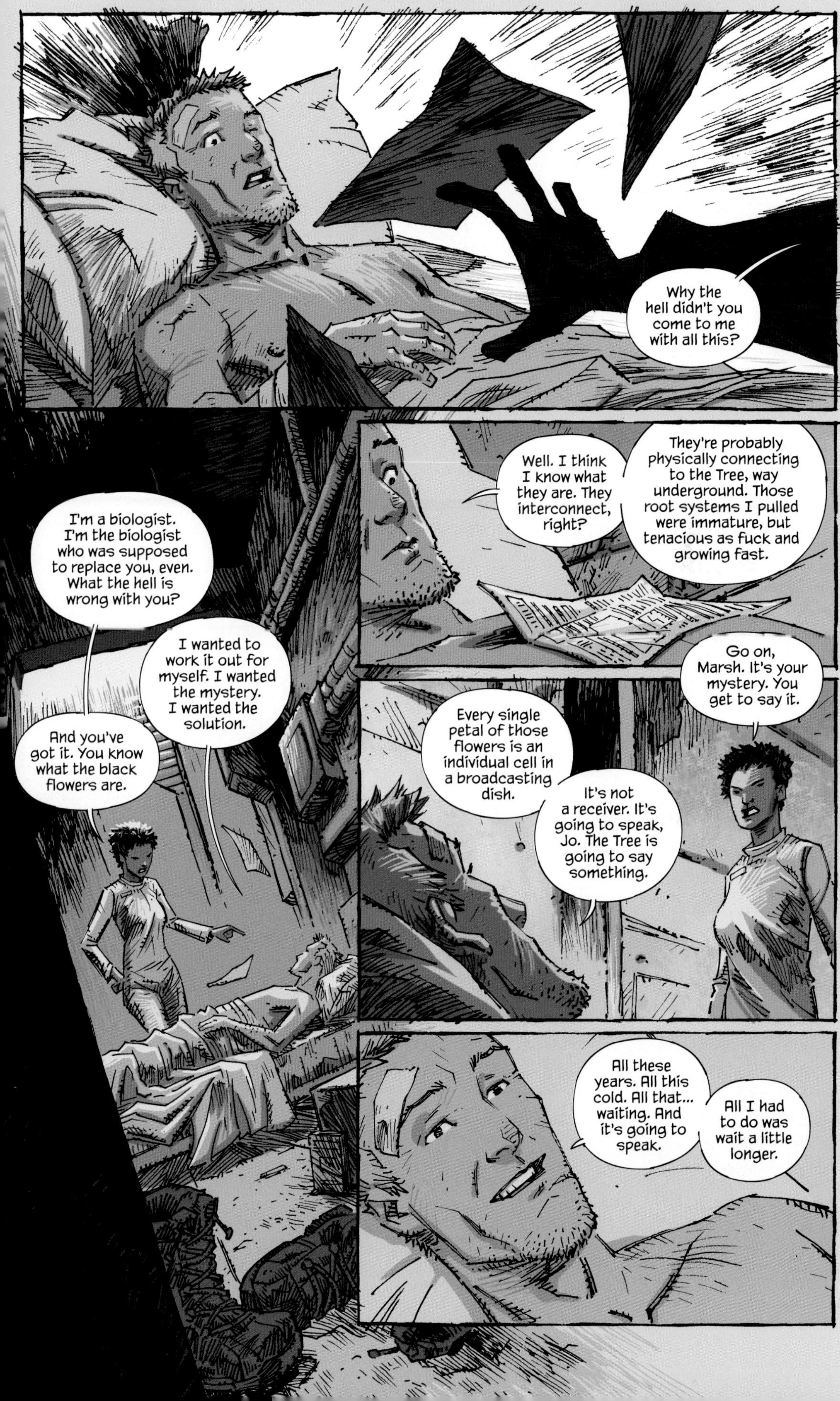
Why the hell didn't you come to me with all this?
I'm a biologist. I'm the biologist who was supposed to replace you, even. What the hell is wrong with you?
I wanted to work it out for myself. I wanted the mystery. I wanted the solution.
And you've got it. You know what the black flowers are.
Well. I think I know what they are. They interconnect, right?
They're probably physically connecting to the Tree, way underground. Those root systems I pulled were immature, but tenacious as fuck and growing fast.
Go on, Marsh. It's your mystery. You get to say it.
Every single petal of those flowers is an individual cell in a broadcasting dish.
It's not a receiver. It's going to speak, Jo. The Tree is going to say something.
All these years. All this cold. All that... waiting. And it's going to speak.
All I had to do was wait a little longer.

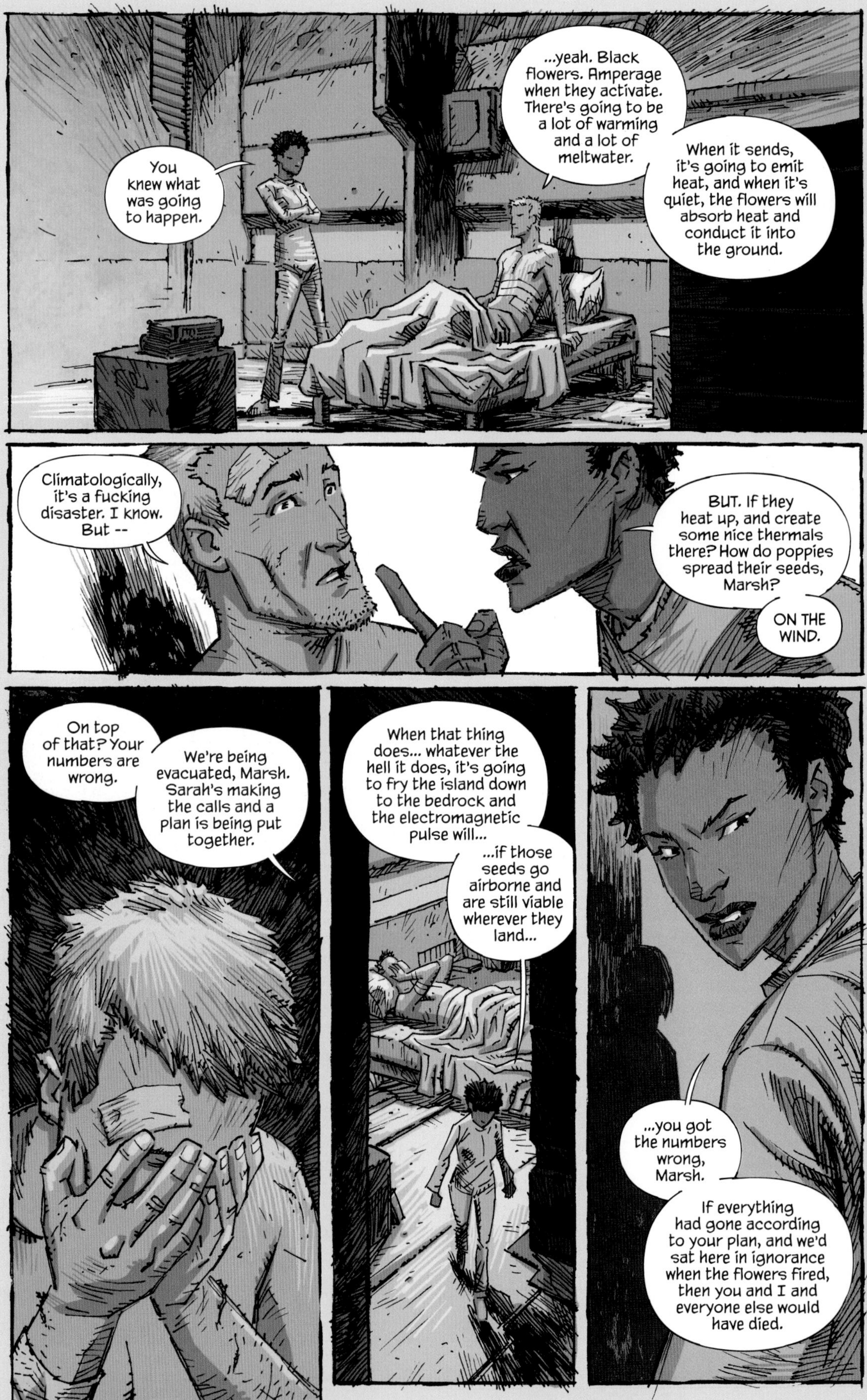

You knew what was going to happen.
...yeah. Black flowers. Amperage when they activate. There's going to be a lot of warming and a lot of meltwater.
When it sends, it's going to emit heat, and when it's quiet, the flowers will absorb heat and conduct it into the ground.
Climatologically, it's a fucking disaster. I know. But --
BUT. If they heat up, and create some nice thermals there? How do poppies spread their seeds, Marsh?
ON THE WIND.
On top of that? Your numbers are wrong.
We're being evacuated, Marsh. Sarah's making the calls and a plan is being put together.
When that thing does... whatever the hell it does, it's going to fry the island down to the bedrock and the electromagnetic pulse will...
...if those seeds go airborne and are still viable wherever they land...
...you got the numbers wrong, Marsh.
If everything had gone according to your plan, and we'd sat here in ignorance when the flowers fired, then you and I and everyone else would have died.

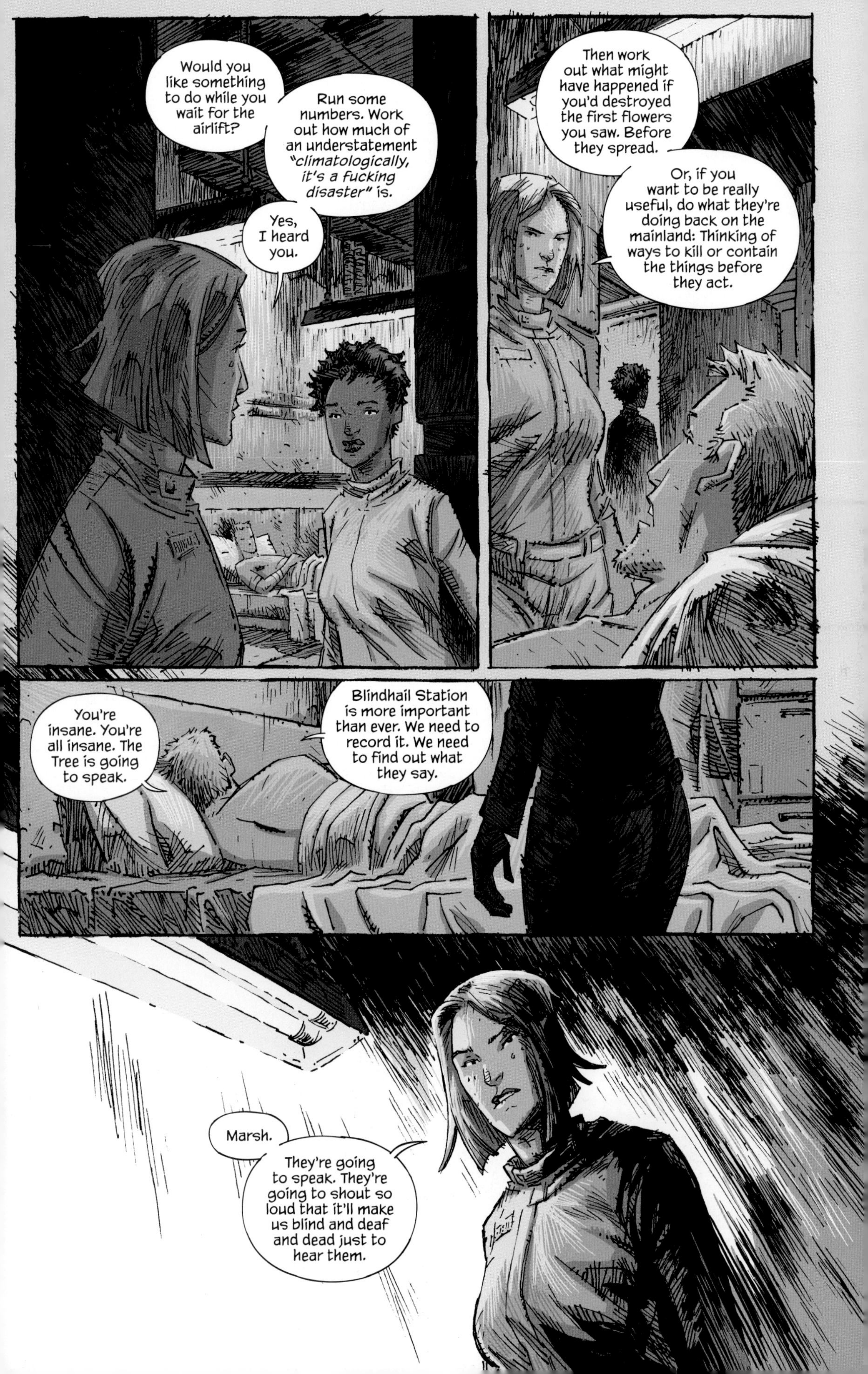
Would you like something to do while you wait for the airlift?
Run some numbers. Work out how much of an understatement *"climatologically, it's a fucking disaster"* is.
Yes, I heard you.
Then work out what might have happened if you'd destroyed the first flowers you saw. Before they spread.
Or, if you want to be really useful, do what they're doing back on the mainland: Thinking of ways to kill or contain the things before they act.
You're insane. You're all insane. The Tree is going to speak.
Blindhail Station is more important than ever. We need to record it. We need to find out what they say.
Marsh.
They're going to speak. They're going to shout so loud that it'll make us blind and deaf and dead just to hear them.

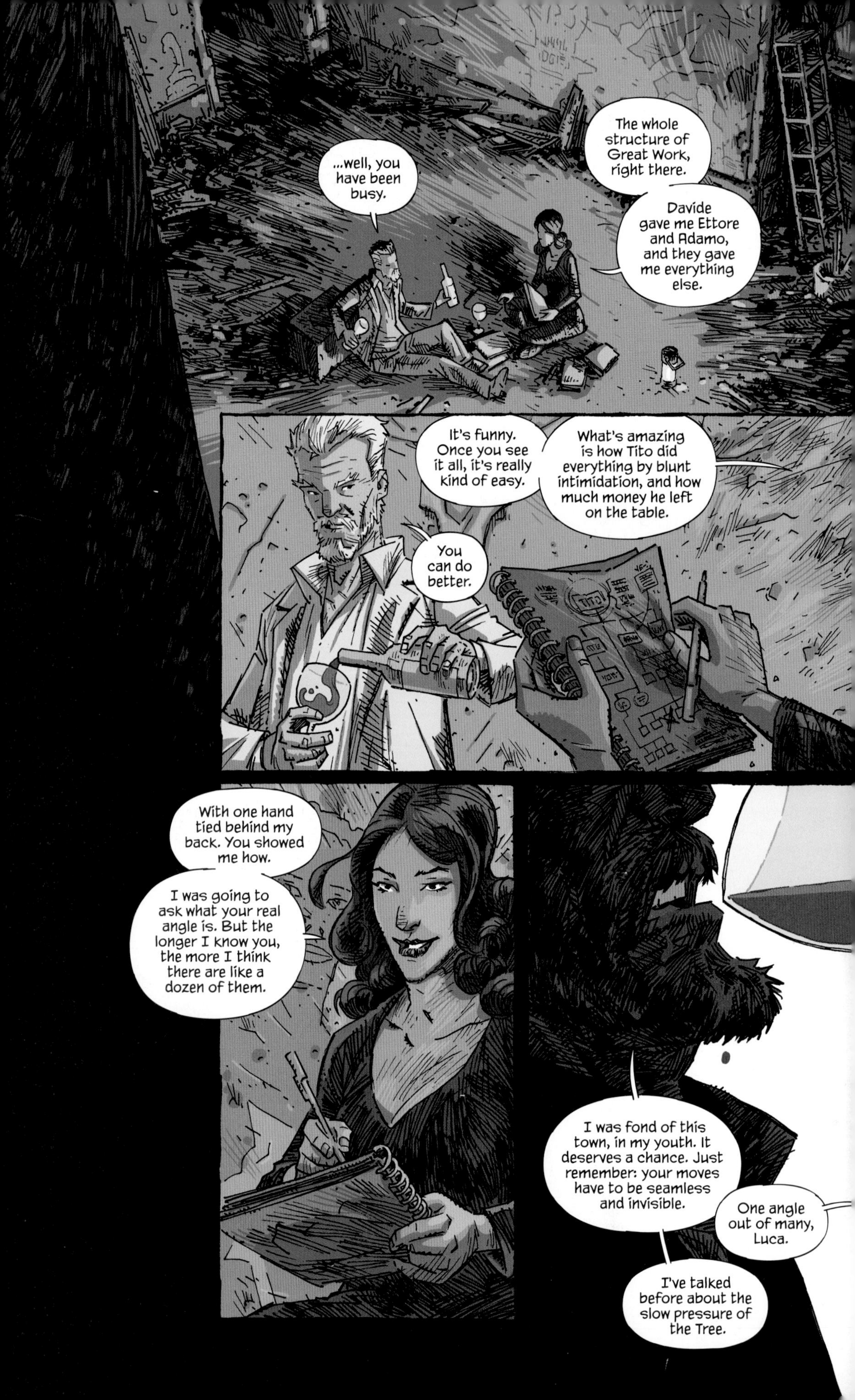
...well, you have been busy.
The whole structure of Great Work, right there.
Davide gave me Ettore and Adamo, and they gave me everything else.
It's funny. Once you see it all, it's really kind of easy.
What's amazing is how Tito did everything by blunt intimidation, and how much money he left on the table.
You can do better.
With one hand tied behind my back. You showed me how.
I was going to ask what your real angle is. But the longer I know you, the more I think there are like a dozen of them.
I was fond of this town, in my youth. It deserves a chance. Just remember: your moves have to be seamless and invisible.
One angle out of many, Luca.
I've talked before about the slow pressure of the Tree.

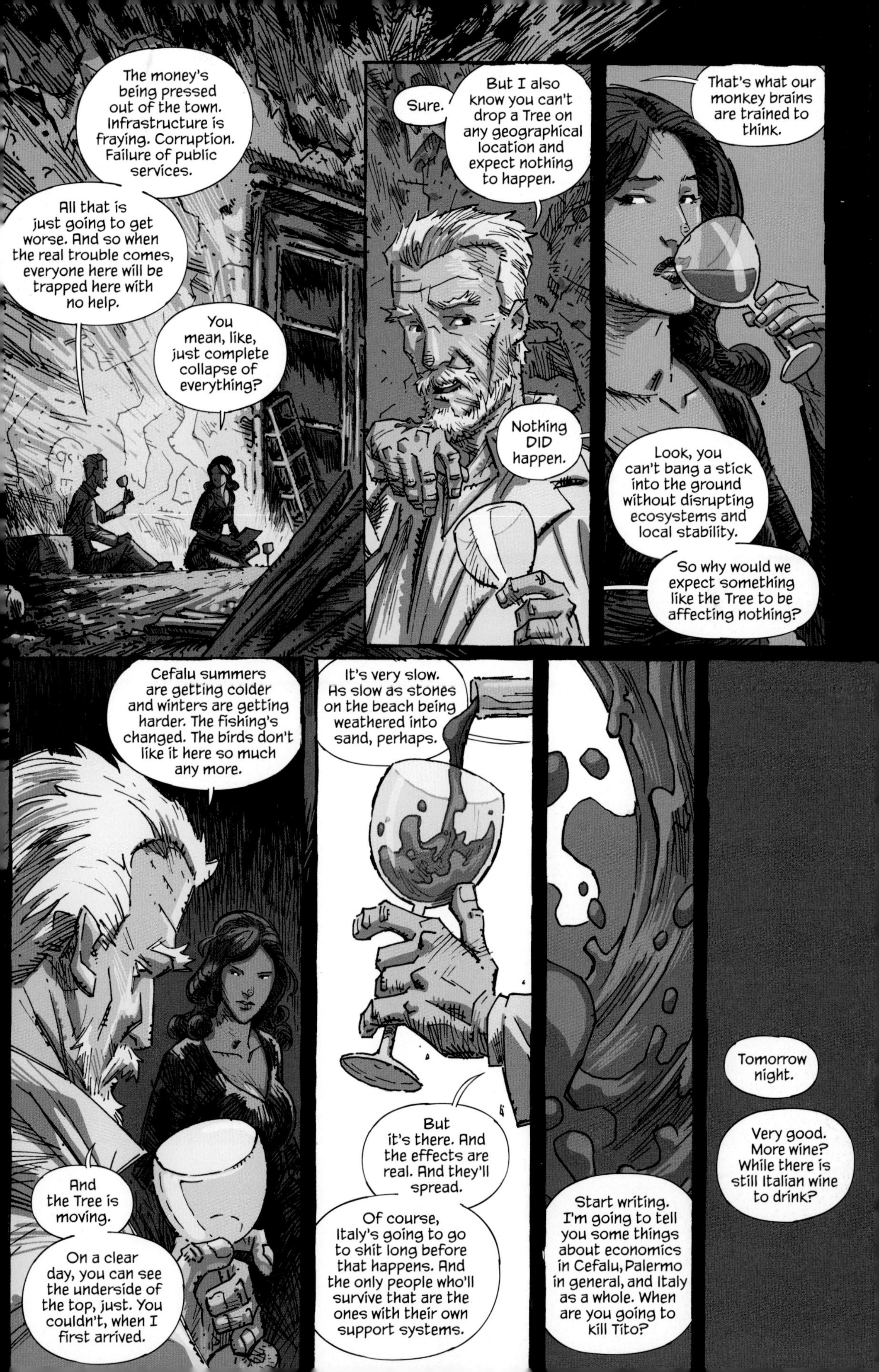

The money's being pressed out of the town. Infrastructure is fraying. Corruption. Failure of public services.
All that is just going to get worse. And so when the real trouble comes, everyone here will be trapped here with no help.
You mean, like, just complete collapse of everything?
Sure.
But I also know you can't drop a Tree on any geographical location and expect nothing to happen.
Nothing DID happen.
That's what our monkey brains are trained to think.
Look, you can't bang a stick into the ground without disrupting ecosystems and local stability.
So why would we expect something like the Tree to be affecting nothing?
Cefalu summers are getting colder and winters are getting harder. The fishing's changed. The birds don't like it here so much any more.
And the Tree is moving.
On a clear day, you can see the underside of the top, just. You couldn't, when I first arrived.
It's very slow. As slow as stones on the beach being weathered into sand, perhaps.
But it's there. And the effects are real. And they'll spread.
Of course, Italy's going to go to shit long before that happens. And the only people who'll survive that are the ones with their own support systems.
Start writing. I'm going to tell you some things about economics in Cefalu, Palermo in general, and Italy as a whole. When are you going to kill Tito?
Tomorrow night.
Very good. More wine? While there is still Italian wine to drink?

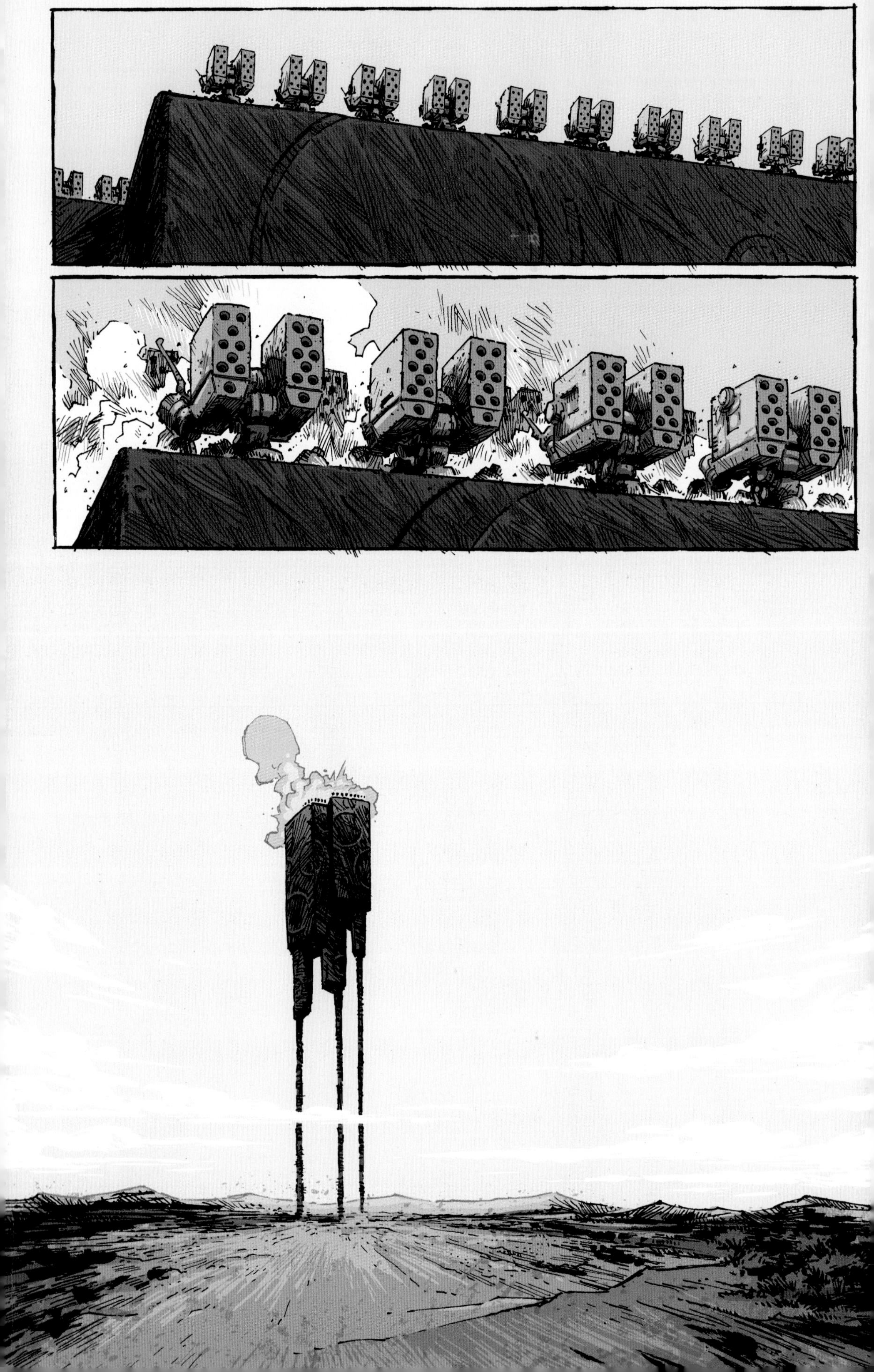

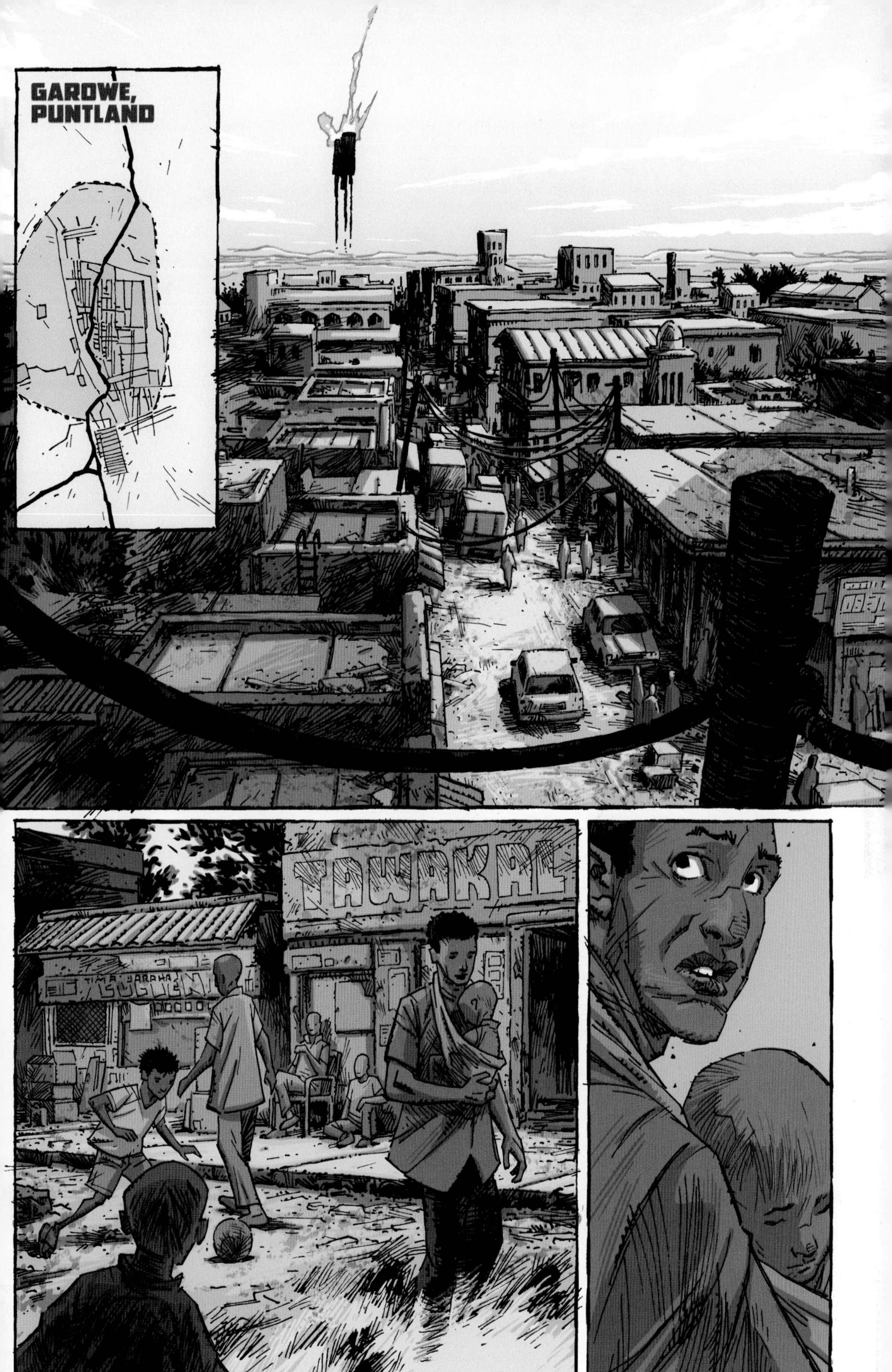
GAROWE,
PUNTLAND
TAWAKAL

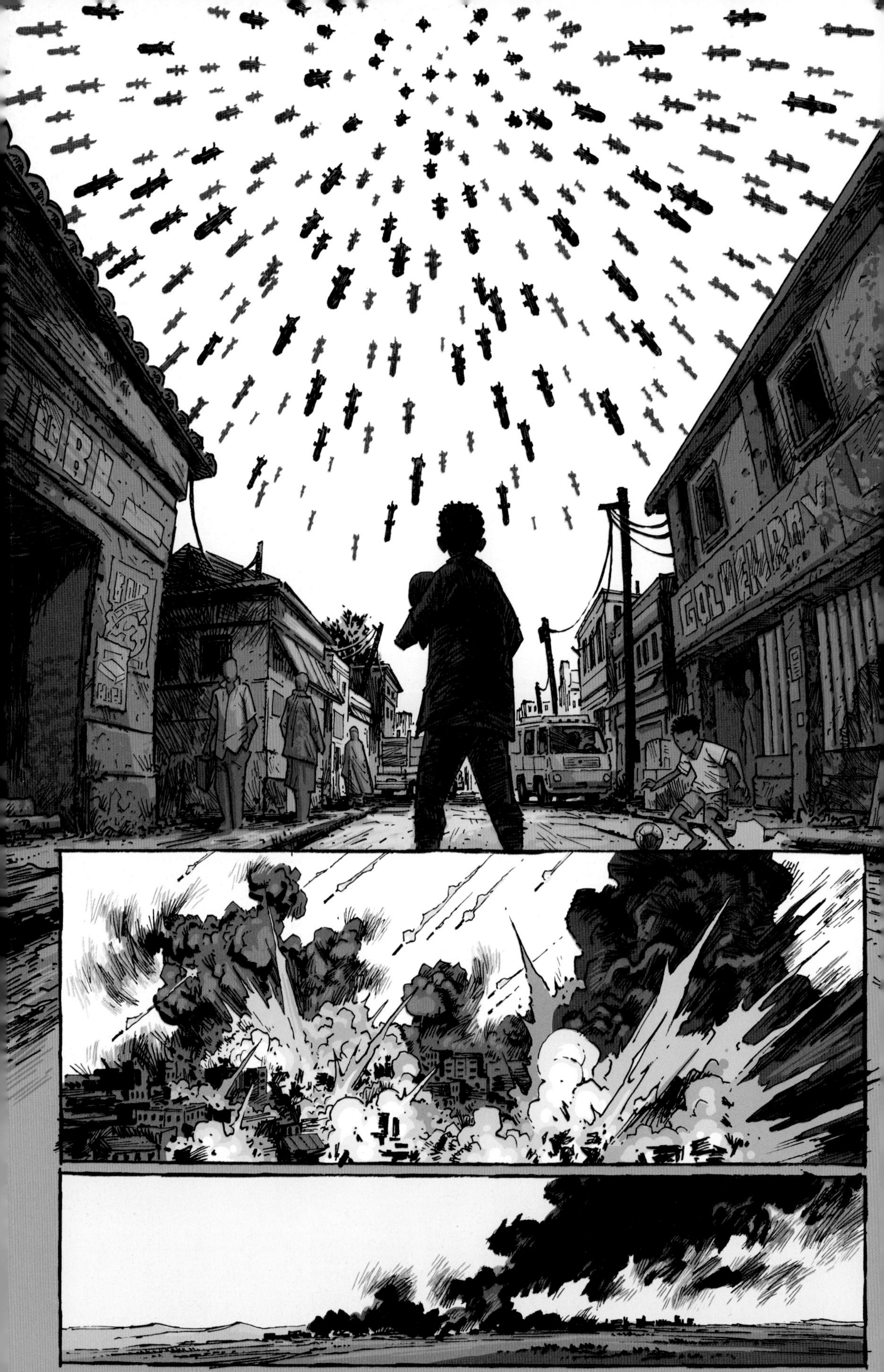

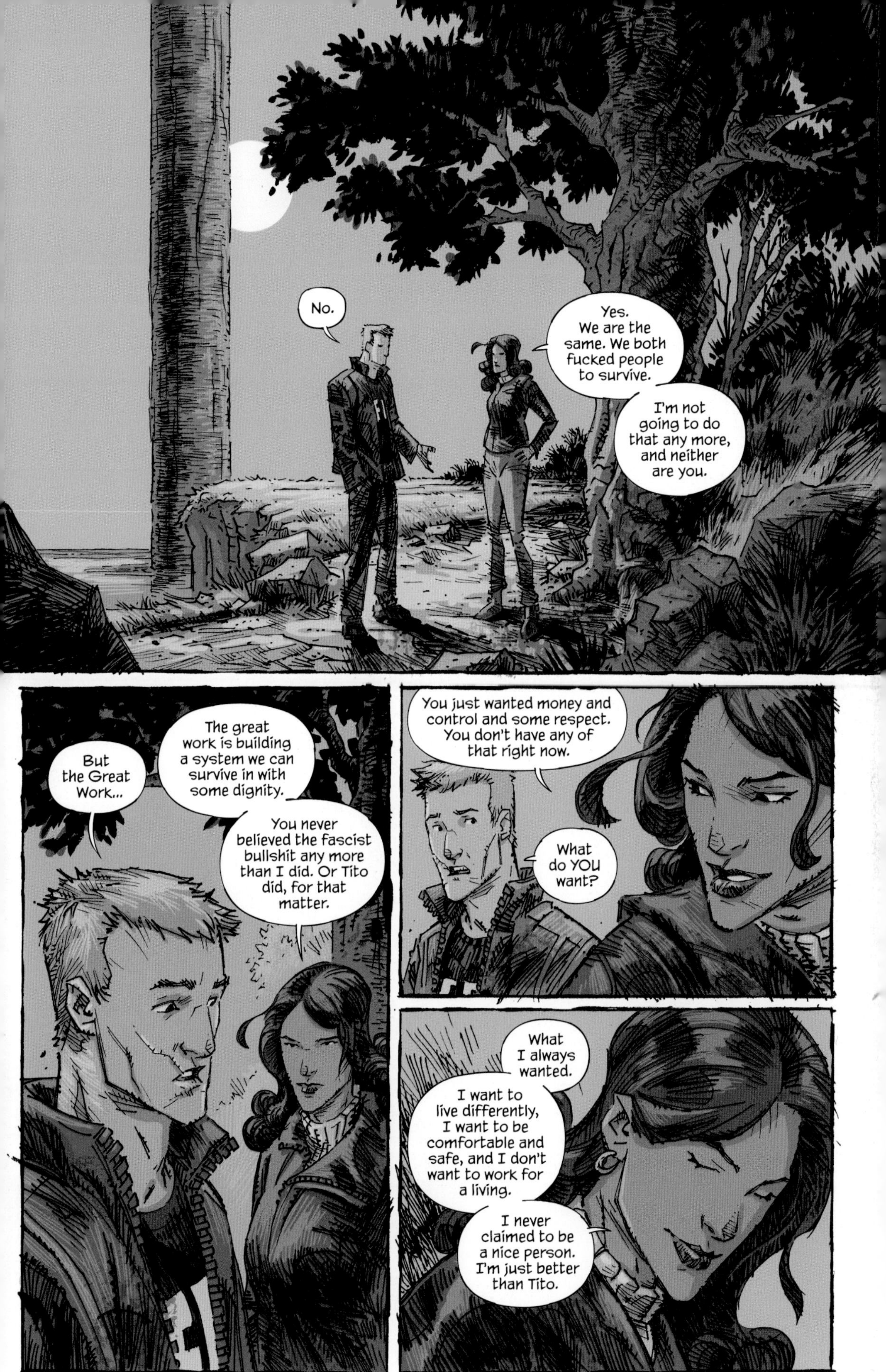
No.
Yes. We are the same. We both fucked people to survive.
I'm not going to do that any more, and neither are you.
But the Great Work...
The great work is building a system we can survive in with some dignity.
You never believed the fascist bullshit any more than I did. Or Tito did, for that matter.
You just wanted money and control and some respect. You don't have any of that right now.
What do YOU want?
What I always wanted.
I want to live differently, I want to be comfortable and safe, and I don't want to work for a living.
I never claimed to be a nice person. I'm just better than Tito.

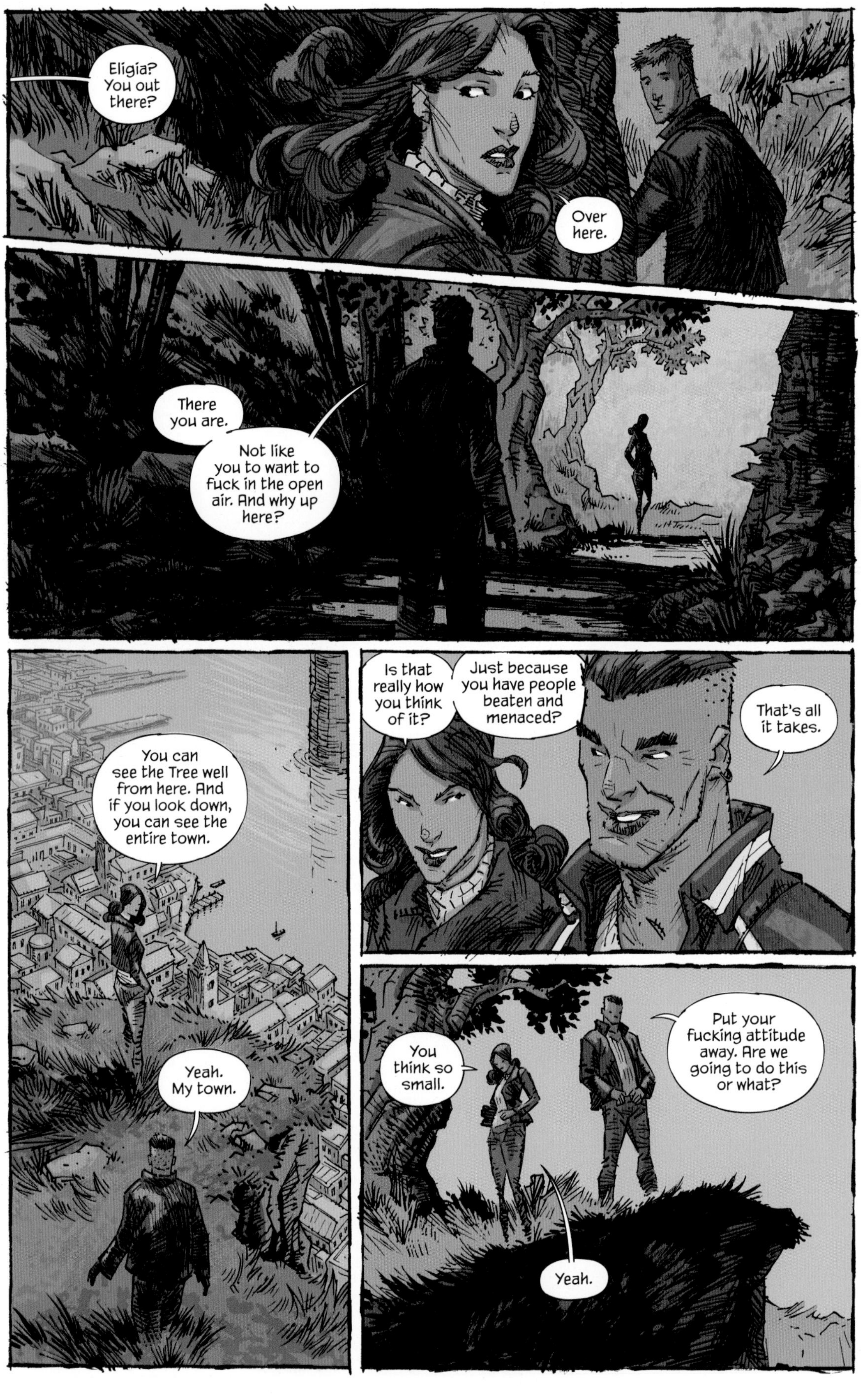
Eligia? You out there?
Over here.
There you are.
Not like you to want to fuck in the open air. And why up here?
You can see the Tree well from here. And if you look down, you can see the entire town.
Yeah. My town.
Is that really how you think of it?
Just because you have people beaten and menaced?
That's all it takes.
You think so small.
Put your fucking attitude away. Are we going to do this or what?
Yeah.

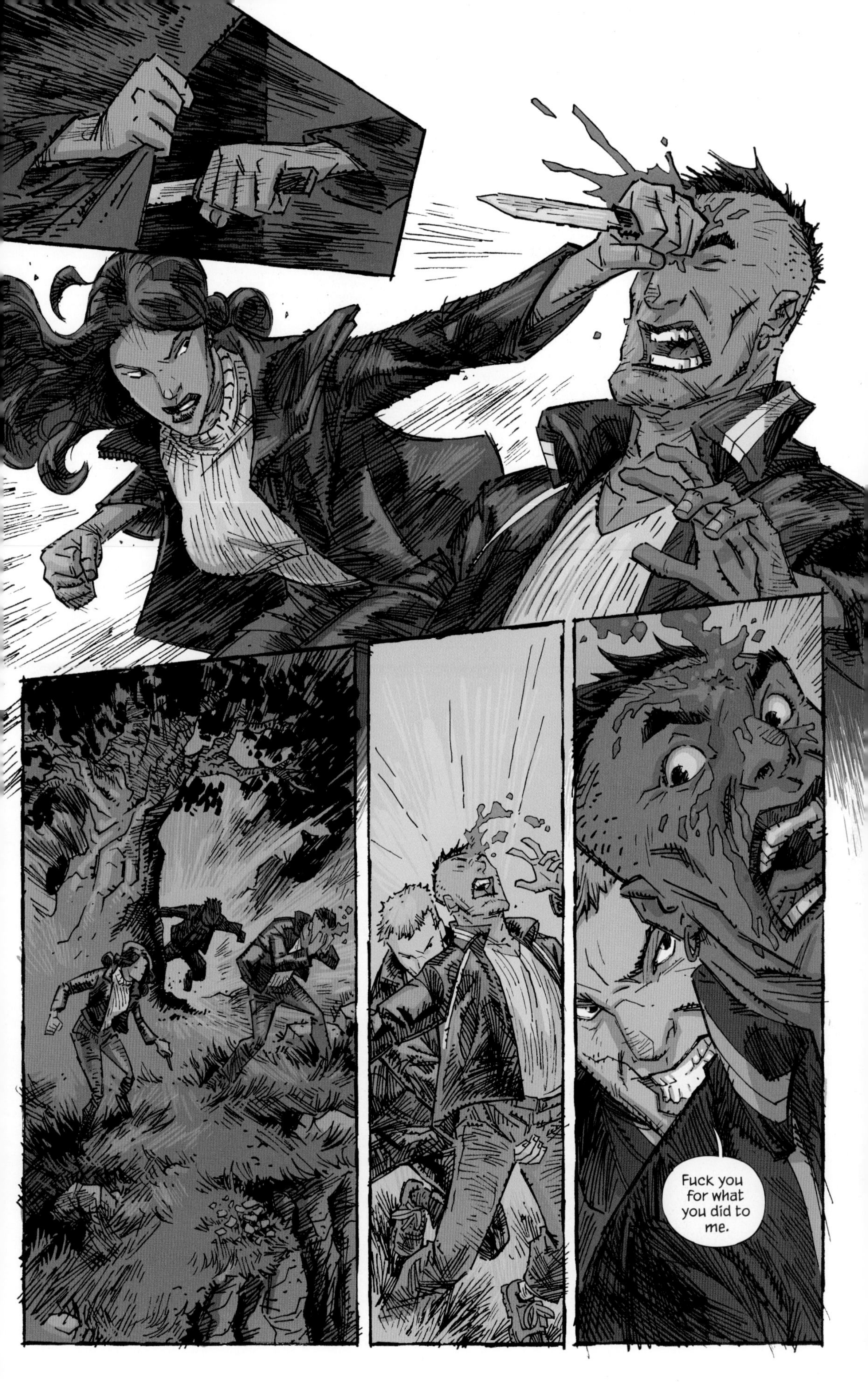
Fuck you for what you did to me.

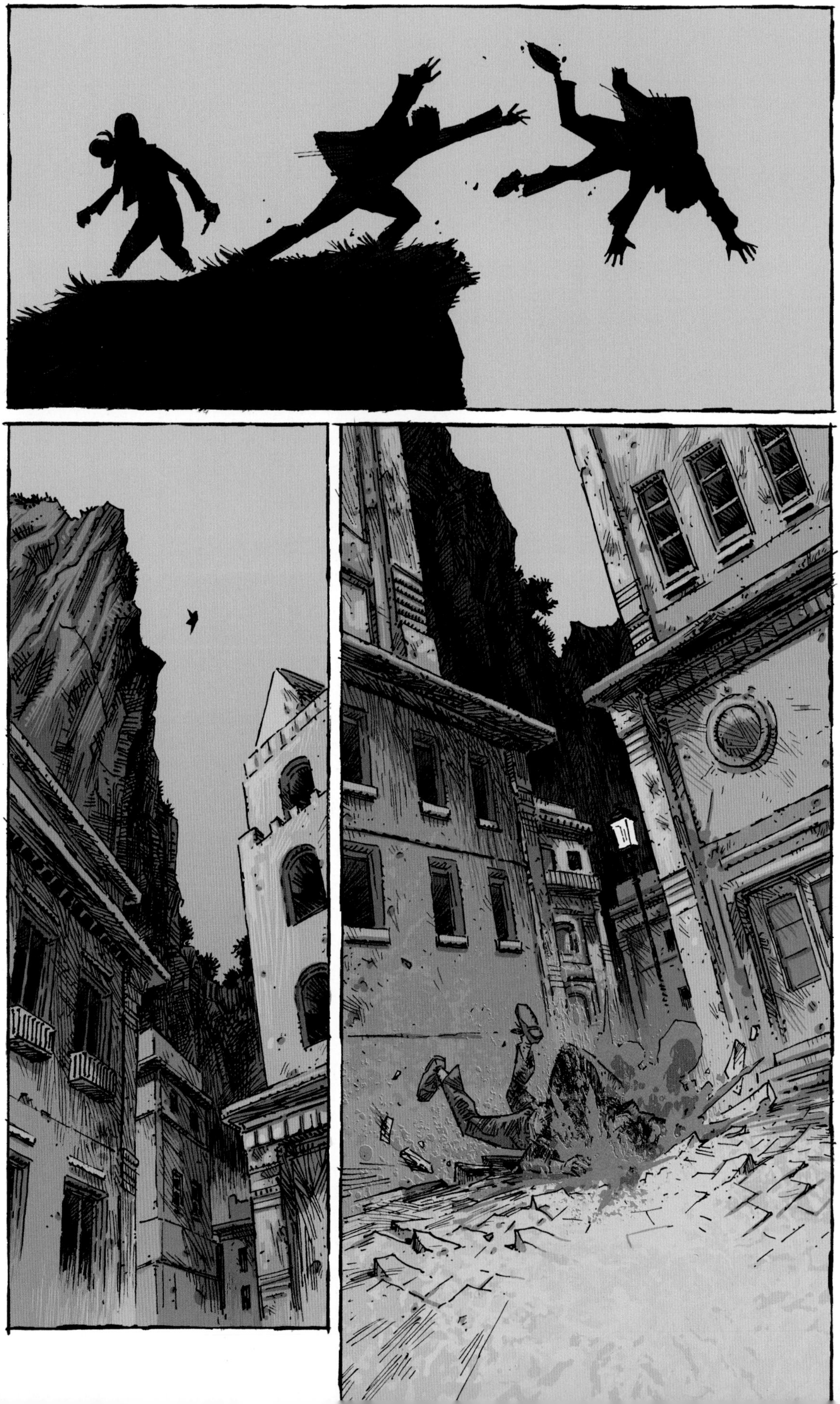

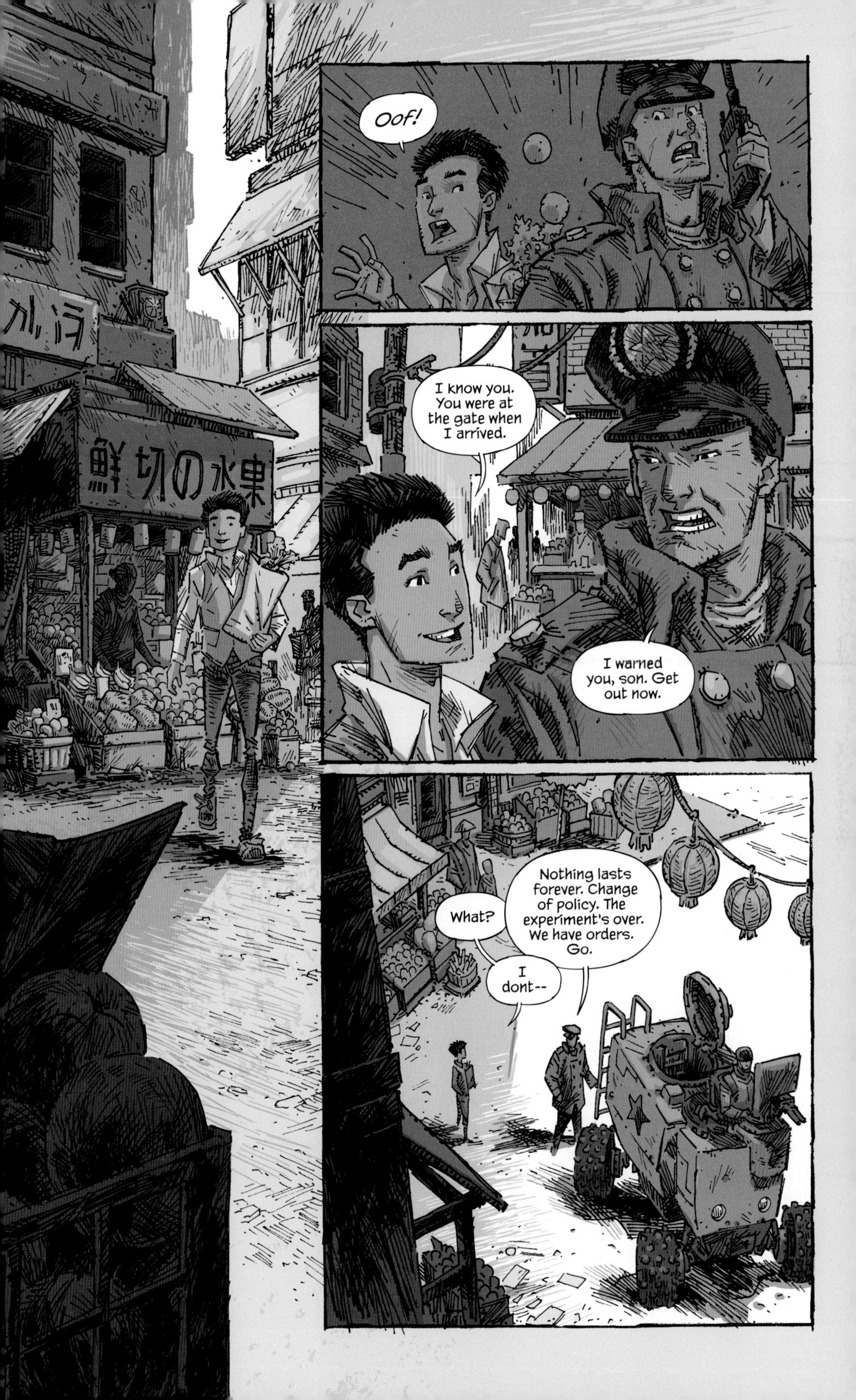
鮮切の水東
Oof!
I know you. You were at the gate when I arrived.
I warned you, son. Get out now.
What?
Nothing lasts forever. Change of policy. The experiment's over. We have orders. Go.
I dont--

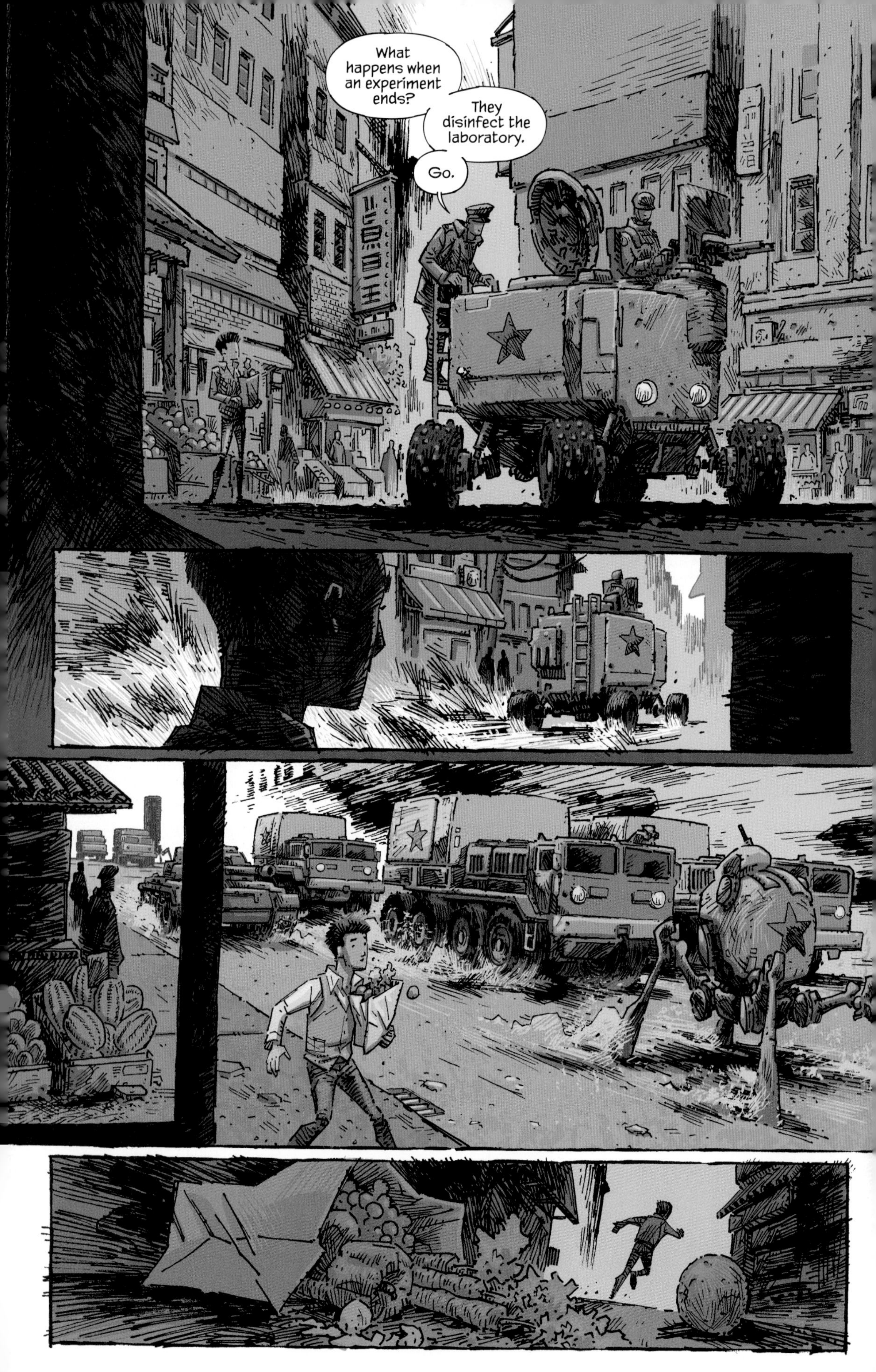
What happens when an experiment ends?
They disinfect the laboratory.
Go.

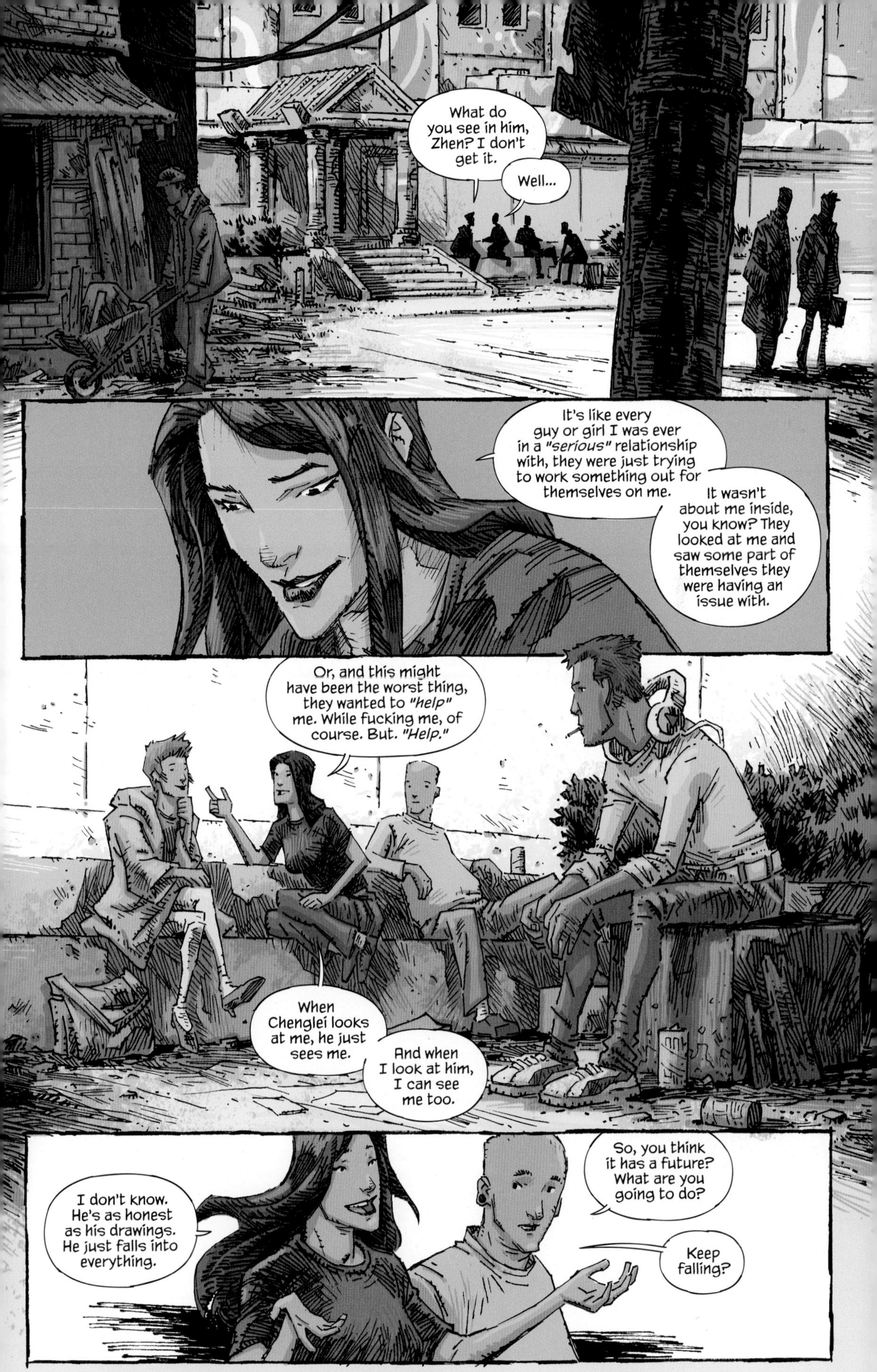
What do you see in him, Zhen? I don't get it.
Well...
It's like every guy or girl I was ever in a "serious" relationship with, they were just trying to work something out for themselves on me.
It wasn't about me inside, you know? They looked at me and saw some part of themselves they were having an issue with.
Or, and this might have been the worst thing, they wanted to "help" me. While fucking me, of course. But. "Help."
When Chenglei looks at me, he just sees me.
And when I look at him, I can see me too.
So, you think it has a future? What are you going to do?
I don't know. He's as honest as his drawings. He just falls into everything.
Keep falling?

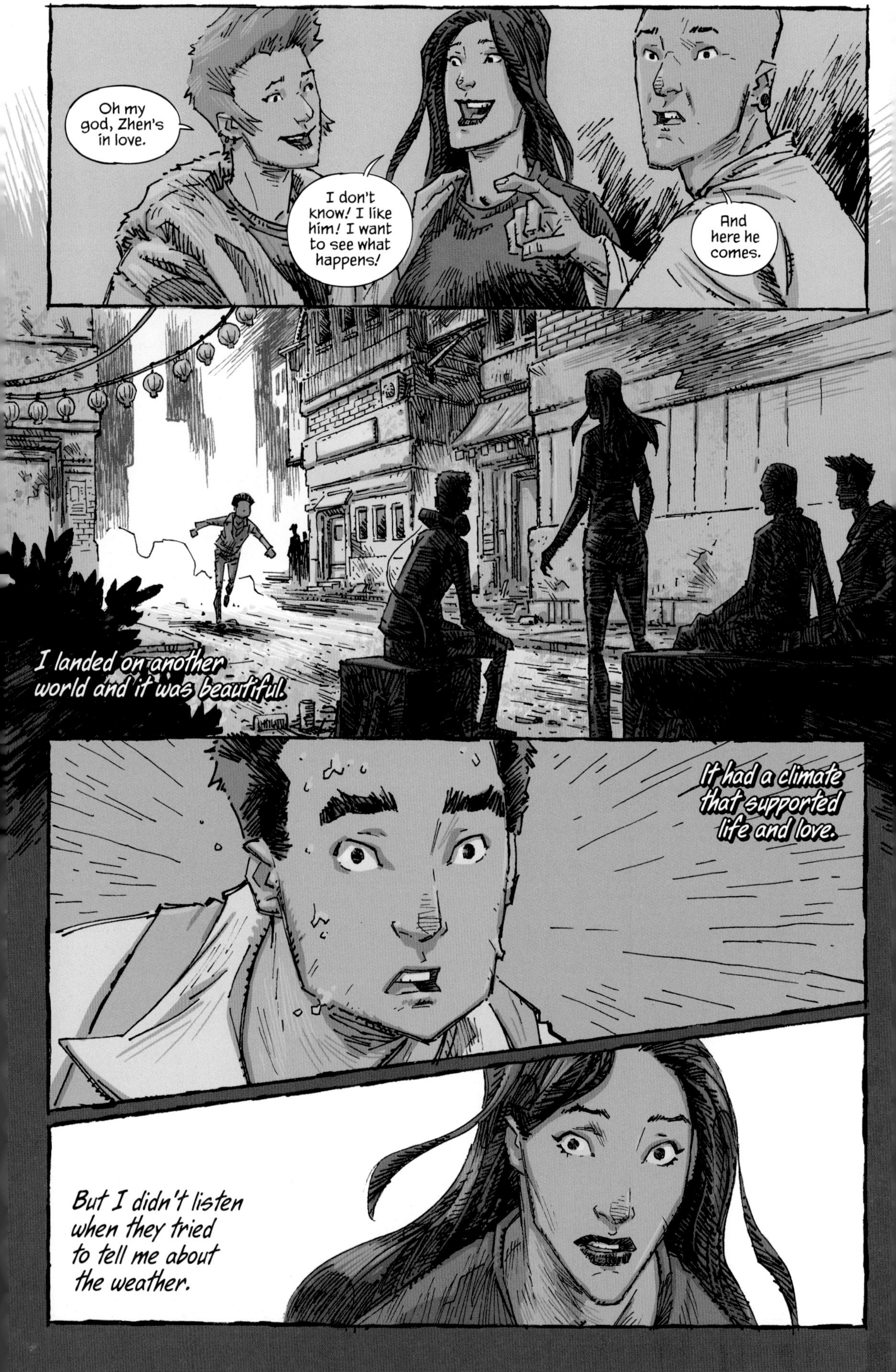
Oh my god, Zhen's in love.
I don't know! I like him! I want to see what happens!
And here he comes.
I landed on another world and it was beautiful.
It had a climate that supported life and love.
But I didn't listen when they tried to tell me about the weather.

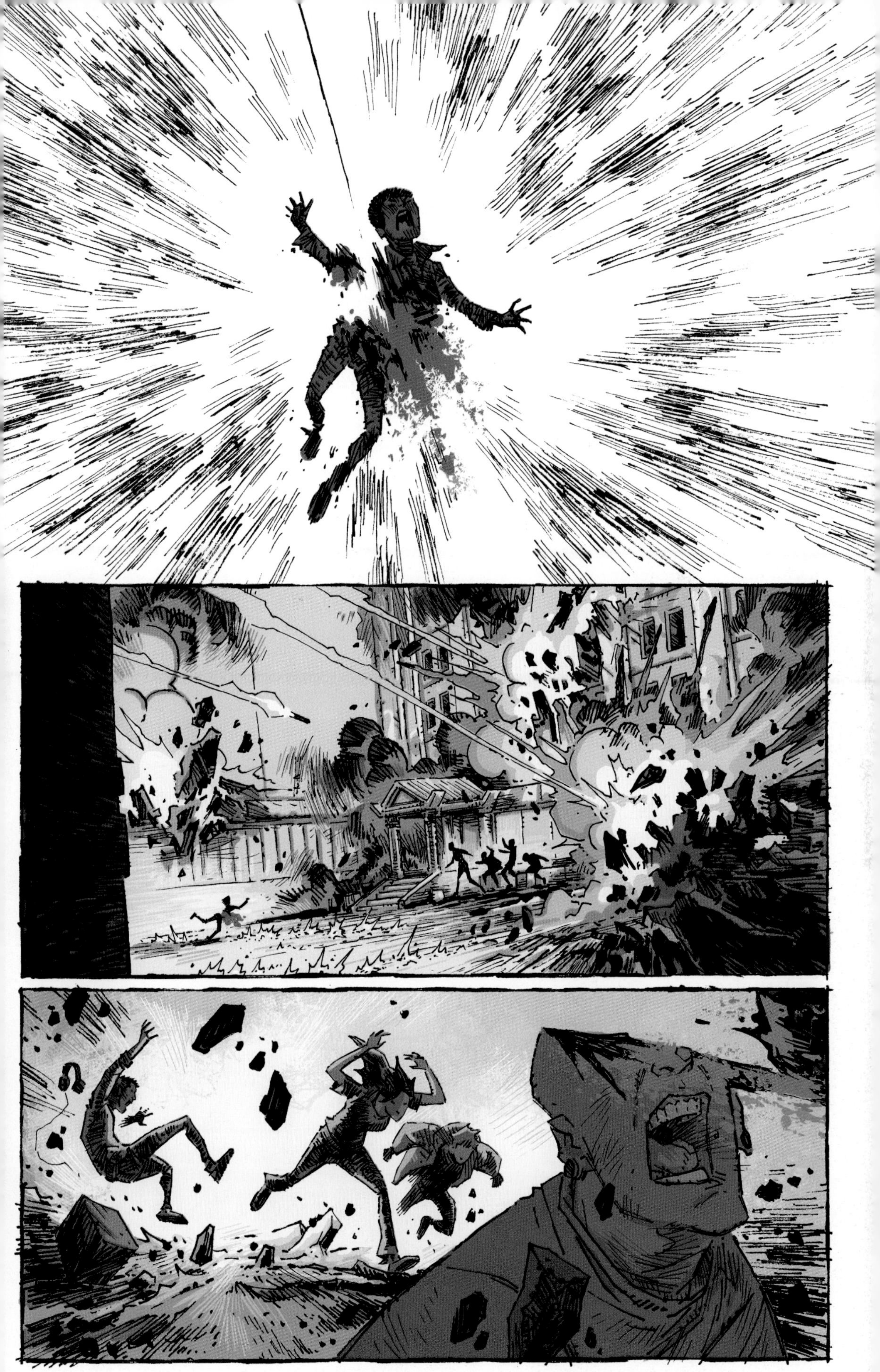

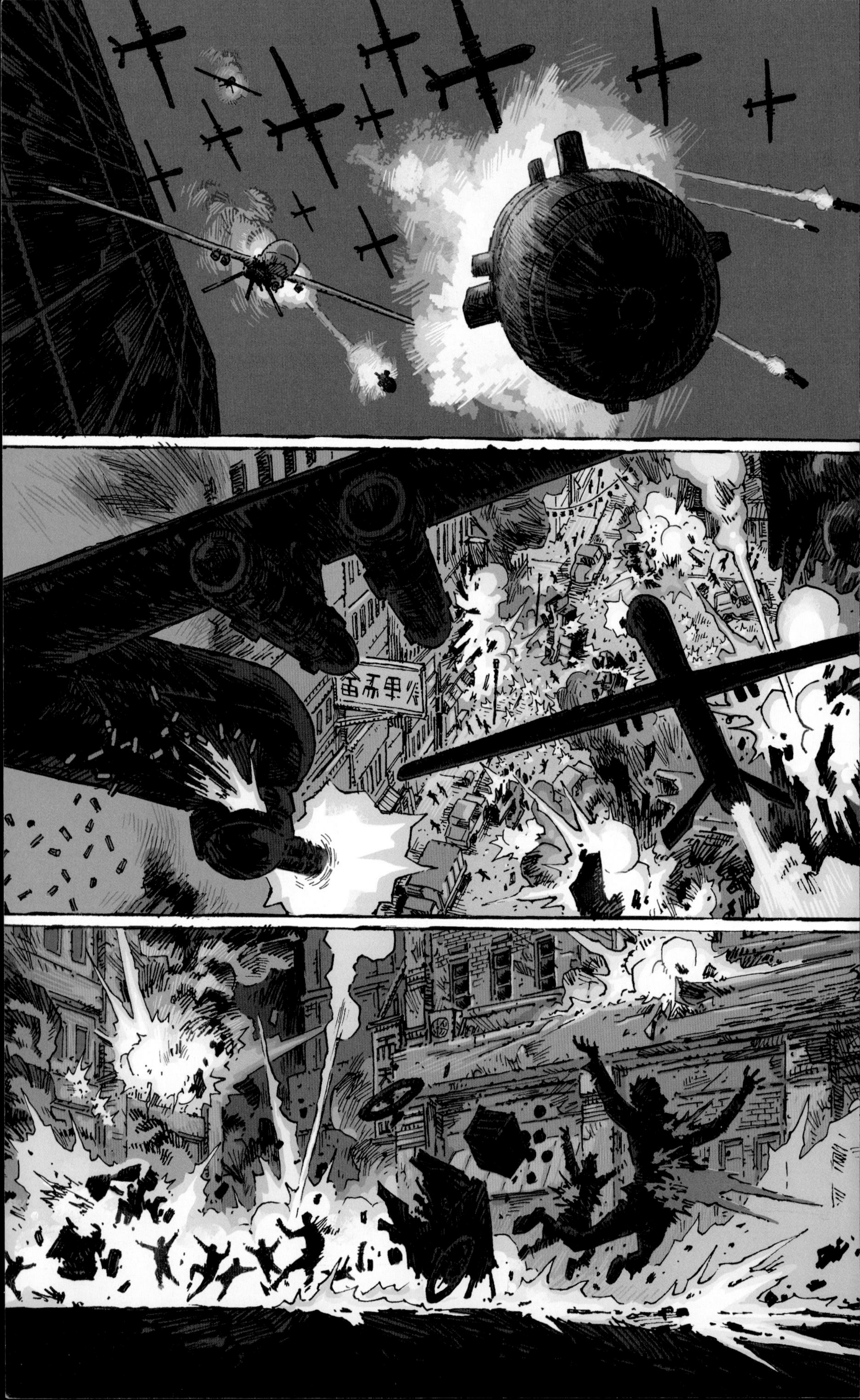

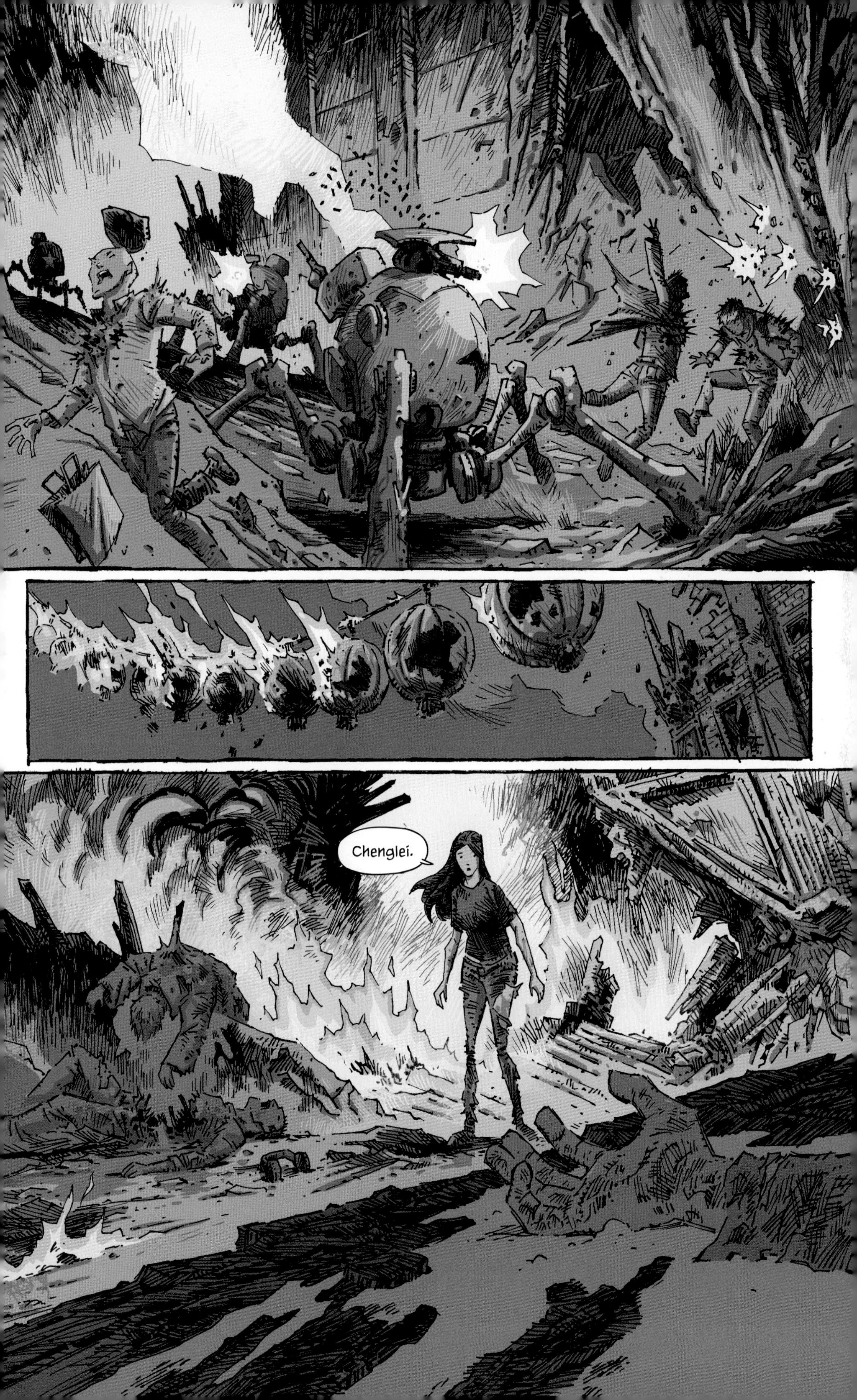
Chenglei.

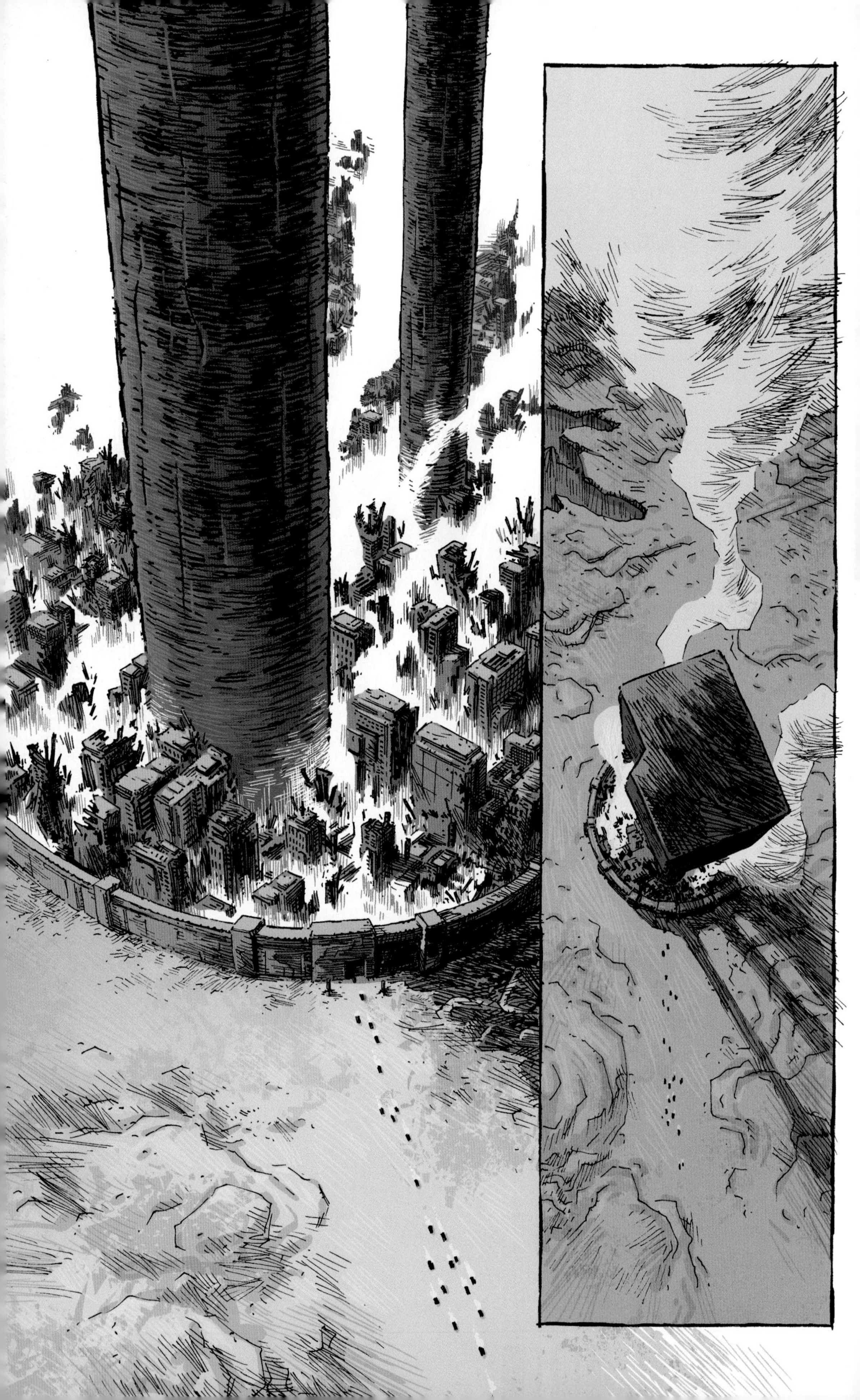

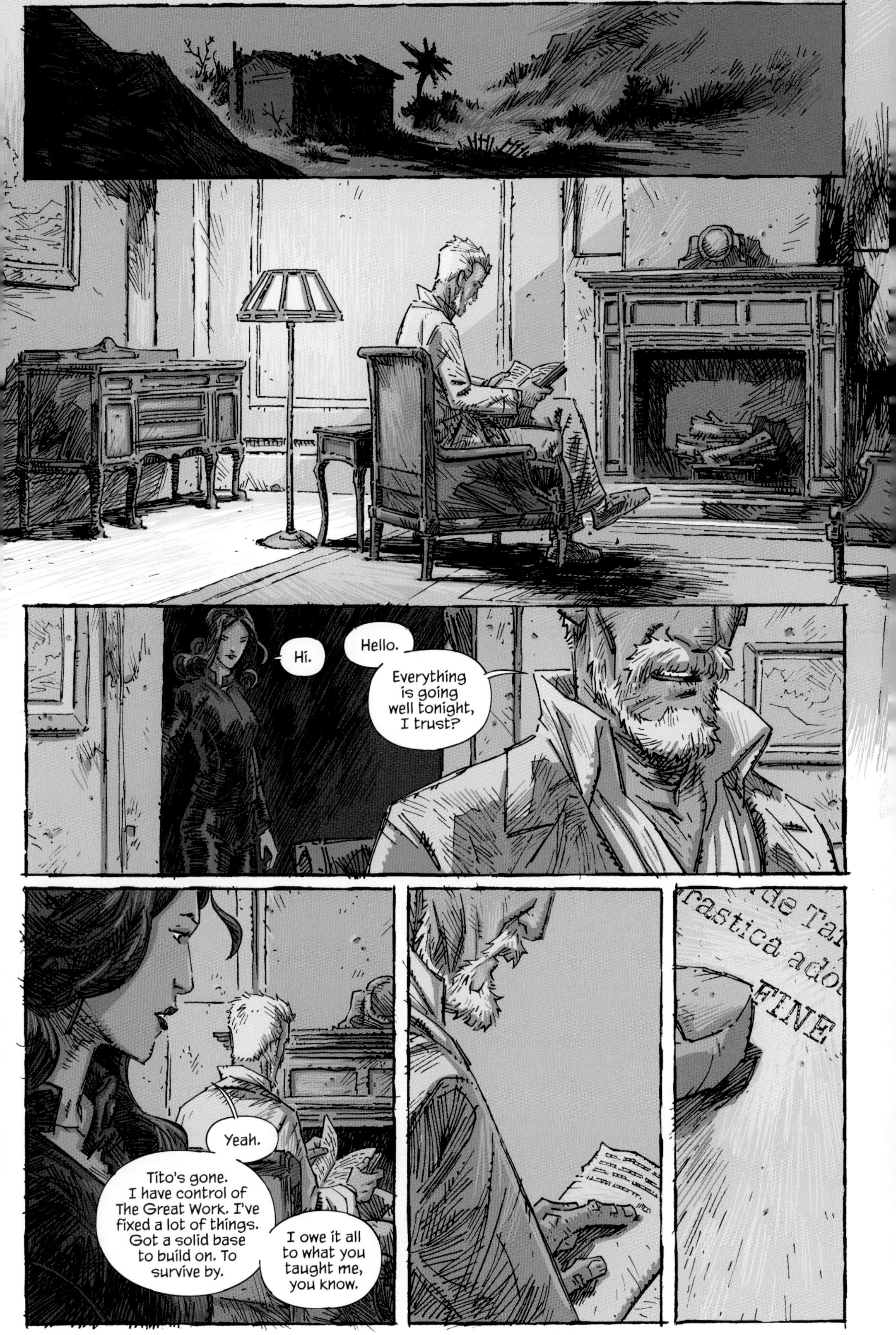
Hi.
Hello.
Everything is going well tonight, I trust?
Yeah.
Tito's gone. I have control of The Great Work. I've fixed a lot of things. Got a solid base to build on. To survive by.
I owe it all to what you taught me, you know.
de Ta
rastica ado
FINE

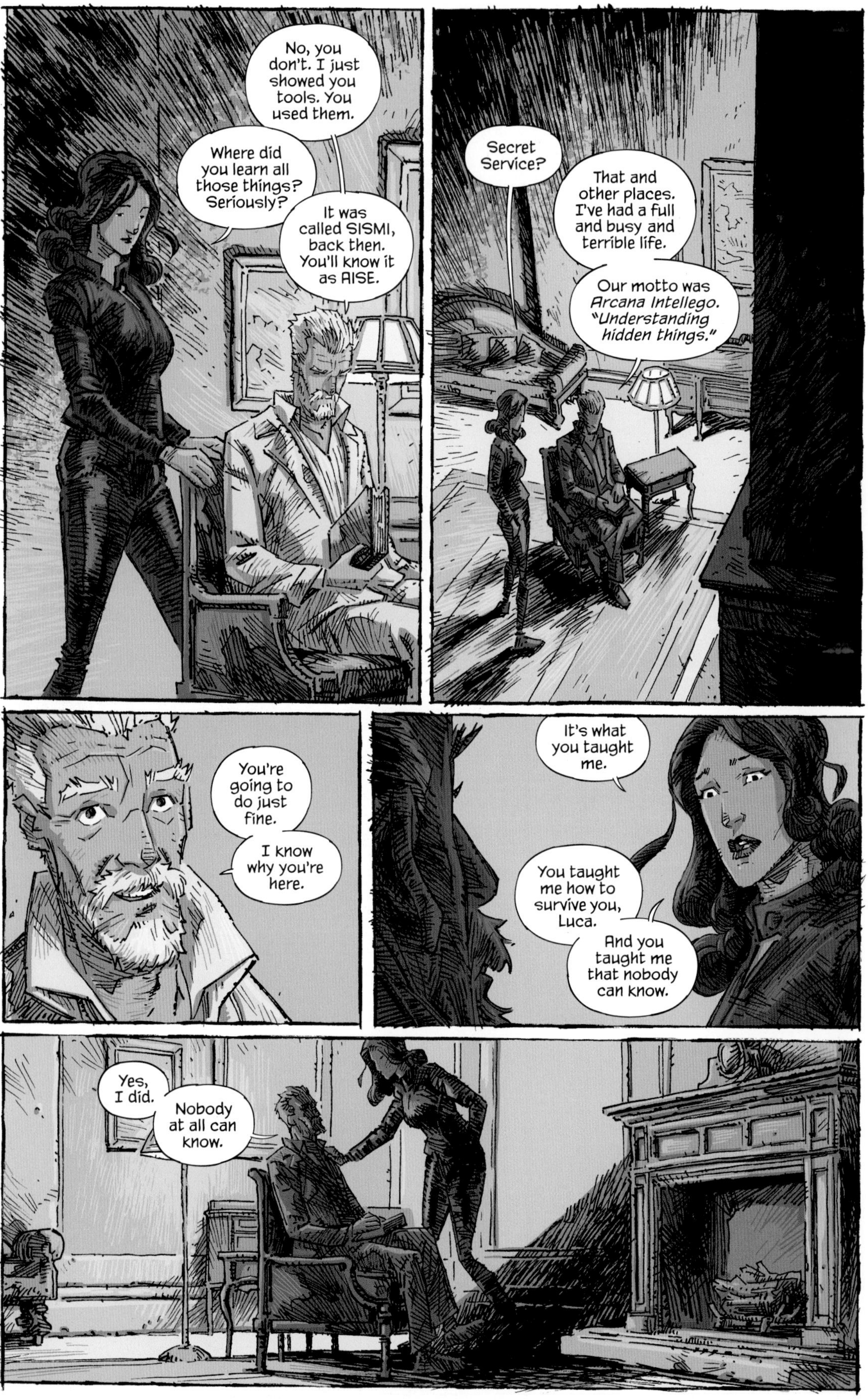
No, you don't. I just showed you tools. You used them.
Where did you learn all those things? Seriously?
It was called SISMI, back then. You'll know it as AISE.
Secret Service?
That and other places. I've had a full and busy and terrible life.
Our motto was *Arcana Intellego.* *"Understanding hidden things."*
You're going to do just fine.
I know why you're here.
It's what you taught me.
You taught me how to survive you, Luca.
And you taught me that nobody can know.
Yes, I did.
Nobody at all can know.

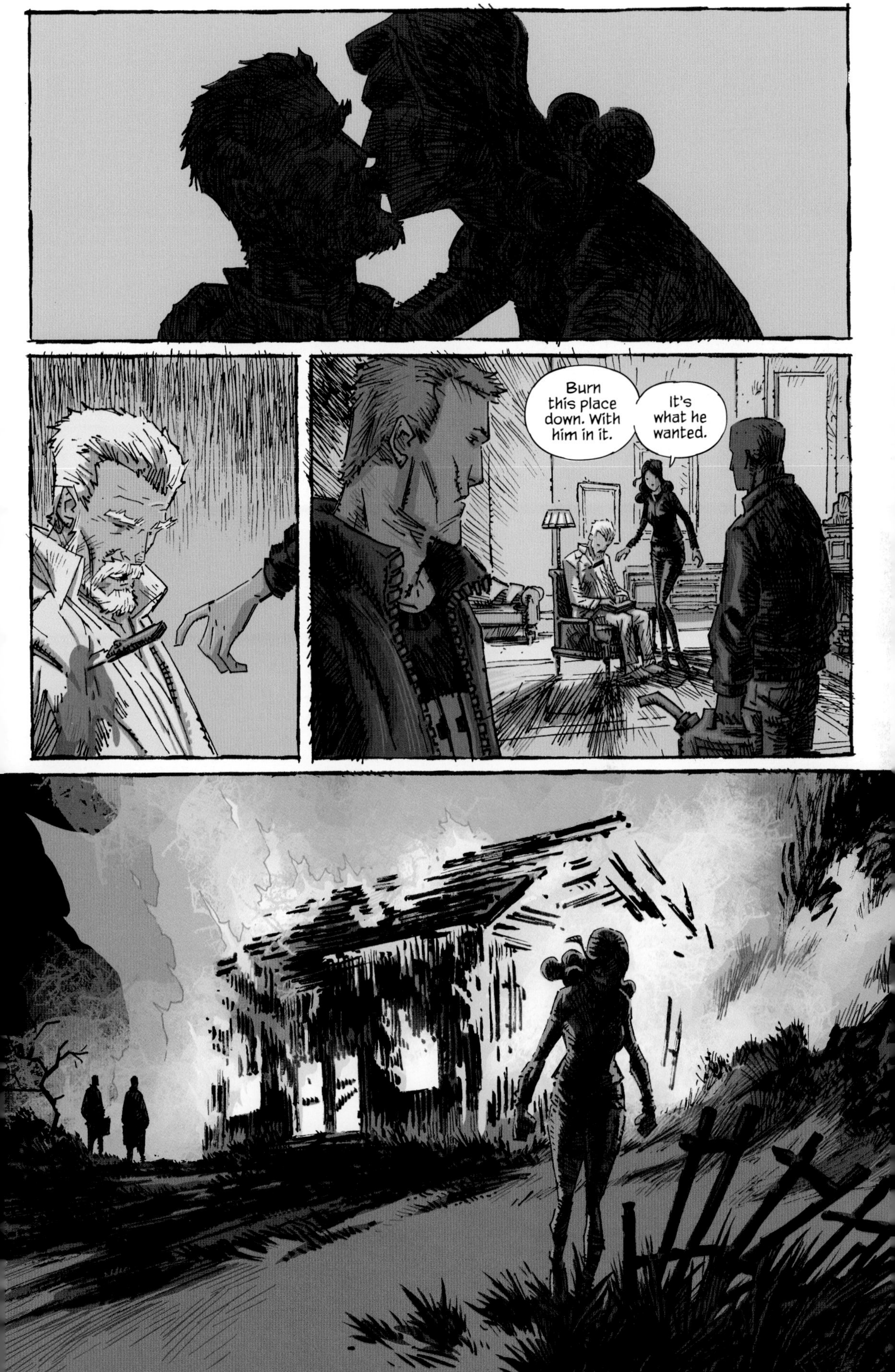
Burn this place down. With him in it.
It's what he wanted.

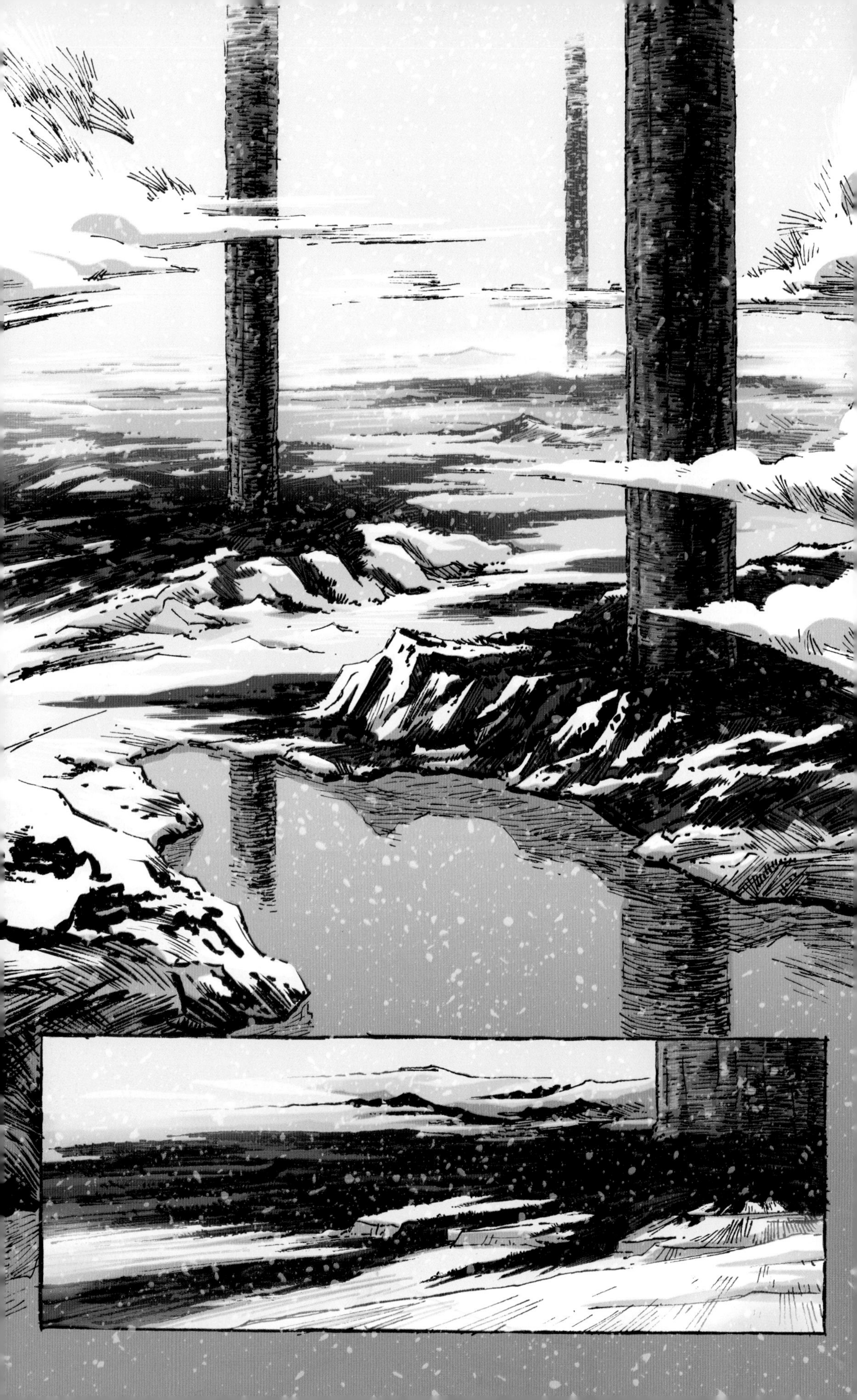

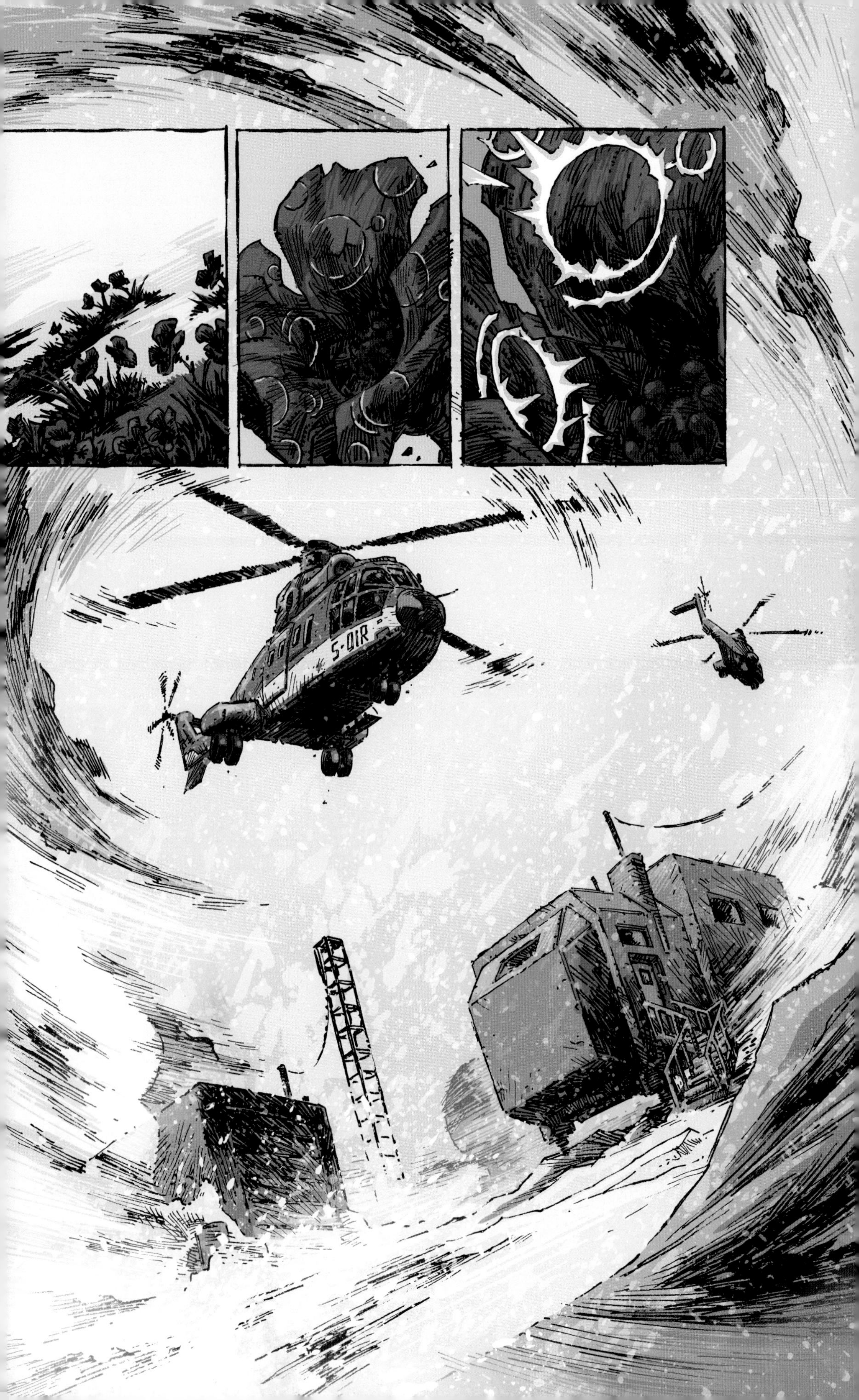
S-OIR

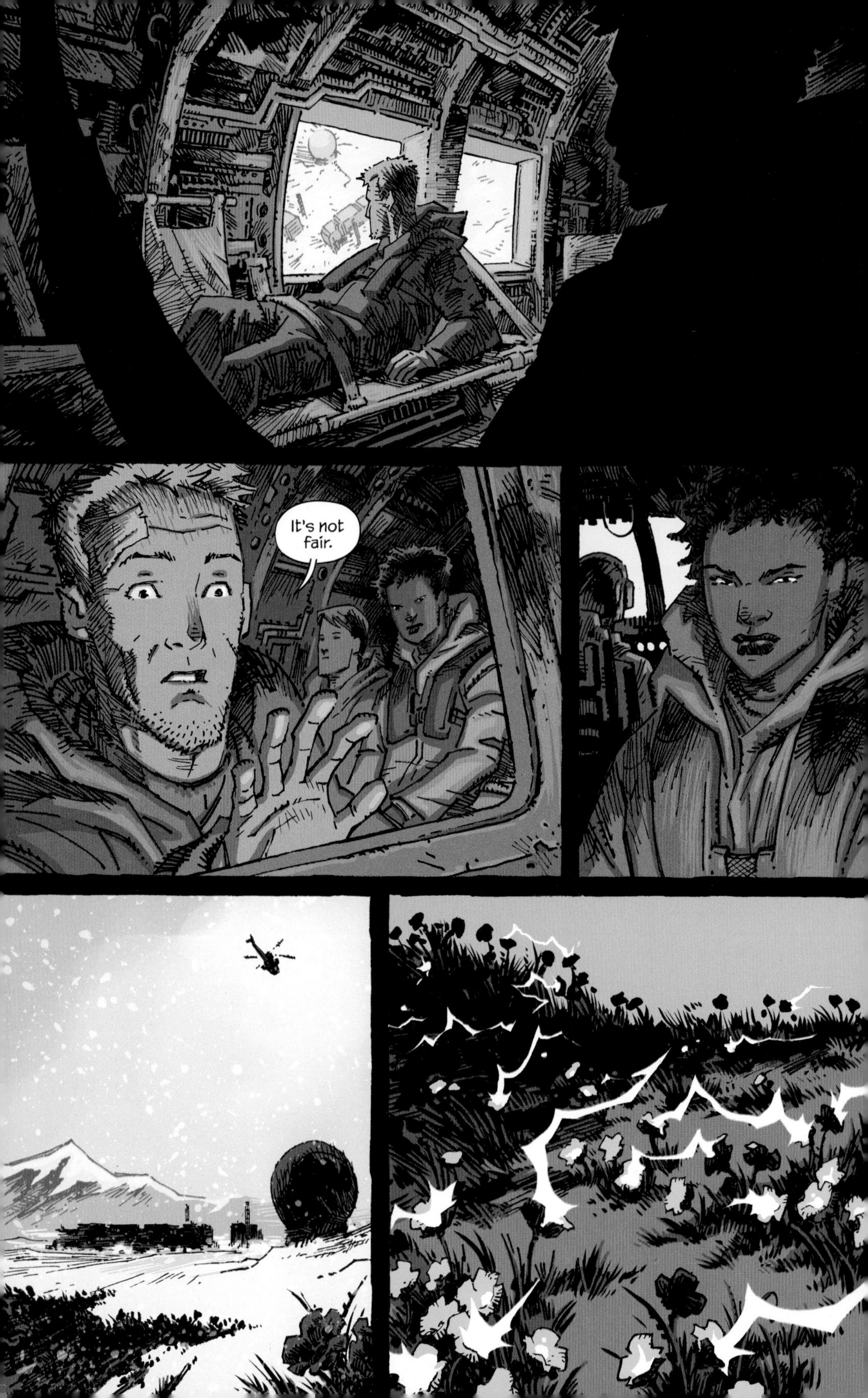
It's not fair.

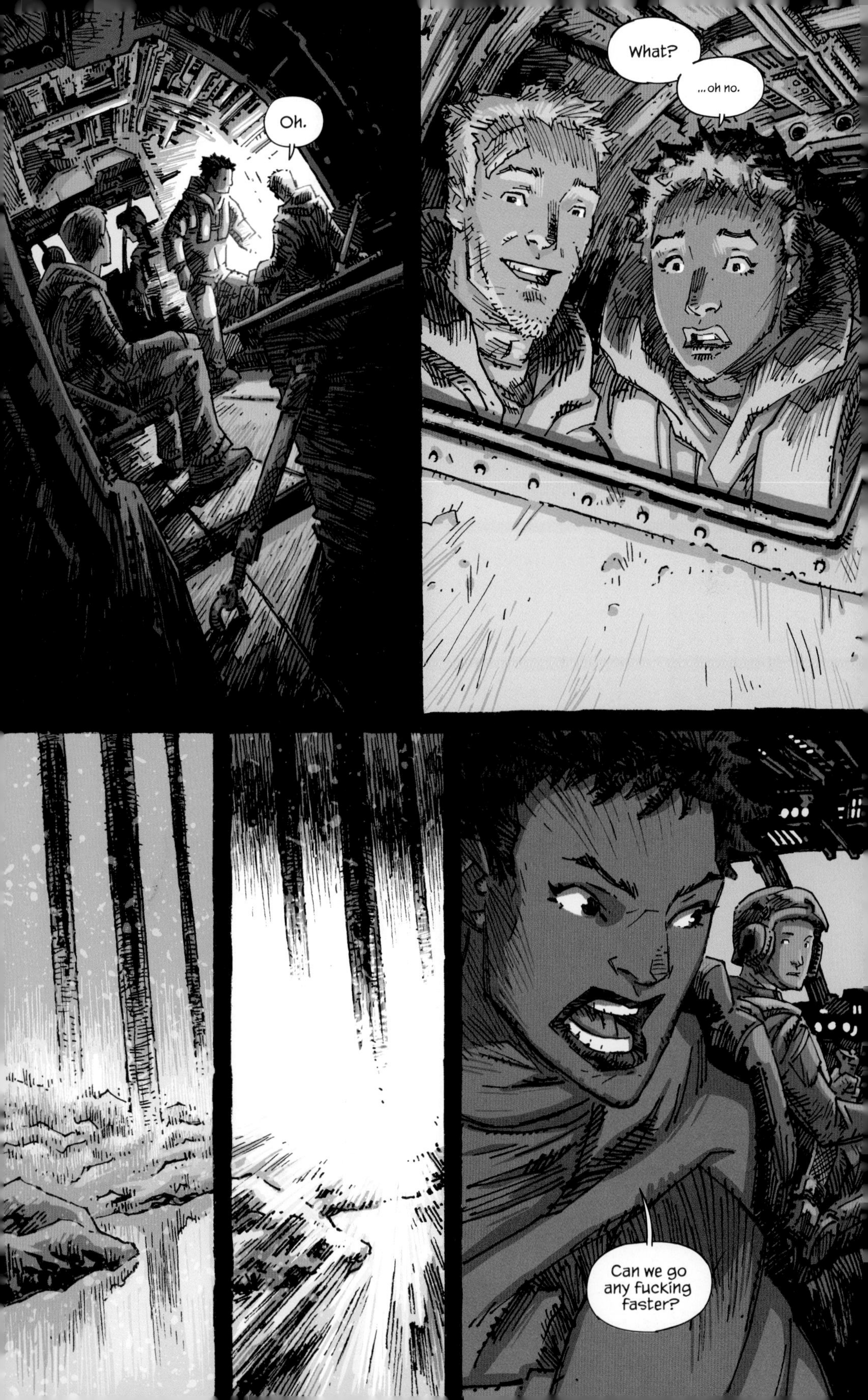
Oh.
What?
...oh no.
Can we go any fucking faster?

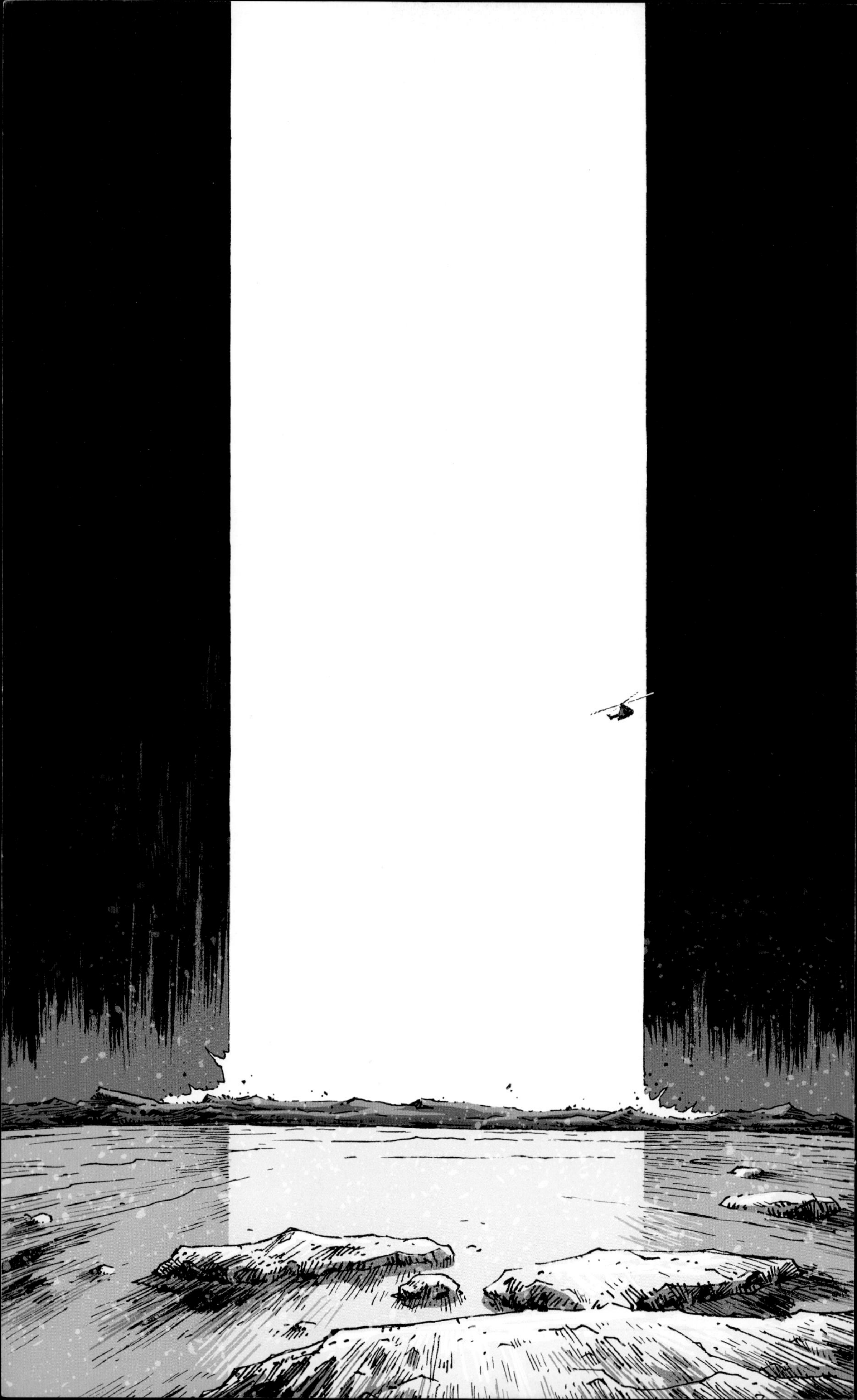

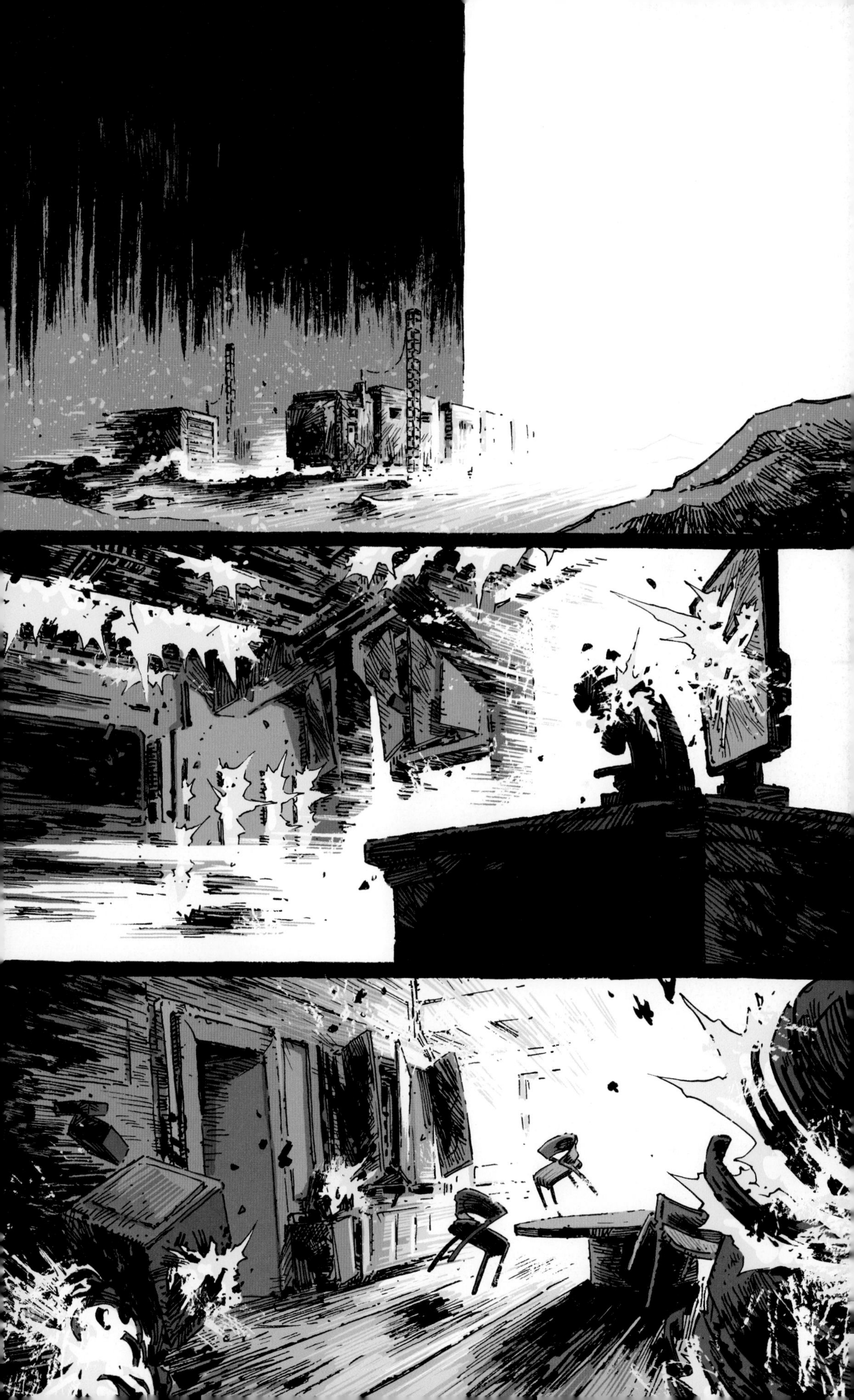

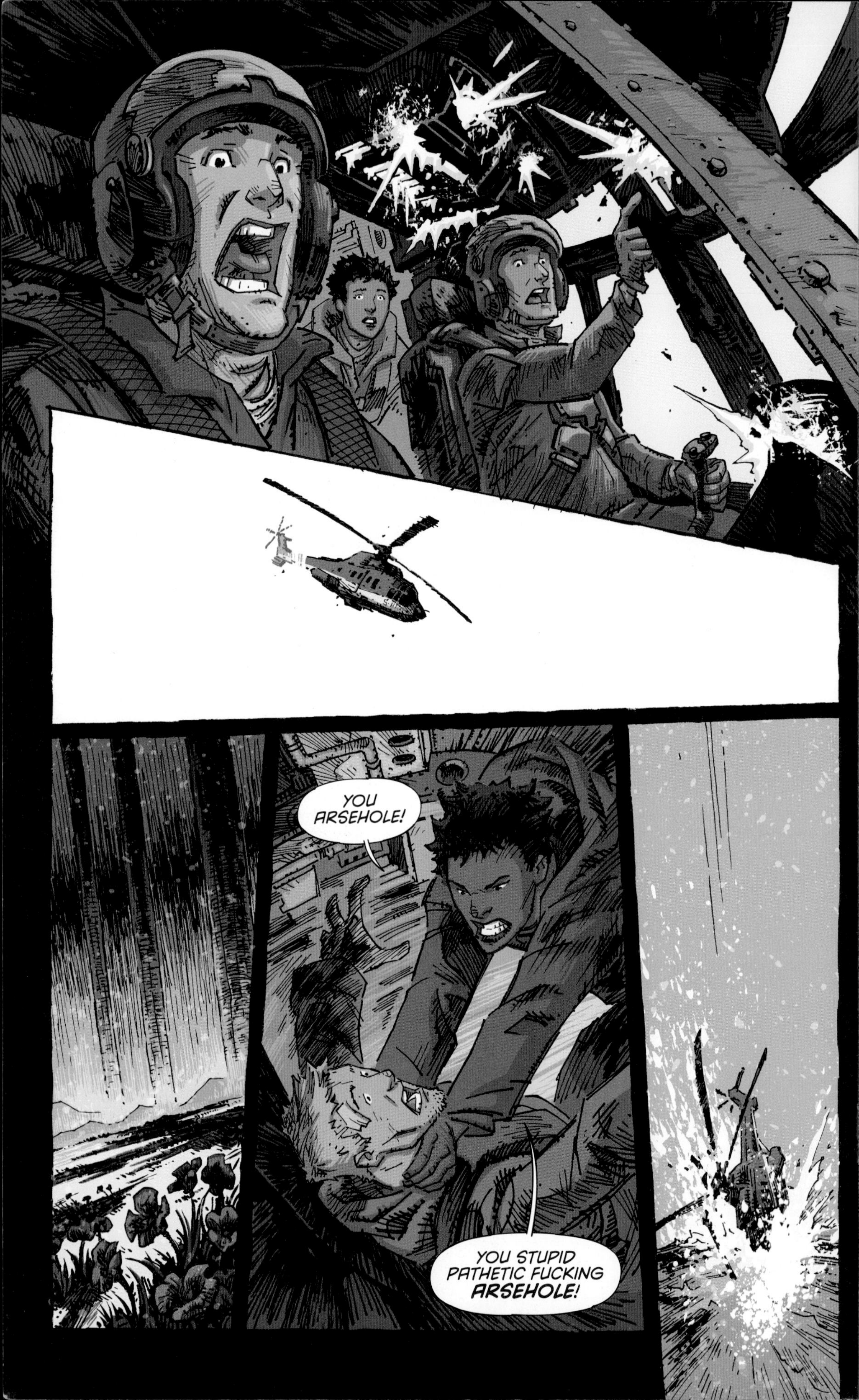
YOU ARSEHOLE!
YOU STUPID PATHETIC FUCKING ARSEHOLE!

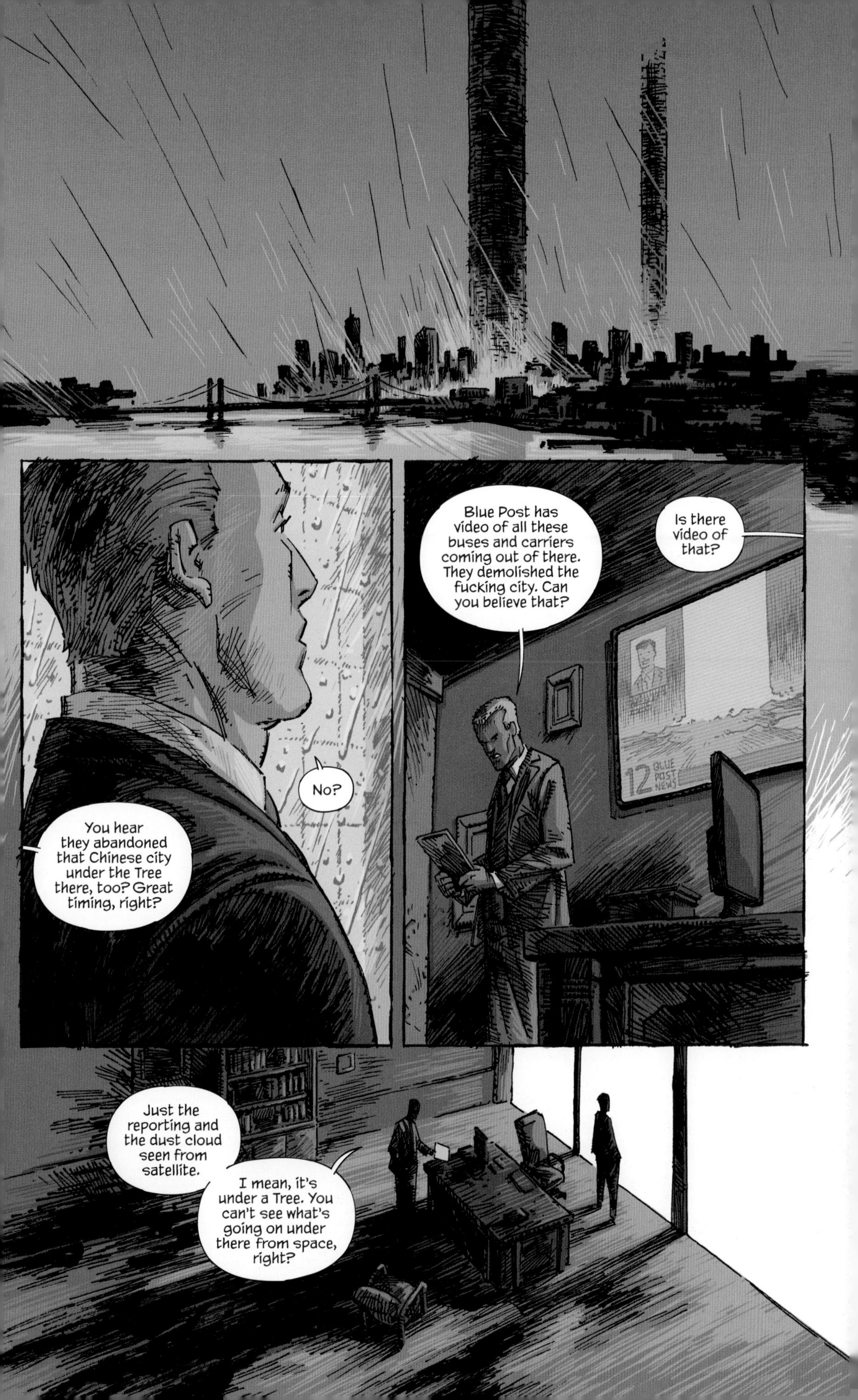
You hear they abandoned that Chinese city under the Tree there, too? Great timing, right?
No?
Blue Post has video of all these buses and carriers coming out of there. They demolished the fucking city. Can you believe that?
Is there video of that?
12 BLUE POST NEWS
Just the reporting and the dust cloud seen from satellite.
I mean, it's under a Tree. You can't see what's going on under there from space, right?

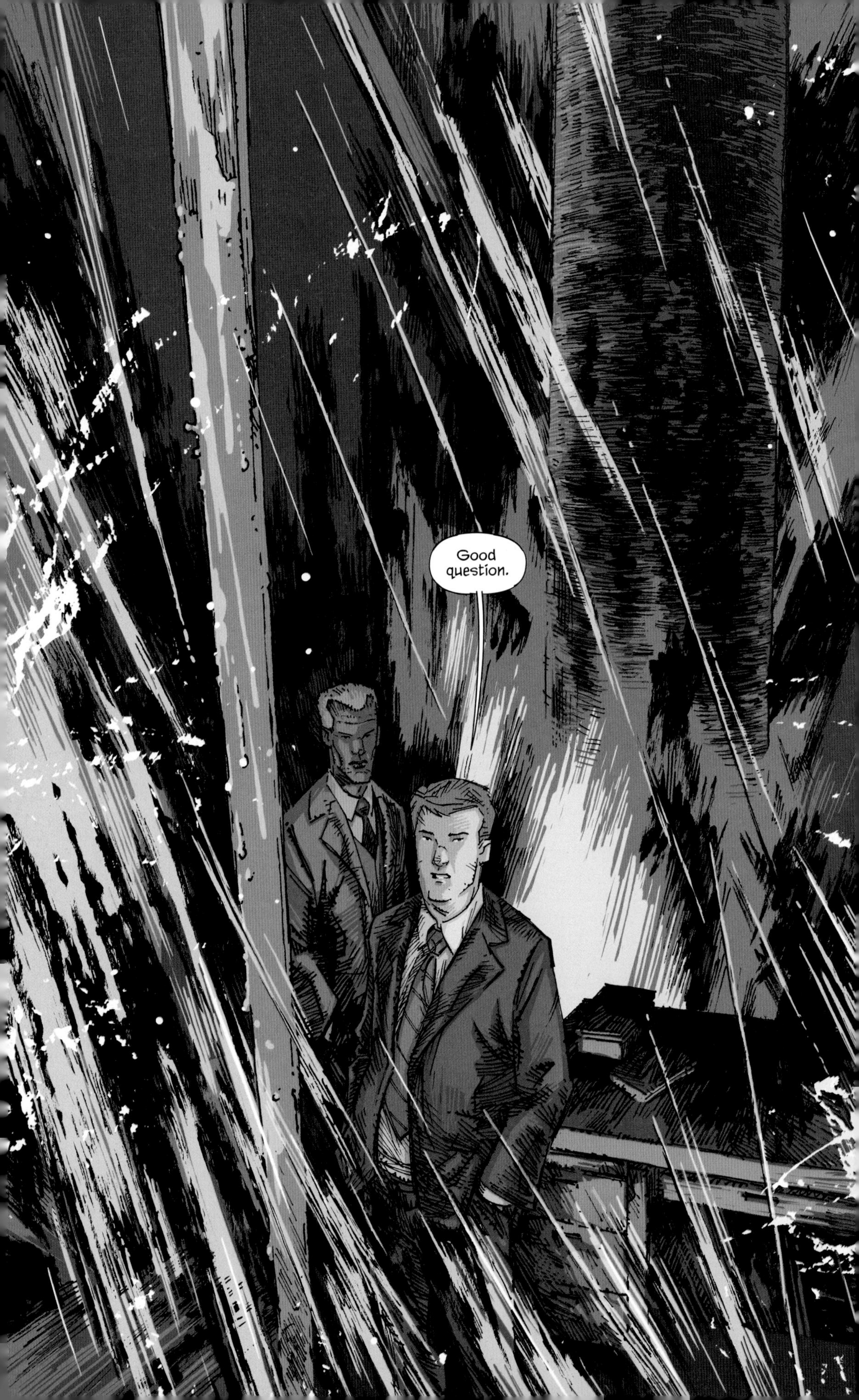
Good question.

NEXT
TWO FORESTS

SERIES COVERS

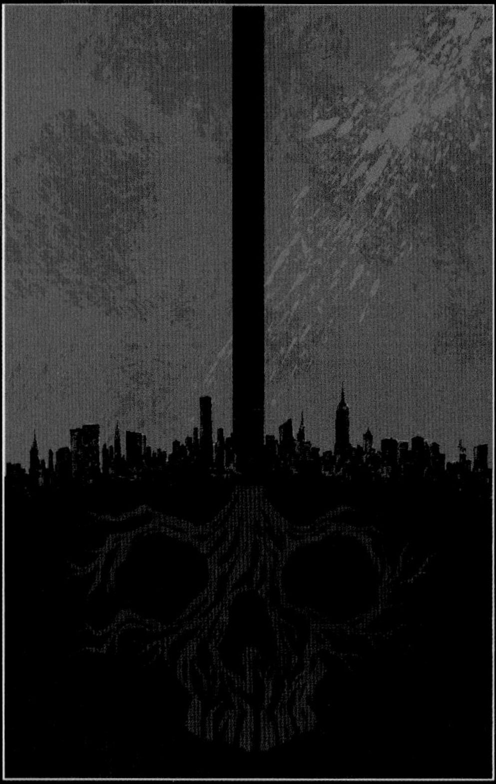

1

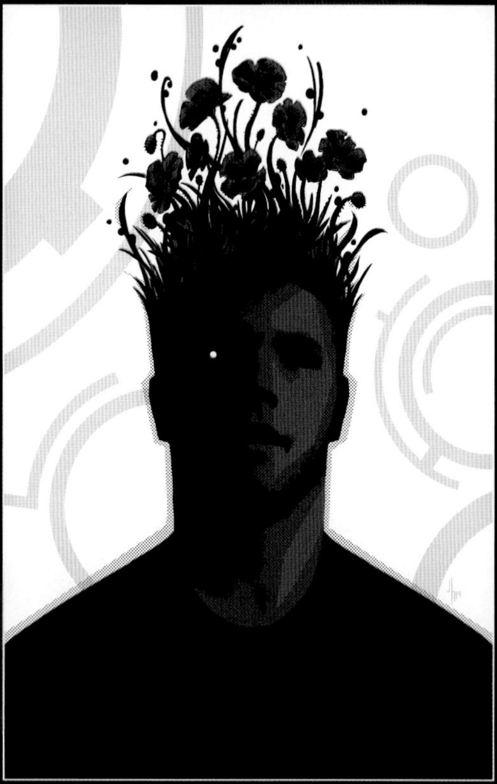

2

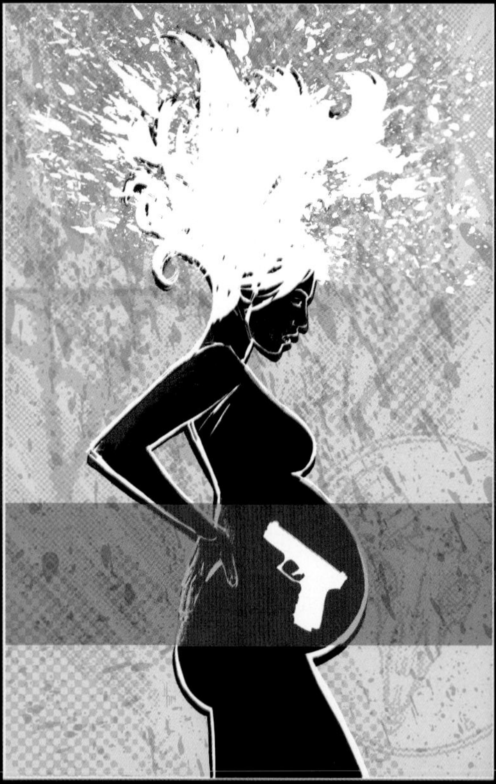

3

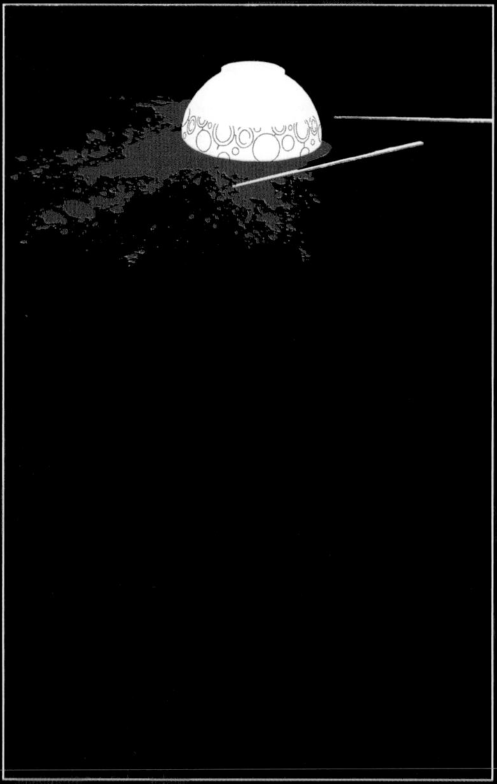

4

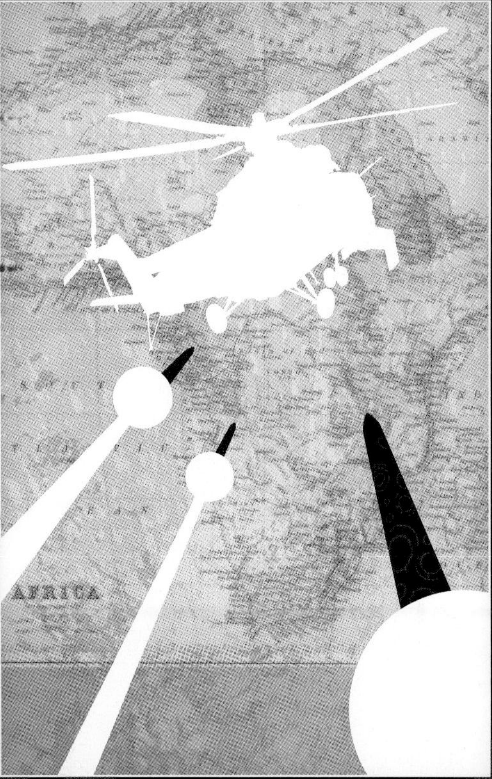
AFRICA
5

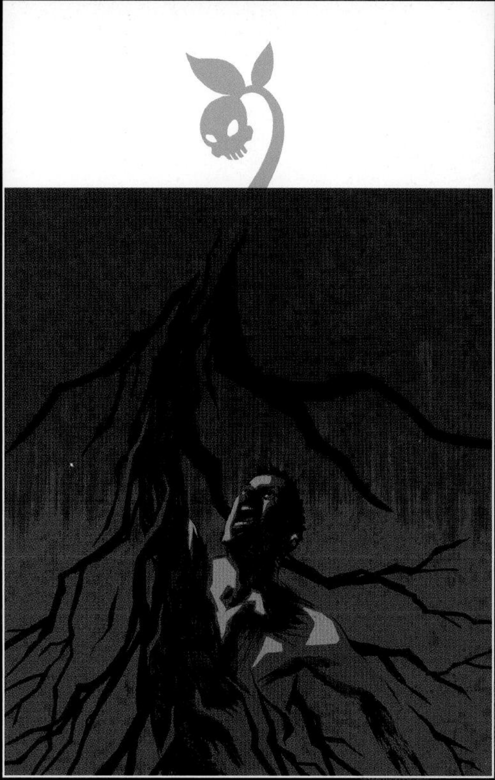
6

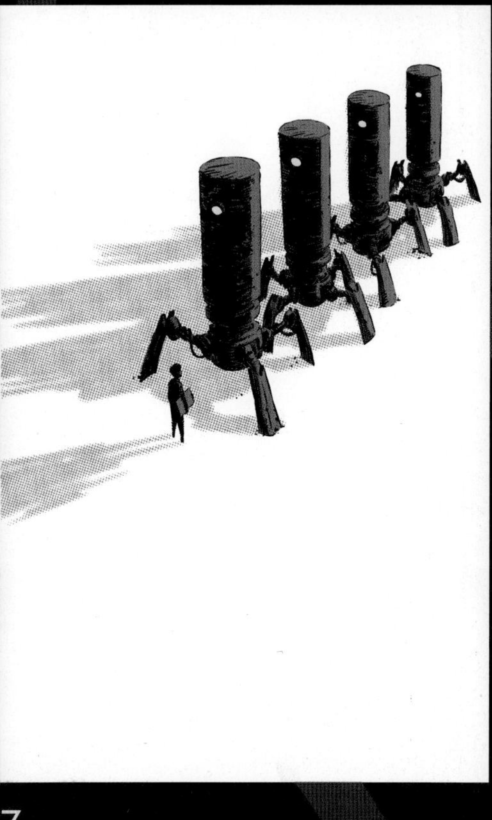
7

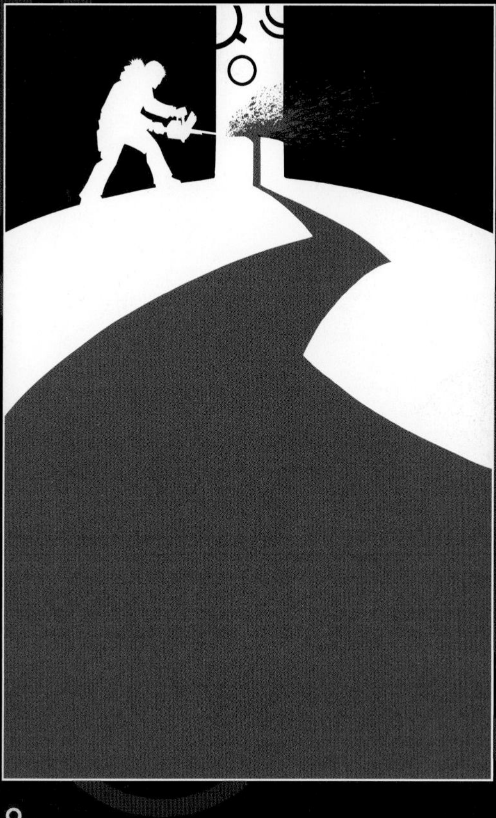
8

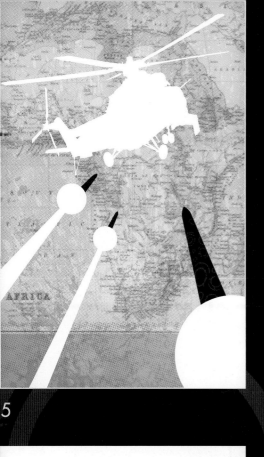

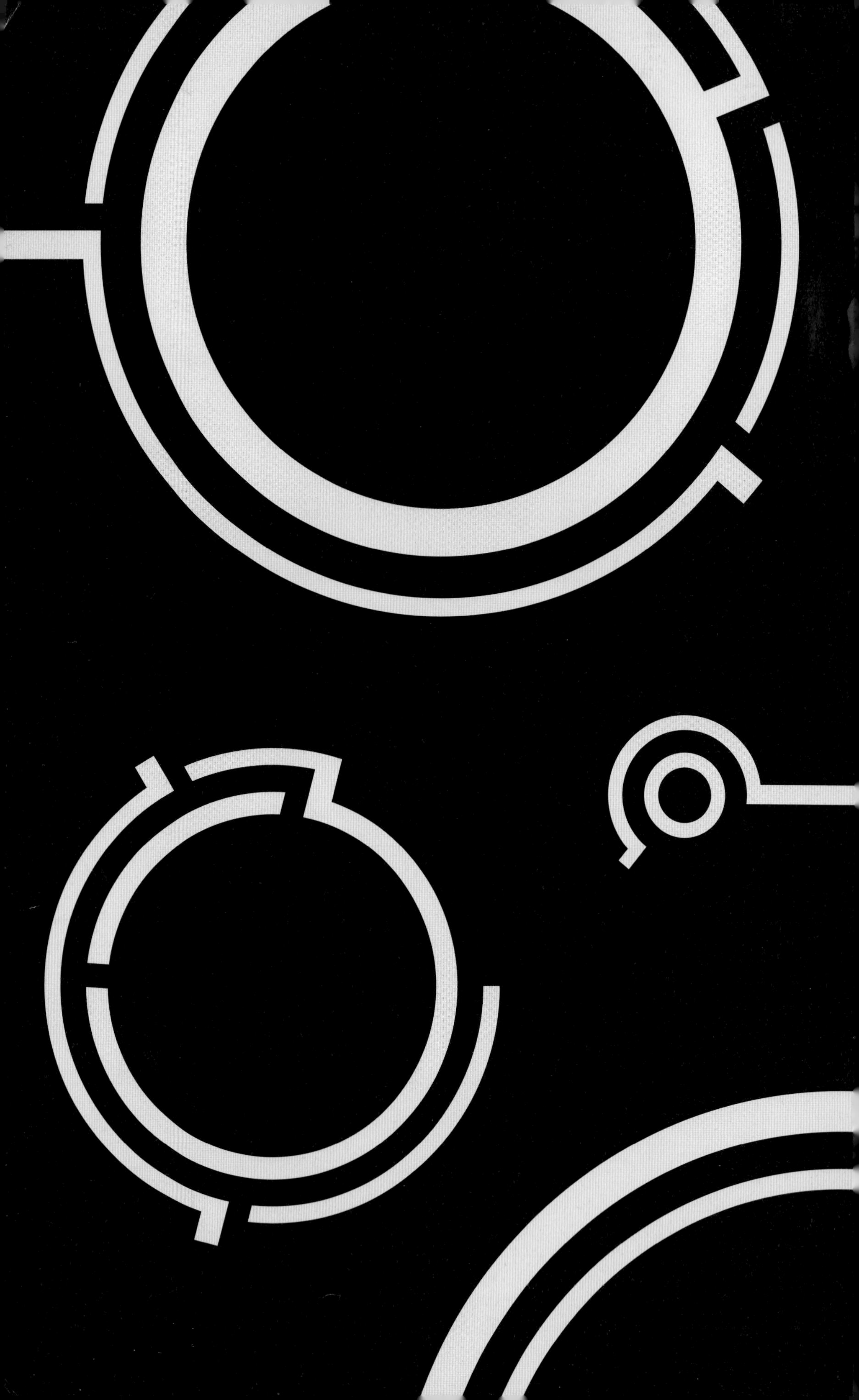